THE SOCIAL PSYCHOLOGY OF TOLERANCE

This highly topical book is the first of its kind to provide a comprehensive theoretical and empirical discussion of the social psychology of tolerance, exploring the importance and drawbacks of a focus on tolerance and discussing how tolerance can be stimulated in a range of contexts.

The importance of tolerance for a diverse, equal, and open society is increasingly recognised by social and behavioural scientists. When people are aware of salient differences and disagree about the value of various viewpoints and ways of life, the question of tolerance arises. Not only in relation to religious, cultural, ideological, and viewpoint differences but also concerning everyday things such as annoying habits of one's partner, the views and behaviour of one's children, disagreements at work, and neighbourhood hassles. Verkuyten uses concrete examples to discuss the various reasons for why tolerance is vital for peaceful communities, especially in our increasingly diverse and polarised world.

Providing a thorough examination of the social psychology of tolerance, this is a valuable text not only to social psychologists but also to a range of students and scholars in the social and behavioural sciences more broadly.

Maykel Verkuyten is a full professor in interdisciplinary social science at Utrecht University, the Netherlands. He is also the former academic director of the European Research Centre on Migration and Ethnic Relations (ERCOMER) at Utrecht University. He has published extensively on topics related to ethnic identity, intergroup relations, and cultural diversity.

European Monographs in Social Psychology

Affiliated with the European Association of Social Psychology

Series Editors

Professor Batja Gomes de Mesquita

Leuven University, Belgium

Professor Vincent Yzerbyt

University of Louvain-la-Neuve, Belgium

The aim of this series is to publish and promote the highest quality of writing in European social psychology. The editors and the editorial board encourage publications which approach social psychology from a wide range of theoretical perspectives and whose content may be applied, theoretical or empirical. The authors of books in this series should be affiliated to institutions that are located in countries, which would qualify for membership of the Association. All books are published in English, and translations from other European languages are welcomed. Please submit ideas and proposals for books in the series to Batja Gomes de Mesquita or Vincent Yzerbyt.

The Social Psychology of Ethnic Identity
Second Edition
Maykel Verkuyten

Henri Tajfel
Explorer of Identity and Difference
Rupert Brown

Using Intergroup Contact to Fight Prejudice and Negative Attitudes
Psychological Perspectives
Loris Vezzali and Sofia Stathi

The Social Psychology of Tolerance
Maykel Verkuyten

For more information about this series, please visit www.routledge.com

THE SOCIAL PSYCHOLOGY OF TOLERANCE

Maykel Verkuyten

Routledge
Taylor & Francis Group
LONDON AND NEW YORK

Cover image: © Getty Images

First published 2023
by Routledge
4 Park Square, Milton Park, Abingdon, Oxon OX14 4RN

and by Routledge
605 Third Avenue, New York, NY 10158

Routledge is an imprint of the Taylor & Francis Group, an informa business

British Library Cataloguing-in-Publication Data
A catalogue record for this book is available from the British Library

Library of Congress Cataloging-in-Publication Data
Names: Verkuyten, M., author.
Title: The social psychology of tolerance / Maykel Verkuyten.
Description: First Edition. | New York, NY : Routledge, 2023. |
Includes bibliographical references and index.
Identifiers: LCCN 2022026180 (print) | LCCN 2022026181 (ebook) |
ISBN 9781032370453 (hardback) | ISBN 9781032370439 (paperback) |
ISBN 9781003335030 (ebook)
Subjects: LCSH: Toleration. | Multiculturalism—Psychological aspects.
Classification: LCC HM1271 .V4787 2023 (print) | LCC HM1271 (ebook) |
DDC 305.8—dc23/eng/20220728
LC record available at https://lccn.loc.gov/2022026180
LC ebook record available at https://lccn.loc.gov/2022026181

ISBN: 978-1-032-37045-3 (hbk)
ISBN: 978-1-032-37043-9 (pbk)
ISBN: 978-1-003-33503-0 (ebk)

DOI: 10.4324/9781003335030

Typeset in Bembo
by Apex CoVantage, LLC

CONTENTS

ACKNOWLEDGEMENTS

Many people have directly or indirectly influenced my interest in, and thinking about, tolerance and diversity. I am very grateful for their support, suggestions, and stimulating contributions. Several of my colleagues have been involved in specific studies that, in one way or another, addressed issues related to tolerance. In this regard, I am indebted to Sabahat Çiğdem Bağci, Saptarshi Chowdhury Barua, Marcel Coenders, Ester Driel, Jessica Gale, Borja Martinovic, Jolanda van der Noll, Anouk Smeekes, Olivia Spiegler, Tobias Stark, and Jochem Thijs.

I also have had the pleasure of working with a number of graduate students who chose to study with me for their master's theses or for extracurricular research. Thank you, Magdalena Hirsch, Rachel Kollar, Sander Sleijpen, and Luuk Slooter. Furthermore, several PhD students have joined me in examining tolerance and intolerance from various perspectives and with different approaches, and I am very grateful for all their inspiration, input, and work: Sara Cvetkovska, Marija Dangubić, Maike Gieling, Paul Hindriks, and Evi Velthuis. Levi Adelman joined the tolerance project as a postdoctoral researcher, and in the four years of his stay at Ercomer, he made indispensable contributions to the theoretical thinking and empirical investigations, in addition to his lively presence and sociability. The research has benefitted greatly from his creativity and commitment, and he has also co-supervised one of the PhD students. One of the real pleasures of this project was the opportunity to work closely together with Kumar Yogeeswaran. In 2015, I visited Kumar in New Zealand during my sabbatical, because I was impressed by his work on multiculturalism. And working together for the past seven years, only made me more impressed by his dedication, cleverness, and excellent scholarship. It turned out that we worked together very well and formed a great team, and when Levi later joined, the team became only stronger.

Finally, I want to acknowledge that the work on this book and on the related research programme was supported by a European Research Council (ERC)

Advanced Grant under the European Union's Horizon 2020 research and innovation programme (grant agreement No 740788). I want to thank the council for giving me the support and opportunity to delve into the social psychology of tolerance.

Maykel Verkuyten
Zeist, May 2022

1

INTRODUCTION

Diversity and tolerance

Walzer stated, "Toleration makes difference possible; difference makes toleration necessary" (1997, p. xii). This statement nicely encapsulates the key message of this book and can therefore be considered its guiding motto. A motto, however, can easily become an empty slogan that attracts attention but has little use for practical and analytical purposes. After all, what exactly is meant with "toleration" and with "difference", and what do we mean with related terms such as "diversity", "inclusion", "recognition", "acceptance", and "respect"? What sort of tolerance and which type of differences are we talking about? Diversity is a fact of life but is the implication that we need to tolerate all sorts of differences, also those that are unsettling or even harmful to others or society more generally? And can tolerance not lead to indifference and a distancing towards those who think, feel, and act differently? And how does toleration relate to social justice and equality? Making difference possible is useful, but in how far does toleration contribute to inclusion, equality, and equity or rather to justifying existing power relations? And do differences not require recognition, appreciation, and respect, rather than mere toleration?

These are all relevant questions that require serious consideration. A precondition of tolerance is that there must be a difference that in one way or another is considered relevant or important. Tolerance is based on diversity and therefore an option that people have when there are differences in opinions, beliefs, worldviews, commitments, or ways of life.

Many countries, cities, neighbourhoods, organisations, institutions, and schools around the world face the question of how to manage diversity. The continuing increase in the degree and types of diversity makes this a hotly debated topic. In these debates, some express concerns about too much diversity undermining social cohesion, unity, and the functioning of communities, organisations, and society. Diversity would lead to a lack of shared values and norms and to "us vs. them"

DOI: 10.4324/9781003335030-1

thinking with feelings of outgroup threat and intergroup competition with the related tensions and conflicts. Others argue that diversity implies opportunities for intergroup contact, cultural learning, and cognitive adaptations that lead to innovation, less stereotyping, and higher outgroup acceptance. Thus, some would rather like to reduce diversity for communitarian reasons, while others want to support diversity by encouraging and embracing it (e.g. multiculturalism). And still others want to ignore diversity in favour of individual characteristics (e.g. colour blindness) or focus on the dominant majority group for rejecting diversity (e.g. assimilation).

Much is at stake in these debates, and it has become clear that there is not one best way for managing differences, independent of the type of diversity, the domain of life, and the social situation and broader societal context. It is not very useful to argue in favour or against diversity without knowing what the diversity is about and why that sort of diversity would be valuable or rather problematic in a particular situation. Demographic diversity is something else than worldview diversity; diversity in preferences and tastes differs from moral diversity; diversity in sexual orientation is not the same as religious diversity; racial diversity differs from linguistic diversity; cultural diversity in organisations is something else than ideological diversity in politics; and diversity in global cities and liberal democracies is something else than in rural areas and autocratic societies (e.g. Haidt et al., 2003).

Diversity might be good or might be bad, but it certainly is not easy. Diversity can mean different things to different people with liberals, for example, perceiving demographic diversity as more relevant and conservatives focusing on viewpoint diversity (Howard et al., 2022). Diversity raises complex questions and implies challenges and opportunities, struggles, and uncertainties, especially for common people who actually live with forms of diversity in their everyday lives (e.g. Bell & Hartmann, 2007; A. Harris, 2012; Wise & Velayutham, 2009). The term "diversity" is also increasingly used in combination with terms such as "inclusion", "recognition", "equity", and "social justice". An inclusive, equal, and just society would require that differences are acknowledged, appreciated, and genuinely accepted; that every person and group should not merely endure and condone but rather respect and esteem the lifeways of others.

However, this is more easily said than done, because there can be substantial and deep, even irreconcilable differences in convictions, beliefs, values, and practices. These sorts of differences will be difficult to fully accept, let alone appreciate, when they conflict with one's own convictions and way of life. Afterall, each person tends to believe in the rightness and sensibilities of their values, beliefs, and convictions. Thus, not all beliefs, values, and practices can be simultaneously affirmed and confirmed because of their "propositional content that implies a distinction between true and false, right and wrong, beautiful and ugly" (Joppke, 2004, p. 242). Pro-life activists will not appreciate and embrace the convictions and beliefs of pro-choice activists (and vice versa); orthodox religious believers will find it very difficult to fully accept homosexuality; some feminists consider the Muslim headscarf as a symbol of oppression; antivaxers believe that vaxers are misguided and wrong (and vice versa); and liberals will not appreciate and embrace conservative policies (and vice versa).

A diverse, equal, and peaceful society depends, however, on people's willingness to allow others to have and express their own opinions and beliefs and to let them live the life that they want. It requires that people have to learn to put up with things they disagree with, dislike, or disapprove of, also with things that are antithetical and incompatible with their own convictions, commitments, and worldviews. In short, it requires tolerance as forbearance: or as the philosopher, Bertrand Russell puts it in a BBC interview,[1]

> In this world, which is getting more and more interconnected, we have to learn to tolerate each other. We have to learn to put up with the fact that some people say things that we don't like. We can only live together in that way.

Tolerance is considered "indispensable for any decent society – or at least for societies encompassing deeply divergent ways of life" (Oberdiek, 2001, p. 23); it is "the cost we pay for our adventure in liberty" (Dworkin, 1993, p. 167), and "the price we pay for sustaining any enduring human relationship" (Jones, 2010, p. 39). It is "one of the few viable solutions to the tensions and conflict brought about by multiculturalism and political heterogeneity: tolerance is an essential endorphin of a democratic body politic" (Gibson, 2006a, p. 21), and

> like the incest taboo, tolerance is an essential prerequisite to justice and democracy, an ethos and practice of coexistence required before it is even possible to inaugurate the project of sharing power and rule, settling law, and respecting all human beings as ends.
>
> *(Brown, 2015, p. 6)*

When people are aware of meaningful differences and disagree about the value of various viewpoints and ways of life, the question of tolerance arises. Not only in relation to religious, cultural, viewpoint, and ideological differences but also concerning fairly mundane things such as annoying habits of one's partner, the "risky" views and behaviour of one's children, family disputes, being a principled vegetarian and having meat-eating friends, irritations and disagreements at work, neighbourhood hassles and disputes, and also in relation to dissenting beliefs and actions of *in*group members. Tolerance gets at the heart of what it means to be human and is an indispensable attribute of a free and peaceful society and enduring social relationships.

Tolerance as a buzzword

It is not a novel idea that the management of diversity requires tolerance, but in the last few decades, this idea had become a prominent narrative in many settings. Tolerance became a buzzword in national, international, and organisational settings for establishing multicultural justice and peaceful coexistence. The importance of tolerance for a diverse, equal, and open society is widely recognised, and there is, for example, a *Museum of Tolerance* in Los Angeles and in Jerusalem, and *Tolerance Centres* in cities such as Amsterdam, London, and New York. The importance of tolerance has only increased in our polarised times in which people from opposing sides refuse to listen to each other at best and try to silence and threaten each other, at worst. An indication for the importance of tolerance is provided by a search with Google Books Ngram Viewer.[2] This is a tool for estimating the prevalence of words of interest (as a percentage of all words) among the more than 40 million English language books that have been digitised by Google. The prevalence of the word "tolerance" shows a steady increase up to around 2010, followed by a small decrease. Similarly, the relative prevalence of the word "intolerance" demonstrates a rise starting in the mid-1970s to the mid-2000s. These patterns of change correspond to that of the phrase "cultural diversity" which became more prevalent around the 1980s to rise until the mid-2000s, before declining somewhat.

The importance of tolerance for a diverse and equal society is also recognised by leaders from various countries and across a diverse ideological and left-right political field. For example, in relation to the US, the then president Obama stated, "all of us have to send a clarion call and behave with the values of tolerance and diversity that should be the hallmark of our democracy" (Obama, 5 August 2014), and talking about the middle east, the then president Trump stated, "We must practice tolerance and respect for each other once again – and make this region a place where every man and woman, no matter their faith or ethnicity, can enjoy a life of dignity and hope" (Trump, 5–2017 Saudi Speech Islam). To give some further examples: in 2004, Latvia presented a "National Programme for the Promotion of Tolerance"; the state programme "Youth of Azerbaijan" aimed to promote "national-religious tolerance"; the British Educational Council is advised to consider "tolerance" as one of the fundamental British values that schools should promote[3]; the president of the country with the largest Muslim population (Joko Widodo of Indonesia) has expressed a strong commitment to and argued for the need of a moderate Islam that propagates tolerance; the United Arab Emirates declared 2019 as the year of tolerance and appointed a Minister of State for tolerance; and the "International Organization of Parliaments" chose in 2009 the theme of "Democracy and political tolerance" for the International Day of Democracy in order to highlight the importance of creating a culture of tolerance in society, and political life in particular.

Additionally, the African Union, the European Union, the United Nations, and nongovernmental organisations have all emphasised the importance of policies that promote tolerance. For example, the United Nations Educational, Scientific and Cultural Organization (UNESCO) published in 1995 the *Declaration on the Principles of Toleration*. And in 1996, the UN General Assembly invited Member States to observe 16 November as the "International Day for Tolerance", following from the "UN Year for Tolerance" in 1995. The African Union has promulgated tolerance as a foundational element for social justice, sustainable peace, and preventing recurrence of violence.[4] In Europe, there is a "European medal of tolerance", and the "European day of tolerance"; the former German chancellor Angela Merkel (13 November 2018) declared, "Tolerance is the soul of Europe and an essential basic value of the European idea", and tolerance has been defined as one of the four core features of European culture.[5]

There are also documents like "Promoting tolerance in the EU",[6] and there is the European "*Model National Statute for the Promotion of Tolerance*"[7] which is based on the assumption that "Tolerance must be seen as the glue that enables a pluralist democratic society to function successfully". Furthermore, the Council of Europe proposed making tolerance part of the national school curriculum and all member states agreed (Barrett, 2020). Similarly, religious and civic associations as well as schools worldwide promulgate tolerance, and according to some, a "diversity and tolerance industry" has permeated schools (Weissberg, 2008). For example, the national Dutch Education Council (2021) published "*Set limits, allow freedom*" as a normative framework for freedom and tolerance, within the outer limits of the principles of a democratic society. Magazines such as "*Teaching Tolerance*" started to appear, and in the aftermath of 9/11, the lesson plan "*Tolerance in Times of Trial*" was developed by Public Broadcasting Service for increasing tolerance towards Muslims and Islam. Furthermore, in the academic world, tolerance of different perspectives and methods has been argued for as being necessary for psychological research (Zitzmann & Loreth, 2021) and for preventing science moralisation and (self-)censorship (Krylov, 2021).

Drawbacks of becoming a popular notion

When a particular notion such as tolerance becomes popular, two things are likely to happen. First, the meaning of the notion is extended to capture qualitatively different phenomena, and the original meaning can even be substituted by a new one (Haslam, 2016). There is always the danger that one takes the topic of study too far and overstretch its relevance and importance. Identity researchers, for example, tend to consider all things having to do with people's mental world as identity questions (see Verkuyten, 2018a), and prejudice researchers tend to interpret all outgroup criticisms as forms of subtle, indirect, or covert expressions of prejudicial attitudes (see Tileagă et al., 2021). The understandable passion that scholars have for their topic of interest can turn into a sort of academic imperialism in which meaningful conceptual distinctions are blurred; a range of different phenomena are considered to be similar; and the own favoured approach is turned into a normative position about what should and should not be examined. In the literature, terms such as "identity", "diversity", "prejudice", "racism", and also "tolerance" and "intolerance" are used extensively, in a wide range of situations and in many different ways. As a result, there is a tendency for these terms to lose all significant and coherent meaning which might make them useful for rhetorical and political ends but not for analytical and scientific purposes (Machado & Silva, 2007).

The important idea of tolerance as forbearance and putting up with things that you disagree with, dislike, or disapprove of is often replaced by tolerance as appreciation and full acceptance of diversity. This can be seen in various statements, policy proposals, and educational initiatives and is already apparent in UNESCO's declaration: "tolerance is respect, acceptance and appreciation of the rich diversity of our world's cultures, our forms of expression and ways of being human". This reinterpretation of tolerance as appreciation means that the critical notion of tolerance as forbearance is lost sight off. This is unfortunate theoretically but also for learning to live with diversity and managing differences that really matter to people. Theoretically, forbearance with the related self-restraint is something else than appreciation, and in everyday life, people will not embrace differences that go against their own deeply felt beliefs and commitments. Tolerance as appreciation is a synonym of being open-minded and non-prejudiced, and this cannot replace the much-needed and indispensable notion of tolerance as forbearance.

The second thing that is likely to happen when a notion becomes popular is disappointment and increased criticism, because it does not seem to deliver what it mistakenly is taken to promise. The concept of tolerance goes back to classical antiquity in ancient India and Greece and was developed further in 17th-century Europe as a pragmatic approach for managing religious conflicts and disputes about deeply felt beliefs, convictions, and practices. With the Peace of Westphalia in 1648, the notion of tolerance was proposed as a solution for dealing with religious diversity and for individual claims of consciousness against church and state authority. Conflicting religious claims were not settled or reconciled, but the practice of toleration was institutionalised, as in the English Toleration Act of 1689. With the enlightenment and the development of humanitarian principles in the 18th century, the notion of tolerance was gradually extended to differences in ideological and political views and to the freedom to express and live by these views. Furthermore, tolerance nowadays also involves the acceptance of people expressing views and engaging in the related practices that one considers morally wrong, such as abortion, euthanasia, pornography, and same-sex marriage.

In all these cases, tolerance is suitable and critically important for the task of managing diversity and preventing conflicts. However, similar to multicultural approaches, intergroup contact interventions, and prejudice reduction strategies, tolerance is not a panacea or silver bullet that provides an answer to all questions related to managing diversity. Extending the concept of tolerance inappropriately will lead to disappointments and some unpleasant surprises in the form of backlashes and unintended consequences. A focus on tolerance cannot replace anti-racism and prejudice reduction strategies, but these strategies also do not make a focus on tolerance superfluous. A cure meant for a particular "illness" will not work for another "disease", and it does not make sense to criticise the cure for not doing so.

However, when a notion becomes popular, it is likely to receive increased criticism. Not only because it is considered to fail to deliver (what it never promised) but also because of the always existing limitations that become visible and obvious. As a result, the notion of tolerance is more and more replaced by terms such as "inclusiveness", "full acceptance", "equity", "appreciation", and "social justice". As one illustration, in the beginning of 2021, the popular magazine "*Teaching Tolerance*" changed its name to "*Learning Justice*", because "even we have admitted that 'tolerance' is an imperfect term", and the new name reflects the focus on "celebration of identity and diversity".[8] Another example is the discourse of COC Netherlands (mainstream Dutch LGBTQ+ organisation) that for a long time focused on the need for tolerance but changed its language to full acceptance and inclusion.

In contrast, the discourse of tolerance is also considered as being too indulgent and accommodating for dissenting views and practices and as too demanding for majority members, because it requires them to show self-restraint in putting up with things that go against what they sincerely value and belief. Thus, a focus on tolerance is criticised for either being too little and something we should go beyond or rather being too much and something we should restrict. An example of the former is the Canadian prime minister Trudeau stating:

> The third pillar of peace and security is the advancement of human rights, liberty, and tolerance – the very touchstones of our societies. Although, even the word tolerance is something that I'd like to think we can get past. Because use the word tolerance in a sentence; I tolerate that you exist. Doesn't sound very warm, I mean, there's no religion in the world that says tolerate thy neighbor. I mean, there are places in the world where a little tolerance will go a long way, but I think in countries like Canada and the United States, and Atlantic democracies, we need to move beyond putting up with each other, towards words like friendship, acceptance, and yes, love.
>
> *(the Atlantic Council Global Citizen Award Gala Dinner, 19 September 2017)*

An example of the latter is the then prime minister of the UK, Cameron, stating at a political party conference:

> For too long, we've been so frightened of causing offence that we haven't looked hard enough at what is going on in our communities. This is passive tolerance. And I'll tell you where it leads: To children, British children, going to Pakistan in the summer holidays, before they've even started their GCSEs, and forced to marry a man they've never met . . . children, British children, having their genitals mutilated, not just in a clinic in Lagos but the backstreets in Britain. This passive tolerance has turned us into a less integrated country; it's put our children in danger. It is unforgivable. So let me say it right here: no more passive tolerance in Britain.[9]

Both prime ministers question the relevance and usefulness of tolerance for plural societies, but for different reasons. For the one, it is outdated and not going far enough, and for the other, it tends to go much too far. For Trudeau, tolerance is demeaning and falls short of truly affirming and accepting, or even loving, each other, and for Cameron, tolerance can lead to culpable indulgence concerning the mistreatment of those who are vulnerable within minority communities.

Tolerance is not *the* answer to all the complex questions of diversity, and the different points of criticisms are not without merit. However, throwing out the baby with the bathwater does not help. If something does not always work, it doesn't mean that it never works; and if something is useful sometimes and for some purposes, it doesn't mean that it is useful all the time and for all purposes. Tolerance as forbearance is an incredibly valuable idea that is indispensable for a diverse society: it is a necessary condition for peaceful coexistence but obviously not a sufficient one. Trudeau's plea for friendship, acceptance, and love is of course valuable, but there will always be beliefs, values, and conduct one disagrees with, dislikes, or disapproves of: e.g. an atheist objecting to religious schooling, a religious person who is convinced in the wrongness of abortion, a vegan who finds meat eating morally repugnant, a climate activist who objects to the continuing use of fossil fuel, a libertarian who opposes governmental policies. People cannot, will not, and should not appreciate and celebrate all forms of diversity, but they should accept that others have the equal right to live the life that they want. Already young children do not accept and appreciate everything but can tolerate what they do not find desirable (Wainryb et al., 2001). They can describe some persons as misguided, ignorant, or immature and nevertheless judge that person's beliefs and acts should be tolerated.

Tolerance might be considered minimal, but this also makes it crucial, and probably even more so in our times of increasing diversity and sectarianism and polarisation that threatens liberal democracies (Finkel et al., 2020). It is rather ironic that "mere" tolerance is increasingly criticised just when intolerance is considered one of the most pressing problems in contemporary western societies[10] with opponents using social media and other forms of communication for name-calling, shaming, silencing, harassing, and threatening with violence.

The importance of toleration is that others can live according to their own commitments and values, without you yourself having to compromise or give up on what you believe in and are committed to. In the words of the former US president John F. Kennedy, "Tolerance implies no lack of commitment to one's own beliefs. Rather it condemns the oppression or persecution of others". Or as the African American writer, James Baldwin, said in an interview, "We can disagree and still love each other unless your opinion contributes to my oppression and the denial of my right to exist". Differences in beliefs, convictions, viewpoints, and practices are inevitable, but silencing, cancelling, oppressing, discriminating, and violence are not. Legally, for example, the European highest court has ruled that opinions and views which "shock, offend and disturb" fall under the right of free speech, but discrimination and hate speech do not. Tolerance is what keeps criticisms, disagreements, dislikes, and disapprovals from becoming negative actions that interfere with the freedoms and rights of others.

Psychology of tolerance

In (social) psychology and the social sciences more generally, there is a large literature on prejudice and racism. Thousands of studies have been conducted examining the nature of prejudice and racism, various forms and manifestations, generalised and target-specific aspects, underlying causes and conditions, and the implications and consequences for the targets concerned. Prejudice towards gender, racial, ethnic, linguistic, cultural, national, age, religious, sexual, immigrant, and ideological target groups have been examined, and more. In contrast to this large body of work, there is very little systematic psychological theorising and empirical investigation into toleration in which differences are endured. Already 45 years ago, Jackman (1977) argued that this is unfortunate.

> A shift in emphasis in the ethnic attitudes literature from prime concern with intergroup feelings (however measured) to equal concern with intergroup *tolerance* would broaden the scope of the literature from both a theoretical and a policy perspective, increasing both its sensitivity to and its relevance for the general problem of multigroup coexistence in a democratic society.
>
> *(p. 167, emphasis in original)*

This plea for focusing more on tolerance has not been followed up by many scholars. In contrast to the extensive research on tolerance in political science, there is still little systematic work conducted on the (social) psychology of tolerance. Vogt's (1997) assessment nearly 20 years ago is still accurate and forms a main reason for writing this book.

> Although social psychology has contributed crucially to our understanding of phenomena related to tolerance, such as stereotyping and prejudice, the theoretical work on tolerance itself in social psychology is so underdeveloped that almost any systematic investigation is likely to be productive.
>
> *(p. 237)*

The lack of psychological theorising and research is unfortunate for several reasons, with the critical importance of tolerance for diversity and plural societies being the most important one. Another reason is that a focus on tolerance draws attention to concrete beliefs, norms, and practices, and to the notion of citizenship which is a subject that is little addressed directly by psychological theory and research (Andreouli, 2019). In diverse societies, the hotly debated questions and issues evolve around foreign dress code, language use, dietary requirements, Mosque building, freedom of speech, same-sex marriage, and many other religious, cultural, moral, and ideological beliefs and practices. It is around concrete issues that diversity is put to the test, ways of life collide, and the need for toleration is discussed. Similar to the endorsement of free speech, most people will support the general idea of tolerance but can react negatively when facing the practical, concrete consequences of endorsing tolerance or free speech.

Fortunately, in recent years, social psychologists have shown a growing interest in understanding and examining the psychological underpinnings of tolerance (e.g. Crawford, 2014, Skitka et al., 2013; Simpson et al., 2018; Sullivan & Transue, 1999), and the research discussed in this book is based on our own programme of research and the "forbearance model of tolerance" that we developed. In this research, we have examined when and why people are tolerant, and how people define the boundaries of tolerance. The model proposes that tolerance involves the weighing of reasons for objection with reasons for acceptance. Additionally, the model considers how people draw the boundaries of tolerance by prioritising reasons to reject disapproved of beliefs and behaviours over reasons to accept these beliefs and behaviours. Furthermore, there are various individual differences in tolerance judgements and behaviours, and all sorts of situational circumstances that make tolerance less or more likely. We also have considered in our research how the notion of tolerance can be (mis)used for strategic political reasons and for making ingroup favouring distinctions between "us and them". Finally, we have considered whether, when, and why the experience of being tolerated – of being an object of toleration – might have positive and negative psychological meanings and consequences, especially in comparison to experiences of being rejected and being appreciated. Toleration is likely to have more positive implications than being rejected but might also have negative implications, because it can be considered patronising and lacking appreciation.

Our research

In our research, we have used different methods, ranging from in-depth interviews and ethnographic work to surveys, online experiments, and neuropsychological studies. However, most of our empirical work involves well-powered survey-embedded online experiments among national samples in the Netherlands and Germany. These between-subject experiments have the advantage of combining representative samples and random assignment making it possible to draw more generalisable conclusions, compared to laboratory experiments (Sniderman, 2018; see also Schlueter & Schmidt, 2010). These experiments are especially valuable in light of the continuing debate in psychology about the weaknesses and questionable societal relevance of experimental laboratory research that focuses on internal validity (e.g. Diener et al., 2022; Lin et al., 2021), and the pitfalls of using convenient online samples such as Amazon Mechanical Turk rather than a (national) sample from the population of interest (Zhou & Fishbach, 2016; but see Mullinix et al., 2015).

In studying tolerance, we have focused much on perceived religious differences in relation to Muslim minorities. Historically in Europe, the need for tolerance was discussed and developed in relation to religious difference, and the increasing number of Muslim citizens has given a renewed urgency to the notion of tolerance. The migration of Muslims to Western societies has led to strong public and political debates also within Muslim communities, especially since the beginning of the 21st century. What citizens think about Muslim immigrants and their non-immigrant children has important implications for intergroup relations, civic cohesion, the acceptance of immigration and asylum policies, and political responses to Muslim societal participation and integration. And what Muslim minorities think about Western liberal democracies has implications for their orientation towards and participation in those societies.

In contrast to, for example, the United States, in the relatively secular European countries, religion is often viewed unfavourably, and various Muslim minority beliefs, practices, and behaviours[11] tend to receive broad public disapproval (Verkuyten, 2021) making debates around religion especially relevant for studying processes of toleration. In Europe, religion is typically considered a barrier to the inclusion of Muslims; "religion is at the heart of concerns about immigrant integration in Western Europe, and the central issues have to do with Islam" (Alba & Foner, 2015, p. 118). Bright boundaries would characterise the European context for Muslim minorities, and it has been suggested that the disadvantaged minority status of Muslims in Europe resembles most closely that of African Americans (Suarez-Orozco, 1991).

Islam is often construed and viewed as a threat to Western liberal values and democracy, and there is an increasing number of discriminatory, hostile, and violent actions against Muslims and Islamic facilities. In the US, Muslims experience various forms of discrimination, including being treated with suspicion, singled out by airport security, or called offensive names.[12] In Australia, Muslims have been found to experience discrimination at three times the rate of other Australians.[13] And in Europe, Muslims are discriminated in the areas of employment and education, and their rights to freedom of religion and of expressing their religious identity are sometimes restricted (Amnesty, 2012). Furthermore, there is widespread public support for a restriction, or even ban, on Muslim immigration (Marfouk, 2019). Furthermore, research indicates that anti-Muslim prejudices are fairly widespread in Western societies, although there are important country differences (e.g. Ogan et al., 2014; Shaver et al., 2016). For example, a large-scale representative survey in different countries found that majorities (>65%) in Hungary, Italy, Poland, and Greece express unfavourable views about Muslims, while these views were less common in Northern and Western Europe and in the United States (around 25–30%, PEW, 2017) and in Australia (around 10%).[14]

Almost all Muslims living in Western countries are of immigrant origin, and West Europeans tend to think about Muslims when thinking about the category of foreigners and newcomers (e.g. Wallrich et al., 2020). However, in addition to the prejudices and discrimination faced by immigrants, Muslim have to cope with prejudices related to their religious background. In the media and in political and public debates, Muslims are construed negatively as a "suspect community" (Richardson, 2009; Matthews, 2015; Van Meeteren & Van Oosterdorp, 2019) and singled out as the prototypical negative other (Zolberg & Woon, 1999), and greater news exposure has been found to be associated with stronger anti-Muslim attitudes (Ogan et al., 2014; Shaver et al., 2017). Furthermore, in Europe, there is fairly widespread public support for the idea that "Islam is fundamentally incompatible with our country's culture and values", ranging from 53% in Italy to more than 40% in Germany, The Netherlands, Denmark, and Switzerland.[15]

Yet the fact that anti-Muslim prejudices exist does not mean that all people are negative about Muslims and that they cannot have genuine concerns about specific Muslim beliefs and practices, or that critique of Islam cannot have other sources

(Zuquete, 2008). These concerns and criticisms are fuelled by orthodox Islamic clerics and a substantial group of devout Muslims with anti-democratic beliefs: for example, 47% of Muslims in Germany and 72% in Austria considered following Islamic religious command as more important than following the laws of democracy, and 37% of Muslims in Britain preferred to live under Sharia law (see Wagner, 2021). Freedom and tolerance are under pressure when too many majority people think that Islam does not fit into democracy, and too many Muslim minorities think that democracy does not fit into Islam.

Although some of our research has been conducted in various West European countries and also in the United States, most of the research that I will discuss has been conducted in Germany and the Netherlands. The particular national context has an impact on the topics and groups considered, the questions asked, the research conducted, and the results found (e.g. Van Bavel et al., 2016). This is true for any national context, including the United States, where most psychological findings are produced. The theoretical, conceptual, and empirical work in the US has resulted in a substantial and rich body of social psychological literature that, understandably, reflects the particular history and context of the country. For example, the American history of immigration and slavery, with its pervasive "colour line", differs from the history of non-settler European countries, and American biparty politics and the strong religiousness of the country[16] differ from the multi-party politics and the more secular nature of many European societies. Furthermore, the United States and Europe do represent, of course, only a small fraction of the world population and do not reflect the large range of cultural, religious, economic, and political contexts that matter for people's thinking, feeling, and doing in various parts of the world (Arnett, 2008; Henrich et al., 2010).[17]

The relevance of the particular national context also relates to the terms that are used and how they are understood. For example, in continental Europe, the term "race" is used much less than in the United States, and Europeans are sometimes quite surprised when an American person who "looks white" defines themselves as black because of the "one-drop rule". The sensibilities and discourses of US race relations are often transferred and applied in ways that show little sensitivity to different systems of meaning and little understanding of other historical, political, and cultural contexts. As a result, not contextualising "race" can lead to misunderstandings of European and other non-US contexts (Siebers, 2017), and the same applies to the use of terms such as microaggression, native, multiculturalism, and colour blindness (Guimond et al., 2014).[18]

However, despite the important differences, there are also similarities in processes and findings. For example, forms of exclusion, intolerance, and discrimination against minorities are well documented in many countries around the world, and similar types of coping responses seem to be operative among different minority groups in different settings trying to deal with these negative circumstances. And whereas the topics of debate and concern and the related disagreements and objections can differ greatly between cultures and societies, the psychological processes involved in toleration can be quite similar. Those aspects of the claims made about toleration that have a certain generality to them can be more theoretical than empirical. Existing notions and theories can be used as starting points from which to examine tolerance and diversity, and in the process of doing so, the notions and theories themselves can be scrutinised and evaluated. However, this does not mean that descriptive findings are not important and that there are no normative and moral issues to consider.

Describing and explaining

Finding that people are on average reluctant to accept immigrants or critical of Islamic practices and beliefs or that a relatively high percentage of the population has anti-immigrant or anti-Muslim sentiments is something else than explaining why this is the case. A descriptive question and finding should not be confused with an explanatory question and result. Ignoring the distinction between these two question is a logical fallacy and can easily lead to a "jumping to conclusions", such as (tacitly) assuming that differences in outcomes (e.g. in education and labour market) imply differences in opportunities (e.g. discrimination), that opposing less strict immigration policies is based on xenophobia, that objections to Islamic primary schools are driven by Islamophobia, that pushing against Christian normative values and practices implies hatred of Christians, or that criticising and condemning the national (e.g. US) government for their actions abroad is driven by unpatriotic feelings (e.g. anti-American). These types of explanations can certainly be correct, but they do not follow from describing what people's views and attitudes are. Racist motives can underlie opposition to government programmes to assist minorities, but there can be many other reasons for why people are opposed to such policies. Blurring the distinction between descriptive and explanatory questions distorts academic, public, and political debates.

Social psychologists often have the tendency to ignore descriptive findings in favour of hypothesis testing for examining explanatory processes and mechanism. This is unfortunate, because descriptive findings give us an idea about what it is that we are talking about. There are many social psychological studies that, for example, examine the correlates and causes of prejudicial attitudes among (student) samples that on average do not express negative attitudes at all, with the majority of participants scoring on the positive side of the scales (Henry, 2008). And there is research on generalised prejudice that was developed around the finding that attitudes towards different minority groups are strongly correlated and thus have a common component (Akrami et al., 2011; Bergh & Akrami, 2016). However, a high degree of commonality does not have to indicate generalised negativity but might also indicate general positivity or an overall relatively neutral stance towards various minority groups: "In other words, the analyses are blind to the magnitude (or even existence) of prejudice across target groups" (Meeusen et al., 2017, p. 646). Nevertheless, interpretations about what drives prejudices are made, as are recommendations for ways to address prejudicial attitudes.

When using large, representative samples, descriptive findings provide critical information about the generality of attitudes and behaviours. This information allows us to establish how widespread a phenomenon is and thereby prevents from either overemphasising what is exceptional or ignoring what is common. There are always individual differences and it matters for society and research whether, for example, 80% or rather 20% of the population favours more strict immigration policies, or 70% rather than 30% supports the religious freedoms of Muslim minorities. Some social psychologists have argued for a greater emphasis on description, because it directs us to what is particularly worth studying ("phenomenon detection"), and for its foundational role in theory formation ("phenomenon-driven research"; Cooper, 2015; Funder, 2009; Haig, 2013; Rozin, 2009). Describing a phenomena and knowing how broadly and robustly it exists are very useful, even if there is no clear theory that explains it. I therefore will present in various chapters descriptive findings wherever these are informative and useful.

Obviously, arguing for the relevance of descriptions does not mean to denigrate or eschew the central goal of explanation in almost all sciences, including psychology and research on intergroup relations, prejudice, and tolerance in particular. The aim is to provide answers to "how, why and when questions", but for doing so, sufficient knowledge about robust phenomena in the world is needed (Eronen & Bringmann, 2021). Furthermore, whereas finding material and social external causes for attitudes and behaviours is relatively easy, finding psychological internal causes is often extremely difficult (Eronen, 2020). It requires clearly defined concepts and a recognition that there are typically multiple mental processes that interact in various ways, especially in the real world outside of the lab setting. And there is the danger that theories and lab experiments become wedded to each other with theories describing experimental findings leading to further experiments that increasingly lose touch with reality and our ability to understand real-world group differences and disparities (Cesario, 2022; Lin et al., 2021). The use of different methodological approaches, survey-embedded experiments, and conceptual replications reduces these dangers and allows to examine various explanations at different levels of analysis. In that way, it hopefully is possible to separate substantive and methodological issues and make reliable and valid contributions to the understanding and explanation of tolerance and intolerance.

Blaming and truth

There is another issue that I briefly want to discuss, because it can make theoretical explanations difficult and contested, especially in intergroup research and in studying politically and morally charged topics such as diversity, equality, racism, prejudice, and tolerance. The issue is relatively sensitive but cannot be fully ignored in a book on tolerance and diversity, and for understanding the argumentation and contribution.

In our qualitative research among poor working-class whites in inner city neighbourhoods, we have sometimes been asked why scholars tend to use a double standard in accepting the perceptions, feelings, and experiences of ethnic and religious minority group members for what they are, while the framework of justifications, rationalisations, and hidden biases is used for their own perceptions, feelings, and experiences: why their perceptions and concerns are treated with suspicion and considered disingenuous, whereas those of minorities are considered genuine and not to be unwarranted. They felt that only their feelings and views were not considered genuine expressions about how their lives were being transformed, but rather disqualified with accusations of racisms as yet another means of controlling and silencing poor people (Verkuyten, 1997).[19]

These questions resonate with the debate on politicised, activist scholarship in the humanities and social sciences, and the liberal confirmation and coverage biases in the behavioural sciences (Duerte et al., 2015; Pluckrose & Lindsay, 2020). In social psychology, there is empirical evidence for these biases, for example, with the use of measures that comprise ideological values, conservative people being described more negatively than liberals, and conservatism being more often the focus of explanation than liberalism (Chambers & Schlenker, 2015; Eitan et al., 2018; Sniderman & Tetlock, 1986). Scholars tend to view things that diverge from their own liberal position as deviance to be explained and there is a tendency in the social sciences to consider vulnerable groups as "sacred victims" leading to one-sided analyses (Horowitz et al., 2018).

The debate about activist scholarship and the liberal bias in the social sciences involves different issues, and confirmation and coverage biases also occur, of course, among politically conservative scholars. The result is a tendency to perceive particular findings and explanations as justifications, or rather as accusations, and therefore as moral rather than epistemic issues. This has to do with the tendency to equate cause and blame, and to evaluate interpretations and explanations according to the level of blame attributed to the groups concerned (Felson, 1991). Empirical findings are sometimes dismissed, because these would blame the victim or rather because they would morally brand (poor) whites as (covert) racists. Findings, interpretations, and explanations are not evaluated according to their accuracy but the extent to which they blame disadvantaged or rather advantaged groups: "a theory or explanation is evaluated according to the identity or image it projects for certain groups" (Felson, 1991, p. 8). Whatever the facts, an interpretation can be rejected, because it attributes some role to disadvantaged minority groups which would cause offense or harm, or rather because it passes moral-political judgement on advantaged group members (being "mad and bad").

In doing so, the relevance for particular outcomes of both more distal and proximal processes and the combination of external and internal factors is typically ignored. Blaming the system implies a focus on more distal societal factors (e.g. "structures"), and blaming the victim involves an emphasis on more proximate subjective ones (e.g. "lack of effort"). For example, for the one person, lower educational outcomes of minorities are explained in terms of systemic discrimination and structural disadvantages, and right-wing populist voting in terms of voters xenophobia and racism. For the other person, populist voting is explained in terms of economic decline and globalisation, and minority lower educational outcomes in terms of language and home environment deficits. Both explanations selectively ignore or dismiss structural and systemic conditions or rather people's agency and the role of their beliefs and behaviours and the social networks in which they live their lives.

These forms of blame attributions go together with name-calling (e.g. "political correct", or rather "racist") in which scholars are discouraged to examine controversial issues and ad hominem arguments replace scholarly debate. Being aware and recognising that descriptive findings and causal interpretations can be used in various ways to blame various groups is very important and a requirement for responsible scholarship. However, not telling how it is might actually cause more harm that accepting the facts of the matter. Societal and scientific progress in understanding and addressing critical issues related to diversity, equality, and justice is not served by one-sided, group-serving causal analyses, ignoring inconvenient facts and findings, ideological interpretations, (self-)censorship, and wishful thinking (Loury, 1994). Being a scholar and truth-seeker is something else than being a prophet or a politician, and being a teacher is something else than being a preacher. What is required is intellectual integrity and open and respectful debate about divergent findings, viewpoints, approaches, and interpretations: a debate that toleration makes possible and that can lead to the further development of shared knowledge (Rauch, 2021).

Afterall, scientific progress involves increasing the acceptability of truth claims which depends on further and better reasoning about a range of issues, including theories, methods, data, analyses, and interpretations. Researchers should be able to argue for, justify, and explain their claims about reality for an imaginary, virtual, or actual audience of colleagues. Argumentation in which claims are attacked and defended, refuted, and justified is central for making scientific progress. Discover the truth is the *raison d'être* of scientific work and the mission of institutions such as universities and research centres. However, there is debate about what "truth" means and also whether "truth" is an exact enough criterion.

The first point relates to statements that "truth is relative", or, more modestly, that "truth has a historical or a cultural or a partisan and political dimension". These sorts of statements are often well-intentioned but typically imply mystification resting on a reification error. The problem is that the term "truth" can be grammatically expressed as a noun, and therefore, it is often assumed to have substance, like a kind of thing, like a house. Discussions can then revolve around the question of whether it is ultimately unchanging in its own nature or might change with contexts, circumstances, and time. But a substantive abstract truth in its own right does not exist. Truth does not have substance, in the way concrete things have, or in the way abstract terms like "collectivity" or "consciousness" have. The term's meaning just refers to statements which are thought to "have" truth, in the sense of being true (an adjective word and a qualifier). The concept of "truth/true" qualifies judgements in a particular way; not as "attractive" (personal preferences), not as "good" (moral evaluative), but simply as "true". A true judgement attributes characteristics to an object which correspond with the characteristics the judged object in fact possesses. The concept is about a relationship between a subject (i.e. researcher) and a phenomenon (discrimination, racism) in which a judgement by the subject is made about the phenomenon; a judgement of a particular kind, in which the subject wants to know (seeks knowledge) about characteristics actually possessed by the phenomenon (e.g. whether there actually is discrimination, how it looks like, how extensive it is). If the judgement is factually right in that way, the attribution tallies; *ergo* what the subject says in this respect about the object is true. If not, what they say is untrue, false. The distinction between true and false is not only critical for being able to function in the world, in everyday social interactions, and in institutional contexts (e.g. legal courts), but especially also for scientific progress.

Second, people can believe that something is true but for the wrong reasons. Someone can, accurately, believe that 1% of the richest persons own 99% of the wealth. But if they think that the reason for this is that this 1% is genetically predisposed to be super rich, they believe a true thing, but for the wrong reasons. Knowledge does not only imply that one is correct but also that one's claims are justified in the right way, are formed by the right kind of process. What is needed are theoretical notions, adequate data, and good arguments that provide a correct understanding and explanation of the phenomenon one is interested in. Knowledge implies that one is able to provide reasons and arguments for why you think something is true. It requires the willingness to exchange views and justify one's claims, and correct these if they turn out to be wrong, because others provide more adequate and compelling reasons for their truth claims. This applies to all programmes of research including the research that is discussed in the current book.

An outline

Tolerance is a much-discussed notion in different academic disciplines, in political and policy debates, in institutions and organisations, in educational contexts, and in everyday life. However, it is also a notion that is increasingly criticised, with its relevance for plural societies being questioned. In Chapter 2, therefore, I first discuss various reasons for why tolerance is an indispensable ingredient for living with all sorts of differences. Additionally, I will discuss and evaluate several key points of criticism, namely that tolerance would be of limited use, that it is demeaning, and that it is a depoliticising discourse. I will argue that recognising these critical points does not make tolerance superfluous or inadequate, but rather raises questions about the scope of tolerance, the construal of tolerance, and for empirical research.

After considering the relevance of toleration for plural societies, I turn in Chapter 3 to the question how tolerance can be conceptualised and what it involves. I will make a distinction between tolerance as appreciation and tolerance as forbearance and will discuss the latter more extensively, because this is the distinct meaning that we have focused upon in our research. I will explain the "forbearance model of tolerance" that we developed and that relates to "objection, acceptance, and rejection" as the three central aspects of the tolerance process. Furthermore, tolerance implies that there must be something to tolerate, which means that it is important to discuss the question what sorts of things are the proper objects of tolerance. Additionally, tolerance can be considered an attitude, belief, virtue, action, or behaviour, and for being tolerant, one must be in a position to do so. Hence, I will also discuss various dimensions of tolerance and the importance of power relations.

In Chapters 4–8, the focus is on the empirical research of particular questions and issues that we examined. I will not discuss all the technical details of the different studies and describe all findings, because these can be found in the various published journal articles that are indicated in the text. Rather I am concerned with the examples and the evidence that these studies provide in relation to the tolerance process. The intention is to discuss the nature, meaning, and processes of tolerance in relation to various real-world examples, the research conducted in different fields, and the findings from our research that examines the different aspects of our forbearance model of tolerance. In this way, it should become clear what psychologically is involved in tolerance, how people determine the boundaries of tolerance, when and why intolerance of differences become less or more likely, and what the implications are of being a target of toleration.

Chapter 4 is concerned with the question whether objections towards particular practices and beliefs can reflect not only prejudicial attitudes but also more principled concerns and considerations. This is an important question, because there is little room for tolerance if criticism, disagreement, dislike, or disapproval is driven by group-based antipathy. If that is the case, then the focus should not be on tolerance but rather on understanding forms of prejudice, racism, and discrimination and on evaluating prejudice-reduction, anti-racism, and anti-discrimination approaches. The empirical research that I will discuss clearly demonstrates that disagreements, dislikes, and disapprovals of specific beliefs, practices, and behaviours often do not simply reflect underlying group-based prejudices and therefore raise the question of tolerance.

In Chapter 5, the focus is on the psychological processes involved in practicing tolerance. Individuals differ in their general tendency to be tolerant and in their more pragmatic and principled reasons for toleration. Furthermore, a dual-process model argues for the importance of deliberation in the tolerance process and the implications of this model, and the related empirical research will be discussed. Additionally, tolerance depends on the motivations that dissenting others have for engaging in behaviour that is criticised, disliked, or disapproved off. Moreover, tolerance does not only depend on how we understand and evaluate the dissenting behaviour of others but also on how we understand ourselves as group members. The content of the ingroup identity and the degree of ingroup identification matter, and can also lead to higher rather than lower tolerance.

No individual, group, or society can be tolerant of everything, and the boundaries of tolerance are found where reasons for rejection of the objectionable practice or belief are considered more important than the reasons for acceptance. Chapter 6 deals with the ways in which people draw the boundaries of tolerance by considering things to be intolerable. Specifically, these reasons involve, first, the harm and rights principle and the related processes of moralisation and the weighing of moral values. Second, there is the importance of group continuity and collective autonomy that sets limits to what can be tolerated. And third, people consider reciprocity and maintenance of the democratic order as important boundary conditions for what can be tolerated. However, the toleration discourse with its boundaries is malleable and can be used for different purposes, also for oppressive ends. This will also be discussed and demonstrated empirically.

It is not easy to put up with things that you disagree with, dislike, or disapprove of. Some people are better able to do this than others; some dissenting practices and beliefs are more easy to tolerate than others; and in some situations, it is more difficult to be tolerant than in other situations. Chapter 7 discusses some important individual differences that matter for tolerance, and slippery slope beliefs in particular. Additionally, the importance of perceived threats for the tolerance process will be explained and discussed, with a special focus on power threat and political tolerance of Muslim minority members together with the role of dual citizenship. Furthermore, threats can disappear, fears can fade, and differences that were considered reasons for concern can gradually be seen as common and even interesting. This means that adjustment and gradual changes over time as well as cultural and country differences are important to considered.

Chapter 8 is concerned with the question of the social psychological implications of being the target of toleration: what it means to be tolerated. On the one hand, tolerance is useful for minorities as a critical defence against censorship, discrimination, and persecution of minority voices. It allows minority members to express their views and beliefs and to enact their identities, provides access to resources and rights, and protects them from violence. However, on the other hand, tolerance might also have unintended negative consequences for those who are tolerated. Critics argue that we should go beyond *mere* tolerance, because tolerance is patronising and demeaning and can function as a subtle social mechanism contributing to domination and inequality and the depoliticisation of diversity. This chapter discusses these different arguments and our qualitative, quantitative, and experimental research that aims to systematically examine the possible unintended negative implications that being tolerated can have.

Finally, in the last chapter of the book, I bring the main points and arguments together. Tolerance is indispensable for any plural setting and I discuss how social psychology can improve our understanding of the tolerance process, and that increased attention to tolerance also has benefits for social psychology in raising novel theoretical and empirical questions. I also discuss some possible practical implications and suggestions for policies and in relation to education for increasing tolerance.

2

WHY TOLERANCE MATTERS

To illustrate why tolerance is important, I start with four real-world examples that relate to different domains of life: social, political, academic, and professional.

Living together

In 1998, 300 Kurdish refugees landed on the coast of Riace and received help from local inhabitants. Ever since this small Southern Italian village of some 1500 local people has been home to migrants and refugees (at times, up to 400) who bring new life into this once-dying Calabrian "ghost town", left behind by local emigrants looking for work elsewhere. Over time, NGOs collaborated with the municipality to develop an extensive settlement programme, the so-called "Riace model" (Driel & Verkuyten, 2020). The main aim of the Riace model is not only the reception of refugees but also the development and the revival of the local community. The programme is intertwined with work projects that revitalise local ancient crafts, with solidarity tourism projects, and with programmes for sustainable agriculture and restoration of the old town. These projects promote collaborations between inhabitants from many different ethnic and religious backgrounds and inspired the foundation of national systems that provides financial support for refugees' local and integrated reception.

Riace is considered a successful multicultural community that has attracted the interest of national and European policymakers, journalists, and scholars from around the world. Between 1998 and 2018, the story of Riace received national and international fame for the successful settlement and accommodation of refugees. Riace has been widely presented and discussed as an example of an integrated community in which inhabitants of different cultural backgrounds peacefully live and work together. This does not mean that there are no social inequalities, group stereotypes, ingroup-based friendships, and spatial segregation, but there is an

DOI: 10.4324/9781003335030-2

everyday friendliness and tolerance that serves as a critical "social glue" for the Riace community (Driel & Verkuyten, 2022).[1]

A protest

Each year on 5 December, people in the Netherlands celebrate Saint Nicolaus fest. It is a centuries-old tradition with young children believing that they get presents from St Nicolaus and the older ones, as well as adults, giving presents to each other "in the name of St Nicolaus". In the last 15 years, this feast has become the topic of heated debate and intense controversy,[2] even leading to a report of the United Nations Committee on the Elimination of Racial Discrimination stating that even a "deeply rooted cultural tradition does not justify discriminatory practices and stereotypes". The debate is about the figure of black Pete who is the friendly assistant of St Nicolaus (an old white male with a long white bread) who makes jokes and hands out candy. The controversy has to do with the very stereotypical representation of black Pete played by white people painting their faces black, with large red lips, curly hair, and wearing an earring. For the opponents of black Pete ("kick out black Pete"), this is an unmistaken form of racism, whereas for a majority of the public (at the time 65%), it is part of Dutch tradition and not racist at all. For the former, continuing with black Pete is a clear case of intolerance, but for the latter, the opponents are the intolerant ones in not respecting Dutch culture.

The controversy also leads to protest demonstrations and confrontations between pro-black and anti-black Pete supporters, whereby the former are predominantly white and sometimes try to silence and interfere with the civic rights of the latter who tend to be minority members. For example, in 2017, the national arrival of St Nicolaus was in Dokkum, a small city in the North of the Netherlands. Beforehand, the mayor had indicated that protesting against black Pete would be possible, and in the city, a separate section was reserved for doing so. Anti-black Pete supporters planned to use this opportunity to demonstrate and on the day three busses were on their way to Dokkum. However, when a group of locals heard about this, they decided "spontaneously" to stop and block the buses on the highway, and they did so some 50 miles outside of Dokkum. There was a small confrontation, the police arrived, and there was a long traffic jam. Hearing about the event and the related chaos, the mayor decided that he could no longer guarantee everyone's safety and cancelled the demonstration. The three busses turned around and with police escort returned to their place of departure. This was not the end of the story, however, because the event turned into a legal case in which the locals who had blocked the highway were charged, among other things, with violating the right to demonstrate and sedition. The court, and then the court of appeal, decided that the locals were indeed guilty of obstructing a lawful protest and exercising coercion. The court argued that the right to demonstrate is a constitutional right and that obstructing this right and taking matters in one's own hands cannot be tolerated in a democratic rule of law.

Academic freedom

In 2020, the University of Cambridge proposed a plan with guidelines and rules for upholding free speech at campus. The proposed rules required staff, students, and visiting speakers to remain "respectful" of the views and identities of others. However, the proposal prompted concerns and complaints from some academics, headed by a reader in philosophy Arif Ahmed who argued that differing views should be tolerated rather than respected. It was argued that with the proposal, controversial opinions or subjects could be blocked if these were accused of being disrespectful or causing offence, and that one would have to be respectful to claims and concerns regardless of merit. Requiring "respect" would undermine the freedom to examine controversial views, including those that might be considered offensive. A focus on respect, diversity, and inclusion could mean that subjective feelings are placed above academic freedom. These concerns appeared to be widely shared, and in response, the university's governing body voted by a big majority (80%) in favour of an amendment that introduced a commitment to "tolerance" rather than "respect". On 9 December 2020, the university approved of the revised guidelines in which the word "respect" was replaced by "tolerance".

> The University fosters an environment in which all of its staff and students can participate fully in University life, and feel able to question and test received wisdom, and to express new ideas and controversial or unpopular opinions within the law, without fear of intolerance and discrimination. In exercising their right to freedom of expression, the University expects its staff, students and visitors to be tolerant of the differing opinions of others, in line with the University's core value of freedom of expression. The University also expects its staff, students and visitors to be tolerant of the diverse identities of others, in line with the University's core value of freedom from discrimination. While debate and discussion may be robust and challenging, all speakers have a right to be heard when exercising their right to free speech within the law.

Professional work

The moral and religious beliefs of professionals such as teachers, lawyers, doctors, nurses, therapists, and social workers can have an impact on them being able to obtain and maintain employment and to publicly share their views. For example, various countries have seen strong debates over LGBTQ+ rights and freedom of conscience of devout Christians, and freedom of speech of university students and faculty for expressing conservative beliefs. An example is the high-profile case of Felix Ngole which attracted much media attention in the United Kingdom (Ngole, 2018).

Ngole originates from Cameroon and is a devout Christian who was a second-year master's student on a social work course at Sheffield University. In 2015, he posted a series of comments on Facebook in relation to a prominent news story concerning an American registrar who, because of her religious beliefs, had refused marriage licenses to same-sex couples. After he posted several comments based on his interpretation of the bible (e.g. "same sex marriage is a sin", "homosexuality is a sin", and "it is an abomination"), these comments were brought anonymously to the attention of the university by another student. What followed was a disciplinary hearing and then an investigation by the Faculty of Social Sciences Fitness to Practise (FTP) Committee. In the meeting with the committee, Ngole was asked whether he believed in what he had posted which he saw as a direct attempt by the university to entice him to renounce his Christian faith or censor his views (Ngole, 2018).

The outcome of the investigation was that he was excluded from further study on the course, had to return his university badge, and had his university account terminated. By publicly posting his views, Ngole would have been offensive and disrespectful, damaged public confidence in the profession, and compromised his ability to carry out his role as a social worker, since service users might perceive him as not treating them with dignity and without discrimination. Ngole appealed to a higher appeal committee in the university on the grounds that the decision was an interference with his rights to freedom of speech and freedom of religion, but the FTP panel's decision was upheld. The judge of appeal argued that the university was not concerned about his religious beliefs but about making these beliefs publicly accessible for service users "who would perceive them as judgemental, incompatible with service ethos, or suggestive of discriminatory intent". Subsequently, Ngole appealed the university decision in court, and in 2019, the Court ruled that his removal from the course was "flawed and unfair" and a disproportional restriction of his freedom of consciousness and expression. The Court remitted his case for reconsideration and a new hearing before a differently constituted FTP Committee.

The case involved university regulations and legal procedures but also sparked a strong public debate about Ngole's fitness to practice as a social worker, about (in)tolerance, and whether the university decision was correct. On one internet forum, an online debate[3] was started with Ngole explaining his views and accusing the university of being intolerant with its "new political orthodoxy" that bars religious people and forces them to forswear their beliefs to prevent exclusion, and also arguing that Britain does not live up to its own credo of tolerance and religious freedom. Others, however, argued that Ngole was the one who is intolerant, because his homophobic views would go against the full acceptance and appreciation of minority identities that would be required of a social worker. However, there were also responses in support of Ngole, and some participants in the debate expressed a nuanced position. The forum included a polling question and of the forum visitors 51.3% agreed that "expelling this student is the right decision", while 48.7% disagreed (see Verkuyten, 2022a).

Why we need tolerance

In these four examples from different domains of life, the question of toleration plays a role. It is relevant in relation to social (Riace), political (black Pete protest), academic (Cambridge University), and professional (Ngole) issues. Whether certain opinions, beliefs, behaviours, and practices should be tolerated and why and when are discussed and debated drawing upon various considerations and with various possible outcomes.

The first example of Riace clearly demonstrates the importance of social tolerance. It is hard to imagine how without tolerance people in Riace could peacefully live together. In situations of "super diversity" (Vertovec, 2007), there are inevitably disagreements and tensions around differences in views, beliefs, practices, and interests, making tolerance as everyday friendliness and endurance indispensable for community life (Driel & Verkuyten, 2022). A diverse, egalitarian, and peaceful community does not require that we all like and agree with each other, but rather that people can live together despite irreconcilable differences. The need for tolerance can only be reduced by reducing diversity or liberty or by favouring hostility and violent conflict above compromise, everyday friendliness, and peace. If only for pragmatic reasons, tolerance cannot be missed.

The second example about white majority members blocking the anti-black Pete demonstration relates to civil liberties and political tolerance. The importance of tolerance is relatively easy to understand in the domain of democratic politics and political scientist have conducted many empirical studies on political tolerance. In contrast to authoritarian regimes in which dissenting viewpoints are silenced, oppressed, and persecuted, tolerance is a central pillar of a liberal democracy. Within the boundaries of the law, people have the right to express their ideological viewpoints and interests, and a liberal democracy requires that you allow political activity and the full legal rights of citizenship to your adversaries. Political *in*tolerance related to ideological polarisation is considered one of the pressing problems facing liberal democracies. Trying to silence, exclude, or oppress people you strongly disagree with or disapprove of goes against civil liberties of all and makes free debate, demonstration, and organisation impossible. The importance of political tolerance is obvious if one's own freedom of expression and demonstration and political participation is at stake; if the "rules of the game" are not equally applied to you or your group. Civil liberties are not only for yourself or your group members but also for adversaries that have equal rights and can compete openly for political influence and power.

Tolerance and freedom of expression are not only important in the social and political domains, as the example of Cambridge University demonstrates.[4] As discussed by John Stuart Mill (1859), free debate is important in academic circles but also in everyday life with its "tyranny of social opinion". Mill recognised that people tend to be overconfident that they themselves or their community are right, tend to search for evidence that will confirm their existing ideas and beliefs, and are inclined to see what they want to see. The only reliable antidote towards these confirmation and desirability biases is to tolerate and interact with those who have opposing ideas and beliefs. There are three main reasons for this: the other person could be right; you can further develop why you are right; and both you and the other could be partly right.

First, another person's idea or proposition might turn out to be correct, however controversial it may seem at first and however how certain you are about your own views ("The opinion may possibly be true"). Second, being challenged allows you to develop and reason your own point of view better, defend it against possible objections, and prevent it from becoming an unquestioned dogma rather than a living truth ("He who knows only his own side of the case, knows little of that"). And third, opposing views and beliefs about the complexities of the world will often be partly true and therefore need to be reconciled and combined rather than being silenced and suppressed ("Conflicting doctrines share the truth between them").

All three reasons point at the importance of letting others speak their mind and a willingness to listen. Nobody is right about everything or all of the time and people can learn from others if they allow them to express views that they disagree with, dislike, or disapprove off. In contrast, intolerance of heretical and heterodox views prevents us from further developing and grounding our own beliefs and convictions and to the possibility of altering our opinions, views, and beliefs for engaging with the social world. Tolerating dissenting opinions, views, and beliefs provides the opportunity for developing and testing contrasting beliefs and for confronting ethical dilemmas and thereby for society's intellectual, social, and moral progress.

The fourth example of Felix Ngole relates to religious and moral beliefs and the importance of being able to maintain these and live by them. People can have their own deeply felt beliefs and convictions that make their life meaningful, are part of their conscience, and guide their judgement and conduct. This is also clearly expressed by a young Turkish Muslim living in London (in Barbacan, 2022, p. 146).

> I do not agree with British people who think alcohol or homosexuality is fine. You know we have to accept lesbians, gays, trans-genders. I respect what they are. We should tolerate differences. That is fine. I have to accept them because who they are is none of my business. But then they, kind of, order that we have to encourage or support their being gay or lesbian. I cannot support homosexuality because my religion forbids it. I could say, okay, you are going to be a transgender or a gay – I don't mind – but do not make me encourage or support you. I go against all these practices. The difference between me and others is that I grew up as a Muslim and learnt morals of a Muslim. I respect other aspects of society, but you cannot force what society believes to be right or wrong on others. I respect your preferences and expect you to respect mine.

Giving up on what you sincerely believe in and are committed to, what gives purpose and meaning to your life, is very difficult and something that can and, perhaps, should not be expected or asked for. A religious person can approve of the life of non-religious people or a Christian can approve of the way of life of a Muslim (and vice versa), but not without reservations: "There are aspects of the other's practices, attitudes, and beliefs that each of them must take exception to, must disagree with" (Raz, 1994, p. 150). The case of Felix Ngole and his religious beliefs forms a striking example of this. And there are debates and examples of the exercise of conscience in health care and the refusal to participate in specific medical services, such as abortion, sterilisation, and euthanasia (L.H., Harris, 2012; Murphy & Genius, 2013).

The importance of toleration is that it implies that others have the right to live according to their own deeply felt commitments and beliefs, even when they are in conflict with your own. There are two sides to this. On the one hand, tolerance allows dissenting others to exercise their individual autonomy by expressing their own beliefs and act in accordance with them. On the other hand, to be tolerant does not require that you give up or dilute what you belief or that you should have a lack of commitment to your own beliefs. It is useful to discuss these two sides a bit further, because this helps us to understand why also from a psychological perspective tolerance is an important option in plural societies that afford persons individual liberty.

Beliefs, morality, and diversity

Most parents want to transmit their beliefs and convictions to their children. They consider it important that their children believe in the same things, internalise the same values and norms, and live by the same principles and rules. More generally, they want their children to live a meaningful live with sincere convictions, commitments and moral beliefs that provide purpose, direction, confidence, and a secure sense of self. Around the age of four, children also gradually develop the ability to understand that other people have their own mental states, perspectives, and emotions. This "theory of mind" skill makes them appreciate that others have their own viewpoints which do not only differ from their own but can also be opposed to what they themselves sincerely belief and value.

Children will inevitably encounter people who have different preferences, opinions, and values and beliefs. Some of these differences will be interesting, nice, enjoyable, and enriching, but others will be challenging, unsettling, confusing and threatening. Diversity is like cholesterol; while the right type helps the body stay healthy, the wrong type can lead to a heart attack. Some types of diversity are fun, inspiring, challenging, and productive, while other kinds are disturbing, threatening, and disruptive. Diversity of preferences and tastes is good for living an exciting life, and diversity of views and idea is good for a vibrant and innovative community, but moral diversity can raise very difficult questions. It is difficult to approve and appreciate those who value self-interest and competition, if one has learned from early on that you should take care of others and help those in need (and vice versa).

Appreciation of diversity becomes very difficult when things are defined in terms of contrasting and even incompatible worldviews and morality. It is easy to accept that some people prefer to eat couscous and listen to rap music over the local hot-pot stew and classical music. But the case is quite different if some people deny the equal position of man and woman or favour the death penalty. Moralised conflicts are difficult to reconcile. If I say that I stand for gender equality, but that others in my community do not necessarily have to agree, it becomes a matter of personal preference. When I say that in our society, we stand for gender equality, but other societies may think differently about it, then it becomes a matter of social convention. But if I consider gender equality a moral principle, I stand for it everywhere and everyone else should too. If people from another community or group disagree, there is a problem. A sort of problem that goes beyond differences in preferences, taste, habits, and conventions which can be solved with mutual understanding and reasonable accommodations. A moral principle is typically considered to have general validity (Skitka et al., 2021). You can argue about its interpretation and applicability, but not about the principle itself. For instance, you can disagree about what equality really entails, how it relates to other principles like freedom, and whether something is a matter of equality at all. But if you say that you are in favour of gender equality but are happy to live in a country where that is not guaranteed, it is not a moral principle but a matter of convention and tradition, or of personal preference and opinion.

The conception of "belief" can be considered to apply to things "that" we believe and to things "in which" we believe (Treanor & Sweetman, 2021). The former epistemic meaning relates to matters that one holds to be true. Believing something is taking it to be so and this conception of "belief" does not only apply to the physical ("I believe it rains") and social ("I believe he is lazy") world, but also to the religious domain ("I believe God exists").

To believe *in* something implies that one binds oneself to a particular principle or doctrine which determines how one understands oneself and others. Ideological, religious, and moral beliefs are connected to actions by meaningfully governing one's life and sense of self. People cannot be forced to believe in something and acting on one's conscience and exercising moral autonomy implies following one's own beliefs and convictions.

Not all beliefs, values, and practices can be simultaneously appreciated and endorsed. Their propositional content means that beliefs and convictions are not like personal preferences or social conventions that can be considered to have equal value (Crane, 2017; Turiel, 2002). The ideological and moral beliefs that people hold are often "sacred", and subjectively considered categorical and objectively correct (Skitka et al., 2021; Zmigrod, 2022). To the extent that individuals consider their own ideological and moral position as self-evidently right and objectively grounded, they will view other positions as wrong, misguided, or even immoral (Wright et al., 2014). While diversity of preferences, opinions, and ideas is good for a vibrant, innovative, and strong community, different moral beliefs and worldviews may be difficult to reconcile and accept. Research on *protected values* (Baron & Spranca, 1997), the *value protection model of justice reasoning* (Skitka, 2002; Skitka & Mullen, 2002), the *sacred value protection model* (Tetlock, 2003), the *worldview defence model* (Brandt et al., 2014; Brandt & Van Tongeren, 2017), and *moral convictions* (Ellemers, 2017; Haidt, 2012) demonstrates that not all cultural, religious, and ideological beliefs and practices can exist comfortably side by side. It is very unlikely that people who hold a strong conviction, be it cultural, religious, or ideological, will come to accept and approve of beliefs and practices of others who strongly subscribe to an alternative worldview.

Everything cannot be considered just as worthy as anything else, and one cannot genuinely say "yes" to everything. It is not only logically but also psychologically impossible to really value everything equally and at the same time to be committed to one's own moral norms and beliefs: you cannot believe that your own beliefs are irrational or morally wrong. Morality requires that some things are considered wrong and horrendous, and a moral code that excludes nothing has no force. It is thus highly unlikely – a fantasy (Weissberg, 2008) – that people who hold a strong conviction will come to appreciate, approve, and even celebrate others who strongly subscribe to an alternate worldview. For example, if someone sincerely believes that abortion is murder due to their religious beliefs, or if someone is deeply committed to abortion rights from a commitment towards women's freedoms, it is unrealistic to try and convince them to be open-minded and accept the "other side's perspective". In one case, this would mean asking people to permit what they consider murder, and in the other case, it would mean asking someone to relinquish concerns for women's fundamental rights. Similarly, it will be difficult to persuade an atheist to sincerely appreciate religious beliefs, and to persuade a religious believer to genuine appreciate atheism.

I have discussed various examples and arguments in favour of the critical importance of tolerance in different domains of life. People cannot and will not value and appreciate everything and therefore everyone will need to tolerate at least some things some of the times. However, similar to prejudice-reduction strategies or initiatives focusing on inclusion and equity, tolerance is not the sovereign formula for all the complex questions surrounding forms of diversity. It is important to recognise the difficulty of tolerance and its possible drawbacks, and to consider various points of criticism.

Criticising tolerance

Together with the increased popularity of the notion of tolerance, there is increased criticism. Tolerance as forbearance would be an important ideal in the past, it is argued, but inadequate for achieving social justice and full inclusion in the present. Tolerance is rejected for being far too negative and for being repressive and hampering societal change, or rather for having gone much too far in leading to a culture of permissiveness and a lack of social cohesion. The different points of criticisms are common enough and not without merit, and I will empirically examine several of these in later chapters. However, we should not throw out the baby with the bathwater, because some of these criticisms are based on different understandings of what tolerance means and on particular aspects and usages of the discourse of tolerance. It is useful to discuss three main points of criticisms.

Limited use

According to some critics, tolerance can go, and has gone, too far in its focus on self-determination and the accommodation of cultural diversity. So-called passive, excessive, or mindless tolerance would have led to moral indifference and segregated communities, and would constitute a slippery slope to a society that lacks normative and moral guidelines. Tolerance is blamed for the ascendancy of competing and incompatible norms, values, and lifestyles that threaten liberal values, and "passive or hands-off" tolerance is blamed for condoning the oppression of vulnerable minorities (children, women, sexual minorities, dissenters) within (religious) minority communities (e.g. Okin, 1999; O'Neill, 1999). For example, concern for Jewish children lead some people to argue for the banning of non-medical Jewish male circumcision (Munzer, 2015), and "mindless tolerance" has been blamed for arranged marriages, honour killings, and child mistreatment among some Muslim minorities.

Tolerance would also undermine the substantive bonds that hold communities together, "we want to be a tolerant society, but we don't want to live in a divided society".[5] What would be required is an end to "excesses of tolerance" and the "ideology of tolerism" in favour of articulating clear standards of what is acceptable (Rothberg, 2013). There would be a threshold to tolerance and "we" would have been tolerant enough and even too indulgent and "soft" towards dissenting others which undermines not only social cohesion but in the end also "our" liberal values. It would be paradoxical, for example, to expect people in a liberal society to be committed to gender equality and at the same time to accept unequal gender arrangements among some minority groups in society (Ivarsflaten & Sniderman, 2017). It is argued that being too indulgent and lenient towards dissenting others would mean that tolerance gradually becomes "meaningless or empty" by turning into indifference ("do not care"), resignation ("give up"), an excuse for doing nothing ("it will not matter"), or a permissive relativism ("anything goes"). Thus, for a cohesive community and in order to maintain "our" tolerance and liberal values, we should not lead things slide by and recognise that meaningful tolerance depends on determining what is tolerable and what is not. Ignoring these limits would mean that there is no longer a shared normative and moral compass and that "we" compromise on the continuity of "our" core self-defining liberal values and therefore subvert our group identity.

This first point of criticism has similarities with criticisms on forms of multiculturalism that are considered to be divisive by contributing to essentialist and reified group differences, intergroup conflicts, and a fragmented society (Cobb et al., 2020; Verkuyten & Yogeeswaran, 2020). However, research shows that multiculturalism can have many beneficial effects in some respects, while being less useful in others. There is a complex trade-off of costs and benefits that depends on the way in which multiculturalism is construed and implemented. Similarly, an emphasis on tolerance can work out in various ways and does not imply an unlimited acceptance of competing norms and values with the related danger of parallel societies. Rather, tolerance is based on a shared identity (e.g. citizenship), can instil a sense of pluralist unity, and makes it possible to live together despite important differences among people.

Tolerance is demeaning

A second point of criticism is not that tolerance has gone too far but rather that it does not go far enough, and is even demeaning and disrespectful. Tolerance would imply accommodation at best, which would be hurtful for those who are tolerated and a poor substitute for the necessary recognition, appreciation, and respect that people need and deserve, especially minority group members. These criticisms are often summarised with the term "*mere* toleration", and with adding qualification such as "genuine", "true", "full", and "non-judgemental" appreciation and acceptance to indicate what is actually needed. The demand for more than mere tolerance "is a demand that what one is or does no longer be the object of the negative evaluation that is an essential ingredient of toleration" (Horton, 1996, p. 35).

Tolerance would set the bar too low. It would be patronising, condescending, and offensive, because it judges people rather than fully affirming, appreciating, and validating who and what they are: it involves "the marking of subjects of tolerance as inferior, deviant, or marginal, or undesirable by virtue of being tolerated" (Brown, 2006, p. 13). In the past, tolerance might have been an instrument of civic peace by providing protection against violent persecution of religious dissidents, the argument goes, but in modern plural societies, we should no longer criticise and judge people but rather welcome them and appreciate, embrace, and value them for what they are and want to be. The concept of tolerance would be an instrument of cultural domination that has the capacity to wound and should therefore be rejected and replaced by unconditional affirmation and respect (Ramadan, 2010). Or the meaning of tolerance should be revised and transformed to that of recognition and appreciation of differences in the public sphere (Galeotti, 2002). The negative aspects of criticism, disapproval, and non-interference should be replaced by the positive meanings of recognition, full acceptance, and inclusion.

In these criticisms, tolerance tends to become a form of appreciation and celebration of difference for its own sake, a near blank-check appreciation of diversity (Weissberg, 2008). The nature of the differences does not seem to matter and the only thing that is considered not acceptable is questioning the benefits and "sacred value" of diversity itself. Tolerance as appreciating others and being non-judgemental does not seem to apply to those who think differently about the value of diversity policies and, for example, express conservative and communitarian concerns. Also proponents of inclusion and respect have outgroups with very different values and beliefs to which they are intolerant and discriminate against (e.g. Bizumic et al., 2017), which leads to counter-accusations such as towards supporters of same-sex marriage being intolerant towards those who oppose such marriages (Jowett, 2017). Activism in the name of inclusion and diversity can imply intolerance of other viewpoints: "Ironically, the very effort to tolerate and value diversity constitutes a license to hate those who disagree" (Baumeister, 2001, p. 182). This double standard is similar to people arguing that we should value, appreciate, and embrace all (minority) cultures, while making many negative judgements about their own society. There is a tendency to apply tolerance selectively and this inconsistency has been discussed in terms of "the intolerance of tolerance" (Carson, 2012), turning pluralism in purism (Rauch, 2021), and as forms of censorship (e.g. no- and de-platforming, cancel culture) in which recognition and appreciation of diversity is considered to trump the right to criticise, evaluate, and judge (Campbell & Manning, 2018).[6]

Furthermore, in this criticism, the question of dealing with the difficult issue of living with cultural, religious, and other differences tends to be avoided. Yet many people are struggling with this question, because it is impossible not to judge and compare: "one cannot appreciate everything or nothing" (Weissberg, 2008, p. 45). There are practices and beliefs that cannot and ought not to command our appreciation and respect because these are, for example, harmful, unfair, and evil (e.g. slavery, genital mutilation, and child marriage). To be respectful of them would be to abandon moral sense, so that a completely tolerant person would be left without guidelines. People have their own commitments and beliefs and everyone will disagree, dislike, or disapprove of some things and therefore has to consider reasons for not interfering with dissenting, even contrasting, views and practices. Avoiding these issues or a reluctance to confront them does not make them go away and might even be a symptom of giving in, intellectual disengagement, and a failure of making moral choices about what should be tolerated and what not. Being told to appreciate, value, and celebrate lifestyles that may even be antithetical to your own does not solve the difficult questions of meaningful differences and does not make tolerance as forbearance superfluous. Rather, "tolerance is a constant project of being human . . . in navigating all the things one objects to, is annoyed by, even offended by" (Brown in Di Blasi & Holzhey, 2014, p. 46).

This criticism of tolerance being demeaning also tends to prioritise the affirmation of people's subjective feelings and the possibility that they feel offended and hurt over other considerations such as the open and free exchange of views and beliefs. How people feel becomes the measure of things and defines whether particular actions and beliefs are considered offensive, intolerable, and therefore beyond discussion ("you can't say that"; "it is not OK"; Barrow, 2005). However, it is hard to imagine any statement or argument that cannot be construed as offensive and hurtful to someone, including white parents claiming that social studies and history lessons in school about racism and forms of critical race theory cause discomfort, anguish and other forms of psychological distress among their children.[7] Furthermore, it is likely that both proponents of affirmative action in higher education and those who argue that this negative impact on merit-based promotion can feel offended by the other side. Additionally, whereas some consider wanting to culturally and economically protect the nation as being xenophobic and racist, others consider it common sense and resent being labelled "racist" that prevents their experiences, concerns and grievances being taken seriously (Gest, 2016). Furthermore, meaning is contextual and the same statement or question ("where are you from?"; "this is a land of opportunity") can be experienced as a form of microaggression by some minority members or rather as an expression of interest or encouragement by other minorities, also depending on the situation, context (cultural, national), and speaker.

There is no way of questioning the subjective claim of being offended and hurt, and there often are no good reasons for doing so. Yet feeling offended is not an argument as such, does not settle a debate, does not in itself give people certain rights, and does not relieve people from the responsibility to explain their view and reasoning, and respond to critics. Not all offensive ideas have value, but the value of an idea cannot be judged on the basis of whether it offends. There are of course very good reasons for not trying to offend someone and hurt their feelings. These reasons of kindness, politeness, and civility also matter for perceptions of rational argument and outgroup evaluations (e.g. Popan et al., 2019), but they do not imply an obligation of the offending party to not speak out and refrain from expressing their critical opinion, view, or belief.

Simply claiming that words or particular viewpoints are offensive, hurtful, or unnecessary divisive undermines open debate about contentious issues, silences alternative opinions and ideas, and leads to a culture of wariness and victimhood with negative implications for social progress, moral development, work contexts, academic freedom, and scientific advancement (Campbell & Manning, 2018; Ceci & Williams, 2018; Rauch, 2021). It replaces thinking about what exactly is being claimed and argued with a focus on who is saying it and how you feel about it.[8] The claim of being offended can also be a self-serving act since,

> Taking offence, when it means treating one's personal hurt as ground for punitive response, involves a refusal to show tolerance, to allow freedom or fair play – for why should you be allowed to say what you want when others are denied that right by you.
>
> *(Barrow, 2005, p. 273)*

Tolerance is about providing a basis from which to mitigate meaningful, deep differences and engage in debate about substantive issues, rather than about avoiding the discomfort of disagreement, criticism, disapproval, and contestation. According to Aristotle, those who misunderstand toleration "praise everyone with a view to pleasing them and oppose nothing, but rather suppose they ought not to cause pain (*lupedo*) to anyone they may meet" (Avramenko & Promisel, 2018, p. 855). Tolerance does not involve unconditional appreciation and a desire to please others but also not unreasonable criticism and a desire to hurt others.

A depoliticising discourse

A third point of critique is that tolerance is a "velvet glove" that has a depoliticising effect on social justice movements and that the discourse of tolerance creates biased intergroup differentiations (e.g. "tolerant" West/white majority vs. the "intolerant" East/Muslim minorities). Tolerance would be part of the velvet glove that as a sort of trick masks power relations (Jackman, 1994), and the discourse of tolerance would contribute to maintaining and justifying asymmetries of power (Brown, 2006). Part of this criticism goes back to Marcuse's (1969) well-known essay on "repressive tolerance". Tolerance would be repressive, because it protects the already-established and the related political realities: it implies normativity and is considered a strategy or tool for regulating aversion and managing the presence of the undesirable. Hence, tolerance is examined as a depoliticised conflict reducer that prioritises the status quo and leads to a retreat from social justice ideals by giving the misleading impression of equality, fairness, and inclusion. When the discourse of tolerance is prominent, it would be more difficult for minority groups to stand up against inequalities and disadvantages.

These critical points are important and certainly have merit and I will examine some of these empirically in later chapters. However, these criticisms are in part arguments against particular forms of democracy and can also lead to striking conclusions. For example, Marcuse argued for the need for a "liberating, pure tolerance" which according to him adds up to censoring (even up to and including the use of violence) movements from the political right in favour of movements from the left. Others argue for the need to go beyond tolerance which seems to imply forcing societal change and reversing power relations by radical protest and violent actions, even if the democratic majority does not agree.

However, the fact that a discourse of tolerance can have dominating and depoliticising effects does not mean that it cannot also be used for progressive and emancipatory ends. The discourse of tolerance and intolerance might be useful for resisting domination and can serve the societal and political interests of minorities. For example, the accusation of intolerance with the related victimhood claim can function as moral capital: it can be used to place majorities in a morally accountable position and to induce guilt feelings which can lead to majority support for change (Moscovici & Pérez, 2007). Furthermore, immigrant minorities can put forward that explicit or implicit demands for mainstream assimilation are forms of intolerance that contradict western commitment to diversity, tolerance, and civil liberties (Omlo, 2011). Similarly, in the account about his exclusion from further study, Ngole explained that he migrated to Britain because of the opportunities he "thought it offered". He defines British identity in terms of tolerance in which the protection of individual autonomy is central. He finds his exclusion from the social work course shocking, because it would imply that the country does not live up to its own credo of tolerance and religious freedom (Verkuyten, 2022a).

Muslim organisations can also use the discourse of tolerance to argue against the societal demand for change and reform in the direction of a "Euro-Islam" or "Europeanised Islam" that for them would subvert or fundamentally alter the core of their religious identity (Bilgrami, 1992; Tibi, 2002). In response to the societal demand to develop a Euro-Islam, they argue that this demand actually means that Western societies do not live up to their self-proclaimed and self-defining tradition of tolerance and religious freedom (Yildiz & Verkuyten, 2012). Therefore, Muslim organisations can resist societal demands for change, reform, and assimilation by mobilising the discourse of tolerance that appeals to principles and standards of conduct that European states themselves profess to have developed in response to religious differences and conflicts.

Furthermore, the critical points about depoliticising effects are mainly concerned with the ways in which tolerance is represented and used in societal discourses and in public and political debates. For example, in her book "*Regulating Aversion*", Brown (2006) formulates one of the strongest and most extensive critiques of tolerance. However, she focuses on the political discourse of tolerance and not on people practicing tolerance, and she agrees with the indispensability of tolerance in society and everyday life: "the work I've done on tolerance is not against tolerance: rather, it is intended to be a critique of existing tolerance discourse" (Brown, in Di Blasi & Holzhey, 2014, p. 13). Critically examining how the discourse of tolerance is rhetorically (ab)used and functions in intergroup relations and society more generally is something else than trying to understand the psychological processes and reasons that people have for demonstrating tolerance, and when and why they consider some things intolerable. This understanding of tolerance is according to Brown a crucial and regular part of life, because it is about

> how, for example, my teenager and I survive each other's taste in music; it is how devout Hindus, Muslims, Christians and Jews can be peacefully neighbours. It is, I think, the basis of the constitutional principle . . . that guarantees freedom of speech, freedom of worship, freedom of conscience.
>
> *(Di Blasi & Holzhey, 2014, p. 17)*

To conclude

With the increase in forms of diversity and of polarisation in most societies, there is also an increasing number of statements and initiatives on inclusion, appreciation, full acceptance, and embracing differences. There is no doubt that these are very important, but it is not always clear what exactly is meant by it. Accepting and respecting others as having equal dignity and moral autonomy are critical, but this does not have to imply that one needs to accept and respect different viewpoints, beliefs, or practices. However, what can be expected in such situations is the approach of tolerance, where we do not surrender our own convictions and beliefs, but rather show forbearance by putting up with something that we sincerely disapprove of or are negative about.

People cannot and will not value and appreciate everything and therefore everyone will need to tolerate at least some things. Tolerance might be considered minimal in providing the weakest form of positive relations between persons and groups, but "precisely because it is minimal, it is crucial" (Vogt, 1997, p. xviii). It forms a barrier against discrimination, oppression, exclusion, hostility, and conflict, and a critical condition for discussion and debate, and for citizenship and democracy.

Tolerating things we find abhorrent does not imply that we can do nothing other than refrain from interfering. We do not lose our freedom of expression and our rights to campaign, lobby, organise, and demonstrate. It is part of the deal that others also have to tolerate us and this is what a diverse and democratic society requires and makes possible. Tolerance provides others and ourselves the freedom and equal right to follow and act on our own conscience and exercise our moral autonomy (Furedi, 2011). However, tolerance is not the only answer to all complex questions of living with diversity and there are serious points of critique that should be considered in evaluating the relevance, importance, and limits of tolerance.

3

THE MEANING OF TOLERANCE

In 2019, we asked a representative sample of Dutch adults about their views on parents refusing to vaccinate their children against polio. In contrast to, for example, Belgium, there is no obligatory vaccination in the Netherlands and a minority of especially orthodox religious parents do not want to vaccinate their children. The great majority of the public was negative towards non-vaccination (84%) and agreed that it should not be tolerated. However, there was also a small section of the public with negative attitudes towards non-vaccination but indicating that it should nevertheless be tolerated (14%). They considered personal choice and religious freedom to be more important than public health concerns.

The question of vaccination often leads to attempts to silence, censor, and attack the "other side" (e.g. Kata, 2012), and a strong discussion about non-vaccination occurred in the second part of 2021 in relation to Covid-19. Not getting vaccinated against Covid-19 led to heated public and political debates, with some countries (Austria, Germany, Greece, Australia, and New Zealand) deciding (at the time) to make vaccination obligatory and other countries taking measures such as having to show QR codes or negative tests before being allowed to enter public buildings, theatres, restaurants, and so on. In the Netherlands, 43% disagreed with compulsory vaccination, 36% agreed, and 19% was undecided (December 2021; I&O).

The debate was about the weighing of opposing considerations and many people struggled with deciding which considerations should have priority. On the one hand, there was the importance of individual liberties, privacy, and physical integrity, which are guaranteed in the constitution, and, on the other hand, there was the safety, well-being, and the liberty of others. Individual freedom and physical integrity had to be weighed against the freedom of others and public health. Prioritising the former considerations led to a call for tolerance of the non-vaccinators and prioritising the latter led to a plea for zero-tolerance. This weighing of considerations also changed over time with the population increasingly showing less

DOI: 10.4324/9781003335030-3

understanding of those who were not vaccinated, and a similar change was apparent in political debates. Political parties that initially stated to be categorical against obligatory vaccination gradually changed their view because of starting to weigh the different considerations differently. What also mattered in these debates about whether non-vaccination should be tolerated were the reasons for not being vaccinated. Non-vaccinators who were unwilling received less understanding ("egoists" and "irresponsible") than those who were insufficiently informed or had reasons to not fully trust authorities and the government (e.g. immigrants, lower social classes).

This example demonstrates what is involved in tolerance, namely the weighing of different reasons and concerns: reasons for objection towards non-vaccination and reasons for acceptance of non-vaccination. Tolerance is the outcome when the latter reasons trump the former, when individual freedom and bodily integrity are considered more important than public health and safety. In contrast, when the reasons for objection are given priority, zero tolerance of non-vaccination is the result.

However, not everyone interprets this dilemma situation as a matter of tolerance, and when the word tolerance is used, it is not always used in the same way. This is not specific for this particular dilemma. Tolerance is a word that has various meanings and that is used in different ways when thinking about difficult questions related to forms of diversity and polarisation. Furthermore, other terms are used such as "respect", "recognition", "appreciation", and "acceptance", sometimes in addition to "tolerance" ("tolerate and respect") and sometimes to indicate that tolerance is not enough ("not tolerance, but respect"). However, also these other terms have multiple meanings and are used in quite different ways (e.g. Conover, 2009; Fraser, 2003; Laegaard, 2010a). For example, "acceptance" is used as a passive term and equated with tolerance to indicate enduring something one disagrees with, dislikes, or disapproves of (King, 2012), but also as an active term to indicate wholehearted, genuine or "full" acceptance in which people are not judged but rather embraced for what they are (Scanlon, 2003). This latter meaning is similar to the way in which the term "respect" is often used, but also this term can be understood in different ways depending, for example, on what it is that is respected (Honneth, 1995; Taylor, 1992).[1] Recognition of other's basic human dignity, as members of humanity, and unconditional respect for their personal autonomy, is something else than respecting and valuing their specific achievements, views, beliefs, commitments, and practices. The former is a requirement for tolerance, whereas the latter is not. Acting respectfully towards others as equals does not have to imply the appreciation of (parts of) their particular way of life.

The different terms that are used and the different ways in which the same term is used can lead to misunderstandings, ambiguous descriptions, inadequate explanations, and misguided recommendations. So it is important to make conceptual distinctions that enable us to distinguish between specific phenomena and to describe and explain them (Machado & Silva, 2007). Discussing how particular concepts are used makes it clear what the argument is about and gives the reader the opportunity to disagree and voice criticism.

Two key meanings of tolerance

In 1976, Ferrar noted, "The concept of tolerance is in disarray" and "The tolerance label is typically pasted over conglomerate indices of attitudes, opinions, behaviors and beliefs which assume some unspecified definition of tolerance" (p. 63). He continues by saying that within the literature there are distinct definitions of tolerance which are by no means identical or interchangeable, such as the approval and appreciation of a wide range of beliefs and practices and the allowance of a range of rights and privileges. Similarly, King (2012, p. x) notes a general impression of confusion because tolerance "simply disgorged too many different, contradictory, unsystematic understandings" and this prevents getting the analysis right. He argues that tolerance is considered an attitude, a belief, a virtue, a value orientation, a discourse, and a practice. Other scholars have also discussed tolerance as a complex, paradoxical, and multidimensional construct, and various forms and distinctions have been proposed. For example, Walzer (1997) argues that there are five types of tolerance of cultural and religious differences, which vary from resigned acceptance for the sake of peace to enthusiastic endorsement of diversity (see also Ricoeur, 1996). Similarly, Forst (2013) makes a distinction between four conceptualisations of tolerance: the permission, coexistence, respect, and esteem conception. Others make a distinction between tolerance in the distinct domains of politics, social relations, and moral issues, and empirical research in different countries demonstrate that these are considered different matters (Erisen & Kentmen-Cin, 2017; Lee, 2014; Mather & Tranby, 2014).

One main and recurrent distinction is between the modern understanding of tolerance as appreciation and the classical understanding of tolerance as forbearance.[2] The key psychological differences between these two understanding are presented in Table 3.1, and the distinction can be further explained with an example.

The Netherlands is well known in the world as being a tolerant society, and already in 1579, the freedom of religion was guaranteed in the Union of Utrecht. Compared to other countries, the young republic had in the 17th century great freedom and was a refuge for freethinkers from all corners of Europe, including for Pierre Bayle who wrote a "Treatise on universal toleration". Nowadays, Dutch people still consider "tolerance" a self-defining national trait (de Hardt et al., 2019)

TABLE 3.1 Distinguishing the psychology of appreciation tolerance and forbearance tolerance

	Appreciation tolerance	*Forbearance tolerance*
Affective state	Positive outgroup feelings and beliefs	Disapproval of outgroup beliefs and practices
Psychological process	Flexible thinking, being well-disposed, open-minded	Balanced thinking, weighing contrasting moral reasons
Behavioural outcome	Approving, recognition	Allowing, non-interference

Source: Adapted from Verkuyten et al. (2022a)

which would be demonstrated, for example, by the fact that the Netherlands was the first to allow euthanasia, legalise same-sex marriage, and allowed coffeeshops that sell soft drugs. However, it is not fully clear what is meant by claiming that the Dutch are tolerant, because it can at least refer to two different understandings. On the one hand, it can mean that the Dutch disapprove of little and appreciate much, and on the other hand, that they disapprove of many things which they nevertheless endure. Thus, the Dutch can allow more because they object to less (appreciation tolerance) or because they put up with more (forbearance tolerance).

Tolerance as appreciation

The former – modern – meaning implies that the Dutch are relatively broad minded, open, and non-judgemental. This is the meaning that is put forward in UNESCO's (1995) declaration on tolerance that was mentioned in the Introductory chapter. In this understanding, tolerance is equated with recognising and appreciating forms of diversity, and intolerance with dogmatism and prejudice. Also social psychologists tend to explicitly, or tacitly, equate tolerance with appreciation and liking of different ways of life, and intolerance with prejudice as a generalised negative feeling, belief, and behavioural orientation towards a group of people (e.g. Dunn & Singh, 2011; Ganzach & Schul, 2021). They use a prejudice-tolerance continuum, whereby tolerance is conceptualised as the "tendency to be generally free of prejudice" (Duckitt, 1992, p. 8). For example, cross-national research introducing a new individual difference measure of tolerance, conceptualises tolerance as a value orientation and generally positive response towards difference (Hjerm et al., 2020).

A tolerant or non-prejudiced person is characterised by open-mindedness, mental flexibility, acceptance of ambiguity, empathic ability and self-security (e.g. Togeby, 1998; Van Zalk et al., 2014). In contrast, prejudiced people are narrow-minded because of their need for structure and definiteness. They are characterised by cognitive inflexibility, low integrative complexity, and a desire for simplicity, certainty, and security (for a review, see Roets & Van Hiel, 2011). The prejudiced person has difficulty in accepting the differing views, beliefs, and practices of other people because of a need for closure and a lack of openness to experience, and feelings of fear and uncertainty (Jost et al., 2003). This results in a pattern of generalised (explicit and implicit) prejudice towards multiple types of minority groups, that has been found in many studies (Hodson & Dhont, 2015).

Tolerance as non-prejudice is also discussed by Allport in his classical book on "*The Nature of Prejudice*" in which he considers a tolerant person as someone who is appreciative, open-minded, and "on friendly terms with all sorts of people" (Allport, 1954, p. 425). According to this understanding, it would be odd to say that a person who is favourably disposed towards minorities is not tolerant of them, or a person who accepts more and values diversity more is less tolerant. Claiming that a person or group (e.g. the Dutch) is tolerant would not mean that they endure many things that they dislike or disapprove of, but rather that they disapprove of little. Tolerance in this understanding implies a positive response to diversity itself, a signifier of appreciation and affirmation, and intolerance is equated with dogmatism, closed mindedness, and prejudice more generally.

Tolerance as forbearance

The second, classical meaning of tolerance is not about the Dutch disapproving of little, but rather that they disapprove of many things which they nevertheless condone and endure. In the same Allport (1954) book that provided the aforementioned quote, another section says, "When we say that we tolerate a headache, or our shabby apartment, or a neighbor, we certainly do not mean that we like them, but merely that in spite of our dislike we shall endure them" (Allport, 1954, p. 425). This meaning is central in the philosophical and political science literature that focuses on tolerance as forbearance; putting up with things that one objects to or is negative about (Cohen, 2004; King, 2012). In this understanding, tolerance involves acceptance despite objection whereby the latter is a critical ingredient: "one cannot tolerate ideas of which one approves" (Gibson, 2006a, p. 22). Differences to which people are indifferent or which they like and enjoy, do not require tolerance.

Tolerance is an option only when one disagrees, dislikes, or disapproves of something. It implies a prior act of judgement (Sandel, 1996) and is not about putting up with what is endurable but putting up with what one actually finds difficult to bear. Tolerance requires self-control and a more tolerant person is more likely to accept conduct that they continue to object to. The reason for acceptance is that the disapproval of the practices or beliefs of another person or group (e.g. annoying behaviour, non-vaccination, ritual slaughter of animals) is considered less important than the reason to nonetheless accept those practices or beliefs (e.g. self-determination, physical integrity, religious freedom). This understanding also implies the existence of boundaries because not everything can and should be tolerated, such as injustice, oppression, and harming others: tolerance is not an unlimited good.

Two common lay understandings

These two main understanding of the meaning of tolerance do not only appear in academic writings but are also two common cultural understandings that are used in everyday life and public discourses (Verkuyten & Kollar, 2021). Research on "culturomics" uses computational methods for examining semantics in large corpus of data and focuses on the range of other words with which a target word is collocated (Bybee, 2010; Michel et al., 2011). This approach relies on dense representations of words (embeddings) that result, for example, in visual representations such as "word clouds". This work has resulted in two different word clouds for "tolerance". A first one has words such as "multicultural", "friends", "happy", and "respect", and is similar to the modern understanding of tolerance.[3] A second one contains words such as "endurance", "forbearance", "restraint", and "self-control", and therefore is in line with the classical understanding of tolerance.[4]

For intolerance, there is only one main type of word cloud in which terms such as "prejudice", "biased", "racism", and "discrimination" are prominent.[5] Thus, whereas tolerance seems to have two different cultural meanings, intolerance seems to be commonly associated with negative words and not as a response to normatively intolerable beliefs and practices.

These word clouds tell us something about the broad cultural meanings that exist but little about how common people understand situations of tolerance and intolerance. To gain insight into this, we included an open-ended question in a survey on a national sample of Dutch adults (Verkuyten & Kollar, 2021). Participants were asked randomly to share a concrete example of either tolerance or intolerance that they had experienced themselves or heard about. Subsequently, they were asked to explain why they considered this an example of (in)tolerance and then to indicate when this would no longer be a case of (in)tolerance. In the introduction to the open-ended question, half of the respondents were given the classical definition of (in)tolerance as (not) putting up with something one disapproves of, while no definition was provided to the other half of the respondents. The reason for this distinction was to examine whether people's spontaneous understanding is similar or rather differs from their guided understanding.

Some of the examples given for tolerance by the participants referred to openness and respecting who and what others are and want to be. Tolerance would imply withholding opinions or judgement and being favourably disposed towards those who are different. This modern understanding of tolerance was evident in around 20% of the descriptions. However, most of the descriptions were in line with the classical understanding as putting up with someone's behaviour when one disapproves of it, or when others endure one's own annoying behaviour. This classical understanding was evident in 73% of the examples when no definition was given and in 88% of the examples after a definition was provided.

In the condition without a definition, people predominantly explained that the situation was an example of tolerance because it had to do with endurance, patience, or putting up with something that one objects to because of the respect for other people as individuals or their freedom to be who they are ("I disapprove of something she does, but I accept her"). With a definition, the explanation was similar in emphasising acceptance, self-control, and putting up with things that bother you, and the types of examples given in the two conditions were also quite similar:

> My colleague is a Muslim and prays several times a day. During these times I receive his calls for him and I think he has a right to this time. Other colleagues disagree but they go for smoke for every hour and I also tolerate that.
>
> *(without definition)*

> I live in a town with very religious people. I don't agree with their beliefs but I do accept and respect them.
>
> *(definition given)*

In both versions (with and without a definition), it was explained that if the behaviour in the situation crosses certain unacceptable boundaries (e.g. hurting others, forcing your will on someone else, and disrespecting others), it would become a non-tolerable situation. Thus, in line with the classic understanding, boundaries of tolerance were recognised:

> If they would push their faith on me and I wouldn't be able to live my normal life anymore.

> Lack of respect from the other side, however much you disagree with someone reciprocal respect is a mark of civilization.

In contrast to the examples given for tolerance, the majority of examples (84%) for intolerance were in line with the modern understanding of narrow-mindedness and prejudice (Figgou & Condor, 2006). Intolerance was represented as a negative emotional reaction towards difference. The situations described were considered examples of intolerance because of a lack of empathy, being overly critical, or discriminatory, and the examples most often related to ethnicity, but disabilities, sexual orientation, and difference of opinion were also mentioned. Furthermore, although there were more people who did not give an example when there was no definition presented than when a definition was provided, the types of examples were similar:

> It happened in the store where I work. A customer came and saw that there were two male customers standing holding hands. She then literally said to the men that she didn't think that they should publicly hold hands in the store.
>
> *(without definition)*

> A lot of people say, when they read about a break-in or a hit and run "it was probably a Moroccan or a Turk or a Polish person".
>
> *(definition given)*

The solutions mentioned for turning the situation of intolerance into a case of tolerance were also more in line with the modern understanding of tolerance. Empathy and perspective taking were most often described as antidotes to intolerance. It was explained that empathy and perspective taking can be increased by positive experiences or similar hardships that place you in the other person's shoes. In addition, openness and understanding were suggested as solutions that would turn an intolerant situation into tolerance. However, perspective taking and understanding could also serve the cause of forbearance tolerance in learning one to endure what one continues to disagree with or find wrong.

> If you think about why something is done. If you do your best to understand the other. You may still not agree or still think their approach is wrong but you did try to understand them. You looked beyond your own world and showed respect.

Tolerance as forbearance

The classical term tolerance derives from the Latin word *tolerabilis* which implies the existence of a burden, originally a physical one, and later also a mental one. The burden requires forbearance, as the intentional choice not to negatively interfere with beliefs, behaviours and practices to which one objects (Cohen, 2004; Forst, 2013). Three clarifications of this description are important that together form the distinct conceptualisation of tolerance. The three aspects of "objection, acceptance and rejection" relate to different psychological processes and form the core of our social psychological "Forbearance Model of Tolerance" that is presented in Figure 3.1 and that will be discussed and elaborated upon in the various chapters. Here, I will consider each of these three aspects and subsequently discuss three other issues related to tolerance: the object of tolerance, dimensions of tolerance, and power relations.

Objection

First, tolerance is not an unwillingness to judge or criticise, but implies judgement in the sense of making considered decisions about views, beliefs, and practices that one cares about and objects to (Sandel, 1996). It makes little sense to say that we are tolerant to things that we like, approve of, agree with, or are neutral or indifferent ("who cares") about. Mere non-interference (e.g. "leaving them alone", "ignoring things", and "turning a blind eye") or supporting things one agrees with or promotes, therefore, are not reflective of toleration. Thus, tolerance is not the same as recognising, appreciating, embracing, and celebrating forms of diversity. Rather, there is always an objection (disagreement, criticism, disapproval, or dislike) which is the initial aspect of the tolerance process, such as when outgroup or ingroup members, strangers or friends, outsiders or family members, engage in practices or voice ideological beliefs that are unappealing, unsettling, or uninviting. The

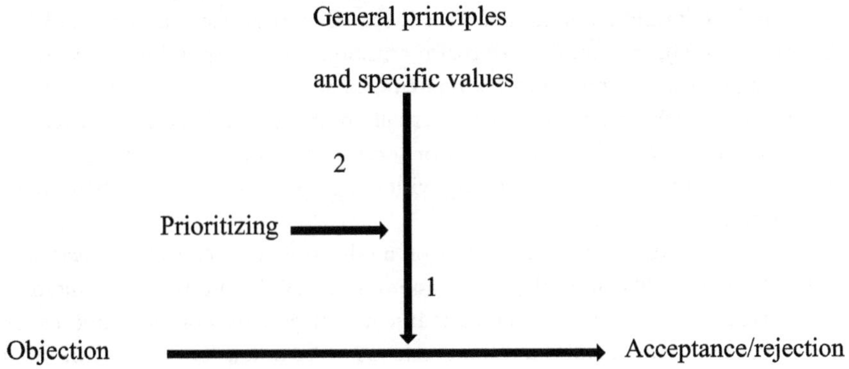

FIGURE 3.1 The forbearance model of tolerance

Source: Adapted from Verkuyten et al. (2020a)

objection can be rather intuitive, for example, drawn from gut feelings of dislike or moral emotions, or it may be based on reflective thinking about the meaning and implications of unfamiliar or opposing values, beliefs, and practices (see Chapter 5; Verkuyten et al., 2022a). Importantly, the objection should not simply reflect group-based prejudice but needs to have some value, as we will discuss later and examine empirically in Chapter 4.

Acceptance

Second, tolerance implies self-restraint in not acting on the negative attitude that one has towards a dissenting belief, behaviour or practice. The self-restraint requires effort because of the continuing nagging feeling of disapproval and the temptation to act upon this. Tolerance involves "the suppression of the tendency to suppress" (Schuyt, 1997, p. 169) which has been described as "painful", "to suffer", and as being at once "necessary and impossible" (Tønder, 2013; Williams, 1996). With tolerance, the negative attitude does not translate into negative action aimed at interfering or stopping what one objects to, and sometimes even involves active support for the rights of dissenting others. The self-restraint is based on having principled (e.g. equal rights) or pragmatic (e.g. coexistence) reasons or endorsing specific values for voluntary accepting what one objects to or is negative about. This makes tolerance the opposite of discrimination in which distinctions and differentiations are made based on reasons that are normatively considered irrelevant and inappropriate.

However, mere non-interference or non-discrimination is not enough because there are many reasons for this. The non-interference and acceptance should not be coerced or based on fear, social disapproval, possible sanctions, or concerns over self-image. And it should not be a matter of resigning and giving up because this would mean that you do not value the non-interference bur rather, for example, are pessimistic about the possibility of dialogue and change (Cohen, 2004). This makes tolerance different from, for example, expressing non-prejudicial views for reasons of conforming to ingroup norms to secure ingroup acceptance (Crandall & Eshleman, 2003), or from the external motivation not to respond with prejudice, or the suppression of prejudice for reputational reasons (Plant & Devine, 1998). People are tolerant when they have internally motivated and value-based reasons (e.g. concepts of equality or freedom, or social cohesion, or peace) to intentionally refrain from negatively interfering with disapproved of beliefs and behaviours (conditional path "1" in Figure 3.1).

In other words, there is a process of moderation whereby the objection is overridden by deliberative thinking about value-based reasons to not interfere (Verkuyten et al., 2020a). Tolerance is intentional because one does not act on principles by accident and one cannot tolerate what one is ignorant of. In other words, there is a system of priorities (King, 2012) whereby the intuitive or more reflective objection is overridden or balanced by deliberative thinking about warranted reasons to not interfere.

We must value our non-interference as something that we do for the right reasons. The presence of these reasons matter because it determines whether a person is tolerant or not. An example can illustrate this point. Imagine that you learn of a neighbour wanting to burn the national flag, an action you strongly disapprove of. You can decide not to interfere because you value freedom of speech, or rather because you think there is nothing you can do about it, or that it isn't worth the effort, or that you fear your neighbour's reaction. The difference is that with the first reason the non-interference is principled, based on a value, whereas the latter reasons indicate resignation or permissiveness rather than tolerance. With the first reason there is the feeling that one is doing the right thing by doing nothing, while with the second type of reasons, doing nothing feels like the wrong thing to do.

Rejection

Third, tolerance requires that there is no action aimed at preventing the disliked or disapproved of conduct, and if one does interfere in the behaviour, one clearly fails to tolerate it. Obviously this is a matter of degree and people can be less or more tolerant depending on how strongly they disapprove of the behaviour and on the type of interference (e.g. from trying to discourage it to taking concrete steps to stop it).

However, there can be additional reasons for not tolerating behaviours that are considered intolerable. The requirement to accept other beliefs should not turn into the requirement to have no genuine beliefs or moral convictions on the basis of which opposing beliefs are considered seriously misguided and wrong. It is difficult to imagine that anyone would tolerate everything. This would imply a complete lack of any guiding beliefs, commitments and principles. Tolerance differs from relativism ("anything goes") and unlimited appreciation of diversity since there are boundaries to what can and should be accepted, as indicated, for example, with the use of the term "zero tolerance" for hate crimes, theft, oppression, and so on (Kim & Wreen, 2003; Lukes, 2008). There are always beliefs, behaviours and practices that are considered intolerable, for example, because these are considered morally unacceptable or as threatening the freedom of others, or undermining the maintenance of group identity, or promoting social disorder and threatening peaceful coexistence. So one cannot praise a person simply for being tolerant because they may condone oppression, unfairness, cruelty, or violence, which would imply culpable indulgence. And although intolerance is typically not acclaimed, one cannot condemn a person simply for being intolerant because they may be intolerant of these negative practices. The fact that people cannot and do not tolerate everything forms one of the central aspects of toleration: drawing a line between what should and what should not be tolerated.

Already young children (5-years-old) use nonrelativistic criteria for evaluating beliefs that reflect disagreements, and their judgements of relativism differ from their tolerance of divergent beliefs (Turiel, 2002; Wainryb et al., 2001). Furthermore, people tend to view moral convictions as absolute and universal (Skitka et al., 2021). Thus, there can be additional reasons not to tolerate a certain behaviour (e.g. harmful, oppression, and violence) that take priority over the reasons for accepting what one objects to (e.g. religious freedom), making the particular belief, practice or behaviour not to be tolerated. For those who favoured obligatory Covid-19 vaccination, public health and a fully functioning society did trump arguments of individual choice and body integrity (conditional path "2" in Figure 3.1).

Furthermore, associations such as a church, a school, a private company or a political movement can decide not to tolerate voices that challenge or deny essential aspects of its core beliefs and values. They can have good reasons for this because "religious groups and political movements would lose their point if they had to include just anyone" (Scanlon, 2003, p. 194). People who try to transfer the group identity into something that is very different from what it is meant to be, can be considered intolerable. For example, in June 2021, the party leadership of the Socialist Party in the Netherlands voted in favour of no longer recognising their youth branch "Red" as part of the party because it would be too radical in trying to change the party in the communist direction. Similarly, a school might want to maintain its religious identity which can mean having a denominational closed admission policy that trumps the freedom of choice of parents and children.

The meaning of intolerance

The term *in*tolerance is not only used for things that are considered unacceptable (e.g. oppression and violence) but also for interfering which what one actually should accept (e.g. equal civil rights of all). This can be confusing, but the distinction between the two meanings is similar to the distinction between differential treatment and discrimination. This latter distinction has to do with whether there are, or are not, good reasons and arguments for differentiating between persons and groups. Treating categories of people (women, Muslims, sexual minorities) differently on the basis of reasons that are considered irrelevant is something else then treating categories of people (e.g. children, the elderly, and the sick) differently for relevant reasons: the former is discrimination, the latter is differential treatment. There can be good reasons to make distinctions between categories of people that differ in relevant ways. In the legal domain, there is the doctrine of reasonable classification, because the application of law cannot be universal or general in character but depends upon various aspects, such as the nature of the case, group, place, and circumstances.

Obviously, what are considered good reasons can change and can differ between individuals, groups, cultures, and historical periods. Yet this does not take away the fact that the distinction is a critical one. Things that are considered equal should be treated in the same way and things that are different should be treated differently. The term intolerance is most often used in the sense of discrimination when there are no good reasons to interfere, but also in the sense of differential treatment when there are good reasons to interfere in what is considered unacceptable. The latter meaning concerns the question of the boundaries of tolerance which is discussed in Chapter 6, and the former one is discussed in Chapter 7.

The object of tolerance

With tolerance there must be something to tolerate, but it is not directly obvious what sorts of things are the proper objects of tolerance. In the literature, there are different views on this and in particular on the question if tolerance applies to persons per se, or rather to beliefs, convictions, viewpoints, lifestyles, behaviours and practices. This is a difficult question because in everyday life, and also in empirical research, it is often not easy to make a distinction between the two. However, this empirical difficulty does not imply that it can be ignored conceptually and that people never make a distinction between a person per se or a category of people as people, and the beliefs, viewpoints and practices that individuals or groups of people hold or are engaged in.

The fact that there can be overlap is not a reason for ignoring the analytical usefulness of making a distinction and dismiss the democratic principle of differentiating between ideas and beliefs that one disagree with and combat, and respecting the person expressing these ideas and beliefs as an equal citizen. Such a distinction is in fact a critical aspect of tolerance: treating and respecting all people as equally valuable, without treating all viewpoints, beliefs, and practices as equally valuable. All persons are equal and worthy of respect but "The idea that all views or opinions are worthy of respect is entirely false" (Crane, 2017, p. 178). In the words of the philosopher Peter Kreeft, tolerance is about "being egalitarian towards people" together with "being elitist about ideas": respecting people as autonomous and equal human beings while considering some ideas, views, and beliefs as better or more valuable than other ones.

Tolerance differs from forms of racism and prejudices because it involves recognising others as autonomous persons and treating them with equal dignity and respect, or as "different equals" (Simon, 2020). It implies thinking well of others as equal persons, in spite of their beliefs, viewpoints and practices that one disagrees with, dislikes, or disapproves off. What should be respected is others' autonomy and right to determine for themselves the life that they wish to lead. In the European *Statute for the Promotion of Tolerance*, it is explained that tolerance means both respect (as an active term) for the human dignity and rights of others, and acceptance (as a passive term) of dissenting peculiarities of others. Thus, tolerance implies that one should respect others as autonomous persons, as full members of a common community and equal human beings, but without having to appreciate their views, commitments and beliefs.[6]

Research shows that people are able to make a distinction between practices and beliefs they disapprove of, on the one hand, and respecting persons in virtue of their shared humanity, on the other hand, at both the explicit and implicit mental levels (De Keersmaecker et al., 2021; Uzarevic et al., 2020; Veenvliet, 2008; Wenger & Daniels, 2006). This distinction is broadly recognised, including by minority members as illustrated in the next quote taken from one of our interviews[7] with a trans person talking about the relationship with their partner and their grandmother's response.

> so I feel like she was respectful, just really couldn't wrap her head around us being together so she tolerated it and tried her best to just well show interest in us. . . . Yeah, I think that's kind of where I feel like that to me shows like okay they do, they might not accept it or agree with it but they do respect you as a human being and feel like they need to kind of like show that they do see you as a person.

Tolerance signifies an approach towards dissenting others "insofar as it pertains to beliefs and opinions and forms of behaviour linked to them" (Furedi, 2011, p. 11; Bader, 2013). This is vitally important for a culturally diverse, polarised and peaceful society, but also means that the concept of tolerance should not be inappropriately extended to situations in which it is not suitable. Unfortunately this happens frequently and for understandable reasons, but expanding the meaning and purpose of tolerance is not very helpful. Specifically what tends to happen is that tolerance is directed towards categorical distinctions based on demographic characteristics such as race and gender. However, whereas tolerance is appropriate for specific beliefs, views, and practices, it is not adequate for solving tensions and conflicts between social categories or classes of people.

Tolerance does not address intergroup biases that result from categorical distinctions between the ingroup ("us") and outgroup ("them"), or forms of racism, sexism, or group-based prejudices more generally. A categorical distinction between ingroup ("us") and outgroup ("them") does not make the outgroup ("them"), by itself, a subject for tolerance. Making an "us-them" distinction provides a necessary condition for ingroup favouritism and can go together with outgroup dislike (Diehl, 1990; Tajfel & Turner, 1979). Social categorisation is, thereby, a key factor in intergroup animosity with stronger group boundaries often leading to greater intergroup bias (but see Park & Judd, 2005). However, intergroup biases resulting from social categorisation is not thought about as being redressable by tolerance. Categorical distinctions with the related psychological processes of perceiving less difference within categories and stronger differences between categories, stereotypical generalisations, a general tendency to value and trust those who belong to the same category as oneself, and outgroup prejudice, differ from the processes involved in tolerance. I will discuss this further in the next chapter, but for now, it is important to explain why persons or groups per se are not the appropriate objects of tolerance.

It makes little sense to say that one must dislike or hate women or a racial group, to be able to be tolerant of them. This would imply that one has to be a bigot in order to have the possibility of being tolerant and that a more racist person showing self-restraint is more tolerant and virtuous (Forst, 2013; Horton, 1996). One implication would be that prejudice and racism are turned into acceptable and valid objections that only need to be restrained: "It turns a blind prejudice into an ethical judgment" (Forst, 2001, p. 194). However, a misogynist or a racist who refrains from acting upon their sexist or racist feelings and beliefs does not tend to demonstrate tolerance, and a more racist person showing self-restraint is not a more tolerant person. The possibility of being tolerant does not depend on being a bigot, and bigotry should not be addressed by stimulating tolerance, but rather by anti-racism and prejudice reduction strategies (Verkuyten et al., 2020a). Thus, a racist, homophobe or misogynist should not learn to be tolerant but should work towards stop being a racist, homophobe or misogynist.

Tolerance is based on diversity but not all differences are similar. Ideological positions, worldviews, and religious beliefs are something else than demographic characteristics such as race and gender. The former are things that one believes in, is convinced about and committed to, and which one practices. These involve explanations and interpretations of the world and differ in the extent to which they are discussed, imposed and complied with. These matters of belief and understanding can in principle be contradicted and criticised and this is likely to occur regularly, depending on the freedom to do so. Groups that are bound together by religion, viewpoint, or ideology can be tolerated, and in those cases, tolerance refers to the beliefs and practices of members of those groups, or what the group stands for. However, people of a different gender or race should not be tolerated on the basis of their categorical belonging but rather recognised and respected as similar human beings.

Markers such as race and gender may in some contexts indicate similar experiences but do not imply a shared worldview which means that there is no legitimate reasons to question someone's gender or race. There are racist, sexist, and prejudicial reasons for doing so, and these should be considered and addressed for what they are: "It is not tolerance toward different races that we generally wish to promote but the recognition of the intrinsic moral irrelevance of racial differences" (Horton, 1996, p. 34). With tolerance, the objections that one has should be considered reasonable (e.g. not arbitrary and not prejudiced) and not without value (Forst, 2013). Arguing that someone should tolerate a category of people because "blind hatred" of these people is wrong, is not really arguing for toleration at all. So strictly speaking terms such as "racial tolerance" or "gender tolerance" are misleading because the proper objects of tolerance are not social categories per se but rather specific beliefs, behaviours and practices that one objects to (Horton, 1996).

Although various "ascriptive" characteristics are not in themselves objects of tolerance, they often become so when they are connected, by insiders or outsiders, to specific cultural features, stereotypical traits, and particular behaviours, rituals and practices. When racial differences are culturalised and essentialised, the question of tolerating racial groups arises. People can hate Jews, look down upon women and dislike immigrants, but what is at issue in tolerating Jews or women or immigrants are the beliefs, values, norms and acts held to define them. Thus, social categories become the proper focus of tolerance if accompanied by a defining set of group values and beliefs and a community of practitioners. An example, is opinion-based groups (being pro or anti an issue) that involve a social identity based on shared opinion with the related behaviour (Bliuc et al., 2007).

However in principle, the objection involved in tolerance is not focused on social categories per se, but rather on specific dissenting beliefs and practices. It is around concrete issues (e.g. dress-code, religious education, language use, dietary requirements, sexual practices, ideological beliefs, Mosque building, and parenting approaches) that ways of life collide and the need for toleration arises. Furthermore, the question of tolerance can also arise in relation to *in*group members that one favours or for family members and friends that are involved in practices that one objects to. Similar to parents finding that certain practices of their children should not be tolerated (e.g. smoking and drinking), people can wish to deny forms of freedom of expression (e.g. burning of the national flag and forms of hate speech) to fellow ingroup members. Furthermore, one can reject a specific practice (e.g. ritual slaughter of animals) of a group (Jews and Muslims) to whom one has neutral or even positive feelings (Hurwitz & Mondak, 2002; Sniderman et al., 1989).

Accepting the existence of a different view and respecting the right to hold a particular difference, is not the same as accepting and respecting the difference itself (Balint, 2010; Carson, 2012). To accept that a different view exists and respect others' attachment to it, does not have to imply that one approves of the view, let alone appreciate it. A person's passion for a dissenting conviction or principle can be a sign of integrity which makes one respect the person while still rejecting the belief (Zlatev, 2019). It is possible to disagree with someone without being disagreeable, and having a critical debate can be a sign of respect rather than a display of disrespect (Bendersky, 2014). Tolerance is about respecting, for example, Fatma as an equal citizen and not about valuing her Islamic religious beliefs, or accepting that John, as a born-again Christian, has the same rights as everyone else and not about appreciating born-again Christianity. To be tolerant implies a commitment to accept, and perhaps even actively support, the right of different equals their exercise of choice: to not negatively interfere and restrict their personal or collective autonomy (Kachanoff et al., 2021).

Dimensions of tolerance

Various scholars distinguish between tolerance as an attitude, belief or a virtue, and toleration as a practice, action or behaviour, while others argue that we should not worry too much about these distinctions (King, 2012; Vogt, 1997; Walzer, 1997). Both "tolerance" and "toleration" are nouns and both terms are reduced to the same verb "to tolerate" when used for acts of toleration and to the same adjectival form "tolerant". However, the term "tolerance" is also used to refer to a moral attitude, a belief, and to a general predisposition to endure things one dislikes. Furthermore, the psychological literature clearly indicates that attitudes and beliefs are important for actions, but that the latter typically depends on much more. So for reasons of clarity it seems best to use the term "toleration" for the activity and "tolerance" for the psychology. This makes it possible, for example, to consider dispositional tolerance as the general psychological tendency to allow others to live the life that they wish, and to examine whether and when this predisposition is translated into actual behaviour.

Yet things might be a bit more complicated than this because tolerance generally means behavioural *inaction*, namely endurance, forbearance, and non-interference. Furthermore, tolerance can also be considered and empirically examined in terms of an assessment or judgement. A judgement can be purely a private matter but is often expressed, either in real life or in the context of a research. According to speech act theory (Littlejohn, 2009) and discursive social psychology (Augoustinos & Tileagă, 2012), an expressed judgement is a form of verbal behaviour, a performative social act. Much of social life is about talk and debate, and words make things happen. People use language to define, justify, criticise, explain, blame, persuade, promote, and exclude others. Many actions are performed through statements and utterances which means that actual behaviour does not have to be more meaningful or "real" than words that are expressed. In everyday life, words are rarely "merely words" and ticking a box in a questionnaire is also an action, like ticking a box for a candidate in a political election. Stating that one tolerates or not tolerates specific beliefs and practices of minority groups is socially meaningful. It defines the nature of groups and the related subject positions (e.g. tolerator and tolerated) and can work, for example, in the direction of justifying less or rather more strict measures and supportive minority policies.

Tolerance implies deliberation about reasons to tolerate things that one disagrees with, disapproves of or dislikes. It involves a weighting of different considerations and the resulting assessment can be expressed and thereby can have profound social and political consequences. This means that the distinction between tolerance and toleration is not always as clear-cut as the distinction between attitude and behaviour seems to suggest. Furthermore, toleration as an action, or an inaction, cannot be studied without an examination of attitudes and beliefs. Toleration implies a prior negative attitude about what is to be tolerated, with self-restraint that is motivated by particular values and beliefs. Thus, attitudes and beliefs are an integral part of the tolerance process, and tolerance assessments and judgements about dissenting beliefs and practices are the primary focus of the research in this book.

Research on tolerance judgements finds a difference between political and social tolerance (e.g. Erisen & Kentmen-Cin, 2017; Lee, 2014), that people can be tolerant in some contexts but not others (Velthuis et al., 2022b), and also relatively weak associations between tolerance of different practices of the same minority group (Van der Noll, 2014; Verkuyten & Slooter, 2007). These findings indicate that actual tolerance judgements do not simply reflect an underlying dispositional orientation but also depend on information about whom, what, why, and when people are asked to tolerate dissenting beliefs and practices (e.g. Chanley, 1994; Stouffer, 1955). Some people will be more inclined to be tolerant across dissenting practices and a range of situations, but tolerance also varies depending on domain of life, practice, and context. People can tolerate the expression of political ideas that they disagree with but be intolerant towards the enactment of minority identities and practices that they consider immoral (e.g. forced marriage). And people might tolerate certain practices (e.g. wearing of a headscarf) and not others (e.g. building of minarets) of the same minority group (Muslims), and they may agree with the same practice (Muslim headscarf) in some contexts (public life) and not in others (as a civil servant). Or they might tolerate activities less when these directly affect their everyday life compared to society more generally, such as the building of minarets in their neighbourhood versus in a distant city (Chanley, 1994).

The domain-, activity-, and situation-related variance in tolerance indicates that a tolerant judgement does not simply reflect an underlying predisposition to be tolerant but involves various considerations and concerns that differ depending on the case at hand. Questions of political tolerance raise considerations of democratic procedures and rights, while questions of social tolerance can involve concerns about intergroup fairness and equality. And whereas civil servants wearing a headscarf might raise concerns about state secularism, the establishment of Islamic schools can be considered in relation to religious freedom. Tolerance involves deliberate thinking about reasons for not interfering in what one disapproves of and these reasons will differ depending on the domain, activity and situation.

However, this does not mean that predispositions do not matter. For example, Stenner (2005) proposes an "authoritarian dynamic model" in which two major factors in union "produce manifest expressions of intolerance: authoritarian predisposition and conditions of threat" (p. 7). Thus, on the one hand, there is the importance of (perceived) characteristics of groups and practices and of the situation and context that influence how people perceive, evaluate and act in the world. On the other hand, there are individual differences in predispositions that make people more or less prone to act in a particular way or evaluate something in a positive or negative way; e.g. individual differences in cognitive flexibility, open-mindedness, and dispositional tolerance or rather in dogmatism, social dominance orientation, and authoritarianism. Both situations and dispositions are important to consider, especially in combination with each other.

Power relations

Scholars writing about tolerance agree that tolerance requires being in a position to be able to interfere (disrupt, suppress, and censure) with what you object to. Refraining from interfering should not be because of legal prohibitions, a lack of power, or lacking the means for doing so. Thus, it is typically up to the more powerful to tolerate the powerless, to those who are well of to tolerate the less fortunate, and for dominant majority groups to tolerate minorities. When one is in a position to indulge others, there is also the option not to do so. The power to tolerate implies the power not to tolerate and the likelihood of intolerance can be higher towards less influential minority groups (Gibson et al., 2020a). In contrast, being a minority typically means that one is not in the position to negatively interfere with the behaviour of the majority, making the question of tolerance less relevant. In a situation of powerlessness, there can be acquiescence and giving in, but little tolerance.

However, power comes in varied forms which is not always easy to determine in real-life settings, and people are hardly ever powerless in all domains of life (e.g. they can determine what happens in their own homes). Furthermore, what is important for tolerance is not so much the actual ability for negatively interfering in the lives of others but rather whether the person or group believes to have that power. There can be all sorts of cases in which one thinks to be able or has the right to interfere with the disapproved of behaviour, without this being the case. These situations are also cases of tolerance because the person or group involved believes that they can interfere. Furthermore, for examining tolerant judgements, people can imagine, or asked to imagine, situations in which they would be able to censor or stop the opposed behaviour. Thus, also minority members can be asked about their judgements of tolerance: what they would do *if* they had the power to interfere with things they object to (Horton, 1996).

When investigating questions of tolerance, we also should be careful not to unthinkably apply the schematic framework of societal powerful-powerless, oppressor-oppressed, or majority-minority. This framework is extremely useful and analytically powerful and therefore dominates much of the thinking and research in social psychology and the social sciences more generally. Arguably, the majority–minority distinction has become a self-evident and productive framework for many social psychological questions, topics, and findings. Yet, despite its great usefulness, there are also drawbacks and limiting implications, since it can function as easy labels and result in a binary bias in which multifaceted social situations are simplified to two (coherent) groups that are diametrically opposed, like villains and heroes, or perpetrators and victims, with nothing in between (Verkuyten, 2018b). In relation to tolerance and the psychological research, there are four issues that are useful to briefly discuss. This discussion is not meant to nuance the critical importance of existing power relations and societal hierarchies, but rather to demonstrate that questions of tolerance and intolerance are very relevant in a range of situations with different types of relationships and forms of power, and not only in relation to how the societal majority reacts towards minorities.

Minority influence

First, research on minority influence (Gardikiotis, 2011) indicates that minorities can be more influential than they are often considered to be. There are different ways in which, for example, ideological minority groups capture the attention of media and influence how news organisations and politicians frame demands (Wasow, 2020). Activist groups can also try to disrupt or censure beliefs and behaviours they disagree with or disapprove of, such as via social media. For example, small radical religious (e.g. Islamist) and right-wing (e.g. neo-nazis) groups can have a mobilising and (self-)censoring influence on public debates by using social media for harassing, intimidating and physically threatening opinion makers and politicians. And these sorts of groups can harass social and behavioural scientists studying, for example, topics such as victimisation experiences of ethnic and sexual minorities, immigration, and climate change: with, for the scientists, considerable personal consequences and forms of scientific self-censorship (Stein & Appel, 2021). There are an increasing number of case in which these marginal ideological groups try to silence the expression of liberal views, obstruct open debate, influence decision-making, and engage in targeted harassment and violence.

Additionally, there are radical left-wing activists that do not want to be confronted with alternative viewpoints and use forms of cancelling, de-platforming, disinvitations, and naming and shaming to have their way. There are various cases in academics, the arts, sports, and in corporations and organisations in which individuals expressing heterodox views have become the subject of controversy, harassment, smearing and public shaming on social media (Berry & Sobieraj, 2014; Blackford, 2019; Dreger, 2015). Especially in the US and increasingly also in Great Britain and in continental Europe, there have been public denunciations together with demands for public apologies and administrative punishments to which administrators and managers complied. As a result, academic and non-academic employees had not only their reputations destroyed but also had to step down and lost their job and career for expressing their views. Furthermore, novelist (e.g. Germaine Greer; Lionel Shriver; J.K. Rowling), sports figures (e.g. Martina Navratilova), journalists (e.g. Andy Ngo; Kevin Williamson), and public figures (e.g. Maajid Nawaz) have faced forms of outrage and call-out culture.[8] Similarly, there have been successful minority demonstrations, actions and demands for removing monuments, changing names of buildings and laws of physics,[9] stopping alleged cultural appropriation, withdrawing commercial adds,[10] changing artistic content, retracting peer reviewed journal articles, withdrawing (invited) publication offers, cancelling public lectures, and for the use of different phrases, terms, and words.

These events and examples indicate that small numbers of activists across the political spectrum are often not powerless at all, and also face the question whether they should tolerate things they criticise, dislike, or disapprove of. The answer in many of these cases seems to be a dogmatic – and sometimes violent – demand for ideological conformity, "moral purity", and radical change, and of name calling and the excoriation of "heretics" rather than openness, dialogue, and toleration of opposing viewpoints.

Local contexts

There are many local contexts (schools, neighbourhoods, and cities) for which the standard societal majority–minority framework makes less sense. Local situations may differ from the national context and the broader social context is a different matter than the everyday living situation. Relationships in the wider society do interfere in local situations, but they cannot be applied wholescale to, for example, the lives of people in many urban quarters or local schools. In these situations, status and power differences are actively defined and challenged, making a simple majority–minority model not always very adequate for understanding the dynamics of identities and group relations. Groups that in terms of numbers and power are minorities at the national level can be majorities at the local level, and vice versa. And local status can drive perceptions, feelings, and behaviours more than national status. Working in the UK, Modood and colleagues concluded already in 1994 that

> Our research . . . challenges those who think in terms of simplistic oppositions of British – alien or black – white. A significant population on the ground is living in ways that refute these dualisms. It is time for social analysts and policy-makers to catch up.
>
> *(Modood et al., 1994, p. 218)*

Modern-day reality in cities such as London, Brussels, New York, Amsterdam, Los Angeles, Rome, Berlin, Stockholm, and Paris is that there are hundreds of different ethnic, religious, and language groups, which are also heterogeneous themselves, and with the national majority being a local minority in terms of numbers and power. In various European cities, for example, second-generation immigrants are more "native" (born and raised) to their city of residence than their peers of non-migrant parentage of which many come to the city to study or work (Schneider et al., 2012). Additionally, in these cities, second-generation immigrants express strong feelings of local belonging (Fleischmann & Phalet, 2016) and are also relatively more strongly involved in their neighbourhood of residence which they consider their home (Schneider et al., 2012). Furthermore, minorities tend to live together in the same neighbourhoods, send their children to the same schools, and buy their groceries in the same streets. There are many cities, neighbourhoods, and institutions (e.g. schools) that predominantly consist of various ethnic and religious minority groups, and in which there are inter-minority tensions, conflicts, and hostilities. This means that in these contexts, it is not only about the national majority tolerating practices and beliefs of minorities but that the question of tolerance is much more complex and diverse with various groups being both the object and subject of toleration. One example is when in 2011 in areas in London, Islamic extremist were spreading posters with "You are entering a Shariah controlled zone – Islamic rules enforced".[11] The posters suggested that alcohol, high heels, drugs, music, and gambling were forbidden in the area, also for residents from different cultural and religious backgrounds.

Minorities within minorities

This poster example also indicates that societal minority members may feel pressured to adhere to certain norms of behaviour that come from fellow ingroup members. Questions of tolerance and intolerance do not only involve societal majority–minority relations but can relate to important processes within groups and communities. Tajfel points out that for minority group members, not all situations elicit minority–majority comparisons:

> not all "natural" social contexts include the need or the requirement for intergroup comparisons, and a person's idea about himself or herself is at least as much (and probably much more) dependent upon continuous and daily interaction with individuals from the same social group.
>
> *(1978, p. 327)*

This is especially likely for ethnic minority communities that have strongly integrated norms, traditions, values, and functions. Also for religious minority communities (the Amish, Hasidic Jews, and orthodox Muslims), the majority can be considered inherently different and thus partly irrelevant for social comparisons.

Differences and similarities within the own cultural or religious minority community can get a lot of attention in daily life and are much discussed. People make comparisons between subgroups within their community, such as between "established" and recent co-ethnic immigrants, those with a left-wing and right-wing political orientation, integrating and assimilating individuals, and those who are considered "true" believers and those who are not. Newly immigrated Arabs in the United States are found to be aware of their lower social status compared to other Arab groups, and struggle with the discrimination and derogation they experience from well-established immigrant groups (Kumar et al., 2015). And in a study of daily acculturative hassles among Vietnamese-Canadians, there was evidence that intra-group processes, such as feeling isolated from one's ethnic group, being perceived as too white, and pressures to conform to cultural traditions had a significant negative impact on their acculturation process (Lay & Nguyen, 1998).

In other words, there is the important question of toleration of minorities within minorities and of subgroups that are less powerful and dependent on the good will of ingroup members to be able to live the life that they want. In how far, for example, are religious minority communities tolerant towards community members not wearing religious attire (e.g. headscarf for Muslim women), having a specific sexual orientation (e.g. homosexuality), practicing pre-marital sex (by women), and questioning certain doctrines or disaffiliating themselves from the faith (apostacy). Family members, peers, and authority figures can put very strong pressures on women, youngsters, and others who do not fully accept the strict demands of a religious community, up to and beyond implicit or explicit threats, the use of violence and "honour killings". These sorts of questions can matter a very great deal for the freedom that minority individuals have to conduct their own life, and sometimes much more than whether the societal majority tolerates expressions of their faith. The equal rights of women, and of sexual and other minorities are not only threatened by majority members but often also by dominant factions within minority communities. This makes engagement in liminal and debated practices highly dependent on the goodwill of, for example, one's spouse, father, and other male authorities, which severely limits the freedom of these members (e.g. women, girls, and sexual minorities).

Furthermore, minority communities may want to teach their children anti-liberal sexual mores and anti-democratic views. Since 2013, all Dutch primary schools are required to pay attention to "sexual diversity" in society. In 2019, it turned out that the Board of Islamic Schools which represents more than 80% of all the Islamic schools in the country published the lesson book "*Help! I am growing up*". The book has separate versions for girls and boys and is not only about sexual development and diversity but also about marriage, family, infidelity, the need for a strict gender segregation starting with puberty, and that looking at and having contact with someone of the opposite gender is a very big sin ("zina") resulting in great punishment in the afterlife. Additionally, children at Salafist mosque schools are taught that people with a different faith, apostates, homosexuals, and so-called "wizards" deserve the death penalty.[12] And children are told that "this is not our land" and that they should turn away from infidels, Dutch society and the principles of liberty, equality and tolerance.[13]

A Dutch Muslim formulated it as follows:

> As a Muslim I sometimes feel that I am fighting on three fronts. You have that public debate. Then within the Islamic faith you have the extremists who abuse the faith to justify cruel practices. And thirdly, there are fanatic Muslims who regard me as an unbeliever.[14]

This resonates with what is stated in the European Statute for the Promotion of Tolerance, "Members of a group who wish the benefit from tolerance must show it to (aa) society at large, (bb) members of other groups, and also (cc) dissidents within their own group".

Equal relationships

Not all forms of tolerance have to imply an unequal, hierarchical relationship. Forst (2013) makes a distinction between permission and egalitarian forms[15] of toleration. The former refers to intergroup contexts that are characterised by a clear differences in power and status, whereby the majority conditionally permits dissenting minority groups to live according to their way of life. The permission form of toleration is hierarchical, because the majority allows minorities certain exceptions or privileges on conditions specified by them, such as allowing Muslims to pray at work, but not during office hours, or to allow religious expressions and teaching, but only if they do not disrupt the daily functioning of the school. The qualified permission to minority group members to live according to their beliefs affirms the dominant position of the majority and the dependent and disadvantaged position of the minority.

By contrast, the egalitarian form of toleration implies a more equal relationship between different groups in society. While groups can hold very different beliefs about the good life and have different cultural or religious beliefs and practices, they can have a more egalitarian relationship in which the one does not dominates the other. Each group can be recognised in a reciprocal sense and as being guided, for example, by shared democratic norms and rules, including the protection of minority rights. Majority rule in a democracy is not another road to oppression, because minorities have basic rights and freedoms that should not be interfered with or removed. There are many situations in which the power difference is small or less obvious and both sides face the similar question of not interfering or rather trying to interfere with the disapproved of practices and beliefs of the other. The obvious example is the political and ideological polarisation that is currently visible in many western countries.

4
TOLERANCE AND PREJUDICE

A focus on tolerance is misplaced, or at least of limited use, when forms of criticism, dislike, and disapproval are implicit or explicit prejudices, covert or overt negative group-based feelings, rationalisations and justifications of bigotry, or resulting from the mere categorisation in us and them. If this is the case then the emphasis should not be on tolerance but rather on prejudices and racisms and on strategies of prejudice reduction and anti-racism. It is of little use to consider tolerance when the majority of the public is simply prejudiced towards minority groups and tries to justify their group-based antipathy. A focus on tolerance might then even be misleading and apologetic. Thus, objections and opposition to, for example, religious practices of Muslim minorities or providing support for immigrants should be more than simply Islamophobia or xenophobia. In this chapter, I will therefore consider the first critical question: whether people's criticism, dislike, or disapproval of minority's ways of life can be based on something else than prejudice.

Criticism and antisemitism

In 2016, the International Holocaust Remembrance Alliance (IHRA) published a working definition of antisemitism that intended to provide clarity about what antisemitism is in order to equip policy makers with a practical tool to address hate and discrimination against Jews. The aim was to have a clear and uniform standard for the monitoring of antisemitic incidents and for educational and training purposes. The IHRA's Committee on Antisemitism and Holocaust Denial worked to build international consensus around the question what counts as antisemitism, and the developed definition was adopted by the Plenary and also, for example, by the European Union. Added to the general definition of antisemitism ("Antisemitism is a certain perception of Jews, which may be expressed as hatred toward Jews. Rhetorical and physical manifestations of antisemitism are directed toward

DOI: 10.4324/9781003335030-4

Jewish or non-Jewish individuals and/or their property, toward Jewish community institutions and religious facilities".) was a list of 11 "contemporary examples of antisemitism", seven of which related to Israel.

Very soon, the IHRA definition and especially the list of examples became a source of confusion, divisiveness, and contention, because it would brand almost all forms of criticism of Israel or Zionism as antisemitic. The definition would make it impossible to differentiate between legitimate criticism of Israel and Zionism and antisemitic speech and conduct. It would have a negative effect on free speech and academic freedom and would weaken the fight against far-right antisemitism. Therefore, in 2020, a group of international scholars came together to critically assess the IHRA definition and to clarify those aspects that caused confusion and concern. Specifically, it was considered important to provide guidance in deciding whether political conduct and speech about Israel and Zionism should be protected or rather considered antisemitic. After a year of workshops and meetings, the *Jerusalem Declaration of Antisemitism* was published which was claimed to be more clear, coherent, nuanced, and politically neutral. The declaration was endorsed by more than 200 scholars of antisemitism and related fields, including heads of leading institutes in Europe, the US, and Israel. It consists of a preamble, the actual definition of antisemitism, and a set of 15 practical guidelines. Antisemitism was defined as "discrimination, prejudice, hostility or violence against Jews as Jews (or Jewish institutions as Jewish)". Several examples were given that, on the face of it, are not antisemitic, whether or not one approves of the view or action: e.g. "criticizing or opposing Zionism as a form of nationalism", and "supporting the Palestinian demand for justice and the full grant of their political, national, civil and human rights, as encapsulated in international law".

A central concern about the IHRA definition that the Jerusalem declaration tried to address is that in relation to Israel and Zionism, not all forms of criticism of particular actions and proposals for different political and institutional arrangements, are antisemitic. It was stated that in general "the line between antisemitic and non-antisemitic speech is different from the line between unreasonable and reasonable speech". Legitimate criticism of policies, practices, and of political, philosophical, and ideological positions should be possible and dismissing criticism as antisemitic delegitimises the voices of those who disagree (e.g. Palestinians and critical Jews). There should be a space for open and respectful discussion of contested issues rather than moral accusations that silence others.

The tendency to brand, or at least dismiss, critical comments and judgements as forms of prejudice or racism is not limited to the topic of Israel and Zionism. This also happens, for example, in relation to religious criticism, continuing immigration, cultural diversity, minority policies, and populist voting. Critical comments on Islam and its more fundamentalist interpretations are sometimes disqualified by labelling these as Islamophobic, having doubts about immigration as being xenophobic, expressing concerns about diversity as being nativist, opposing minority policies as being racist, and those voting for populist politicians would be bigots.

However, it is rather limited and limiting to consider all forms of disagreement, criticism, dislike, and disapproval as forms of (subtle) prejudice, forms of justice-based opposition as merely masking prejudice, and inaction as the result of suppressed antipathy that waits to be released when the right justification is there. This implies a very pessimistic and one-sided perspective on human functioning and ignores the fact that people, for instance, can and do make a distinction between antisemitism and opposition to Israeli politics (Beattie, 2017; Staetsky, 2012), anti-Muslim feelings and Islam critique (Imhoff & Recker, 2012), between Muslims and Islamic fundamentalist (Sniderman et al., 2014), between anti-immigrant and anti-immigration attitudes (Ceobanu & Escandell, 2010), and that liberal and secular principles can be genuine determinants of opposition to specific religious minority practices (Sniderman & Hagendoorn, 2007), similar to the fact that beliefs about sexual morality and sanctity of life can underlie opposition towards abortion (Rodriguez & Ditto, 2019), concern for justice can be a genuine determinant of opposition to affirmative action (Bobocel et al., 1998), and that political ideology rather than racism, sexism, or islamophobia can underly political candidate evaluation (Bai, 2021).

For example, in Germany and with three representative surveys, it was found that Islamophobia is empirically distinct from gender-based and secular-based forms of critique of Islam (Heyder & Eisentraut, 2016). Furthermore, while attitudes towards Muslims vary little across west European countries, there is a lot of variation in levels of opposition to the headscarf (Helbling, 2014). And an experimental research in the UK demonstrated that anti-Muslim reactions are more strongly determined by people's resistance towards orthodox religious practices and behaviours than towards Muslims as a group of people. Devout practising Muslim were evaluated somewhat more negatively compared to devout Christians but the latter were clearly resented more than the average practicing Muslim (Helbling & Traunmüller, 2020). Thus, people's concerns about Muslim minorities can be more about strict forms of religiosity then about Muslim as a group per se. Ignoring these kinds of distinctions misses out on understanding some of the more principled and nuanced conditions involved in intergroup relations. The critically important agenda to examine prejudice and racism in all its forms, dimensions and facets should not make scholars think that there is nothing else going on and nothing else to see.

People might disapprove of specific minority group beliefs and practices (religious education, building minarets, ritual slaughter of animals), but not of the minority group as a category of people (e.g. Muslims and Jews). They can resist the idea of Muslims establishing an Islamic primary school, not because they feel negatively towards Muslims, but because they believe that religion has no place in education entirely. In one study, we classified Dutch adolescents according to their level of tolerance of Muslims speaking and teaching at their school and their degree of prejudice towards Muslims. All four combinations of tolerance and prejudice were evident, including nonprejudiced and intolerant (12.5%) and prejudiced and tolerant (32.4%) (Van der Noll et al., 2010). People can have, for example, liberal secular values that lead them to support bans on all religious symbols and not only minority religious symbols in the public sphere. There can be a more generic disapproval of the practice itself (Bilodeau et al., 2018; Hurwitz & Mondak, 2002; Sniderman et al., 1989) because things that are considered right are simply right and what is wrong is wrong, independent of who is doing it (Skitka et al., 2021; Turiel, 2002).

Not all forms of criticism, dislike, and disapproval can be productively understood in terms of prejudice, xenophobia, and racism. Doing so is theoretically limited and limiting and therefore does not serve the scholarly aim of understanding and combatting prejudice in general and towards disadvantaged groups in particular. It limits the ability to meaningfully engage with the larger society and prevents from developing a detailed and nuanced theoretical and empirical understanding of people's concerns and considerations in trying to deal with their everyday questions and dilemmas with forms of diversity: an understanding that is needed for wise psychological interventions (Walton, 2014). It becomes difficult to discuss and change people's views when their concerns about diversity or their negative experiences with cultural, religious, or ideological others are disqualified and dismissed as irrational bigotry ("mad and bad"; "deplorables"). Rather, we need to understand the intergroup situation and how people come to think negatively of others with, according to them, sufficient warrant. For example, in her extensive fieldwork among Tea Party supporters in the US, Hochschild identifies a "deep story" in which people feel betrayed in their country:

> strangers step ahead of you in line, making you anxious, resentful and afraid. A president allies with the line cutters, making you feel distrustful, betrayed. A person ahead of you in line insults you as an ignorant redneck, making you feel humiliated and mad.
>
> *(2016, p. 222)*

People want to be morally good persons, but they also are morally outraged when they feel betrayed and when their genuine concerns about, for example, globalisation, immigration, and forms of diversity are not taken seriously, but rather reduced to prejudice and racism (Gest, 2016; Verkuyten, 1997). These interpretations might convey indifference and disrespect towards the views and experiences of common people and can make researchers appear as being guided by non-scientific values and political agendas (Ferguson et al., 2019). To label a particular viewpoint or concern as racist is to pass moral and political judgement and thus a serious matter that is not self-evident but requires clear standards of proof.

Prejudice

There is a large and important literature on the psychology of prejudice, and in our own research, we have tried to make various contributions to this body or work. Much is known about the nature, development, causes, and consequences of prejudicial attitudes, ranging from generalised prejudice to target-specific prejudices, from implicit and covert to explicit and overt prejudices, and about the different ways in which people rationalise and justify their prejudicial feelings and beliefs (Crandall & Eshleman, 2003). Furthermore, there are different theoretical approaches and perspectives for studying prejudice ranging from neurological processes to social structural conditions (see Dixon & Levine, 2012). Prejudice reduction is without any doubt critically important for intergroup relations in pluralistic societies, because it reduces the risk of forms of negative outgroup behaviour and intergroup conflict. However, there have also been various criticism of this literature, for example, for being focused too much on the individual and neglecting the broader societal context (Dixon et al., 2012), and for conceptual unclarities.

Conceptualisation

The meaning of the term "prejudice" is broad and has been expanded over the years to include modern, aversive, symbolic, subtle, benevolent, and non-conscious forms. There are good and valid reasons for doing so, but this conceptual broadening has ambivalent implications (Haslam, 2016). It implies that qualitatively different phenomena are all considered forms of prejudice or racism which makes it more difficult to distinguish between these phenomenon and to describe and understand them. Furthermore, it implies that mild variants of negativity are considered under the same umbrella together with more severe forms for which the concept was originally introduced. When something becomes more exceptional, there is a tendency to expand the concept of it as a sort of moral elevation: behavioural omissions and insensitive questions are increasingly also considered forms of prejudice and racism, similar to the tendency to see innocuous requests as unethical when unethical request become more rare (Levari et al., 2018).

The social psychological literature on prejudice presents and discusses a range of definitions (see Brown, 2010; Duckitt, 1992). Prejudice is sometimes equated with irrationality and sometimes with injustice, sometimes with intention and sometimes with impact, it is sometimes conceived as emotional and sometimes as cognitive, it is sometimes considered to involve implicit and sometimes explicit processes and also as involving both, and it is equated with patterns of negative behaviour and structural inequalities. Furthermore, sexism, racism, Islamophobia, homophobia, xenophobia, and the like are considered special cases of the more general phenomenon of prejudice (Brown, 2010), whereby racism in particular has become the prototypical example of prejudice. Additionally, feelings of uncertainty and anxiety, not engaging in particular activities, and ingroup favouritism without outgroup negativity are also described and interpreted as forms of prejudice. And, although being prejudiced is typically equated with having a negative attitude, some modern manifestations of prejudice involve a blend of positive and negative aspects, with positive attitudes also having unfavourable consequences for disadvantaged groups, such as with benevolent sexism (Glick & Fiske, 2001). Indeed, some perspectives on prejudice and discrimination assert that prejudice can emerge not from antipathy, but rather from perceived incongruity of a person's social role with the stereotypes associated with their group (Eagly & Karau, 2002).

The different aspects, distinctions, and perspectives make the field of prejudice research very broad and difficult to evaluate. However, the fact that a range of phenomena are considered manifestations and forms of prejudice presupposes a certain view of what prejudice entails, which is what the question of conceptualisation is about. Manifestations and forms can be understood only once it is clear exactly what it is that is considered to be expressed or suppressed or rationalised. How else do we know that prejudices are at stake and not, for example, misunderstandings, disagreements, reasonable concerns, or principled beliefs?

There need to be common components of prejudices that allow us to identify some key conceptual differences between the features of prejudice and the objection underlying tolerance. This is important, because it makes it possible to discuss theoretically and examine empirically the nature of prejudice and of tolerance, and when and why both might dissolve and bleed into one another in everyday life. In the empirical world, prejudice and intolerance can be relatively independent but might also become closely connected and hard to distinguish. However, such observations are difficult to make without at least some idea about what prejudice and objection-based tolerance and intolerance are all about. Developing the conceptual distinction between these phenomena gives us the tools to study the nature of the respective processes, and to better understand how and when these exist separately or co-exist together.

Despite the conceptual and theoretical diversity, there is, in general, also a point of commonality in how prejudice is understood. Most often the term prejudice is used for group-based antipathy, in whatever form: "it is a social orientation towards whole groups of people or towards individuals because of their membership in a particular group" (Brown, 2010, p. 4). Thus, prejudice is commonly seen as a form of antipathy towards a group, or members of that group, by virtue of this fact: "an antipathy . . . directed toward a group as a whole, or toward an individual because he is a member of that group"(Allport, 1954, p. 9). There can be various cognitive, emotional, ideological, and structural reasons for this negativity but what matters in everyday life is that the antipathy implies a readiness to push away, reject and discriminate others, only on the basis of their group membership; e.g. for being an African American, Mexican, immigrant, refugee, Muslim, Jew, or sexual minority. With prejudice there is a negative focus on a category of people *as* people.

Tolerance implies objection towards specific beliefs, practices, and behaviours and the objection should not simply reflect group-based antipathy. However, people with more prejudicial attitudes towards outgroups are more likely to oppose particular outgroup beliefs and practices. For example, majority members with stronger anti-Muslim sentiments tend to more strongly oppose the building of Mosques and minarets, Islamic schools, and the wearing of headscarves (e.g. Helbling, 2014; Saroglou et al., 2009; Van der Noll, 2014). And more racist individuals will more strongly oppose supportive minority policies (e.g. Sears & Henry, 2003). Thus, opposition to and rejection of specific beliefs, practices, or policies can reflect a general dislike of Muslims and be used to justify anti-Muslim prejudices, reflect a general dislike of immigrants and be used to justify xenophobic attitudes, or reflect racial antipathy and be used to justify racist views.

However, not all disapproval of outgroup beliefs and practices reflects outgroup dislike, as it can be based on other considerations. Islamophobes will object to the building of mosques and minarets similar to racists objecting to racial minority policies. Yet assuming that the reverse is true is a logical fallacy (*Non sequitur;* "it does not follow"). Criticising or rejecting a practice, a policy, an ideological belief system, or a worldview (liberalism, communism, Zionism, Christianity, and Islam) does not have to imply prejudicial feelings towards a group of people (liberals, communist, Jews, Christians, and Muslims). While racist motives have an impact on support for programmes to assist minorities, opposition to such policies is not racist by definition. Furthermore, criticising specific outgroup beliefs and practices does not have to imply that one does not respect the human dignity of others, does not consider them as having equal rights, and does not think well of them as a group of people.

Following Allport's (1954) classical definition, it has been argued that prejudice is antipathy based on a faulty generalisation. Prejudice would involve misconceptions, inaccuracies, and misjudgements that result from personality dynamics, general cognitive errors, rigid forms of thinking, or unconscious biases. However, many scholars argue against this feature for defining prejudice because it is often very difficult, or even impossible, to establish the "incorrectness" or "veridicality" of prejudicial attitudes (e.g. Dixon, 2017; see also Jussim et al., 2015). Furthermore, even when people may hold generally accurate stereotypes about groups, the application of these stereotypes to individuals still leads to errors and biases (e.g. Jussim et al., 2009).

In addition to this "truth correspondence" problem, it is possible to understand prejudice in terms of what is considered socially reasonable and acceptable. It can be argued that "prejudice occurs when 'we' dislike 'them', and don't have a sensible reason for doing so" (Dixon & Levine, 2012, p. 10). This approach allows one to distinguish between intergroup negativity with or without sufficient warrant: negativity that does and does not seem reasonable and justified. It makes it possible, for example, to distinguish between the hostility that a violently subjugated population may feel towards their oppressors from the hostility that the latter feel towards the former (e.g. the antipathy of Jews towards Germans during the Nazi era, as opposed to the antipathy of Germans towards Jews). Or to distinguish between negativity towards mainstream critical groups (e.g. animal right activists; born-again Christians) and groups that act as adversaries in pitting themselves against the larger society and denouncing Western democracy and its values (e.g. Salafists, neo-Nazis). Conceptualising prejudice as any negative evaluation based on group membership that "does not depend on whether such a prejudice can be justified according some moral code" (Crandall et al., 2002, p. 359) would imply that negativity towards racists, sexists, extremists, oppressors, criminals, and sex offenders are also similar prejudices. But there are groups that one can dislike for the "right" reasons: if this would not be possible, then there can only be unlimited acceptance and holding no moral convictions and beliefs. It would mean that one applies a general rule to all situations when clearly there are exceptions to the rule. By simply conceptualising prejudice as a negative outgroup attitude, the differences between these sorts of situations disappear, and the possibility that negative reactions can be reasonably warranted is ignored (Dixon, 2017).

Obviously, what is considered reasonable depends on social, cultural, and historical circumstances. But this does not mean that there are no general moral principles and no shared social conventions about what is and what is not acceptable. The moral domain is typically concerned with fairness, justice and other's welfare and is considered to apply anytime and everywhere (Skitka et al., 2021; Turiel, 2002). Research with children demonstrates that they interpret issues of fairness, justice and avoiding harm to others as unalterable, general, and not subject to authority jurisdiction (see Wainryb, 2006). And research on moral emotions shows that people exhibit strong intuitive objection to the physical and psychological harm of others and unfair treatment (Turiel et al., 1987; but also see Haidt et al., 1993), and that they tend to reject beliefs and practices that go against basic human capabilities (Turiel, 2002).

As pointed out earlier: treating categories of people (e.g. the elderly, the young, the sick) differently for relevant reasons (i.e. differential treatment) is something else than treating categories of people (women, African Americans, sexual minorities) differently on the basis of reasons that are considered irrelevant (i.e. discrimination). While there can be disagreements about whether particular reasons are relevant in a certain situation, a distinction between reasonable and just versus unreasonable and unjust is often codified in mores and legal rules and regulations (e.g. "beyond reasonable doubt"; "doctrine of reasonable classification"), and is essential in how people think about their social world. Without this distinction, almost all thinking, debate, decision-making, and ruling would become impossible.

Tolerance is not based on prejudice, fear, or hatred, but involves objections that "must be reasonable in a minimal sense" (Forst, 2013, p. 2; see also Cohen, 2004). This means that the objections must not be arbitrary (e.g. use of double standards), unintelligible, and without moral value. It is generally more difficult to argue for and recognise the value and reasonableness of racist hatred and white supremacy beliefs than of anti-abortionists' concern for the unborn life, or the religious disapproval of secular beliefs, euthanasia, and same-sex marriage. People can think that there is nothing wrong with abortion, but still recognise that others may have reasons based on a commitment to a particular belief or value for disapproving of it. And a Christian can be convinced that "Jesus is the only way" and disapprove of Hinduism as a belief system, while remaining egalitarian towards Hindus as a category of people. The prejudiced attitudes and discriminatory actions of a racist or bigot should not be equated with the reasonable concerns and critical remarks about other cultural and religious beliefs and practices (e.g. patriarchal, homophobic, and misogynistic). Conceptualising prejudice in terms of "any negative evaluation" or simply equate it with group-based dislike or disapproval makes the concept rather meaningless. A negative evaluation based on critical discernment is something else than a negative evaluation based on antipathy and hatred. I might sit farther away from someone who is a smoker and think more negatively about smokers than non-smokers, because smokers affect my health negatively and burden our health care system.

Operationalisation

Prejudice research does not only face the question of conceptualisation but also of operationalisation and measurement. Measures should be able to make a distinction between individuals in terms of the degree or intensity of their negativity towards an outgroup. Thus, measures of Islamophobia, for example, are designed to rank order individuals from those who most dislike Muslims to those who least dislike them. And measures of prejudicial attitudes towards immigrants are designed to rank order individuals in terms of their degree of dislike and disdain for immigrants. Measures of antisemitism, racial prejudice, homophobia, and so on are similarly designed to rank order people. Thus, the higher a person's score on these sorts of measures, the more prejudiced that person is. There are numerous empirical studies that use scores in this way and interpret the findings in terms of prejudice with its correlates, causes, and consequences. However, because of the focus on prejudice, it is often not clear what a low score indicates and what people need to answer for not being considered prejudiced. Rather, what typically happens is that a low score is considered low prejudice and thus also described and interpreted in terms of a prejudicial attitude.

Yet, in many studies, people are found to express "lukewarm" or neutral attitudes, and not only because of social desirability concerns (Bamberg & Verkuyten, 2022).[1] For example, in one study, a new measure of Islamophobia was examined in six countries, including Poland, Germany, and the United States (Uenal et al., 2021). Anti-Muslim prejudice was measured with five statements (e.g. "Muslims are not trustworthy" and "The Islamist terrorist find strong support among Muslims") using 5-point scales ranging from 1 (definitely false) to 5 (definitely true). The average score across the countries was on the "false-side" of the scale (2.60), and on measures of negative intergroup emotions (fear, anger, and disgust), the average scores ranged between 1.86 and 2.20, with a score of 1 indicating "strongly disagree". Therefore, on average, the various samples in the six countries did not express anti-Muslim feelings and beliefs, and the possibility of holding positive attitudes was not considered.

Another example is the influential work on integrated threat theory for explaining outgroup prejudices. One of the early studies testing this theory focused on prejudice towards immigrants (Cuban, Mexican, and Asian immigrants in the US) in which "prejudice reflects negative affect associated with out-groups . . . and thus emphasizes antipathy toward out-groups" (Stephan et al., 1999, p. 2225). This definition of prejudice was operationalised by asking about different reactions, like rejection, dislike, hatred, and disdain on 10-point scales (e.g. "no hatred at all" to "extreme hatred"). The highest average score was 3.85 towards Cuban immigrants which is clearly at the positive side of the scale, but the findings are discussed in terms of anti-immigrant prejudices.

Although in these studies bipolar response scales are typically used with a positive and a negative pole, the findings are interpreted in terms of degree of prejudice and the possibility that people have neutral or positive outgroup attitudes tends to be ignored. The result is that the research does not tell us much about the nature of prejudice as antipathy, let alone hatred, but rather about the difference between, for example, individuals who are slightly negative, neutral or rather mild positive about a particular outgroup. Additionally, in ordering individuals from the most to least negative – in practice from slight negative or neutral to positive – this research assumes a linear continuum from more to less prejudice. And research on generalised prejudice across minority outgroup focuses on a linear continuum that captures the commonality between target-specific prejudices (e.g. towards women, immigrants, Jews, and Muslims; e.g. Bergh & Akrami, 2016; Hodson & Dhont, 2015). However, a high degree of consistency and commonality in the evaluation of different target groups does not tell us anything about the degree of negativity, and can also be the result of relative neutrality or generalised positivity and open-mindedness (Meeusen et al., 2017). Similarly, a high degree of consistency in the evaluation of a range of outgroup practices and beliefs (e.g. building of mosques, minarets, Islamic education, and wearing of a headscarf) can indicate Islamophobia but also a positive or neutral attitude towards Muslims.

Based on their in-depth research of many local communities with rapidly increasing ethnic diversity, Grey and colleagues (2009) have proposed a 20–60–20 rule. About 20% of the people tend to embrace diversification, 20% is convinced that it a bad thing, and the majority of 60% isn't sure what to think about diversification. This latter group tends to be generally open to learning more about it, but based on their subsequent experiences, they can develop in either way towards rejection of newcomers or finding accord with them.

Individual profiles

It is also likely that different individuals combine their evaluations of various outgroup practices and beliefs in different ways resulting in different configurations of how the various evaluations are organised *within* individuals (Osborne & Sibley, 2017). For example, using a person-centred approach for examining people's attitudes towards different minority groups, Meeusen and colleagues (2017) found five qualitatively distinct subgroups of individuals that could not be ordered along a linear continuum of more versus less prejudice. And in a nationwide study in Australia, it was found that Australians could be placed in four qualitative different classes based on the perception of Islam (Dunn et al., 2021). In addition to Islamophobes (13% of the population), there was a group of individuals that was unsure about diversity and had some concerns about Muslims (24%), a large group that was positive towards diversity but also had concerns (50%), and a group that had no concerns about Muslims (13%).

Additionally, different subgroups of individuals have been found in person-centred research on political and social tolerance. For example, in a US study on political tolerance, the best model for the data required four categories of individuals rather than a continuum of tolerance (McCutcheon, 1985). In addition to a group of individuals that was consistently positive towards various minority groups and three different practices, and a group of people that was consistently negative, two other categories of people were found. Individuals in these two categories tolerated some groups and some practices, but rejected others. These four categories could not be readily placed on a unidimensional positive–negative continuum, because there was no monotonic change across the four groups of individuals. Rather, they formed four latent classes of political tolerance. Similarly, in examining political and social tolerance among a nationwide sample in the US, four qualitative different profiles were found including subgroups of individuals that were generally intolerant or generally tolerant, and individuals who were politically intolerant or socially intolerant (Mather & Tranby, 2014; see also Lee, 2014).

Critical inclusiveness

Diversity is increasingly discussed in relation to "inclusion": inclusive education, inclusive organisations, inclusive teams, and inclusive leadership are some of the terms that have become popular. Inclusion is considered more than tolerance because it would entail full acceptance in which differences are embraced, valued, and appreciated. However, what exactly this means is not always clear, and the fact that tolerance implies respect for personal autonomy and human dignity is ignored.

In much of the writing, inclusion seems to be a sort of unconditional appreciation of diversity in which one is asked to accept cultural, religious, and ideological practices and beliefs that one might consider misguided and even morally wrong. But there is one exception, namely viewpoints that raise critical questions about the value of diversity. The appreciation and full acceptance that inclusion would entail does not tend to apply to those who have, for example, conservative and communitarian concerns and favour similarity in beliefs, values, and norms: inclusiveness can become the new orthodoxy in which there is little room for heterodox views.

Inclusiveness as valuing diversity seems to imply that one should not judge and be critical, but rather appreciate and embrace differences for what they are. However, this could mean that one has to accept things that one finds unacceptable, in general or at least in a liberal society. In one of our studies, we have examined the possibility that being inclusive towards Muslim minorities does not preclude the possibility of being critical about gender inequality (Dangubić et al., 2022a). The next quote is from a Dutch participant in our research.

> Islamic organizations strive for gender inequality. I do not find this okay and by not giving these organization airtime it becomes less easy to spread these ideas. In addition, this belief is at odds with our norms and values and affects the foundations of our country.

In their empirical study on religion and politics worldwide, Norris and Inglehardt (2004) found a substantial cultural cleavage in social values towards gender equality[2] between the West and Muslim nations. This cultural fault line is also clearly found between majority members and Muslim minorities in West European societies (Diehl et al., 2009; SCP, 2005). Research has found that on average majority members tend to have more egalitarian gender attitudes than Muslim minorities, and this is, for example, reflected in a less traditional division of household tasks and more similar child-raising practices for girls and boys. This average difference in social values is further reflected in majority members believing that Muslim women have fewer rights and liberties than Muslim men, and Muslim minorities believing that European women have too many rights and liberties (Andreassen, 2012; Biliński, 2021; Sniderman & Hagendoorn, 2007). For example, a considerable majority of West Europeans (59%–83%) consider Muslims lacking in respect for women and in four national representative surveys conducted between 1998 and 2009, around 90% of the Dutch population agreed that Muslim men dominate their wives (Gijsberts & Lubbers, 2009). The strong average difference in gender values that exists between the West and Muslim nations, and between majority members and Muslim minorities in Western societies, indicates that this perception of gender inequality is not simply a stereotypical generalisation.

For some majority group members, this perception can lead to feelings of threat that justify, or even increase, their dislike of Muslims and their opposition towards Muslim expressive and civil rights (see Verkuyten, 2021). The survey findings and quoted statement can be read in this way: a focus on gender equality as an acceptable way to express one's prejudicial attitudes towards Muslim minorities and to justify one's exclusionary views (Kalla & Broockman, 2020; Strabac & Listhaug, 2008). People who have negative feelings towards Muslim minorities ("*anti-Muslim individuals*") are likely to reject Muslims' expressive rights and disapprove of various Muslim practices and beliefs (e.g. Helbling, 2014; Uenal et al., 2021).

However, the survey findings and the quoted statement can also, partly, reflect a more principled orientation in which one disapproves of the perceived treatment of women among some Muslims, but without having negative feelings towards Muslims and rejecting their civil rights. That nine out of ten Dutch majority members agree that Muslim men dominate their wives is unlikely to imply that nine out of ten are Islamophobes. Some people might have an inclusive orientation towards Muslim minorities while simultaneously being critical of perceived Muslim gender values and arrangements ("*critical inclusiveness*").

Being inclusive does not have to mean that one cannot be critical. Whether people are inclusive or not depends on how societal inclusion is understood and what being inclusive implies. In general, a societal inclusive orientation can be considered to have two main aspects (Hagendoorn & Poppe, 2011; Ivarsflaten & Sniderman, 2017; Sniderman et al., 2014). First, it involves being unprejudiced and well-disposed towards Muslims as a group of people and respect them as Muslims. Second, it implies that one accepts that Muslims have the same rights as equal members of society, including the right to express and enact their religious identity. Societal inclusion understood in this way, thus, implies thinking well of Muslims and treating them as full members of the common community without them having to hide their identity as Muslims.

However, inclusiveness does not mean that people will not perceive group differences in norms, values, and practices, nor that they will not engage in critical assessments of these differences. An inclusive attitude does not have to imply a sort of cultural relativistic stance in which all practices and values are considered equally valuable and valid. For example, Helbling (2014) found in six European countries that people with secular liberal values felt positively towards Muslims as a group, but also conflicted regarding the legislation of religious practices such as the wearing of the headscarf. In addition, among national samples in the UK, France, Germany, and the Netherlands, a substantial portion of people with a positive attitude towards Muslims supported a ban on headscarves (Van der Noll, 2010; see also Saroglou et al., 2009) and also rejected Islamic education and the building of Mosques (Van der Noll, 2014).

It is likely that people are committed to their own liberal values and beliefs, which make them disapprove of some Muslim minority values and practices. For example, Sniderman and Hagendoorn (2007) employed a covert measure of prejudice (the list experiment[3]), and found that disapproval of some Muslim practices can be based on principled liberal concerns, rather than hidden dislike of the group. In liberal democracies, gender equality is considered a fundamental value and a general principle that is endorsed – although not always practiced – by the vast majority of the population (Roggeband & Verloo, 2007). It would be paradoxical to expect in a liberal society that an individual who is committed to gender equality will be positive towards unequal gender arrangements among some minority groups in society (Ivarsflaten & Sniderman, 2017). It would be nothing less paradoxical to require that majority members support the liberal principle of equality by accepting Muslims and their equal civil rights, but reject that very principle by accepting unequal treatment of women among some Muslims. It is thus likely that there is a substantial proportion of majority members that is critical of Muslim gender values and arrangements, but without having negative feelings towards Muslims as a group or people or rejecting their expressive rights.

However, those who express positive attitudes towards Muslims but are also critical about gender issues might be hiding their anti-Muslim prejudice behind more acceptable reasons (e.g. Chakraborti & Zempi, 2012; Fernandez, 2009). If this is the case, then this group of people would be quite similar to anti-Muslim individuals, except for not expressing their prejudice openly. There are at least two ways to examine this possibility which we used in our research. The first one is to use the list experiment as an indirect or covert measure of prejudice, which allows to assess whether gender critical majority members harbour negative feelings towards Muslims as a group of people and reject their rights. A critical inclusive orientation would imply that one has no hidden prejudices towards Muslims, but does have negative feelings towards gendered practices.

The second one is to examine whether gender critical individuals positively differ from anti-Muslim individuals on three liberal constructs: valuing unconditional respect for others (Lalljee et al., 2007), endorsing civil liberties (Gustavsson et al., 2016), and open-minded thinking (Stanovich & West, 1997). These constructs play a key role in accepting other groups and their practices (Sullivan & Transue, 1999), and can be expected to be more important to those who are critically inclusive towards Muslims.

We used representative samples of German and Dutch majority members and a person-centred approach (latent profile analysis) for identifying qualitatively distinct subgroups of individuals who differ in the way in which they combine their evaluation of Muslim gender practices with their general feelings towards Muslim minorities and their support of Muslim expressive rights. This allows us to examine whether perceiving the lack of gender equality among Muslims is driven by anti-Muslim sentiments or a more general concern for liberal values. Whereas in the former case, the perception of Muslim gender inequality is combined with prejudice towards Muslims and lack of support for their equal rights, in the latter case, it coexists with more positive feelings and the endorsement of their rights. Subsequently we used the list experiment as a covert measure of prejudice to assess if gender critical individuals tend to present themselves in a more positive light and use their criticism as a justification for anti-Muslim sentiments that they do not express openly. Furthermore, we tested whether the different profiles of individuals differ in their support for unconditional respect for people, endorsement of civil liberties more, and open-minded thinking (Dangubić et al., 2022a).

The findings show that in addition to a subgroup of individuals that had anti-Muslim attitudes in every respect (19%; "anti-Muslim"), there was a substantial subgroup of people in both countries (around 33%; "critical inclusive") that felt positively towards Muslims as a group of people and endorsed Muslim expressive rights, but at the same time was critical about Muslim gendered practices. Furthermore, on the covert measure of prejudice, this critical subgroup did not demonstrate any hidden prejudices (0%), but on another covert measure, 36% of this subgroup was negative about Muslims wearing veils in public. The fact that they did not use an opportunity to express negativity towards immigrants covertly but were only negative towards the gendered practice of wearing a veil strongly indicates that, among the public in both countries, there is a substantial subgroup of individuals that is genuinely critical of gendered practices without being negative towards Muslims as a group of people or not respecting their equal expressive rights. This interpretation was further supported by the finding that this subgroup of individuals scored relatively high on measures of unconditional respect, open minded thinking, and the endorsement of civil liberties. The finding that this "critical inclusive" subgroup was the numerically largest one is important, because it is a group that is typically ignored in prejudice research.

Taking a more relativistic stance on gender equality appears to be difficult for most majority members in liberal societies. With a Swiss representative sample and examining various pro and con arguments to wearing a burqa or niqab, it was found that only 18.3% was a consistent supporter and 15.2% was consistently negative (Eugster, 2021). In addition, around one-third (32%) was opposed, because a face veil would be incompatible with western culture, and another third (34.5%) had positive attitudes towards Muslims but also principled objections towards the face veil as a symbol of female oppression. Furthermore, in a large-field experiment conducted in 25 cities, it was found that ethnic German woman discriminate against Muslim women in their helping behaviour, but not when Muslim women signalled that they hold liberal gender attitudes (Choi et al., 2021). Additionally, in an experimental study that manipulated whether Muslims either do or do not support gender equality, anti-Muslim sentiments were found to be reduced in the condition in which Muslims valued gender equality, because this increased people's belief that Muslims share their liberal values (Moss et al., 2019). And in a large-scale study in the UK, it was found that anti-Muslim attitudes are far more negative towards beliefs of orthodox Muslims which are seen as incompatible with western liberal values (gender roles and sexual orientations), compared to the average practicing Muslim and secular Muslim immigrants (Helbling & Traunmüller, 2020). Furthermore, in a qualitative analysis of an open-ended question in a representative population survey in Norway, it was found that depictions of how Muslims treat women is considered the main reason for negative attitudes towards Islam (Doving, 2015).

It could of course be argued that it is prejudicial in itself to use liberal values such as gender equality as a standard for being critical, but it is difficult to understand what this would mean in a liberal society. It seems rather awkward to accuse value-based liberalism of acting according to its own values. It also would lead to the use of double standards in which liberal values are rejected but at the same time are put forward to argue for Muslim minorities having the freedom and right to live the life that they want. And it would imply that one cannot express concerns about Muslim minorities being on average much more rejecting of homosexuality and LGBTQ+ rights than (Christian) majority members (e.g. Röder & Spierings, 2022), and having relatively strong antisemitic attitudes, already in early adolescence (Verkuyten & Thijs, 2010).

Prejudices and principles

Inclusiveness is often presented as going beyond tolerance which would be insufficient and even inadequate for a diverse society. However, a plea for inclusiveness tends to go together with intolerance towards those who think differently, and the findings for critical inclusiveness indicate that inclusiveness does not have to imply appreciation of specific differences. There are various types of diversity, and disagreement, criticism, dislike, and disapproval of particular views, beliefs, and practices are inevitable, also in everyday life in an inclusive setting. Inclusiveness can be critical and cannot do without tolerance. Rather, inclusiveness requires tolerance in which one has objections but does not act upon these, for example, towards those who express concerns about diversity and favour similarity and commonalities.

An important step in examining tolerance is to consider the nature of the objections and to determine whether they meet the non-prejudicial criteria necessary to be considered components of the tolerance process. This is not always easy to do, because an objection to a specific outgroup practice may represent an expression of one's prejudicial attitude towards the group per se, an expression of disapproval of that particular practice, or a combination of these two. For example, majority members can reject the wearing of a headscarf by Muslim public servants, because they dislike Muslims, or because they believe that religion has no place in public institutions, or some combination of both. In our research, we have used four related strategies to examine these possibilities that might drive objections towards Muslim minority practices: (1) statistically controlling for group-based prejudice, (2) considering multiple minority practices, (3) examining double standards, and (4) using a multiple-actor–multiple-act design.

Controlling for prejudice

One strategy for taking the role of prejudice in objections towards outgroup practices into account is to statistically control for prejudicial attitudes. For example, research in Belgium shows that adherence to a conception of human rights induces Islam criticism, independent of prejudice and xenophobia (Elchardus & Spruyt, 2014), whereas values of self-direction and universalism are independently associated with stronger support for Islamic practices (Saroglou et al., 2009; Van der Noll, 2014).

Secularism involves a general opposition to religious interference in public affairs, and this can form the ground for not accepting a role for any religion – including Islam – in, for example, public education and public institutions (Fetzer & Soper, 2003). In a German study, it was found that a desire for the separation of church and state plays a role in opposition to both Christian and Islamic public education, beyond anti-Muslim attitudes (Van der Noll & Saroglou, 2015). Additionally, in a large-scale study in Western European countries, we found, independent of prejudice, that those endorsing secularism were more likely to reject religious symbols and religious public education for both Christians and Muslims (Dangubić et al., 2020). Furthermore, in a study in Quebec, Breton and Eady (2015) showed that while those who hold prejudicial views supported a ban on religious symbols, a majority of people supporting such a ban did so out of secular beliefs.

In addition to secular beliefs, it has been found that people with liberal values can have positive attitudes towards Muslims as a group but feel torn when it comes to religious practices such as the wearing of the headscarf (Helbling, 2014). The reason is that some of these practices are considered to stand for the illiberal values of Islam (patriarchal, gender inequality, and rejection of sexual liberties). One can oppose the headscarf in the name of liberalism, because it is considered a symbol of restricted freedom and inequality. Liberalism might have a more procedural meaning in which one accepts all ways of life or rather a more substantive one in which only those ways of life are accepted that are considered liberal (Gustavsson et al.,

2016). The former interpretation goes together with a more positive view on Muslim veils, while the latter leads to a less positive view.

Multiple minority practices

In addition to statistically controlling for prejudice when examining objections towards minority beliefs and practices, it is possible to examine people's attitudes towards a range of minority practices. Cross-practice consistency can indicate a general disliking (or a general liking) of Muslim minorities, and inconsistencies can indicate more principled considerations or social normative concerns about specific practices (Dangubić et al., 2021; Sniderman et al., 1989). Specifically, some people may display negative feelings towards Muslims and disapprove of a range of practices ("anti-Muslim"), while others have positive feelings and consistently accept all practices ("pro-Muslims"). Additionally, people can accept some minority practices, but not others, and this practice-based inconsistency suggests that they not only consider the group they are asked to tolerate, but also information about the nature of the dissenting practices.

The consideration of multiple practices might demonstrate that people have objections to a particular practice (e.g. wearing of a headscarf) but not towards another practice (e.g. Islamic schools), and also do not have negative feelings towards Muslims as a group of people. A particular practice might raise specific moral concerns, such as the wearing of a headscarf which can evoke the issue of gender equality. However, the rejection of some Muslim practices might also result from social norms that make it socially acceptable to express one's prejudiced feelings by rejecting these practices and not others (Crandall & Eshleman, 2003). Thus, some individuals may be practicing a form of principled objection that emerges from specific values and beliefs held about specific practices, while other individuals may be practicing a form of negativity that emerges from prejudice towards the group that they may be unwilling to openly express.

Using data from five representative samples of Dutch adults, we empirically identified within each dataset subgroups of individuals that qualitatively differ in their subjective constellations of general feelings towards Muslims as a group of people and disapproval of various Muslim practices (Adelman & Verkuyten, 2020a; Dangubić et al., 2020). The latent profile analyses of the different samples indicated that four main subgroups of majority members exist within the public: those who have either consistent liking-based (around 30% of the national samples) or disliking-based profiles (around 20%), those who display more principle-based intolerance (around 20%; neutral to positive attitudes towards Muslims and selective disapproval of some practices) or prejudiced intolerance (around 30%; neutral to positive attitudes towards the group and cross-practice negativity).

Furthermore, these subgroups of majority members differed in predictable ways on, for example, social dominance orientation, authoritarianism, status quo conservatism, cognitive sophistication, perceived outgroup threat, the tendency to engage in anti-discrimination activities, prejudicial feelings towards other minority outgroups, and the disapproval of non-Muslim minority practices. For example, and compared to the other subgroups, individuals in the disliking subgroup were not only more authoritarian and conservative, but also most negative towards refugees and Polish immigrants and disapproved more strongly of homosexual men kissing in public and of gender-neutral practices (Dangubić et al., 2021). Furthermore, individuals in the principled subgroup were relatively more likely to engage in cognitive sophisticated thought, to have lower social dominance orientation, and were more inclined to be involved in anti-discrimination protest (Adelman & Verkuyten, 2020a).

These findings indicate that around half of the Dutch majority population has prejudicial attitudes towards Muslim minorities and that the other half has not. This is similar, for example, to the finding that around half of the public supports a ban of headscarves in Germany, the Netherlands, and Spain, whereas the other half does not.[4] Furthermore, the non-prejudiced half is not consistently positive towards all practices but can also be critical of some practices but not of others. This is similar to research on tolerance of the enactment of dissenting beliefs that indicates that practice-related difference in tolerance is common, as different practices can involve the convergence of different considerations and values (e.g. Chanley, 1994; Stouffer, 1955).

Double standards

> "I have just completed a survey with, among other things, my opinion about the arrival of Islamic schools, political parties and other matters. I have indicated that I am opposed to this. I found it a pity that there was no possibility to give additional information. So I would like to make the comment that I am against these things not because they are Islamic groups, but because they are religious groups themselves. I am against the mixture of religion and things like education and politics, no matter what religion it is. So it is not intolerance towards Islam on that front, but against all religions".

This comment was sent to us by a participant in one of our Dutch national studies. It demonstrates that objections to various practices of a minority group do not have to indicate negativity towards that particular group. There is the possibility that people have more principled reasons for their objections, such as strong secular beliefs, and therefore do not apply a double standard but rather object to the same practice regardless of who engages in it.[5] However, in many studies, people are only asked questions about one specific minority group (e.g. Muslims, immigrants, or Mexicans) to measure their prejudice towards that group (Islamophobia, xenophobia).

Research that focuses on multiple outgroups moves beyond measuring prejudice to the assessment of discrimination of specific groups that as members of society are equally warranted in claiming their rights and benefits (Sniderman, 2018). For example, we found that Dutch adolescents were less tolerant towards Muslims exercising their right to establish their own schools and to demonstrate and protest compared to non-religious groups (Verkuyten & Slooter, 2007, 2008).

Furthermore, the disapproval of particular religious practices (clothing and symbols) can be motivated either by more general anti-religious sentiments or rather by discriminatory attitudes towards Muslims as a group (Mondak & Hurwitz, 1998). If people, for example, are equally opposed to Muslims and Christians engaging in the same act (actor consistent; no double standard), it is more likely that they have general reasons for doing so or hold religion more generally in contempt. But if people apply a double standard and reject a particular act only for Muslims (actor inconsistent), it is more likely that prejudicial feelings towards Muslims are involved. For example, in a study in Quebec (Bilodeau et al., 2018), a distinction was made between individuals who favoured a ban of all religious symbols and those who favoured a religious minority restriction. While the former group of individuals was motivated by secular and liberal values, the latter was motivated by prejudice and feelings of cultural threat. Similarly, in Denmark, Aarøe (2012) showed that those who support secularism do not differentiate between the banning of Christians' and Muslims' symbols for public officials.

Using an experimental design (Havermans & Verkuyten, 2021), we asked Dutch majority members to indicate their positive (tolerate and learn from) and negative (aggress and avoid) behavioural intentions towards either immigrants with a contrasting cultural worldview or co-ethnics with such a worldview. The findings showed no double standard, but rather a similar degree of toleration towards both target groups (also similar intentions for the other behaviours). Furthermore, the possible moderating role of authoritarianism was considered, and there was no difference in tolerance of the two target groups between respondents low or high in authoritarianism. One interpretation of these findings is that belief incongruency is unsettling and that people have a desire for maintaining their cultural worldview. As a result, they tend to react similarly towards both immigrants and co-ethnics whose values and norms conflict with their own, independent of individual differences in, for example, authoritarianism, openness to experience, conscientiousness, and religious beliefs (Brandt & Van Tongeren, 2017).

In another study (Dangubić et al., 2020), we used data from the EURISLAM research project that focuses on national identity, citizenship, and the incorporation of Muslims in six European countries: Belgium, France, Germany, the Netherlands, Switzerland, and the United Kingdom.[6] Adult participants were randomly selected members of the national majority who were asked, for example, whether "Public schools should offer [Muslim/Christian] religious education for those who want it", "Teachers in public schools should not be allowed to wear a veil", and "Teachers in public schools should not be allowed to wear visible Christian symbols such as a cross or a nun's habit". For the question of Muslim religious education in public schools, 52.8% did not support this (47.2% did) which suggests anti-Muslim prejudice. However, of this subgroup, 24.8% also did not support Christian education whereas 28% discriminated against Muslims. Similarly, 77.3% objected to teachers wearing Muslim symbols, but of this subgroup, 38.5% was also negative about the wearing of Christian symbols, and, thus, 38.8% discriminated against Muslim teachers.

Around one-third of the public using a double standard towards Muslims is clearly problematic and reason for concern. It is intolerant, and even outright discrimination, to differentiate between groups that are equally warranted in claiming civic rights and benefits. It implies that Muslims are not treated as full and equal members of society and this is critical: equality is not merely a matter "of thinking well of them, or even also wishing them well; it is, crucially, a matter of treating them well" (Sniderman et al., 2014, p. 120). However, what these findings also demonstrate is that most West European majority members do not use a double standard and thus are inclined to treat Muslims well, or at least not less well than Christians. A majority of the public appears to support the civil liberties and rights of Muslims or is equally critical as towards Christians, a group whose legitimacy in West European societies is not disputed.

To give a further example, in a large-scale research in Denmark, it was found that around three in four Danes supported the civil rights and liberties of Muslims (to demonstrate, debate, and speak at high schools) and to the same extent as they did for other controversial groups such as born-again Christians and the far left and the far right (Sniderman et al., 2014). Additionally, people's support was equally lower for Islamic fundamentalist and neo-Nazis. Furthermore, these findings were not affected by the Mohammed cartoon crisis that was at its height during the data collection. Although this crisis provided a socially acceptable opportunity and convenient pretext for expressing hidden anti-Muslim feelings, the majority of the Danes did not show signs of a backlash against Muslims. A similar finding has been found after the Islamist terrorist attack on Charlie Hebdo in Paris (January 2015): the French public showed even lower rather than higher resistance towards Muslim immigrants in the weeks after the attack (Castanho Silva, 2018; Savelkoul et al., 2022).[7]

Multiple actors and multiple acts

A fourth research strategy is to combine the previous two approaches and simultaneously consider various practices and multiple groups simultaneously. People might reject both Christian and Muslim civil servants wearing religious symbols, but accept Christian primary education while rejecting Islamic primary schools. Or, they might reject both Muslims and Christians across both practices.

Simultaneously considering multiple acts and actors makes an even more detailed and nuanced understanding of people's objections possible. Specifically, it allows us to determine for a range of practices the proportions of people showing equal objection or rather discriminatory objection by using a double standard in disapproving of Muslims, but not, for example, Christians or minority Jews practicing their religion (Hurwitz & Mondak, 2002). We used this strategy in three examinations using national samples from different European countries.

In the first experimental research, we compared Dutch majority members' disapproval of four religious practices of two target groups (Sleijpen et al., 2020; see also Verkuyten & Slooter, 2007). In a first study, the practices were performed by immigrant groups of either Turkish Muslims or Turkish Christians, and we found that people differentiated between the different practices but in a similar way for both groups. Thus, people were most tolerant of wearing a religious necklace and least tolerant of a religious authority giving an anti-abortion speech, independent of the religious immigrant group.

However, people might reject Turks as an immigrant group, independent of whether they are Muslim or Christian (Spruyt & Elchardus, 2012; Strabac & Listhaug, 2008). Therefore, in Experiment 2, we examined tolerance of the same practices for Muslims and Dutch Orthodox Protestants as two numerically small religious communities in the Netherlands that struggle to hold on to their religious values and beliefs (Fetzer & Soper, 2003; Ribberink et al., 2017). The findings again revealed practice-related variation in tolerance but no double standards, except for the anti-abortion speech.

A second research involved the further analyses of the EURISLAM data in which majority members were asked questions about Christians and Muslims (i.e. two target groups) focusing on two separate practices (wearing religious symbols and religious education; Dangubić et al., 2020). With these two actors and two acts combined, there are 16 logically possible combinations of acceptance and rejection and nine of these combinations are presented in Table 4.1 (the remaining seven involve positive discrimination of Muslims which was very exceptional). The table shows that there is empirical support for the existence of similar (dis)approval of two practices for both groups (C1 to C4), next to discriminatory disapproval of Muslims (C5 to C9). Whereas almost four out of ten West Europeans discriminate against Muslims practicing their religion, six out of ten do not make a distinction between Muslims and Christians in their (partial) acceptance or rejection of

TABLE 4.1 Combinations of multiple acts (religious symbols and education) and multiple actors (Muslims and Christians) approach (without positive discrimination of Muslims). Percentages of majority members from five West European countries (N = 1,580)

Combinations	*Symbol*		*Education*		
	Christian	*Muslim*	*Christian*	*Muslim*	
C1.	Accept	Accept	Accept	Accept	Equal acceptance: 16.6%
C2.	Reject	Reject	Accept	Accept	Partial equal
C3.	Accept	Accept	Reject	Reject	rejection: 28.9%
C4.	Reject	Reject	Reject	Reject	Equal rejection: 15.3%
C5.	Reject	Reject	Accept	Reject	Discriminatory
C6.	Accept	Reject	Reject	Reject	rejection: 39.2%
C7.	Accept	Accept	Accept	Reject	
C8.	Accept	Reject	Accept	Accept	
C9.	Accept	Reject	Accept	Reject	

Source: Based on Dangubić et al. (2021)

the two practices. Furthermore, analyses indicate that prejudice towards Muslims was associated with a higher likelihood of displaying discriminatory than equal disapproval, and that those endorsing secularism were more likely to show equal disapproval compared to discriminatory disapproval.

In the third examination using national samples from Germany and the Netherlands, majority members were asked about four different practices and three religious groups (Muslims, Christians, and Jews; Dangubić et al., 2022b). A first finding is that a large majority of the population in both countries (>90%) rejected the exclusion of women on the board of religious organisations, independent of the religious group. Such a practice was perceived to go against the principle of gender equality and therefore considered unacceptable regardless of which religious group was engaged in it.

With latent profile analysis on the other three practices, we found one subgroup that used a double standard by more strongly rejecting Muslims than Christians and Jews engaging in the same practices (discriminatory rejection; 16.3%). Individuals within this subgroup were characterised by prejudicial feelings towards Muslims as a group and strong national identification, and in their self-reported responses, they criticised Muslims and referred to the importance of maintaining national traditions and values.

However, a large majority of the population in both countries did not use a double standard, but rather displayed actor-consistent and act-(in)consistent patterns of responses. This suggests that the rejection of these individuals is guided by other reasons than anti-Muslim prejudices per se. One in six individuals displayed the equal rejection pattern by rejecting all practices for all three religious groups which suggest generalised or common negativity towards religious expressions. These individuals were characterised by negative feelings towards both Muslims and non-Muslim religious groups, and positive feelings towards non-believers. They were also less religiously affiliated and displayed strong endorsement of secular principles.

In contrast to subgroups that rejected various practices, around one-fifth of the population accepted all practices for all three religious groups involved (equal acceptance) which indicates a generalised tendency to value all religious groups. Individuals within this subgroup were more likely to be religiously affiliated, to have positive feelings towards Muslims and non-Muslim religious groups, and to be open minded.

Additionally, around one in seven individuals displayed a partial equal rejection pattern of responses by accepting some practices and rejecting others, but equally for all three religious groups. The existence of this subgroup most clearly indicates that there can be practice-based variation in ratings that does not reflect generalised prejudice or target-group specific prejudices. Although individuals within this subgroup strongly endorsed civil liberties and accepted some religious practices (e.g. religious education in public schools), they were also strongly in favour of secularism which probably made them reject other practices (e.g. broadcasting time on national television). The two principles of civil liberty and secularism might be relevant simultaneously and combined in various ways in people's thinking (Dangubić et al., 2020; Peffley et al., 2001).

Finally, around one-third of the population in both countries responded in a moderate way by neither clearly rejecting nor accepting the practices, similarly towards the three religious groups ("moderates"). There are several possible reasons for this relatively large subgroup of individuals which was also found in person-centred research on the evaluation of seven different minority groups in Belgium (Meeusen et al., 2017), in Dutch research on the evaluation of various Muslim minority practices (Adelman & Verkuyten, 2020a), and in Swiss research on various arguments for face veiling (Eugster, 2021). In addition to possible methodological reasons, it might mean that around one-third of the population does not have very strong views on whether specific religious practices should or should not be accepted (Sturgis et al., 2014). For example, in the Swiss research and when asked directly, this subgroup was undecided on whether to support or oppose a face veil ban proposal. These findings suggest that very similar ratings of various outgroups and various practices do not have to reflect generalised prejudice or generalised positivity but might also indicate uncertainty, ambivalence, or even indifference. This interpretation corresponds to the notion that the social attitudes of people can be unstable and not clearly rooted in deep convictions or beliefs (Zaller, 1992).

Internal reasons

The findings for the different constellations of attitudes and evaluations within individuals provide a more nuanced, complete, and integrated description of the different considerations that people can have. The results indicate that for substantial numbers of majority members, the nature of their objections meet the non-prejudicial criteria that is necessary to be considered components of tolerance. In addition to individuals that are clearly prejudiced towards religious minority groups and people who are positive and supportive, there is a relatively large critical group that faces the question of tolerance.

However, as discussed in Chapter 3, the self-restraint involved in tolerance should not be coerced or based on fear, social disapproval, possible sanctions, or concerns over self-image. Tolerance is different from expressing non-prejudicial views for reasons of conforming to ingroup norms and secure ingroup acceptance (Crandall & Eshleman, 2003), or from the external motivation not to respond with prejudice or the suppression of prejudice for reputational reasons (Plant & Devine, 1998). People are tolerant when they have internally motivated reasons to respond without prejudice and discrimination, such as self-endorsed egalitarian and liberal values, and equity beliefs.

Research among children demonstrates that children as young as 7 years understand the difference between having external and internal reasons for outgroup evaluations (Hughes et al., 2016; Jargon & Thijs, 2021). External reasons include the desire to conform to social norms and avoid disapproval, while internal reasons stem from personal beliefs about equality, harm, and fairness. Internal reasons tend to be associated more strongly and consistently with outgroup acceptance than external reasons, which indicates that promoting the "right reasons" for outgroup acceptance is important.

Using large representative samples of majority members in the Netherlands and Germany, we examined the constellations of internal motivation and external motivation to respond without prejudice towards immigrants (Bamberg & Verkuyten, 2022). Again with latent profile analysis, we found four subgroups of which three were validated by a different pattern of the proportion of negative individuals on an indirect or covert measure (list experiment) as well as the average level of self-reported prejudice.

First, there was a subgroup of "*equally unmotivated*" individuals that was characterised by the highest proportion of negative people on the indirect measure, and the highest average self-reported prejudice on the direct measure. Around 10% of the majority population belonged to this profile, which is similar to the percentage that voted for a far-right party in the 2019 parliamentary elections in the Netherlands (10.9% for FVD) and Germany (11% AFD).[8] This suggests that around one in ten majority members did not fear negative social consequences of appearing prejudiced and also were not personally dedicated to egalitarianism.

We further identified a large subgroup of "*equally moderately*" motivated individuals of which 48% was negative on the indirect measure and which on average was moderately prejudiced on the direct self-report measure. The fact that six out of ten majority members were found to belong to this subgroup indicates that most peoples' motivation to respond without prejudice stems from both a personal dedication to egalitarians and a concern about the negative consequences of appearing prejudiced towards minority members, and immigrants in particular. Thus, a constellation of motives in which both internal and external motivations are moderately important appeared to be the most common pattern among the majority population in the two countries. This constellation does not prevent many of the individuals in this group to express prejudices on the direct and indirect measures, but also implies that many other individuals in this group do face the question of practicing tolerance or not.

A third subgroup consisted of "*predominantly internally motivated*" individuals (around 21%) of which one in three was prejudiced on the indirect measure and had on average a neutral score on the self-reported prejudice measure. This pattern of findings indicates that an internal motivation to respond without prejudice that stems from personal values goes together with a lack of prejudice towards immigrants, also for two in three individuals on the indirect measure. Thus, the internalisation and personal dedication to egalitarian values appear to be important for eliminating people's prejudice towards this minority group and imply the possibility to deliberate about reasons to tolerate things that one dislikes or disapproves of. Yet one-third of this subgroup indicated to be annoyed by the number of refugees in the country, and this might indicate subtle prejudiced feelings but also pragmatic and societal concerns about the accommodation of increasing number of refugees applying for asylum. These concerns might also be considered as relevant reasons for considering whether certain measures, policies, practices, and beliefs should or should not be tolerated (see Chapter 6). This raises the question of what exactly is involved in practicing tolerance.

5
PRACTICING TOLERANCE

Reporting on a trip to the Netherlands in 1988, the famous Italian novelist Claudio Magris wrote,

> In a large square something like a festival or a mass of universal tolerance took place. Countless closely spaced pavilions, stalls, kiosks, and counters presented, offered, propagated, preached, and spread their gospel, their ever-and-one-sacrifice truth. Political parties, churches, associations, clubs, movements and groups peddled their various and often completely opposite remedies for our mental, physical, social, metaphysical, sexual, cultural, gastronomic health; everyone had something to say and a message to proclaim: the antimilitarists, the military veterans and the health apostles as well as the adherents of strict diets or erotic techniques, esoteric cults or gymnastic exercises, ascetic or orgiastic practices – practices in the direction of community building but also of wild anarchic individualism; people explained the advantages of collective insurance or, conversely, the abolition thereof.
>
> *(in Terpstra & de Wit, 2019, p. 246)*

During the trip, he attended a festival where there was a kind of general tolerance on display in which a range of clearly contrasting beliefs, practices, and worldviews were demonstrated side by side. There was a general atmosphere of mutual acceptance of very different people expressing their specific views, enacting their identities, and arguing their case.

In several of our studies with large representative samples from the Netherlands and Germany, we have used four items that tap into the predisposition to endorse tolerance in general (e.g. "I accept it when other people do things that I wholeheartedly disapprove of" and "I am tolerant of people who have a fundamentally different way of life"). Across these studies, we have found in both countries that

DOI: 10.4324/9781003335030-5

around two in three (~ 68%) score on the positive side of the scale and thus endorse tolerance in general, and one in eight (~ 12%) tends to be intolerant by scoring on the negative side of the scale (and ~ 20% "neutral").[1]

These percentages indicate a relatively strong general commitment to the notion of tolerance in these two societies.[2] Furthermore, this commitment appears to be reliable and valid, because this general measure of tolerance is empirically distinct from the endorsement of cultural relativist beliefs ("One can only judge the norms and values of another culture from that culture itself") and indifference ("I do not care if people want to live differently than me"), and is associated in expected ways with, for example, established measures of open-mindedness, deprovincialisation, dogmatism, authoritarianism, educational level, and political orientation.[3]

Hence, many ordinary majority members appear to support the core liberal democratic notion of everyone being able to live the life that they want, especially those ways of life one disagrees with, dislikes, or disapproves of (e.g. Sniderman et al., 2014). In other words, there is a clear positive force (tolerance) in favour of accepting dissenting beliefs and practices, in addition to the negative forces (e.g. prejudices, structural discrimination) working against minorities. This positive force will certainly not simply prevail over the negative ones, but that does not mean that it can be ignored or considered meaningless. Tolerance forms a critical minimal condition for a peaceful diverse society, and the fact that most majority members endorse tolerance in general indicates that an appeal to people's values and beliefs is possible.

However, and similar to the difference between the endorsement of principles such as freedom and equality and their practical (policy) implications, the general support of the notion of tolerance does not simply translate in actual tolerance. For the evaluation of concrete situations and cases, not only a person's predisposition is relevant but also various other considerations and concerns. In our studies, we find that the endorsement of tolerance in general is a reliable separate predictor of actual tolerance in concrete situations, but far from the only or main thing that matters.[4] There is, as always, a person by context interaction, and the endorsement of general principles is something else than the evaluation of specific cases, and this is also true for tolerance. Research has shown that there often is a difference in the way in which people judge abstract reasons and general notions in comparison to concrete cases and specific situations (Dixon et al., 2017). It is one thing to agree with the general notion that people should have the freedom to live the life that they want, but another to accept, for example, same-sex marriage, abortion, apostacy, building of a mosque with minarets in one's neighbourhood, or Muslim teachers in public schools wearing a headscarf. Furthermore, there tends to be an asymmetry in the tolerance process.

An asymmetry

Research indicates that it is easier to convince tolerant people to give up their tolerance than to persuade intolerant people to become more tolerant (e.g. Gibson, 2006a; Gieling et al., 2012; Peffley et al., 2001), especially in relation to transgressive groups (Petersen et al., 2011). With intolerance, the negative judgement about a dissenting belief or practice is in agreement with rejecting those beliefs or practices: you reject what you object to. Being tolerant, on the other hand, implies putting up with actions and practices that you consider wrong: you accept what you object to. Such a scenario may elicit dissonance and uneasiness (Festinger, 1962) and makes tolerance more fragile than intolerance. The difficulty is that with tolerance, competing values and principles are at stake, which require complex decision-making.

Using the action-based model of dissonance (Harmon-Jones & Mills, 1999), we used electroencephalography (EEG) to examine the implications of practicing intergroup toleration. Specifically, non-Muslim participants were encouraged to either identify Muslim practices they disapproved of and then consider reasons why they may nevertheless tolerate such practices (tolerance condition) or only identify practices they disapproved of (control condition). Data suggested that for politically liberal participants, practicing tolerance (relative to the control condition) led to more cognitive conflict, and in turn, more positive reactions towards Muslims. However, politically conservative participants experienced less cognitive conflict, and in turn, reported more negative reactions towards Muslims when asked to practice toleration relative to when they were not asked to tolerate Muslim practices (Yogeeswaran et al., 2021). These diverging findings among liberals and conservatives suggest that encouraging toleration may have varied consequences depending on people's own ideologies and motivations (Jost, 2017). An emphasis on tolerance might not only lead to greater acceptance, but might also backfire and have unanticipated consequences.

The asymmetry of tolerance and the thinking involved in practicing tolerance suggests that it is a challenge to try to stimulate tolerance. In our research, we found that majority Dutch adolescents became less tolerant when considerations against Muslim minority practices were presented, whereas tolerance was not affected by considerations in favour of tolerating the practices (Gieling et al., 2012). Other research has found that the communication of a tolerant social norm was only effective among those whose initial attitudes towards the tolerated Muslim minority practices were more positive (Van Doorn, 2016). Thus, providing tolerant norm information only led to tolerant norm perceptions when the norm was in line with the initial attitude. Other research has also found that a call for tolerance can help build support for public policies among the already tolerant, but simultaneously weaken the support among the intolerant (Djupe et al., 2015).

However, this asymmetry might also depend on the question about the main reason that people have for endorsing tolerance in general: *why* they in general accept that dissenting others can affirm their dissenting views and live their life accordingly. Two main reasons are, first, avoiding societal conflicts and, second, respecting the equal standing and rights of others. These two reasons are similar to two forms of tolerance that have been put forward in a historical and conceptual analysis by Forst (2013), namely coexistence tolerance and respect tolerance.[5] These forms of tolerance differ in how strongly they are based on pragmatic or principled concerns, and therefore correspond to the distinction between principled and pragmatic ways in which people reason about societal issues (e.g. Colombo, 2021), and the distinction between instrumentality-based (for the functioning of society) and respect-based cultural diversity beliefs (Kauff et al., 2020).

Pragmatic and principled reasons

The development of the notion of tolerance in 16th- and 17th-century Europe was mainly for pragmatic reasons. These centuries were characterised by vigorous state repression and doctrinal Christian divisions that inspired violent conflicts and wholescale slaughter. John Locke's "*A letter concerning tolerance*" (1685), written while in exile in the Netherlands, was one of the classic defences of tolerance. Locke argued for condoning dissenting religious dogmas and practices since the alternative of perpetual civil war was far worse. Establishing tolerance would be a practical matter to avoid endless conflicts, also because genuine religious belief is voluntary and cannot be forced upon people, even not with torture.

Forst (2013) uses the term *coexistence tolerance* for the more pragmatic acceptance of dissenting ways of life in order to avoid conflicts and to find and maintain peaceful cohabitation (Kirchner et al., 2011). The focus is not so much on the rights of other groups as such, but rather on the inevitability of having to live together.[6] Coexistence tolerance is considered instrumental to the attainment of the value of maintaining social harmony and peace, and things that go against this should not be tolerated. Its instrumental and more conditional nature makes it morally less imperative than respect tolerance and in some situations also people with prejudicial feelings might be willing to accept others in order to prevent conflicts and secure peaceful coexistence. They may think that in given circumstances, it is in society's best interest to tolerate dissenting others to live the life that they want, rather than suppress and exclude them. This could mean that the endorsement of coexistence tolerance partly reflects outgroup prejudice, whereas this should not be the case for the endorsement of respect tolerance. However, and independent of prejudice, a pragmatic tolerant person can prefer to refrain from negatively interfering with dissenting practices because of the values of peace, public order, and societal harmony (Haidt, 2012).

Historically, the notion of *respect tolerance* was developed much later and in relation to the increasing importance of liberal principles of human dignity and personal autonomy. Respect tolerance is based on the principled Kantian belief that all people are autonomous individuals with equal rights, which is considered important already by children from a variety of cultural and national contexts (Helwig, 2008). Although there are sometimes "deep" cultural, religious, and ideological differences in ways of life, others are tolerated, because they are respected as equal citizens with the same dignity, rights, and civil liberties (Simon, 2020). When people respect members of another group as equals, it is likely that they are not strongly negative towards this group. In research among Tea Party supporters (Simon et al., 2019), it was found that respect for homosexuals and Muslims as equal fellow citizens goes together with more positive attitudes towards those outgroups. Respect for outgroup members as equals fosters tolerance as has been found in survey, longitudinal and experimental research among different groups and in different countries (see Zitzmann et al., 2022).

We investigated these two main reasons for being tolerant in relation to the acceptance of specific minority practices in four studies using five national samples of Dutch majority members (Velthuis et al., 2021).[7] We first examined in all samples whether the expected empirical distinction between the endorsement of coexistence tolerance and respect tolerance[8] exist and how these relate to group-based prejudice. Additionally, we used a random experimental design to test whether the meaning and endorsement of the two forms of tolerance is immigrant category specific or rather similar across immigrant groups. Furthermore, we examined whether the two forms of tolerance are positively associated with the acceptance of concrete Muslim minority practices, independent of prejudice.

Among the five samples, we clearly found that the two forms of tolerance are empirically distinct in relation to dissenting people in general and cultural minorities in particular. Furthermore, both forms had a similar meaning and similar levels of endorsement in relation to various immigrant categories that feature in public and political debates (Western, non-Western, Muslim, and non-Muslim immigrants). This means that both forms are more general rather than group-specific conceptions of tolerance. The distinction between the two forms of tolerance was further supported by their different relations with the endorsement of tolerance in general and with prejudicial feelings. Across the five studies, there was a robust negative relation between respect tolerance and prejudice, and although coexistence tolerance was also negatively correlated with prejudice this association was much weaker or did not appear when controlling statistically for respect tolerance.

Higher coexistence tolerance was quite strongly associated with higher respect tolerance (see also Klein & Zick, 2013) which indicates that people who consider it important to tolerate minorities and cultural others for reasons of peaceful cohabitation also tend to respect them as equal citizens. Supporting the ability of minorities to live the life that they want for reasons of societal harmony and peace seems to partly reflect reasons of equal dignity and respect. However, the latter reasons appear to be more important than the former, because coexistence tolerance was not independently related to the acceptance of Muslim minority practices. It is likely that the more instrumental nature of coexistence tolerance makes it less morally imperative than respect tolerance and therefore more contextual. Pragmatic reasons for tolerance could more strongly shift back and forth depending on what the situational context and pragmatic motives are. Emphasising tolerance to avoid conflicts may in some situations be a useful or even the best possible option, but it remains a pragmatic and not principled solution.

Stimulating respect tolerance might be particularly helpful for improving intergroup relations in culturally diverse societies (Zitzmann et al., 2022). Respect tolerance was endorsed relatively strongly in the national samples and more strongly than coexistence tolerance. Thus, most majority members (around 65%) tended to agree with the principle that immigrant-origin minorities are autonomous citizens with equal rights and therefore have the freedom to live the life that they want. Furthermore, stronger respect tolerance was not only a general, abstract belief but also associated with the acceptance of concrete Muslim minority practices. Thus, respecting people with an immigrant background as fellow citizens did go together with higher acceptance of concrete practices, also among majority members who expressed concerns about the continuity of their ingroup culture and identity, and among those with prejudiced feelings.

The tolerance process

In practicing tolerance, there is a combination of objections towards particular beliefs and practices, while nonetheless holding a positive judgement of and behavioural intention towards accepting these practices and beliefs. This inconsistency between the negative attitude (objection) and positive intention (acceptance) requires deliberation and self-restraint.

In one of our neuropsychological studies, people were asked to reflect on different scenarios related to dissenting practices and beliefs of disliked and liked groups[9] that evoke tolerance-related processes (Nash et al., 2022). For example, in one scenario, people were first asked to think about a belief or practice in society that they disapproved of, before then considering reasons why despite their disapproval they should nevertheless tolerate it in society rather than ban or forbid it. During the tasks, EEG (electroencephalography) activity was recorded for comparing (source localised) brain activity during the engagement of tolerance against brain activity during disapproval. Results showed that engaging in tolerance was associated with increased activation in the right insula, the right dorsolateral prefrontal cortex, and the anterior cingulate cortex. These brain regions are all key in cognitive control and deliberative processes and together suggests that thinking about tolerating dissenting beliefs and practices implies increased control and deliberation. In other words, our brain appears to engage in effortful deliberation to restrain our initial negative reactions when we think about tolerating beliefs and practices that we view as problematic.

The deliberation involved in tolerance implies the recognition of relevant reasons for accepting cultural, religious, and ideological beliefs and different modes of conduct that one disagrees with, dislikes, or disapproves of. In such cases, one's spontaneous or more reflective objections towards dissenting beliefs and practices (e.g. building of mosques) is overpowered by considerations to nonetheless allow those beliefs and practices in society (e.g. religious freedom; see Figure 3.1 the first moderation path).

Respect for others as equals appears to be an important consideration for tolerance. A stronger tendency to unconditionally respect others as human beings with intrinsic worth has been found to be associated with stronger positive action tendencies and weaker negative action tendencies towards ethnic and religious (Muslim) minority outgroups (Lalljee et al., 2009). In one study, we found that respect of others in virtue of being human is associated with higher tolerance of Muslim minority practices (Dangubić et al., 2022a). And in a further study among Dutch adolescents, we examined the endorsement of the equality of cultural groups in relation to tolerance of four specific Muslim minority practices (e.g. wearing of a headscarf, Islamic public schools) together with the feelings towards the respective Muslim actors (Thijs et al., 2021). The analysis revealed that there was a significant direct effect of cultural equality on tolerance. The endorsement of the equal status of cultural minority groups was associated with higher tolerance, independent of minority outgroup feelings.

The respect of others as equals is grounded in a common higher-level category membership (fellow citizens or fellow humans; Simon, 2020) and does not preclude the possibilities to object to what they believe and how they live their lives. As discussed in Chapter 3, tolerating other citizens' divergent beliefs and practices (e.g. "respecting their equal civic right to hold particular beliefs and act according to it") is not the same as considering these beliefs and practices as equally valid (e.g. "valuing what they believe and practice"). Tolerance involves an act of judgement, but this does not serve to censor "wrong beliefs" or intervene in dissenting practices because tolerance demands respect for the equal rights and freedoms of others to hold and express their own beliefs and live their life accordingly. As indicated earlier, research has shown that people may be tolerant of beliefs and practices they disapprove of because they endorse liberal and democratic values (Gibson, 2006a; Saroglou et al., 2009; Sullivan & Transue, 1999).

Deliberating about disapproved of conduct

Beyond the importance of holding specific values such as equal respect and civil liberties for the tolerance process, we also examined the importance of recognising relevant reasons for why others engage in disapproved of behaviours, as part of determining what to tolerate and what not to tolerate.

> Whenever I see a woman in a full burqa, I feel personally offended. But it is an important part of what I believe: what I feel personally is irrelevant. It does not matter what I feel, nobody should abide by what I feel.
>
> *(Richard Dawkins, in an interview, 18-2-2015)*

In this quote, the evolutionary biologist and self-declared atheist, Dawkins, indicates that in the presence of relevant (actual or imagined) triggering conditions, he has a negative gut reaction towards a particular practice. The reaction is intuitive, without any intention on his part, and does not have to involve dislike of Muslims as a group of people. However, there is also a reflective process that involves his moral beliefs, as Dawkins is opposed to a burqa ban, because he considers this a violation of individual liberty.

> I think there are good reasons to not accept the wearing of a burqa in our Western society, but that there are even better reasons to nevertheless condone it.
>
> *(anonymous contribution to online discussion, 21-4-2018)*

Similar to Dawkins, this person does not support a burqa ban, but whereas Dawkins seems to restrain his negative gut reaction, this person appears to have been involved in deliberative thinking about the pros (e.g. social integration and security) and cons (e.g. religious freedom and egalitarianism) of such a ban.

Psychologically, tolerance is rather paradoxical and far from easy, because one intentionally refrains from obstructing or interfering with conduct that one objects to, despite having the perceived ability to do so. Tolerance involves a sequential reasoning process in which the reasons for non-interference trump one's dislike, disapproval, or disagreement to the ways of life of other people. On the one hand, there is what you feel or believe to be misguided or wrong that makes you want to censor, repress or regulate it, but on the other hand, there are reasons like equal respect, peaceful coexistence, personal autonomy, and civil liberties, which encourage you to grant others the right to live their own lives. However, the two quotes indicate that psychologically there are two main ways of being tolerant: tolerance processes based on intuitive (Dawkins) versus reflective (anonymous contribution) objections (see Figure 5.1). This distinction can be understood through dual-process theories, which are leading theoretical frameworks for understanding thinking in both cognitive and social psychology. Although the different theories within psychology have varied origins, make differing assumptions, and propose various defining and correlated characteristics, all argue for a qualitative distinction between two types of cognitive processing: a relatively intuitive process that is autonomous and rapid versus a more deliberate process that requires working memory and cognitive control (see Evans, 2008; Evans & Stanovich, 2013; Greene, 2013).

There is converging evidence from psychology and neuroscience for the dual processing distinction, which has been applied to various domains of thinking such as decision-making, learning, and moral judgement. In the latter domain, moral intuitions and the reflective use of normative rules are considered to concurrently drive moral decisions and positions (Greene, 2013; Haré, 1981; Trémolière et al., 2018).

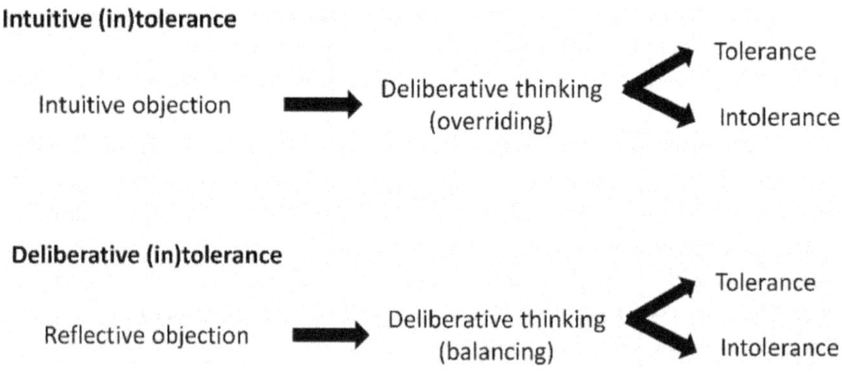

FIGURE 5.1 The sequential process model of the two forms of forbearance tolerance and intolerance

Source: Verkuyten et al. 2022a.

Most of these models propose a sequential form of cognitive processing, rather than a parallel form (Sloman, 1996). Intuitive processes provide a default moral intuition, which may or may not be overcome by subsequently reflective processing. The assumption is that deliberative processing "requires access to central executive resources in order to suspend or inhibit the intuitive response to a problem for the time it takes to produce a reflective response" (Trémolière et al., 2018, p. 576). In support of this assumption, research has found that a reflective moral response takes longer than an intuitive moral reaction, and that time pressure or cognitive load decreases the likelihood of a reflective moral response (Trémolière et al., 2018). Similarly, experimentally encouraging people to trust their gut feelings reduces reflective moral responding, and a stronger individual tendency at rational thinking is more likely to elicit a reflective moral answer (see Evans & Stanovich, 2013; Trémolière et al., 2018).

However, unfamiliar practices and behaviours can not only trigger intuitive responses but can also spontaneously initiate reflective thinking whereby one tries to make sense of what is happening (Thompson, 2013; Thompson et al., 2011). Sometimes we do not know how to feel about novel beliefs or practices without some thinking about what it means and what its implications are. Furthermore, research on moral dilemmas has found that sacrificial dilemma decision-making (e.g. trolley problem[10]), which is typically considered to be primarily driven by intuitive emotional responses to causing harm, can also arise from cognitive reflection (Byrd & Conway, 2019; McPheters et al., 2018). This indicates that reflection need not always entail overcoming initial intuitive responses, but can result from the wish to consider dilemmatic and novel situations extensively (Baron et al., 2015).

Moral intuitions can be shaped by prior reasoning and debate, leading people to moralise particular issues (e.g. smoking, drunk-drinking, abortion) that then trigger intuitive moral emotions (Skitka et al., 2021). Furthermore, reasoning not only plays a post-hoc role in moral justification (Haidt, 2012) but also in deliberative thinking about real-world moral issues that people debate (e.g. gay marriage, apostasy, the building of minarets, risky behaviour of one's children, offensive speech, and wet markets). There does not have to be immediate gut reactions as to whether these practices are right or wrong, which makes reflective reasoning about moral principles critical (Cushman et al., 2006; Pizarro & Bloom, 2003). For example, mindful thinking can foster tolerance, while cognitive depletion leads to lower acceptance (Baumgartner & Morgan, 2019). The implication is that in thinking about unfamiliar events, practices, and dissenting conduct, two or more deliberative processes might be involved; these may either converge into a single conclusion or give rise to competing considerations. In other words, there can be a deliberative–deliberative conflict between contrasting values and norms that one subscribes to, which requires balanced reasoning or weighing in deciding whether to accept or reject particular dissenting practices and beliefs.

The dual process model of moral judgement provides a useful framework for understanding the processes involved in tolerance, where one's objections to dissenting conduct are weighed against reasons not to interfere. However, the process it takes can emerge in two distinct forms (Figure 5.1). A necessary condition of tolerance is that there is dislike, disapproval, or disagreement with the beliefs and practices of others, and one can be tolerant of conduct regardless of their feelings towards those enacting them. For example, parents can tolerate risky behaviour (smoking, drinking) of their children, or one can tolerate certain annoying behaviours of their partner, and people can be intolerant of conduct from their ingroup members (e.g. flag burning and hate speech). However, the objection (dislike, disapproval, and disagreement) can derive either from intuitive reactions (disgust, fear, and anger) or from thoughtful reasoning. In the former case, tolerance is the outcome of the default-overriding dual-process model (intuitive processes, overpowered by deliberate processes). In the latter case, both the objection and reason to tolerate are based on reflective thinking in which there is a weighing of the reasonable objection to dissenting conduct and the reason to nevertheless tolerate it (deliberative processes, overpowered by other deliberative processes). Thus, even if the outcome of behavioural non-interference is the same, there are psychological differences between these two ways of being tolerant that correspond to the distinction in moral philosophy between moral intuitions and moral reasoning (Dellantonio & Job, 2012). In the next section, I will first discuss our research on the first process, and in the subsequent section, I consider the second process.

Intuition and deliberation

We tested the default-overriding dual process model in multiple online studies using an experimental design for manipulating intuitive versus deliberative thinking (Capraro et al., 2019; Levine et al., 2018). We examined the key prediction that deliberative thinking leads to higher tolerance of minority practices and beliefs, compared to intuitive thinking.

In one study, we focused on political tolerance of immigrant-origin individuals with dual citizenship (accepting that they, e.g. "hold public demonstrations", "give public speeches", and "found their own political organisations") (Verkuyten et al., 2022a). Citizenship is a critical marker of legal and political community membership that provides security, protection, and equal civil, social, and political rights and responsibilities (Bloemraad, 2015; Marshall, 1964). Although an increasing number of countries permit dual citizenship for immigrants (Harpaz, 2019; Harpaz & Mateos, 2019), continued worries about divided loyalties and political trustfulness of dual citizens frequently boil up, leading to forms of political intolerance. In the Netherlands, for example, a majority of the population (60%) does not support dual citizenship (Vink et al., 2019), and similar reservations have been expressed in other European countries (Jasinskaja-Lahti et al., 2020). Furthermore, experimental research has found that immigrants' dual citizenship (compared to host country citizenship only) elicits suspicions of divided loyalties because these immigrants are perceived as being more loyal to the country of origin and are considered deviant members who compromise national unity (Jasinskaja-Lahti et al.,

2020; Kunst et al., 2019). Dual citizenship can trigger loyalty concerns and the public tends to think more in terms of divided loyalties than multiple loyalties with the result that dual citizens can be intuitively treated with "double standards" resulting in political intolerance.

As expected, the experimental findings indicated that participants in the deliberative condition were more tolerant than participants in the intuitive and the control conditions. Furthermore, the means of tolerance in the control condition did not differ significantly from those in the intuitive condition which is in line with the notion that in online surveys participants tend to respond to these kind of questions based on their gut reactions and without much reflection (Krosnick, 1999). Thus, the results support the theoretical prediction that deliberative thinking can lead to higher tolerance: political tolerance of immigrant-origin individuals with dual citizenship was higher when participants were invited to give a balanced judgement compared to intuitive thinking. This finding was robust across demographic categories such as gender, age, religiosity, educational level, and also across ideological constructs such as political orientation and authoritarianism. Hence, deliberative thinking led to higher tolerance similarly for older and younger participants, religious and non-religious affiliated individuals, higher and lower educated, those with a more left-wing or right-wing political orientation, higher and lower national identifiers, and those with a stronger and weaker authoritarian predisposition (Verkuyten et al., 2022b).

However, it should be noted that the results in terms of effect sizes were small (Cohen, 1988) and this is probably due to the use of survey experiments that tend to have relatively weak experimental manipulations (Sniderman, 2018). Participants simply were instructed either to respond directly or rather to reflect before answering. Yet small effects can be of theoretical and practical importance (Götz et al., 2022) and similar low effect sizes have been found in experimental research on dual process models of moral judgement (Capraro et al., 2019) and intolerance (Baumgartner & Morgan, 2019). The fact that our manipulation showed the expected effect suggests that even simple online instructions can influence the degree to which individuals are willing to politically tolerate individuals with dual citizenship. It is likely that more extensive procedures in which people more deeply reflect on reasons for being politically tolerant towards those with dual citizenship may yield stronger effects.

In a second random research, we conducted three studies focusing on tolerance of Muslim minority practices, of gender debated issues (e.g. installing gender-neutral toilets) and for other contested issues such as changing the black-faced helper (black Pete) in the Saint Nicolaus fest (Verkuyten et al., 2022a). Since all these practices and issues tend to evoke negative reactions among many Dutch majority members, they are suitable for examining the importance of deliberative and intuitive thinking for tolerance. Furthermore, focusing on Muslim minority practices and the other types of practices and issues makes it possible to examine whether the role of deliberative thinking for tolerance is specific for an immigrant-origin group (Muslims) or rather generalises across various debated practices.

In the first study, we examined whether deliberative thinking leads to higher tolerance compared to intuitive thinking and a control condition. This was found to be the case in relation to both general debated practices and Muslim minority practices, and also across various demographic groups of respondents. In line with dual-process theories, this again suggests that tolerance is more likely when people engage in a deliberative cognitive process, which corresponds with previous empirical findings on the role of deliberative thinking for moral judgement (Marcus et al., 1995; Pennycook et al., 2014).

Yet, unlike intuitive thinking, which relies on gut-level reactions, within deliberative thinking, there are many different reasoning pathways for people to take when being asked to consider whether certain dissenting practices should be tolerated. More specifically, and as discussed earlier, there are two main types of reasons that generate tolerance: valuing and maintaining social harmony and peace, and respecting the equal standing and rights of others. In two further experimental studies, we examined whether reflecting on these more pragmatic or more principled reasons has different implications for tolerance, or rather if both lead to increased tolerance compared to intuitive based reactions.

We found that people took relatively more and equal time in answering the questions in the two deliberative conditions and, again, that deliberative thinking increased tolerance. This higher tolerance occurred regardless of whether people were asked to deliberate over more pragmatic or more principled reasons for acceptance. Furthermore, the findings were similar across a range of minority practices and again robust across participants' gender, age, educational level, and political orientation (Verkuyten et al., 2022a).

Both pragmatic and principled considerations emphasise that cultural "others" should be able to live the life that they want but for different reasons: reasons of societal harmony and peace or reasons of equal dignity and respect. Tolerance can be increased by asking people to think about more principled or about more pragmatic reasons for accepting debated minority practices. For tolerance judgements, it might thus be important that individuals recognise their intuitive disapproval, and are encouraged to "stand still" and engage in reflective thinking. This can increase the likelihood of tolerance which makes debate and dialogue for finding solutions for living with diversity possible.

However, it is important to recognise possible backlashes. Reflecting about these reasons and what they mean in everyday life does not always have to lead to higher tolerance. Thinking about the social implications of high-level dissenting minority practices and beliefs might also trigger considerations about possible negative consequences for social cohesion and public order which can lead to lower tolerance (Adelman et al., 2021a; Chong, 1994; Kuklinski et al., 1991). And thinking about principled reasons might also lead to lower tolerance of practices (e.g. gender inequality) that are considered to go against key liberal values and therefore are considered intolerable (Adelman et al., 2021a). In other words, people can also reflect on the reasons that define principled and pragmatic limits or boundaries of what can be tolerated. I will discuss this further in Chapter 6.

Recognising relevant reasons

The earlier anonymous quote about the burqa indicates that people can recognise that there can be better reasons to nevertheless accept – in this case – the wearing of a burqa than reasons for banning it. Both the objection and reason for acceptance are based on reflective thinking in which there is a weighing of the reasonable objection to dissenting conduct and the reason to nevertheless tolerate it. This process of recognising relevant reasons to tolerate something we disapprove of involves not only reasons that people themselves have for being tolerant but also the perceived reasons that others have for their actions.

What most conceptualisations of rationality have in common is the notion of reason: "for a belief to be rational is for it to be based on reasons" (Crane, 2017, p. 147). A belief or action is rational when there are conventions, principles, or values which count in favour of believing or doing it (Scanlon, 2004). People appeal to these reasons when making arguments about what they themselves or others (should) believe or do. Reasons and arguments can be considered good or bad in the sense of being perceived to be a relevant or not relevant consideration in favour of believing or doing something. For example and as discussed earlier, treating categories of people (Muslims, sexual minorities) differently on the basis of reasons that are considered irrelevant is discrimination, and this differs from differential treatment in which categories of people (e.g. children, the sick) are treated differently for relevant reasons.

Good (vs. bad) reasons can be traced to some understandable or normatively acceptable source, and rationality refers to the process of employing these reasons for forming one's beliefs. Actions and beliefs that have an unacceptable normative basis are considered unreasonable and irrational, whereas actions and beliefs that are perceived as socially acceptable and having value, are considered reasonable and rational. Obviously, what are considered good reasons can differ between individuals, groups, and situations, but there is a strong first-person dimension in that the person themselves must belief that there is an acceptable and relevant basis for a particular belief or course of action.

People can be expected to be more tolerant if they think that there are good reasons to accept what they continue to object of. On the one hand, there is what one thinks is false or wrong, but on the other hand, one must be able and willing to allow others to live the life they want. There need to be relevant reasons to endure the objectionable behaviours or beliefs that trump one's objection. With three studies among national samples of Dutch majority members (Verkuyten et al., 2022b), we tried to provide a conceptual replication (Crandall & Sherman, 2016) of the expected role of recognising reasons for tolerating disapproved of conduct by focusing on Muslim minorities and orthodox Protestants as an established religious minority group, by considering a range of minority practices and in two contexts, by using different measures of tolerance, and by focusing on self-reported and perceived reasons.

In the first two studies, we examined whether the self-recognition of relevant considerations impacts the process of weighing the objection against reasons to nonetheless demonstrate acceptance. Specifically, we considered the importance of thinking about reasons for tolerance by testing the prediction that individuals will be more tolerant when they themselves recognise that there are relevant considerations for supporting a broad range of practices and events that they are negative about. In the first study, we focused on tolerance of Muslim minority practices (e.g. "Imagine that at the secondary schools of your children, it is considered, at the request of Muslim parents, to give swimming lessons separately to boys and girls", "Some Muslim organizations want Dutch hospitals to have an arrangement that – if possible – men are treated by men and women by women"), while in the second study, we considered religious minority practices of Orthodox Protestants ("Recently there was a discussion about Orthodox Protestant schools refusing to hire homosexual teachers" and "Recently there was a discussion about Orthodox Protestant organizations that refuse women on their board"). The focus on these two numerically small religious groups allows us to assess whether recognising additional reasons matters for the tolerance of practices of an immigrant-origin group (Muslims) that often is perceived as threatening national culture and identity, similarly applies to a historically established religious minority group (i.e. orthodox Protestants) aligned with the majority population.

In both studies, participants were first asked to think about the specific practice or event and to indicate on a binary scale whether they were more positive or more negative towards it. Depending on their answer, they were subsequently asked to indicate if there are arguments to nevertheless not to support the practice or rather to support the practice. Then, participants were presented with a behavioural intention question measuring tolerance. In both studies, the great majority of participants were negative towards the various practices (84.2% up to 95.4%), which indicates that all scenarios are relevant toleration cases for most people. Furthermore, of those with a negative attitude, many did not think that there were additional reasons for supporting it. However, there was a substantial minority of participants that despite their negative feelings did recognise that there were also relevant reasons for support (11.3%–35.9%) and these people overall were more tolerant. Depending on the specific practice, the self-reported reasons to tolerate had to do with the importance of principles of free speech, freedom of education, religious freedoms, and minority rights, as well as pragmatic considerations of coexistence and peaceful cohabitation. Thus, these participants used more principled and pragmatic reasons for tolerance, which is in line with what was discussed earlier.

In general, people were more negative towards the practices and events of orthodox Protestants than Muslim minorities, which suggests that these were considered more controversial, despite the enacting group being a native minority group. Furthermore, we presented people with scenarios that differed in the degree of required majority group accommodation and some of these practices were perceived as more demanding than others. Yet, although the degree of tolerance differed, the role of recognising relevant reasons for tolerance was similar towards orthodox Protestants and Muslims, across less and more demanding minority practices, as well as practices that affects one's personal life and the broader society.

This conceptual replication supports the theoretical proposition that values and principles can overpower negative beliefs, and thereby enhances our confidence in the reflective process underlying tolerance. However, it is important to note that a majority was intolerant and did not think that there were relevant arguments to nevertheless accept the dissenting practice.

In a third study, we experimentally tested whether perceiving others to have relevant reasons for a controversial action leads to higher tolerance of that action. Based on our previous research (Adelman & Verkuyten, 2020b), we focused on protest to the reception of refugees and the perceived reasons that the protester gives for the action. For the experimental manipulation, we used the familiar distinction between irrational (prejudicial) and rational (relevant) bases for negative outgroup evaluation (Billig, 1988). This distinction refers to whether a judgement or action is, or is not, based on clear thought and reason, and it is commonly used by people for criticising as well as justifying their negative attitudes towards minority groups (e.g. Kleiner, 1998; Verkuyten, 1998), including refugees (Capdevila & Callaghan, 2008; Figgou & Condor, 2006). We expected the experimental manipulation to affect the perceived reasonableness of the protest action which in turn will have an impact on tolerance. Thus, we examined perceived reasonableness as the underlying mechanism between the (ir)rational nature of the protest action and tolerance. Furthermore, we considered the perceived offensiveness of the protest action for assessing whether participants did indeed disapprove of the action and thus whether it involved for them a question of tolerance.

Participants read a brief description of an act of controversial criticism, modelled on a newspaper-style news article about citizens' responses to the reception of refugees. The scenario described a situation in which a local Dutch male (Johan Kok) in the city of Gouda in the Netherlands had put up a poster in the front window of his house stating, "NO, AGAINST REFUGEES".[11] The person putting up the poster gave either an irrational or a rational explanation for their action. These explanations were based on public debates and lay person's own accounts (e.g. Capdevila & Callaghan, 2008; Verkuyten, 1998) and either involved more prejudiced feelings and beliefs or argued for considered thought about the impact of refugees on society as an operationalisation of being rational.

The findings demonstrated that participants tended to be more tolerant of a controversial action, if the explanation for this action was perceived to be more rationally based. This effect was found independent of the perceived offensiveness of the action which suggests that perceived rationality caused acceptance more generally. Furthermore, when focusing only on the subgroup of participants who considered the poster offensive, we found that the level of offensiveness did not differ between the two experimental conditions. Thus, putting up the poster was considered equally offensive in both conditions, which means that perceived offensiveness did not explain the reasonableness and tolerance difference between the two conditions. In short, we found that considered thought as a perceived rational basis for a controversial action was considered more reasonable, and therefore, tolerated more, independent of the perceived offensiveness of the action.

Reasons behind dissenting conduct

The findings of the third study indicate that the explanation that people give for their controversial action matters for tolerance. However, an account of dissenting conduct can not only differ in terms of perceived reasonableness since there can be various types of reasons for why people engage in behaviour that is criticised, disliked, or disapproved off. The understanding of these reasons are likely to matter for tolerance. For example, it is likely that parents will become more tolerant of the restless and impulsive behaviour of their child when it turns out that the child has ADHD, and a diagnosis of autism will make parents more tolerant of their child's restricted and repetitive pattern of thought and social behaviour. Furthermore, caring about a contentious social issue signals personal integrity and trustworthiness which even in cases of strong disagreement makes tolerance more likely (Zlatev, 2019). Additionally, research has found that people can be less tolerant towards a difference that results from self-chosen conversion than when given or ascribed (Jones & Bejan, 2021). Defining or challenging a particular action as voluntary (self-determined) or involuntary (others determined) has important consequences, such as in welfare debates about "deserving" and "undeserving" citizens, in accounting for people's health and illness, unemployment, and poverty, and in relation to migrants. For example, the perceived (in)voluntariness of migration has an impact on the support for accommodating immigrants because it differently defines immigrants' own responsibility for leaving their home country. Whether migration is considered voluntary (own free choice, "fortune seekers") or involuntary (no choice, "real refugees") affects the attitude that the public has towards newcomers and their cultural rights (Verkuyten, 2004a; Verkuyten et al., 2018b), not only towards immigrants but also towards emigrants (Gieling et al., 2011; Vink et al., 2019).

An understanding of why exactly people belief what they belief and do what they do matters, also for tolerance and already for young children. Children enter school with their own initial opinions and beliefs on what they prefer and like, how the social world works, and what is right and wrong. Disagreements and conflicts related to the differing opinions, beliefs, and interests are commonly observed among children as young as 4 years of age (Ram & Ross, 2001). Being less or more tolerant towards peers who hold different views might depend on the reasons that these peers have for their views. For example, it has been found that older children and adolescents are more tolerant towards beliefs and practices based on dissenting factual information (about what is) compared to opposing moral convictions (about what is right and wrong; Wainryb, 1993), and that already for six-years-old the reasons behind flag-burning matter for its acceptability (Helwig & Prencipe, 1999). Furthermore, in another study (Wainryb et al., 2004) and across four realms of diversity – morality, taste, facts, and ambiguous facts – children were told about two characters who had divergent beliefs (e.g. moral: one character believes it is all right to hit and kick others, and the other character believes it is wrong to hit and kick others; taste: one character believes chocolate ice cream tastes bad and the other believes it tastes good). From ages 5 to 9 years, children were tolerant about some areas of belief diversity (e.g. taste) and intolerant about other areas (e.g. moral; see also Wainryb et al., 1998; Wainryb et al., 2001). Similarly, 4- to 5-year-olds were more frequently tolerant towards peers with different preferences and tastes compared to different moralities (Danniels & Perlman, 2021). These findings indicate that tolerance depends on the type of practice and the (perceived) reason for why others engage in it. We further examined this experimentally among adults in relation Islamic head covering.

Muslim headscarf

Head covering is one of the most important identifiers of a Muslim woman and in western Europe people associate Muslim women with wearing headscarves (Unkelbach et al., 2010). The Muslim headscarf has led to heated debates in various countries and especially around the question whether a secular state conflicts with Muslim women wearing a headscarf in public positions (e.g. civil servants, police officers, and teachers). In these debates, questions are raised about whether women wear a headscarf out of their own free choice or rather because of religious community pressures (Everett et al., 2015; Fasel et al., 2013). Additionally, the debate involves questions related to religious freedom and cultural diversity because Muslim women can wear a headscarf for religious or for cultural reasons[12] (Howard, 2012).

Using an experimental design and Dutch and German majority members we examined whether a civil servant wearing a headscarf out of personal choice, normative religious community pressures, cultural traditions or religious expression, matters for tolerance (Velthuis et al., 2022a). These different reasons might be considered to resonate less or more strongly with liberal views and beliefs in western societies and therefore can be expected to affect people's tolerance of the Muslim headscarf. A central liberal value is self-determination and the personal freedom to choose how one wants to live one's life: people have a right to make their own choices and these choices should be accepted for what they are. People are likely to value autonomous choice and self-determination more than wearing a headscarf for reasons of normative community pressure, cultural traditions and religion. Thus, we expected higher tolerance for the headscarf worn by a civil servant out of personal choice compared to the other three reasons (normative, cultural, religious).

In western Europe, the Muslim headscarf is sometimes portrayed and perceived as an emblem of community oppression of women, and women being socially pressured into wearing a headscarf is a key argument in favour of a ban on headscarves (Howard, 2012). Muslim women are considered to wear a headscarf because they feel to have no choice and are afraid of the disapproval of other Muslims, and some Muslim women do indeed wear a headscarf for this reason (Legate et al., 2020). People being pressured, controlled and sanctioned by community members goes against the liberal principle of self-determination and personal choice. In contrast, wearing a headscarf for reasons of cultural or religious identity enactment implies the wish to express one's traditions or beliefs. Although this can also involve expectations of community members, it does not have to involve outward compliance and social sanctions. Thus, we also expected lower tolerance for the headscarf worn by a civil servant because of normative community expectations than for reasons of cultural or religious identity enactment.

Additionally, we explored whether there is a difference in tolerating the wearing of a headscarf for reasons of cultural or of religious identity enactment. It might be that people are more willing to accept religious identity enactment than the enactment of cultural identity because the former raises considerations of religious freedom. Religious freedom is a key aspect of liberal democracy and endorsed by most people, whereas cultural differences might be more contested, which is reflected in the declining support of multiculturalism in various west European societies. However, it might also be the case that both forms of identity enactment are evaluated similarly for tolerance of a civil servant wearing a headscarf. In this context, wearing a headscarf for religious reasons might be considered as conflicting with the secular nature of the state, and cultural reasons might be interpreted as symbolic for the unwillingness to integrate and adapt to the secular norms and values of western host societies (Van der Noll, 2010).

The findings in both the Netherlands and Germany showed that acceptance of the headscarf was on average low, implying that people were generally *in*tolerant of a Muslim women wearing a headscarf as a civil servant. However, wearing a headscarf for reasons out of personal choice was highest and tolerance was lowest for normative community expectations, with no significant differences between reasons of religious and cultural identity enactment (Velthuis et al., 2022a). This pattern of findings is in line with the few empirical studies indicating the importance of personal reasons for the tolerance of the headscarf and Muslim minority practices more generally. For example, Everett and colleagues (2015) found that wearing a headscarf for reasons of self-expression led to more positive attitudes compared to normative community reasons. Furthermore, we found that Dutch majority adolescents were more tolerant of the wearing of a headscarf when it was interpreted as a personal choice rather than reflecting a socio-cultural convention (Gieling et al., 2010).

Group identity and tolerance

I have discussed the endorsement of tolerance in general, the pragmatic and principles reasons for this endorsement, the role of deliberation, the acknowledgement of reasons for being tolerant, and that the perceived reasons behind dissenting beliefs and practices matter for tolerance. In all these research works, people are typically asked about what they personally think about dissenting beliefs and practices. However, people can also look at the world as group members and in terms of the meanings associated with that membership. According to the social identity perspective, when people's sense of self is bound up with their membership of a certain social group, they start to feel, think and behave in terms of what this group means and stands for (Reicher et al., 2010). Specifically, it is proposed that thinking about oneself in terms of a particular group membership implies a process of depersonalisation in which people understand themselves in terms of what defines and characterises the ingroup compared to a salient outgroup (Turner et al., 1987). Through this process of self-stereotyping, the norms, values, and beliefs of the ingroup become part of the psychological self, thereby providing the inner guidelines for appropriate intergroup attitudes and behaviour.

In an intergroup context, people are likely to judge and act in accordance with ingroup norms and beliefs and there is much evidence, including neurological, that group identity content determines the way in which people feel, think, and act (Xiao et al., 2016). Importantly, this means that group identification does not necessarily lead to the exclusion of outsiders but can also be associated with tolerance, acceptance and support (e.g. Levine & Manning, 2014; Tarrant et al., 2009). Whether the former or the latter occurs depends on how the group identity is defined and the normative meanings that emanates from it. Prosocial behaviour, such as friendliness, hospitality, care and helpfulness, may be a consequence of how a community understands itself, as with many religious communities. Furthermore, it has been demonstrated that a national identity defined in terms of cultural diversity leads to higher acceptance of minorities and immigrants in Canada (Citrin et al., 2012), and a national identity defined in terms of egalitarianism to lower outgoup hostility (Butz et al., 2007). Additionally, Reicher and colleagues (2006) present a social identity analysis of Bulgarian resistance against the deportation of Jews in World War II. Using historical documents, they show that Jews were helped because "we are the kind of people who help others". Bulgarians were described as a historically generous and tolerant people and antisemitic measures would go against their national character and therefore was construed as something "we simply do not do".

These examples show that "our" reaction towards others is closely linked to how "we" understand ourselves. Tolerance and supporting those in need can define "who we are" and can be the very dimension along which a particular community distinguish itself positively from other communities (Tajfel & Turner, 1979). Thus, when historical norms and beliefs prescribe tolerance of minority groups, group members can be expected to behave accordingly and feel positive about themselves for doing so. An example is our ethnographic research in the small Italian town of Riace, discussed in Chapter 2, and other research examples relate to national identity.

Local identity

In Riace, the large majority of local inhabitants supports the extensive refugee reception programme and considers tolerance and hospitality towards refugees an integral and defining part of the identity of the town (Driel & Verkuyten, 2020). People are "orgoglioso" (very proud) of the ways in which *their* Riace and *their* mayor (Domenico) support refugees and simultaneously stop the socioeconomic decline of the village, and thereby forms a positive example for other towns:

> We, guided by Domenico are somehow really an "avant garde". A small town, that serves as an example of hospitality towards migrants, of different ways to create a social and fair economy. To revive a town. Of this I am very proud.
>
> *(male inhabitant, 28 years)*

Most Riace people strongly identify with the local community which is demonstrated by the fact that they explicitly express their pride to belong to the "village of hospitality" in everyday interactions and on social media. When the locals are asked about their town, they almost unanimously answer to be proud of their Riace, the town of hospitality (see also Rinaldis, 2016; Sasso, 2012). This feeling of pride relates not only to being a positive example for others but is also grounded in a historical narrative.

Locals typically explain the town's tolerance and hospitality by referring to the history of Riace. For centuries, people have been immigrating into the Calabrian region and the town of Riace, but locals also have been emigrating due to poverty, political oppression, and the mafia. Because of the long history of migration, the local inhabitants argue that the welcoming reception of newcomers is in their "DNA", even when being critical about some of the migration policies. The reception of refugees is presented as a continuation of what locals have always been doing. The local identity of tolerance and hospitality is grounded in history making the current welcoming attitude towards refugees a continuation of who "we have always been". The history provides a particular meaning to the local identity that makes help and support of refugees "the most normal thing to do". Everyone in Riace knows these historical narratives by heart, taught by their parents and grandparents.[13]

This local identity is not only a story that is told but also enacted in specific activities and rituals and expressed in symbols throughout the town. For example, local initiatives combine the reception and housing of refugees with restoration and sustainability projects, the revival of local ancient crafts and solidarity tourism. The craft workshops and these projects promote tolerance and hospitality towards newcomers by expressing a strong message of solidarity that refers to Riace's history of migration. A hand painted welcoming sign, for example, reads "*Riace, paese dell'Accoglienza*" ("Riace, a town of hospitality"). The main town square is decorated with murals showing the migration history of Riace, such as a painting that depicts Italians leaving for New York and Argentina, on the left side, and African women landing at the Riace's coast, on the right sight. When entering the historical centre, a colourful gate welcomes people into the "global village" of Riace and next to it a mural shows the nationalities of all Riace's inhabitants. Other expressions are more subtle, such as the solidarity calendar which has portraits of locals and refugees together. The calendar is produced by the reception project and hangs in most offices and houses throughout town.

National identity

Tolerance is considered a self-defining national feature in most liberal democracies. In countries such as France, the United Kingdom, Sweden, and Germany, politicians and the public mention tolerance as one of the things that makes their country to what it is (Tiemeijer, 2021). This national self-understanding is also present in the Netherlands in which the historical self-representation of being a religious tolerant nation is widely endorsed as a core element of Dutch identity (de Hardt et al., 2019).[14] In comparison with other European countries this was indeed the case in the past,[15] and recent cross-national research suggests that the Dutch are quite tolerant, although it depends on what exactly people are asked to tolerate.[16]

Following the social identity perspective, it can be argued that those who understand Dutch national history and identity as one of religious tolerance will show more acceptance of the expressive rights of Muslim minorities. A self-defining history of tolerance implies that different religious groups have always been able to express their identity at the same time. Accommodating Muslim minorities is then not incompatibility with who we are and always have been as a nation but rather a continuation of our national identity. A national tradition of tolerance implies that expressions of Islam are not threatening the historical continuity of the Dutch identity. Rather, the acceptance of Muslim expressive rights fits and confirms the defining historical narrative of religious tolerance.

We examined the relation between historical tolerance and the acceptance of Muslim minority practices and expressive rights in different studies. In one study, we asked two samples of Dutch majority members about their endorsement of Dutch historical tolerance (e.g. "The Netherlands has a long history of religious tolerance" and "Tolerance is a historical achievement that the Netherlands should continue to fulfil") and their acceptance of Muslim expressive rights (e.g. "Muslims should have the right to not only celebrate their Islamic holidays at home, but also in public life" and "In the Netherlands wearing a headscarf should not be forbidden"). In both samples, participants on average endorsed the idea that the Netherlands is a historically tolerant country. Further and in line with the social identity perspective, stronger endorsement of historical tolerance was related to more acceptance of Muslim expressive rights, especially for individuals who relatively strongly identified with the national category (Smeekes et al., 2012, Study 1). This suggests that acceptance of Muslim minorities can be consistent with the national self-understanding of higher identifiers when this understanding is defined in terms of a historical tradition of religious and cultural tolerance. For these individuals, the acceptance of public expressions of Islam confirms the historical national identity of religious tolerance.

In another research, we presented three different samples of Dutch majority members with a brief introduction about the Dutch self-defining history of tolerance which would be still present and visible today (Verkuyten et al., 2022a).[17] Subsequently we asked how strongly people endorse the notion that in order to maintain our tradition of tolerance we should be welcoming towards dissenters and that for maintaining our tolerance we should give others the space to live the life that they want. In all three samples, participants on average agreed that we should welcome and accommodate others for maintaining our tolerant identity. Furthermore, in all three samples stronger endorsement of identity maintenance was associated quite strongly ($r \sim .65$) with higher acceptance of Muslim minority practices (e.g. "the building of new mosques with minarets in the Netherlands" and "Establishing Islamic primary schools"). These associations were found independent of political orientation, national identification, and the general predisposition to be tolerant. This indicates that individuals were more accepting of Muslim minority practices if they agreed that maintaining our tolerant identity requires that we live up to it by welcoming dissenting others.

The likely reason for this association is that in a discourse of national tolerance the accommodation of Muslim minorities is not incompatible with who we are or threatening to the continuation of our national identity. Thus, individuals who more strongly endorse the belief that for maintaining our tolerant identity we should live up to it, might accept Muslim minority practices more because they are less concerned about identity incompatibility and ingroup cultural continuity, concerns that are often expressed in relation to Muslim minorities. In other words, there might be an indirect association between endorsing historical tolerance and the acceptance of Muslim minority practices via lower perceived cultural continuity threat and lower identity incompatibility.

In one survey study among a national sample, we indeed found that stronger endorsement of maintaining our historical identity of tolerance was associated with lower perceived identity continuity threat[18] and via threat to higher support of minority practices (Verkuyten et al., 2022a). In another survey study, we examined the endorsement of historical tolerance in relation to perceived identity incompatibility (Smeekes et al., 2012, Study 2). Individuals who subscribe to a religious tolerant national history should not perceive the acceptance of Islamic schools, Mosques, Islamic holidays, and other visible signs of Islam as incompatible with "who we traditionally are". Thus, endorsing a representation of historical tolerance is likely to be associated with higher acceptance, via reduced perceptions of incompatibility.[19] On average, the endorsement of historical tolerance was again found to be high and positively associated with acceptance of Muslim minority rights. Importantly, this endorsement was negatively associated with perceptions of identity incompatibility, and this subsequently translated into more acceptance of Muslim expressive rights, especially for higher identifiers. Thus, those who consider the Netherlands to be a traditionally open and religious tolerant society did not tend to see Muslim practices as incompatible with "our" way of life. As a result, they were inclined to be more accepting of Muslims expressing their religion in public life.

In a further study, we used an experimental design to examine the causal effects of inducing a representation of historical religious tolerance on the acceptance of Muslim expressive rights and perceived identity incompatibility (Smeekes et al., 2012, Study 3; see also Fairlamb & Cinnirella, 2021). Hence, we tried to show that encouraging people to think in terms of a national history of religious tolerance has a positive impact on perceptions of identity incompatibility and acceptance of Muslim expressive rights. The findings showed that, compared to a control condition, individuals did indeed experience less identity incompatibility with Muslims when their country's history of religious tolerance was salient, and this, in turn, resulted in increased support for Muslim expressive rights, again especially for higher identifiers.

These different studies and findings demonstrate that tolerant understandings of local or national history can elevate acceptance of minority practices and rights. In support of the social identity perspective, people display higher outgroup acceptance when historical tolerant norms and beliefs define the local identity or national category. Furthermore, the reduction of perceived identity continuity threat and of identity incompatibility are mechanisms through which awareness of historical tolerance improves acceptance of minority rights and practices.

Group identification and tolerance

The findings of these studies show that for developing an understanding of intergroup relations, it is important to focus on the content that people ascribe to their ingroup identity, and not only on the extent to which people feel attached to it. However, the social identity perspectives proposes that people who highly identify with an ingroup are more likely to act in accordance with ingroup norms and beliefs. This means that when historical norms and beliefs prescribe tolerance of immigrants, especially highly identified group members should behave accordingly.

As indicated, we indeed found in several of our studies that especially for higher identifiers a national history of tolerance matters for the acceptance of Muslim minority rights and practices. Compared to lower identifiers, higher identifiers displayed similar levels of acceptance when the salience of historical tolerance was high. This pattern of findings provides support for the social identity perspective, because it shows that when the meaning of national identity is shared among group members, differences in outgroup acceptance between higher and lower identifiers are reduced. Similar findings have been observed in other research on intergroup relations (Butz et al., 2007; Jetten et al., 1997), which indicates the generalisability of these social identity processes.

Furthermore, using data from four European countries (Belgium, Germany, UK, Switzerland), we found in another study that Muslims compared to majority members were less supportive of democracy and of liberal sexual mores (e.g. divorce, homosexuality, sex before marriage), not only because they were more religious but also because they had lower national identification (Eskelinen & Verkuyten, 2020). Ideals of democracy and liberal values are embedded in the culture and institutions of West European nations and national identification implies a stronger tendency to think and act in terms of the liberal beliefs and values that characterise the society, which has also been found among Muslim minorities (see Verkuyten & Martinovic, 2012). Additionally, in another study we found among Muslim minorities in the Netherlands (but not in Germany) that higher national identification was associated with higher political tolerance of the group that Muslim participants themselves liked the least (Verkuyten et al., 2014).

However, in different studies we also found that majority members who had stronger national identification were less accepting of Muslim minority rights and practices in general, and also when there was no mentioning of historical tolerance. This indicates that higher identifiers are more inclined to display negative outgroup attitudes as a means of enhancing positive distinctiveness and have a positive sense of themselves as group members (Jetten et al., 1997; Tajfel & Turner, 1979). For example, in a research conducted in Australia, Finland, Germany, and Norway it was found that higher national identification was associated with higher diversity threat which in turn was associated with lower support for religious minority rights in general and for Muslims in particular (Eskelinen et al., 2022). Yet national identification can take different forms, and a strong sense of national belonging can be psychologically less or more secure.

In his classic book on "*The Nature of Prejudice*", Allport (1954) argued that positive ingroup attachment is beneficial for outgroup tolerance. A secure sense of ingroup belonging can form the psychological basis for an open attitude towards others. Developmental approaches suggest that this secure sense of self is the result of an exploration process whereby individuals try to understand how their group membership impacts their life and establish a clear sense of ingroup belonging and commitment based on that understanding (Marcia, 1966; Phinney et al., 2007). Identity exploration typically involves seeking information and having experiences that are relevant to one's group membership via a range of activities such as reading, thinking, and talking about the customs, traditions, and culture of the ingroup (Syed et al., 2013). Individuals can also identify strongly with their ingroup without identity exploration but in that case they have no in-depth knowledge about the meaning of their group membership and how it affects their decisions and life. There is some evidence that exploration-based ingroup commitments do indeed allow individuals to be more tolerant towards others (e.g. Spiegler et al., 2016; Phinney et al., 2007; Whitehead et al., 2009).

We examined the role of identity exploration in five experimental studies among German adolescents and early adults (Spiegler et al., 2022). We focused on the degree of acceptance of immigrants and the findings indicate that the well-known link between higher national identification and lower acceptance is weaker when participants are instructed to explore the meaning of their national identity. Exploration reduced feelings of intergroup threat, increased a more nuanced perspective on German culture, and enabled high identifiers to oppose anti-immigrant group norms. The results of an internal meta-analysis showed that experimentally induced identity exploration allowed high national identifiers to be more accepting towards immigrants. Identity exploration changed the way majority members relate to outgroups, without disconnecting people from their national ingroup or making them less positive towards this ingroup.

We further examined whether a secure and stable sense of national attachment can form the basis for a more accepting orientation towards minority rights and practices, by considering national narcissism (Verkuyten et al., 2022). People's national identification can be more defensive and contingent upon external approval (i.e. defensive national narcissism), or more secure and stable, thereby forming a more self-determined and confident basis for tolerance of other groups (i.e. secure national attachment; Cichocka, 2016; Golec de Zavala et al., 2019; Jordan et al., 2005). According to this theorising, a secure sense of ingroup belonging involves satisfied individual needs that forms the confident psychological basis for an accepting attitude towards others. In contrast, an insecure and defensive national narcissism stems from frustrated individual needs and can produce negative reactions towards others, as it elicits an inflated image of one's nation that is contingent upon external recognition of ingroup worthiness. In research, national identification minus its statistical overlap with collective narcissism can be interpreted as a secure and positive sense of national belonging that does not depend on external recognition (Cichocka, 2016). Thus by taking concerns about the external recognition of the nation's exceptionality into account (national narcissism), it is possible to examine the role of national identification as a secure sense of national attachment and its association with the acceptance of minority practices and rights. For example, in the context of Poland it was found that stronger national identification (net of national narcissism) led to more positive attitude towards refugees and less collective action against refugees (Górska et al., 2022; see also Bertin et al., 2022). Furthermore, higher secure national identity is found to be associated with stronger support for democracy in both the US and Poland (Marchlewska et al., 2022).

We examined the role of secure national identity in two studies using national samples from the Netherlands and Germany. The findings demonstrated that when taking narcissism into account, stronger national attachment was associated with higher tolerance in general and higher acceptance of Muslim expressive rights in particular. Furthermore, stronger political conservatism was found to predict higher tolerance and more acceptance through stronger national attachment, specifically when taking national narcissism into account. Thus, a more conservative political orientation was associated with lower tolerance and less acceptance via stronger national narcissism, but with higher tolerance and more acceptance via stronger national attachment. In other words, higher national identification commonly found among politically more conservative individuals does not only have to work against tolerance of minority rights and practices but can also provide a confident basis for acceptance.

To conclude

People are able to think about the complexities of living in a diverse world in which disapproval, dislike and disagreement are inevitable, but allowing others to live the life that they want is indispensable and necessary. Doing so requires self-restraint which often is not easy, but not impossible and in fact something that people engage in on a daily basis. Putting up with things that you object to is a common experience for many people in many situations and in all sorts of relations. Those who hold an objection to dissenting practices but see good reasons for not transferring this in a rejection are the ones engaged in toleration for a peaceful plural society. However, this engagement also requires the recognition of boundaries to what can and should be tolerated. Tolerance is not a boundless sort of relativism because there are always also good reasons for why certain things go too far and are, or become, intolerable.

6

THE BOUNDARIES OF TOLERANCE

In November 2021, the Council of Europe launched a campaign to promote societal inclusion of Muslims minorities. The Council aims to uphold human rights, democracy and the rule of law and part of this campaign involved posters and a video with images showing, for example, a woman wearing a hijab, together with statements such as "Beauty is in diversity as freedom is in hijab", "My headscarf, my choice", and "Celebrate diversity & respect hijab". However, a week after releasing the video the campaign was pulled after strong criticism on social media and by politicians, especially in France ("Hijab Campaign Tweets"). The campaign was not considered to promote diversity and religious freedom but rather as going against secular and liberal European values in encouraging women to wear religious garment and by justifying the religious community oppression of women.

Not tolerating something can be the outcome of a trade-off between reasons for accepting versus stronger reasons for rejecting specific practices and beliefs (Figure 3.1). For example, social injustice, harming others, or undermining others' self-determination is often considered more important than one's own freedom to live the life that one wants. In these cases, intolerance (i.e. zero tolerance) is considered a reasonable and necessary response to what is considered intolerable: according to article 1.4 of UNESCO's declaration, "the practice of tolerance does not mean toleration of social injustice"; political leaders state, "we have no tolerance for racism in America. We have no tolerance for violence inspired by racism",[1] and "we cannot – and will not – tolerate any expressions of hatred and discrimination in our communities"[2]; organisations and institutions state that sexual harassment "in whatever form, is one too many and we should definitely not tolerate it"[3]; and forms of cultural appropriation can be considered unacceptable types of cultural thievery (Lenard & Balint, 2020; Mosley & Biernat, 2020).

The *European Model National Statute for the Promotion of Tolerance* has a separate section on boundaries of tolerance. Three main limitations are discussed, whereby

DOI: 10.4324/9781003335030-6

the first one has more of an absolute cutoff point for what is acceptable leading to zero tolerance in which even minor normative and moral transgressions or infringements are considered unacceptable. The other two focus more on the severity of the transgression and degree of acceptability to determine how intolerable particular behaviour is considered to be (Kessler et al., 2010).

First, society must show zero tolerance[4] of, for example, oppression, injustice, group libel and hate crimes which are considered completely unacceptable in any form and circumstance. From a human rights perspective, accepting, for example, honour killings, female genital mutilation, domestic violence, and forced marriage would imply culpable indulgence and not tolerance. In these cases, toleration would infringe on the harm principle and the rights of others. For example, the United Nations Sub-commission on the Promotion and Protection of Human Rights has declared 6 February as an international *Day of Zero Tolerance for Female Genital Mutilation*. And as an amendment to several existing acts including the Immigration and Refugee Protection Act, the Canadian government introduced in 2015 the "*Zero tolerance for barbaric cultural practices act*" intended to prevent polygamy, forced marriage, and honour killings. Similarly, multicultural Sweden was one of the first European countries to pass a Bill against female genital mutilation and polygamy, and to criminalise honour crimes. Thus, also countries that have adopted a more multicultural policy deem some aspects of minority cultures as unacceptable for being illiberal and repugnant (Tawat, 2014).

Second, tolerance of diversity should not lead to undermining or changing society in a fundamental way: "Diversity should not affect the fundamental identity – or the shared values and history and aspirations – of society" (Model National Statute). Tolerance is considered the glue that enables pluralist democratic society to function successfully and this means that tolerance should be promoted in society but without weakening its common bonds. One can draw on the analogy of medical intolerance, such as those seen with lactose, gluten, and histamine intolerances. Allergy symptoms appear when trigger foods are eaten because particular enzymes make the body sick rather than healthy and strong. Similarly, social "bodies" such as democratic communities, religious groups, or political movements that include those with strongly divergent views (theocrats, atheists, and ideological opponents, respectively), would lose their meaning and purpose and gradually cease to exist. Becoming too tolerant ("passive" or "hands-off" tolerance) should be avoided, because it can mean that the identity continuity of the community, organisation or institution is at stake.

Third, it is argued that respect for diversity "should not weaken the common bonds of responsible citizenship within a democratic and open society" (Model National Statute). It is argued that in a liberal democracy, tolerance must be reciprocal and there is no need to be tolerant towards the intolerant, such as radical groups that that try to subvert peace and security, incite hatred and violence, and transgressive groups that completely want to segregate themselves from society. Tolerance must not be used as a means for condoning those who themselves are intolerant because this would undermine the very notion of tolerance. For example, tolerating the so-called "extremist counterculture" of Islamist Salafism will have negative implications for a liberal society, and in particular for the freedoms of other religious minorities, apostates, atheists, women and sexual minorities.

Justified intolerance

No individual, group or society can be tolerant of everything, such as so-called low-value actions (child pornography, criminal behaviour, threats with violence, cruel treatment of animals, domination of women). The boundaries of tolerance are found where reasons for rejection of the objectionable practice or belief are in line with the negative gut feeling or are considered more important than the reasons for acceptance. Cognitive research has shown that having the opportunity to engage in reflective thinking about an initial, intuitive response does not necessarily change that response and can even make people more confident of it (Shynkaruk & Thompson, 2006; Thompson et al., 2011). Thinking can confirm and strengthen the intuitive response rather than interfere with it. This means that people can be intolerant because they believe that they have good reasons to not show self-restraint, but rather, follow their negative gut reactions. For example, the intolerance can be based on direct moral emotions that people have towards harm, violence, and abuse together with reflective reasoning that these practices violate basic human rights and therefore are unacceptable. The intuitive emotional reaction and subsequent reflective thinking can point in the same direction and form the basis for the intolerant response. However, intolerance can also be the outcome of a reflective trade-off between the various reasons for condoning or rejecting dissenting practices and beliefs. Thinking carefully about the pros and cons of dissenting conduct can lead to the conclusion that the latter outweigh the former and thus that the behaviour is intolerable.

However, psychological research indicates that people tend to rationalise their gut feelings and initial choices (Greene, 2013; Haidt, 2001). Rationalisations are a great enemy of tolerance. It implies that people possess a blind spot to their rejection, which they experience as justified dislike or disapproval of dissenting beliefs or practices. Work on belief bias and motivated cognition demonstrates that people are prone to various forms of biased thinking, cling to false beliefs, and engage in wishful thinking (Molden & Higgins, 2012). Cognitive abilities are not only used for critical and deliberative thinking, but also for all sorts of cognitive biases and rationalisations of which individuals do not have to be aware. For example, belief in the conclusion of a particular argument has been found to determine the strength of political belief bias (Gampa et al., 2019). Individuals engage in reflective reasoning with the goal of protecting or rationalising their worldview. People flexibly use general moral principles (deontological and consequential) to support their preferred moral intuitions that follow from their political orientation (Uhlmann et al., 2009). Similarly, a meta-analytical comparison showed that both liberals and conservatives evaluate identical information more favourably when it supports their political beliefs or allegiances than when it challenges these (Ditto et al., 2019; Kahan, 2012).

There is also a large body of social psychological research that demonstrates that people justify their implicit and explicit prejudices and discriminatory behaviour, for example, by arguing that inequalities no longer exist (e.g. Dovidio & Gaertner, 2004), by free speech defences (White & Crandall, 2017), by genetic attributions (Suhay & Jayaratne, 2013), and by using legitimising myths that, for example, support unequal social arrangements (Sidanius & Pratto, 1999), status-legitimising worldviews (Major et al., 2007), negative stereotypes (Stephan & Stephan, 2000), and perceived procedural and distributive justice (Louis et al., 2007).

These rationalisations stand in the way of tolerance and justify discrimination and exclusion. People can be genuinely motivated to be fair, but tend to favour the fairness option that suits them best. This sort of biased fairness (Greene, 2013) is reflected, for example, in attaching self-serving meanings to the same moral terms (e.g. Kraft et al., 2019) such as liberals interpreting free speech in terms of self-expression and conservatives in terms of its cultural value (Alvarez & Kemmelmeier, 2018). As discussed in Chapter 4, biased fairness is also reflected in the use of a double standard that results in intolerance towards only some people or groups and some practices. For example, several experimental studies have found that people apply double standards when determining the acceptability of critical speech, with being more tolerant of critical speech acts when the speaker is a member of the criticised group (White American criticising Americans, and Arab American criticising Arabs; native Dutch criticising native Dutch, and refugees criticising refugees) rather than an outgroup member (Adelman & Verkuyten, 2020b; Lindner & Nosek, 2009).

However, biased forms of thinking can also be due to prior beliefs that form initial anchors for judgement[5] or a lack of reflection and reasoning, rather than motivated cognition (Pennycook, 2020; Pennycook & Rand, 2019). The fact that rationalisation is a great enemy of tolerance does not mean that tolerance has no boundaries and that people cannot have justified reasons for not accepting what they disagree with, dislike, or disapprove off. There can be better reasons for rejection than for acceptance: intolerance can be the outcome of a trade-off whereby reasons for rejecting dissenting beliefs and practices are considered more important than reasons for condoning them. What is considered intolerable cannot be tolerated and as indicated in the European Model National Statute, the reasons for rejection can relate to (1) the harm and rights principle, (2) group continuity and collective autonomy, and (3) reciprocity and the democratic order (Verkuyten & Yogeeswaran, 2017).

Harm and rights

Beginning with Stouffer's (1955) landmark study on people's support for the expression of nonconformist views, empirical research has typically found practice-related variance in tolerance. The decision whether or not to tolerate specific practices depends on the nature of each practice and the related values and concerns that are considered to be at stake (e.g. Chanley, 1994; Gibson & Gouws, 2001).

As discussed in Chapter 4, people can have reasons for being tolerant of specific dissenting practices, but not of others. Different practices can raise distinct moral, normative, and pragmatic concerns. For instance, wearing a burqa might evoke the issue of gender equality for some, and religious education in public schools can evoke concerns about the secular nature of the state for others (Moss et al., 2019), leading to intolerance of both.

The social psychological literature on morality and moral judgements is quite diverse with different moral foundations being proposed (Haidt, 2012) and different conceptualisations and operationalisations being used (e.g. Ellemers, 2017; Malle, 2021; Skitka et al., 2021). However, most scholars agree that the moral domain is concerned with fairness, justice, and other's welfare. Furthermore, people tend to consider most matters of morality as absolute and to apply anytime and everywhere (Graham et al., 2013; Skitka et al., 2021). Research with children demonstrates that they interpret issues of fairness, justice, and avoiding harm to others as unalterable, general, and not subject to authority jurisdiction (Wainryb, 2006). And when children and adolescents view an issue as moral, they experience more discomfort with divergent beliefs (Wright, 2012). Similarly, in a two-nation study involving China and the United States, stronger moral conviction about contemporary societal issues was associated with lower political tolerance of those not sharing one's views, and also with lower intergroup tolerance in the United States, but not in China (Skitka et al., 2013). Furthermore, research in Lebanon, Morocco, and the United States showed that stronger perceived similarity in moral values of fairness and care was associated with higher outgroup tolerance in all three countries (Obeid et al., 2017).

In general, people are less accepting of divergent beliefs and behaviours that are viewed as problematic moral issues, especially when these beliefs and behaviours are seen as violations of objective moral truths (e.g. Goodwin & Darley, 2008, 2012; Wright et al., 2008). People tend to be moral objectivists in considering divergent moral beliefs and values as violations of objective truths. It is, of course, not always clear whether a particular dissenting practice is interpreted as belonging to the moral domain and is considered objectively true, but when it does, tolerance of the practice becomes difficult. Moralised entities and activities tend to lead to avoidance and rejection rather than toleration because views that differ from one's own are considered objectively wrong and even dangerous and immoral (Kovacheff, 2018). If I consider social justice a moral principle, I stand for social justice everywhere and want everyone else to do so. If people from another community disagree, there is a problem, one that goes beyond differences in tastes, preferences and social conventions that can be solved with mutual understanding and reasonable accommodations. One can argue about the interpretation and applicability of a moral principle, but not about the principle itself.

Research on moral emotions shows that people exhibit strong intuitive objection to the physical and psychological harm of others and to unfair treatment (Turiel et al., 1987; also see Haidt et al., 1993). Furthermore, sacred values make people act in terms of moral principles and to react with moral outrage when the integrity of these values is challenged (Tetlock, 2003). And people also tend to reject beliefs and practices that go against basic human capabilities (Turiel, 2002). Thus, it is likely that tolerance will be harder to achieve if dissenting practices are perceived as causing harm to others (e.g. hate groups) or as mistreating or threatening the freedom and rights of others (e.g. against women and gay rights). Sensitivity to what is tolerable is reflected in, first, the process of moralisation, and, second, the use of specific moral values as boundary conditions for tolerance.

Moralisation

Moralisation refers to the process by which moral significance is attached to specific actions and behaviours, and preferences and conventions are converted into moral beliefs and values (Rhee et al., 2019; Rozin, 1999). In many Western countries, for example, cigarette smoking in public buildings and restaurants is not tolerated anymore because it has changed from a personal preference to a moral violation related to health concerns. Similarly, the refusal to shake hands with someone of the opposite gender by some Muslim civil servants and teachers has led to uproar in Europe. Critics construe the act of shaking hands as a matter of principle because it symbolises the moral equality of men and women rather than a preference or social convention. Defining it as a moral issue makes a compromise much more difficult. We have examined the role of moralisation for intolerance in different ways across various studies.

In one study, we presented early adolescents with four different scenarios about parental behaviour and we asked them whether this should be tolerated (Verkuyten et al., 2018a). One scenario was about homeschooling ("some parents do not send their children to school but educate them at home themselves") and this was rejected by 91% of the Dutch children, and independent of whether the parents were ethnic ingroup or ethnic outgroup members. In the Netherlands, homeschooling is extremely rare and the children explained that it was harmful, unjust, and unfair. In contrast, a scenario in which "parents always send their children to bed early" was rejected by only 32% because the majority considered it something that was up to the parents to decide.

In another study, we presented a sample of Dutch adolescents with four different Muslim minority practices that differ in the extent to which these were expected to elicit moral concern (Gieling et al., 2010). We first found that an imam's speech against homosexuality was considered most strongly as morally wrong with around four in five adolescents considering the statement as harmful. This was followed by the refusal to shake hands with someone of the opposite gender, the founding of Islamic primary schools, and then the wearing of a headscarf which was considered more a personal choice rather than a moral issue. Subsequently, in a next study, a large sample of adolescents was asked whether the responsible authorities (municipality, school) should tolerate or not tolerate the specific practice.[6]

In general, adolescents expressed moderate to low levels of tolerance. However, tolerance was highest for the wearing of the headscarf, which was considered a personal rather than moral issue, and lowest for the imam's speech which was moralised the most. In between these two was the tolerance of the two other practices that were mainly considered social conventional matters and that were tolerated equally. Furthermore, adolescents who endorsed multiculturalism tended to be more tolerant of practices that raised personal and conventional considerations but were less accepting of the practice that was predominantly perceived as a moral transgression. This indicates that valuing cultural diversity is not unlimited and does not imply moral relativism in which all practices and beliefs are judged equally right and good (Lukes, 2008). Finally, there were hardly any age, gender and educational differences in tolerance of the imam's harmful speech, while there were differences for the other, less moralised, practices (e.g. the higher educated being more tolerant).

We also found evidence for the moralisation-intolerable link in two other investigations among large samples of Dutch and German adults. In a first research (Adelman et al., 2021a; Study 1), we examined whether majority members will be less tolerant of behaviours that dissent more from social norms and if this is driven by their stronger moralisation of these practices. In testing this expectation, we controlled for prejudicial feelings towards Muslims as a group of people since people might reject certain beliefs and behaviours because of their group-based prejudice rather than their moralisation of the practices per se. The findings demonstrated that Muslim minority practices that were considered more controversial were moralised more strongly and tolerated less. Increased moralisation explained the effect of normative dissent on intolerance and the results emerged independent of prejudice.

In another study, we further examined the role of moralisation for tolerance of a range of Muslim minority practices that differ in their required societal accommodation and in whether they have an impact on one's personal life or on society as a whole (Adelman et al., 2022a). We found for both contexts that Muslim minority practices that were considered more controversial were moralised more strongly and tolerated less. Furthermore, increased moralisation mediated the statistical effect of normative dissent on intolerance. These findings again emerged when controlling for prejudicial attitudes towards Muslims. Additionally, tolerance was regularly practiced by those with group-based prejudice, and those with positive feelings towards Muslims did identify practices they considered unacceptable.

Furthermore, the importance of moralisation carried over across both active and passive forms of tolerance. Tolerance "most minimally implying the suspension of certain negative acts against the [disapproved of] idea, and involving maximally the active promotion of its circulations" (King, 2012, p. 119). Thus, tolerance can not only take a more minimal ("passive") form of not interfering with the disapproved of conduct of others but can also take a more maximal ("active") form in which one actively supports and defends the rights of others to make their case and practice their beliefs. Active tolerance may also require majority group sacrifices, especially in relation to more zero-sum calculations (e.g. replacing a national holiday connected to a Christian celebration with a national holiday linked to a Muslim one). In this case, to behave in support of a minority goal or practice would require an ingroup sacrifice. The same occurs, for example, when public swimming pools create gender-segregated times to meet the needs of different cultural and religious communities and thereby limit the opportunities and freedoms of others. Thus, active tolerance can involve situations ranging from no ingroup sacrifice to some ingroup sacrifice but is especially marked by the active encouragement and enabling of the minority practice that one disapproves of.

These two forms of tolerance are potentially quite different, because passivity is less demanding and often less risky and blameworthy than activity (Keinan & Bereby-Meyer, 2017; Kordes-de Vaal, 1996). Psychologically, taking no action against what one disapproves of is easier than a positive defence of it, and the negative duties of what you should not do are more stringent than the positive duties of what you must do (Lichtenberg, 2010). For example, research finds that proscriptive morality (i.e. doing what you should not) is considered more blameworthy than prescriptive morality (i.e. not doing what you should; Janoff-Bulman et al., 2009). Similarly, neuroscience research reveals that people have distinct physiological guilt-inducing reactions in response to errors in which they reject the status quo compared to errors in which they accept the status quo (Nicolle et al., 2011). Furthermore, research shows that passivity is considered less costly (Kahneman & Miller, 1986; Kahneman & Tversky, 1982) and also less risky than activity, through a diminished sense of personal responsibility (Keinan & Bereby-Meyer, 2017). Acts of omission tend to be seen as non-decisions, making inaction the safer route to avoid responsibility (Kordes-de Vaal, 1996). Thus, there seems to be a broader trend whereby people prefer acts of omission and the maintenance of a status quo (e.g. Baron & Ritov, 2004), and perceive greater negative effects of erroneous actions than inactions (e.g. Feldman & Albarracín, 2017; Kahneman & Tversky, 1982).

In agreement with these findings, we found that while a significant minority of people engaged in passive tolerance towards various disapproved of Muslim practices (between 19.1 and 33.5%, depending on the practice), very few people were willing to engage in active tolerance (between 0.5 and 5.9%) by pro-actively supporting the enactment of these practices. The difference between active and passive tolerance was found across the various practices and for issues that had a more direct impact on people's personal life as well as for the broader society. Furthermore, also people who did not have a negative attitude towards the specific practice were less likely to show active than passive support (Adelman et al., 2022a). This pattern of findings suggests that the difference between passive and active tolerance reflects a more general psychological tendency to make a distinction between action and inaction whereby one perceives, for example, a greater risk and responsibility in relation to action than inaction.

Importantly, however, moralisation had a similar effect on passive and active tolerance. People who had stronger moral concerns about particular Muslim minority practices were less willing to engage in either active or passive tolerance for most of the different practices and across the personal and societal contexts. Interestingly, in both studies, we also found that increased moralisation of each practice was more strongly associated with lower passive tolerance than lower active tolerance. This suggests that not engaging in passive tolerance can be more difficult and more strongly related to morality than not engaging in active tolerance: not negatively interfering with dissenting conduct is likely to be considered morally more mandatory than actively supporting the rights of others.

In a further experimental study conducted in the Netherlands, we used the multiple-act–multiple-actor approach described in Chapter 4 (Hirsch et al., 2019). In addition to different religious practices, these practices were performed by either a culturally dissimilar (Muslims) or a more similar (orthodox Protestant) minority group. We again used vignettes about specific practices that have caused considerable public debate in Dutch society: founding of religious primary schools, exclusion of women from religious boards, and anti-homosexuality statements by religious authorities. Importantly, these practices have been debated in relation to both Muslims and orthodox Protestants, and in a post-hoc test on a national sample, we directly asked people to what extent their moral principles formed the basis of their views on each of the three practices. The findings indicated that the anti-homosexuality statement was again rated as significantly more moral compared to the other two and that the exclusion of women was considered significantly more moral than the founding of religious schools. Subsequently, the experimental findings revealed that participants used a double standard in expressing discriminatory intolerance for practices when these were associated with Muslims rather than orthodox Protestants, but not when the practice elicits high degrees of moral concern.

The sample included a small share of participants (e.g. Protestants) that had positive feelings towards the practices, which indicates that for them, the issue is not a question of toleration. An analysis including only participants who displayed negative or neutral feelings towards the practices showed that people were equally intolerant of the two practices that were moralised most, namely the exclusion of women and the anti-homosexuality statement. This again indicates that intolerance of specific practices is not just a question of outgroup prejudice but can involve moral disapproval of specific practices independent of the religious minority group engaging in it.

Our findings and those of other studies (see Skitka et al., 2021) demonstrate that intolerance is more likely if dissenting practices are moralised and perceived as causing harm to (ingroup or outgroup) others or as mistreating or threatening the freedom and equal rights of others. However, although some practices are beyond toleration for most people, this is not always easy to determine and often subject to debate. For example, moralisation can depend on whether specific practices and beliefs are psychologically distant or near. People tend to more easily apply their moral values and principles to distant rather than proximal events and behaviours (Trope & Liberman, 2010). Distant events – in time (past or future), space (here or there), or socially (friend or acquaintance) – are represented more abstractly with less contextual details and therefore are more likely to be evaluated in terms of general moral principles. For example, immoral practices are considered as more offensive, and moral practices as more virtuous, when these are psychologically distant rather than near (Eyal et al., 2008). People tend to look with a stronger moralising lens to the past and to other cultures and societies. Furthermore, especially moral principles of harm and fairness towards others are endorsed more strongly when thinking more abstractly (Agerström & Björklund, 2009; Napier & Luguri, 2012).

However, there can be strong disagreements about what these moral principles mean and whether they are relevant in a particular situation. For example, Orlenius (2008) describes how the suspension of a school student with Nazi sympathies led to a strong debate among teachers about liberal democratic virtues and risks. There can also be a debate about what constitutes harm: is it physical (body integrity) or also mental (misrecognition)? Is it to specific practices or whole ways of life? Is it to individuals or institutions? Is it caused by action or by omission? There are different harm principles (Cushman et al., 2006) and the notion of "harm" has become culturally and in psychology much more prominent with inflated meanings of harm-related concepts (Haslam, 2016; Haslam et al., 2021). In general, harm can be interpreted in a more narrow or broad sense. In a broader sense, it can be argued that non-recognition, misrecognition, microaggressions, and forms of speech ("speech is violence") and even silence ("silence is violence") inflict harm to such a degree that it undermines people's psychological well-being and functioning (Lui & Quezada, 2019). Causing harm is an acceptable boundary condition for tolerance and therefore anything that is considered offensive should not be tolerated, but disallowed by speech codes and authorities (see Campbell & Manning, 2018). In such cases, how people subjectively feel define whether particular actions and beliefs are considered intolerable and therefore beyond discussion ("you can't say that"). Subjective impact is considered to trump intentions and social considerations.

However, others have a more narrow understanding of what constitutes harm and consider criticism that might cause discomfort or offense as inevitable and indispensable for public debate in pluralist liberal societies. They also consider harm as a boundary condition for tolerance but mark a much smaller territory as being unacceptable harmful. Furthermore, it is pointed out that the merit of a statement, argument, or perspective cannot be reduced entirely to a metric of whether its causes offense. Doing so would prevent any open debate within a pluralistic society given that moral disagreements and viewpoints differences can inherently cause discomfort (Ceci & Williams, 2018). Intentions and other considerations do matter and are considered to trump the possible subjective negative impact that disagreement and disapproval might have.

Whereas the former group of people seems to argue for moral amplification, the latter argues for a degree of demoralisation or amoralisation (Rhee et al., 2019; Tenbrunsel & Messick, 2004). With moral amplification, intolerance in culturally and ideologically diverse settings becomes more likely, making open debate more difficult. In contrast, demoralisation might make tolerance of dissenting beliefs and practices more likely, but this can have more negative psychological consequences for disadvantaged minority members.

Moral values

People tend to be moral objectivists in holding their moral values and beliefs as being objectively true which makes tolerance and compromise less likely and interference, prohibition and censorship acceptable and sometimes even necessary. Moral issues that are objectively grounded are prohibited regardless of whether it involves one's own group or society or a different group or other society (Wright et al., 2014).

Moralisation can not only differ in terms of its grounding, but moralised acts can also be viewed either unacceptable or acceptable depending on the particular moral value that is at stake. Research typically examines linkages between specific values (e.g. benevolence and humanitarianism) and tolerance judgements (e.g. Roccas & Amit, 2011). However, values tend to be inherently comparative and competitive and the trade-off among multiple values that are simultaneously relevant affects cognition and behaviour. For example, the way in which people rank competing values matters for their political tolerance. Giving relatively higher priority to free speech is associated with higher forbearance (Peffley et al., 2001) and prioritising personal safety and security over liberties relates to lower tolerance (Davis & Silver, 2004).

For tolerance and intolerance, therefore, not only the degree of moralisation matters but also the specifics of the moralisation process: the prioritising of contrasting moral values that are used to evaluate dissenting beliefs, practices, and behaviours (Nelson et al., 1997). For example, for some people, the acceptance of minority beliefs and practices may follow from the freedoms that characterise a liber society. For others, the rejection of these beliefs and practices might stem from concerns about communitarian values of societal cohesion. Thus, tolerance of minority practices can be weighed, on the one hand, by the value placed on individual liberties and religious freedom that are supported by overwhelming proportions of citizens in western democracies (Wike & Simmons, 2015), and, on the other hand, by whether such practices undermine communitarian values of maintaining social cohesion and a unified society which are also endorsed by most citizens (Silver, 2018). These two values can conflict with each other, making it important to consider the relative trade-off that people make between them for understanding their tolerance (i.e. freedom trumps cohesion) or intolerance (i.e. cohesion trumps freedom) of different minority practices. For example, the founding of Islamic primary schools can be understood either primarily as a matter of religious freedom, which could lead to greater tolerance, or primarily as a matter of self-segregation that undermines social cohesion, which could lead to greater intolerance.

Whether a particular value guides one's actual judgement is not only dependent on the relative importance that one in general attaches to it, but also on the situation that makes competing values relatively less or more salient and relevant. Most events and practices trigger multiple concerns and require a psychological balancing of reasons to accept or to reject. For example, people may strongly endorse freedom of expression, but in order for this value to influence their judgement about a particular situation, it should be considered more important than, for example, the value of social peace. Nelson and colleagues (1997) found that when news regarding political actions of right-wing extremist groups was framed in terms of the importance of freedom of speech, participants had higher levels of tolerance for this group compared to a situation in which the importance of public order was emphasised (see also Djupe et al., 2016). Similarly, research has found that preferring liberty to public order is associated with higher political tolerance, beyond the effects of democratic values, open-mindedness, partisan identity, perceived outgroup threats, and emotional reactions to outgroups (Gibson et al., 2020b). Furthermore, among middle-school students greater awareness of individual rights was found to increase political tolerance, while concern for public safety resulted in decreases in tolerance (Avery et al., 1992). And in two experiments, we investigated the role of values of freedom of speech and public order and safety in tolerance for a political rally by extreme right-wing and Islamist groups. For both groups, people who valued order and safety expressed higher tolerance when the rally was framed as a free speech issue rather than a social order issue. Participants who valued freedom of speech showed higher tolerance when this value was either reinforced or contradicted by the media framing (Zilli Ramirez & Verkuyten, 2011).

Assigning higher priority to liberal freedom over social cohesion should make tolerance more likely, while attaching higher priority to cohesion over freedom should make tolerance of minority practices less likely. How this trade-off plays out is likely to depend on the extent to which a specific belief or behaviour is considered normatively dissenting in society. We examined the trade-off between the values of individual freedom and social cohesion, and how the prioritisation of these two values is associated with tolerance of Muslim minority practices that differ in their degree of perceived normative dissent. Specifically, we tested the expectation that people will be less tolerant of more controversial practices (e.g. not shaking hands with someone of the opposite gender) when these are seen as a threat to the value of social cohesion over individual freedom, but people would be more tolerant of less controversial practices (e.g. the wearing of Islamic dress in closed meetings) when they consider the value of individual freedom more important than social cohesion.

In two large-scale studies in the Netherlands and Germany (Adelman et al., 2021a), we found that intolerance was higher in both countries for Muslim minority practices that were considered normatively dissenting, and therefore perceived more negatively. More importantly, this increase in intolerance was related to changes in the relative importance of specific moral values and principles that formed the basis for people's judgements. Specifically, as the practices increased in their perceived normative dissent, participants increasingly emphasised the importance of social cohesion over freedom. Further analyses showed that this change in prioritisation, in turn, increased intolerance towards those practices, all above and beyond the effects of prejudicial attitudes towards Muslims. In contrast, less controversial practices were tolerated more because the value of freedom was considered more important than social cohesion.[7]

This research indicates that increasing perceived normative dissent is associated with higher intolerance of Muslim minority practices through moral prioritisation. In subsequent work (Study 4 in Adelman et al., 2021a), we used an experimental design to examine the causal pathway between morality and tolerance by testing whether moralising a given action through framing it in terms of a specific moral value affects tolerance judgements. Specifically, we focused on one of the high-level dissenting practices that raised relatively strong concerns about societal cohesion (not shaking hands with someone of the opposite gender) and examined whether emphasising the importance of religious freedoms leads to higher tolerance. Following our reasoning about the role of moral values, we expected that this practice would be tolerated more when presented in terms of freedom of religion.

We first found that the intolerance of this practice was similar in a control condition and one emphasising the value of social cohesion. This is consistent with the finding that the refusal to shake hands is considered highly dissenting and prompts prioritisation of the value of social cohesion over freedom. However, when this practice was presented as a matter of religious freedom, people were found to be more tolerant towards this normatively dissenting practice. This demonstrates that emphasising a particular moral value can even lead to higher tolerance of a practice that is considered highly dissenting and challenging for societal cohesion.

These findings demonstrate that beyond the level of general moralisation, the differential weighting of the two key moral values of freedom and of social cohesion determines the degree of (in)tolerance. There were substantial differences between people's feelings towards the different behaviours, and in the trade-off that people made between the liberal value of religious freedom and the communitarian value of social cohesion. Muslim minority behaviours differentially led to prioritisation of competing moral values to be tolerant or intolerant of those given behaviours. Behaviours that were perceived as less normatively dissenting were tolerated more because the commitment to freedom of religion was considered to be more important than concern for social cohesion. In contrast, behaviours that were considered normatively more dissenting were not tolerated, because concerns about a cohesive, integrated society out-weighed the principle of freedom. And prompting people to consider the value of religious freedom leads them to become more tolerant even of highly normatively dissenting practices.

These findings shed a further light on some of the polarised debates about tolerance and intolerance. Earlier I pointed at the disagreement about what constitutes harm and that a broader or more narrow interpretation partly explains why one person considers a particular utterance or belief intolerable and another person as something that needs to be tolerated. In addition to these interpretations of harm, there is the prioritising of different values with the one person, for example, emphasising the higher importance of equality and respect and the other emphasising the critical importance of free speech. Both draw the line between what can and cannot be tolerated differently, because both rank order the relevant values differently. Furthermore, the prioritising of different values occurs not only, in general, as a set of relative predispositions or underlying tendencies to evaluate the world in particular ways, but can also differ by situation and context. Those who consider free speech less important can argue strongly for it when their own ability to express themselves is limited, and those who favour free speech can argue for social unity and cohesion when strong polarisation is the result of people saying whatever they like.

Cultural continuity

The 2009 Swiss referendum decision to ban future constructions of Islamic minarets drew widespread criticism inside and outside Switzerland. The proposal for a ban was supported by 57.5% of the public that voted and it gained majority support in all but four of the 26 cantons. So there was a democratic majority in favour of the ban, and the government which was opposed to the ban nevertheless accepted the outcome of the referendum. As a result, an amendment was added to Article 72 of the Swiss constitution stating, "The building of minarets is forbidden".

The minaret controversy concerned the character of public space and proponents of the ban argued that minarets are a symbol of territorial advancement and increasing Islamisation. A ban would also not infringe on human rights and the principles of religious equality and freedom because minarets are not an essential feature of an Islamic mosque (relatively few mosques have them) and therefore a lack of minarets does not prevent Muslims from practicing their faith and have collective prayer and other rituals be performed. However, the main argument of supporters of the ban was "the historic nation's right to shape public space in a way that reflects its identity and to transmit that identity over time" (Miller, 2014, p. 454). The campaign for the proposal clearly contained overt Islamophobic elements, but political and public debates are also about presenting defensible positions and supporters of the ban succeeded in transforming a legal issue into a fundamental ideological matter of protecting Switzerland against allegedly damaging exterior influences (Vatter et al., 2011). Furthermore, while anti-Muslim feelings clearly played an important role in voting in favour of a ban, so did concerns about the continuity and authenticity of Swiss public culture (Baumgartner & Epple, 2014; Christmann et al., 2011).

Human beings would "have a right to culture – not just any culture, but their own" that they can maintain and transmit over time (Margalit & Halbertal, 1994, p. 491). The *European Model National Statute for the Promotion of Tolerance* states that tolerance should not result in undermining or transforming the fundamental identity of society. Similar to organisations, institutions, and minority and local communities, societies should be able to maintain their self-defining norms and values, history and traditions, and commitments and aspirations. Being tolerant towards other cultural practices, beliefs, and worldviews does not require a relativistic view on one's own culture or turning the national community into a very different kind of society. This is illustrated by the famous quote of Mahatma Gandhi: "I do not want my house to be walled in on all sides and my windows to be stuffed. I want the cultures of all lands to be blown about my house as freely as possible. But I refuse to be blown off my feet by any".

Societies are not static, and a sense of cultural continuity does not imply the absence of change but rather a conceptual thread that is established and maintained against a backdrop of continuing change. In a "culturalist" perspective, the idea of conflicting and non-commensurable values that undermine identity continuity is a key proposition (Morris et al., 2015; Wimmer, 2009). This idea is quite powerful and features in analyses and concerns about "colliding ways of life" (Sniderman & Hagendoorn, 2007) and the confrontational clash of civilisations (Huntington, 1993). It is also prominent in the way in which laypeople think about cultural differences. For example, according to Zolberg and Woon (1999), the focus on Islam in political debates in Western Europe has been related to the fact that the European identity, despite national variations, remains deeply embedded in the Christian tradition in relation to which Muslim immigrants constitute a visible "other" and Islam a "bright boundary" (Alba, 2005). In Europe, there is relatively widespread support for the idea that Islam is incompatible with the country's culture and values.[8] Furthermore, in Western Europe, a majority of the public thinks that in their hearts, Muslims want to impose their religious laws on everyone else in the country.[9] On their part, a public opinion poll found that 30% of British Muslims believe homosexuality should be illegal and 39% believe women should always obey their husbands (compared to 5% for non-Muslims).[10] These percentages represent relatively large numbers of people and fuel the notion of incompatible ways of life.

Different practices, beliefs, and values can be experienced as conflicting and being irreconcilable, because they contradict each other and therefore cannot be simultaneously pursued, or they may be mutually denunciatory whereby taking one seriously is to repudiate the other (Lukes, 2008). Alleged incompatible ways of life are difficult to tolerate because of the feeling that one is no longer able to live by one's ingroup identity (Sindic & Reicher, 2009) or develop a sense of shared community belonging (Martinovic & Verkuyten, 2012). The limits of tolerance can be drawn, for example, in relation to *in*group members. Research on the black sheep effect convincingly demonstrates that normative deviant ingroup members are evaluated more negatively than deviant outgroup members (Marques & Paez, 1994). Furthermore, community factions or subgroups that have contrasting views can create a schism in which they secede from the community to join another group or create a new breakaway group (Sani & Reicher, 1999). Schisms are very common and grounded in the belief that the community identity has been subverted into something that is different from what it meant to be.

The importance of identity continuity is also put forward as an argument against assimilation and in favour of ethnic minority groups and other minority communities being able to maintain and express their minority culture. Minority communities are obviously not homogenous, but the argument is about minority group members being able to freely express and celebrate their cultural identity. However, also majority group members have an interest in maintaining and transmitting a meaningful cultural way of life. In most situations, the majority can "take care of itself" and clearly endures privileges for its culture in the public domain, although there are among majority members very different cultural and religious tendencies that pull in different directions. Furthermore, the notion of preserving and expressing the national cultural and identity is often and typically used in an exclusionary and discriminatory discourse about minorities and immigrants.

Nevertheless, several proponents of interculturalism and multiculturalism have argued that majorities should also be able to express and maintain core aspects of their culture, because they also have the right to cultural identity and personal and collective autonomy (Orgad, 2015; Patten, 2020). For example, in the context of Quebec, a strong case has been made for interculturalism which involves protecting "the interests of the majority culture, whose desire to perpetuate and maintain itself is perfectly legitimate" (Bouchard, 2011, p. 438; see also Taylor, 2012). Contrary to multiculturalism, interculturalism more strongly implies the recognition of the culture and language of the majority group and tries to use this for the development of common ground between the majority and ethnic minorities. And in Britain, well-known multicultural proponents have acknowledged that they have neglected to consider the majority and that "multiculturalists need to show the same sensitivity to change, and identity anxiety in relation to the majority as to the minority" (Modood, 2014, p. 309). For making progress and developing mutual understanding, it would be important to recognise that all groups, including majority members, have legitimate concerns and cultural interests.

Majority members might perceive and experience collective autonomy restrictions that challenge the continuity of their identity (Kachanoff et al., 2021). For example, they can feel that symbolic expressions of their identity are dismantled or replaced, such as the removing of statues of historical figures, changing names of buildings, streets, and public spaces, replacing "merry Christmas" with "happy holidays", and changing the tradition of "Three Kings' days" in Germany and Switzerland, and black Pete in the Netherlands. Symbols play an important role in group relations, because they are means to express and experience core values, beliefs, and ideas, and have the power to stir emotions, moving people to action (Verkuyten, 1995). Majority members can have the feeling that they are pressured by radical minority group members who seek to control and restrict experiencing their majority identity, and that they are gradually losing in various situations their freedom to express themselves (Takahashi & Jefferson, 2021). Populist movements use these alleged symbolic infringements on the majority culture for their own anti-diversity and anti-minority agenda, and discourses about majority rights and alleged minority threats are regularly used for racist ends.

However, the feeling of being able to maintain and transmit one's cultural identity is important. One of the central features of human identity involves a subjective sense of continued existence over time and space. Without a feeling that there is a link between past, present, and future, it is impossible to have a sense of personal or group identity. People tend to attribute temporal endurance to the social groups to which they belong (Condor, 1996; Sani, 2008), and the perception of group continuity provides existential security and plays a role in social well-being (Sani, 2008). Research has demonstrated that people tend to oppose social developments and outgroups that undermine the continuation or future existence of the nature of their group (Jetten & Wohl, 2012; Wohl et al., 2010).

Accommodations and changes that are perceived as undermining or transforming the core of one's group identity are very difficult to accept (Kelman, 2001; Sindic & Reicher, 2009). A sense of continuity provides group identities with meaning, because it helps group members to understand where they come from and what constitutes their common and self-defining cultural heritage (Liu & Hilton, 2005; Sani et al., 2008). Although many groups can provide a sense of continuity, this is particularly likely for ethnic and national groups that are mainly defined and understood as communities that live together through time and have a shared culture and identity that is passed on from generation to generation (e.g. Anderson, 1983; DeVos, 1995). Thus, for majority members, concerns about cultural identity continuity can be a boundary condition of tolerance. For example, increasing numbers of Islamic schools, mosques, veiled women, and other visible signs of Islam can be viewed as undermining society's traditional way of life. We examined the role of identity continuity concerns for tolerance and the acceptance of minority beliefs and practices in different ways in various studies.

Continuity concerns

In one study (Velthuis et al., 2021), we examined whether respect-based and pragmatic-based tolerance (see Chapter 4) are less strongly associated with the acceptance of Muslim minority practices for Dutch majority members who are more concerned about their cultural identity continuity. Controlling statistically for prejudice towards Muslims, higher identity continuity concern was associated with lower acceptance. More importantly, there was a significant interaction between respect and continuity but not between coexistence and continuity. The positive relation between respect-based tolerance and acceptance was weaker at high continuity concern compared to low continuity concern.

In another research, we used data from three national Dutch samples for studying the association between deprovincialisation[11] and support for Muslim minority rights and practices, together with the conditional role of identity continuity concern (Velthuis et al., 2020). We found that deprovincialisation is a unique and robust predictor of support for Muslim practices and rights, above and beyond prejudicial feelings, national identification, political orientation, level of education, gender, age, and religious affiliation. Additionally, higher cultural identity concern was found to significantly weaken, but not remove, the deprovincialisation-support association. Deprovincialisation is not the same as a cultural relativist "anything goes approach", and it appears to be more difficult to support immigrants' cultural practices and rights when the cultural continuity of the ingroup is considered to be at stake.

In an experimental study (Smeekes & Verkuyten, 2014a, Study 2), we further tested whether heightened concerns about cultural identity continuity enhance the intention to preserve the group identity by becoming less tolerant of Muslims publicly confirming and expressing their identity. We manipulated continuity concern by asking participants to write and think about how they would feel when their country would no longer have a shared history and future. We compared this to a control condition in which no writing and imagination tasks were given. The findings demonstrated that when people think about their nation having no longer a shared cultural identity, their sense of group continuity becomes salient and this enhances their intolerance of Muslim minorities expressing their identity.

Culture identity representations

The findings of these various studies focus on the role of identity continuity concerns in general. However, it is also possible to consider the importance of specific culture identity representations for tolerance of minority group practices and rights. In a large-scale study in the United States, it was found that stronger endorsement of Christian nationalism was associated with lower support for civil rights of Muslim-Americans (Dahab & Omori, 2019). Similarly, in one study, we asked majority members how strongly they agree with the Netherlands being historically a Christian nation with Christian roots defining Dutch culture and identity (Smeekes & Verkuyten, 2014b; Study 2). Stronger endorsement of the Christian historical representation was found to be associated with a stronger feeling that the continuity of the Dutch culture is undermined by Muslims practicing their religion and this feeling was subsequently related to lower acceptance of Muslim expressive rights.

Subsequently in an experimental study (Smeekes & Verkuyten, 2014b, Study 3), we found among a national sample that a historical representation emphasising the Dutch Christian tradition and culture leads people to display lower acceptance of Muslim expressive rights, because they were more concerned about the continuity of Dutch identity. However, this was only found among the youngest age cohort (18–35) and not among the older age groups. A possible reason for this cohort effect is that the meaning ascribed to Christian cultural heritage and its relevance for Dutch identity vary between the different generations. For the older generations, thinking about Christian cultural heritage might activate pro-social norms of solidarity, care, and love for fellow human beings, which have positive implications for the acceptance of minority groups (Hunsberger & Jackson, 2005). For the youngest generation, Christian cultural heritage may be more strongly linked to the political discourse on Muslim immigrants in which the continuation of "our" Christian cultural heritage is discussed.

In three further studies (Smeekes & Verkuyten, 2011), we found that a historical narrative defining national identity as rooted in Christianity can trigger opposition towards Muslim practices, also among majority members who ordinarily do not view their national identity as being very important (low national identifiers). Thus, a historical narrative which emphasises the Christian roots of Dutch culture can also make people without a strong commitment to their national identity to become less accepting of Muslims publicly confirming and expressing their identity. Most citizens care about their country's national identity and culture, and also those who do not think that their national belonging is very important will probably have an underlying concern and sense of solidarity with their nation (Billig, 1995). In addition, historical narratives make all nationals part of an ongoing national drama (Reicher & Hopkins, 2001). Thus, it seems understandable that also lower identifiers are likely to respond with non-acceptance to circumstances that are defined as undermining the continuity of the nation's traditional way of life. Islamic schools, mosques, Islamic public holidays, veiled women, and other public signs of Islam can be seen as transforming the historical national Christian culture and the ability to live by it, also for low national identifiers.

Reciprocity and democratic order

Popper (1945, p. 265) famously stated,

> unlimited tolerance must lead to the disappearance of tolerance. If we extend unlimited tolerance even to those who are intolerant, if we are not prepared to defend a tolerant society against the onslaught of the intolerant, then the tolerant will be destroyed, and tolerance with them. . . . We should therefore claim, in the name of tolerance, the right not to tolerate the intolerant.

In addition to harm and rights and to cultural identity continuity, there is the norm of reciprocity and the defence of the liberal and democratic order. The "paradox of democracy and tolerance" and the notion of "militant democracy" are discussed in light of this self-defensive principle (e.g. Accetti & Zuckerman, 2017; Capoccia, 2013; Popper, 1945). These notions relate to the possibility that a democratic order can overthrow itself when it does not restrict the democratic freedoms of those who turn against the democratic principles itself. Groups that play by the rules of liberal democracy should be tolerated, but those that do not and deny others basic and equal rights cannot be tolerated. Reciprocity is central to the idea of toleration because otherwise the practice of toleration is destroyed: being tolerant towards forces that fail to reciprocate undermines the benefits of civil liberties and equality and therefore cannot be tolerated. For example, in the context of South Africa, it is found that both the black majority and the white minority are politically less tolerant towards groups that are considered unwilling to follow the rules of democracy and are considered dangerous to society (Gibson, 2006b). And in the context of the USA, political tolerance is higher for least liked groups that are expected to be more strongly committed to reciprocity (Djupe & Neiheisel, 2022).

Human beings have a general tendency to reciprocate, and this tendency has been used to explain a wide range of phenomena in different disciplines. In almost all societies (Gouldner, 1960), reciprocity is considered a moral norm and implies that people feel obliged to help those who have helped them, and that one can reject those who do not behave in return. For example, people will feel compelled to "accept the rights of groups who themselves observe democratic rights of other groups and feel compelled to reject the rights of groups that do not accept the rights of others" (Petersen et al., 2011, p. 584). In their research among the Danish population, Petersen and colleagues found that people are politically tolerant towards groups that they dislike but that are committed to non-violence and accept the democratic rules and procedures (e.g. Muslims, far-right, and far-left). Furthermore, people who were initially intolerant towards these groups could be persuaded by appeals for tolerance. In contrast, Danish people were intolerant towards groups that were considered violent and non-democratic (e.g. Neo-Nazis and Islamic fundamentalist) and people were very difficult to persuade in the direction of tolerance towards these groups. Similarly, in a large-scale study in the context of the US, people were found to be less politically tolerant towards groups that were perceived to be undemocratic (Gibson et al., 2020a), and to have become more tolerant over the last two decades towards controversial groups but not towards Islamic extremist and racist that use hate speech (Boch, 2020). Thus, people tend to politically tolerate dissenting minority groups but this is not without boundaries, because these groups have to accept the reciprocal democratic rights of others.

In the Danish research, the degree of tolerance of the various groups was relatively independent of the degree of sympathy for the group, with many people displaying tolerance towards non-extreme groups that they have no sympathy for. However, there was one interesting exception: political tolerance towards Muslim citizens was remarkably lower among those with the least sympathy. The majority of Danes perceived Muslims as non-violent and non-extreme, but a small percentage of the population perceived Muslim practices as being in conflict with liberal democratic ideals. This perception is not exceptional for Denmark but also exist in other European countries and is fuelled, for example, by Muslim minorities maintaining strong transnational political ties and some Muslims believing that they are not bound by basic liberal democratic rules when these conflict with their religious tenets (Verkuyten, 2021). For example, a public opinion poll found that 30% of British Muslims want to live under *shariah* law and 68% believe that British citizens who insult Islam should be arrested and prosecuted.[12]

In another large-scale study among the Danish population, it was found that people make a distinction (in terms of being violent and respecting democratic rules) between two categories of controversial groups (Sniderman et al., 2014). One category was called out-of-the-mainstream groups that have views and beliefs that are at odds with those of the broader society (Muslims, born-again Christians). These groups are critical and advocate change but not by non-democratic means. The other category consists of transgressive groups that are considered adversaries which actively pit themselves against society and tend to be anti-democratic (Neo-Nazis, Islamic fundamentalists). For political tolerance, the results showed that around three in four Danes support the civil rights (to debate, demonstrate, speak publicly) of Muslims, similar as their support for the rights of born-again

Christians, the far left and the far right. However, only one in two Danes supported the civil rights of Islamic fundamentalists and Neo-Nazis.

In one of our own studies, we used the least-liked group approach[13] to examine political tolerance among Sunni and Alevi Muslims from Turkey living in Germany and the Netherlands (Verkuyten et al., 2014). In general, we found a relatively low level of tolerance, going in the direction of not accepting the least-liked group to hold public office, teach in schools, make public speeches, and hold public rallies (64% intolerant). The reason for this relatively high level of intolerance is that most of the Sunnis and Alevis selected right wing extremists as their least-liked group. This group tends to stigmatise and demonise Islam and challenges the civil rights of Muslim minorities. Thus, it can be argued that the participants were intolerant towards this transgressive political "enemy". Additionally and despite their more humanistic and liberal interpretation of Islam,[14] Alevi compared to Sunni participants turned out to be more intolerant. This denominational difference was due to the choice of the least-liked group. Compared to Sunnis, Alevis were much more likely to select religious fundamentalists as their least-liked one and their level of intolerance towards this group was high. Alevis in Western Europe and in Turkey tend to define their identity in terms of a continuous historical struggle against the suffering and violence from Islamic fundamentalism (Sökefeld, 2008; Yildiz & Verkuyten, 2011). Alevi identity would be denied and oppressed by the dogmatic and intolerant character of Islamic fundamentalism leading to intolerance of the perceived intolerant fundamentalists.

Transgressive practices

These different studies demonstrate that intolerance varies considerably across target groups, with people being more intolerant towards groups that are perceived as not respecting the civil rights of others or even threatening the democratic order. Another way to investigate the boundaries of tolerance is to focus on people's tolerance of a range of behaviours of the same out-of-the-mainstream, but not transgressive, group. A group can use different strategies for expressing their views and trying to persuade others. Research has found that a social movement's use of nonviolence increases people's willingness to support and join the movement (Orazani et al., 2021). However, some behaviours might be more difficult to tolerate, because these are perceived as being anti-normative, disruptive or even immoral.

In one of our experimental studies, we examined this possibility by having American participants first watch either a video about the social importance of reciprocity ("the golden rule") or an unrelated video. Subsequently participants were asked to select from a list of ten out-of-the-mainstream groups their least-liked one. For this group, they were asked about their acceptance of normative protest actions and non-normative actions. The findings showed a positive effect of the golden rule video on tolerance of normative actions (e.g. have a rally, organise a peaceful sit-in) but not for non-normative actions (e.g. occupy buildings, stop others from speaking in public, and block roads) that were disruptive and in general not accepted.

In other experimental research, we used national samples from Germany and the Netherlands to examine whether people are not only intolerant of moral transgressive protest actions of their least-liked group but also when these protest actions are performed by members of their most-liked group. Typically, research into political tolerance focuses on whether and when people are willing to be tolerant of ideological groups they do not belong to because political tolerance presupposes that the perceiver dislikes the target group. It counts as an act of tolerance when a left-wing activist is willing to extend freedoms to right-wing activists, but not when it comes to extending those same freedoms to fellow left-wing people (and vice versa).

However, whereas negative affect towards an ideological group is considered a precondition for the identification of political tolerance, it is not a precondition for *in*tolerance. It is possible to be intolerant towards a group one likes when a particular act or form of protest is in itself controversial. For example, people can believe that members of their most liked group should not be permitted to burn the national flag, block public highways, or spread hate mail. These sorts of actions might be rejected, independent of the particular group engaged in it, including a group one likes or identifies with. Acts of incivility have been found to erode support, also among those who view the uncivil actor positively (Frimer & Skitka, 2018). Furthermore, observational and experimental research has found that the use of non-normative protest actions are generally perceived negatively and as something that should not be tolerated (Boch, 2020; Chong & Levy, 2018). These actions tend to be considered unreasonable, unsettling to normal life, threatening, and also immoral (Feinberg et al., 2020; Simpson et al., 2018) due to the emotional harm and infringement on the rights and freedoms of others. Transgressive protest can be considered morally problematic which reduces support among strong group supporters and opponents alike (Feinberg et al., 2020), and even when used against a widely reviled group (Simpson et al., 2018). Thus, in general, people can be expected to be intolerant of moral transgressive protest actions, both of ideological groups to which they feel emotionally distant or close.

In a pilot study, we first found that eight different transgressive protest actions were all considered morally problematic rather than disruptive for social cooperation or uncommon in society (Verkuyten et al., 2022a). Furthermore, people made a distinction between information-based protest (giving offensive speeches, stopping other people from speaking in public, sending hate mail, and spreading fake news) and obstructive transgressive protest (blocking roads and occupying public buildings). Then in two experimental studies, we first found that participants were generally intolerant of both forms of protest towards either their most-liked or their least-liked group, with intolerance ranging from 55.5% to 87.3% of respondents, and tolerance from 4.6% to 17.7%. The results thus demonstrate that the German and Dutch public tends to be rather intolerant of protest actions that are considered morally problematic, regardless of whether these are done by their most liked or disliked ideological group (see Feinberg et al., 2020; Frimer & Skitka, 2018). Using offensive speech, stopping other people from speaking in public, blocking roads, occupying public buildings, sending hate mail, and spreading false and biased information were all considered actions that should not be tolerated in society. The specific group involved in these actions was not very relevant to the intolerance of these protest actions, but considerations of group membership were not absent. Participants tended to reject the protest actions of their most-liked group somewhat less, compared to their least-liked group. This suggests that ingroup preferences can reduce, but not fully erase, the extent to which people are intolerant of these protest actions.

Discourses of tolerance

As indicated in the first two chapters, "tolerance" is a discourse that can function in different ways. The notions of tolerance and intolerance have different meanings which can be discursively used to serve the opposing goals of accepting or rejecting forms of diversity (Verkuyten & Kollar, 2021). Sometimes, the struggle for equality, social justice, and inclusion will benefit from deploying the tolerance discourse, and sometimes this discourse is used for repressive and depoliticising ends (Brown, 2006). For example, Insel (2019) argues that in contemporary Turkey, widespread contempt and discrimination against ethnic, religious, sexual, and political minority groups are ignored and covered up by the majority group's self-claim to tolerance. The majority would argue that their tolerance is an example of virtue and generosity, but inequalities endure and minorities are only tolerated until they question and challenge the reasons for the inequalities. Similarly, Wemyss (2006) argues in relation to the British context that "tolerance" is a discourse of coercion and power that is hidden behind the representation of tolerance being an act of benevolence and a common-sense positive national quality. And in relation to the principle of "militant democracy", it has been argued that an appeal to this principle can justify banning an expanding range of actions and actors as going against the stability and viability of the democratic order, including the wearing of religious attire (Accetti & Zuckerman, 2017). For example, an examination of speeches by the US President and UK Prime Minister about Muslim minorities before and after an Islamic terrorist attack shows that the notion of tolerance is used to justify stretching actions towards "intolerable Muslims" beyond practices that are typically acceptable in liberal democracies (Solomon, 2016). Furthermore, the claim that a group is "undemocratic" is an easy justification for rejecting the political rights and activities of one's adversaries. Groups and activists that are construed as being "anti-democratic", "disloyal", "immoral" or "violent" are delegitimised as political actors that do not have to be tolerated.

The toleration discourse is malleable and can be appropriated and used for different purposes, similar to general moral principles (Uhlmann et al., 2009), diversity ideologies such as multiculturalism (Ng Tseung Wong & Verkuyten, 2018) and colour blindness (Knowles et al., 2009), and notions of group essentialism

(Verkuyten, 2003). For example, essentialist group beliefs are typically examined as justifying prejudice and discrimination against minorities and as rationalising social hierarchies and existing social arrangements (Haslam et al., 2002; Jost & Banaji, 1994). However, cultural essentialism is an important political tool for ethnic minority groups (Hodgson, 2002; Morin & Saladin d'Anglure, 1997). Culture is the socially right category on which to rest the claim for group rights and to argue for toleration of one's authentic group identity. For example, in the context of multicultural Mauritius, higher perceived cultural essentialism is associated with stronger social and political tolerance of one's least-liked group.[15] Research has also shown that minorities use group essentialism to counter the denial of their identity and assimilation pressures (Morton & Postmes, 2009; Verkuyten, 2003), and that majority members reject essentialism when they argue against multiculturalism (Verkuyten, 2003) and when it is used to exclude them (Morton et al., 2009).

To give another example, in France, the concept of *laïcité* refers to a type of secularism in which the value of neutrality for achieving equality and inclusion is central. Although the principle is most strongly supported by the political left, the majority of the French population considers *laïcité* a fundamental value of the French republic. However, in the last decades, the notion of *laïcité* has been reworked and a "new *laïcité*" has emerged that is less egalitarian and more exclusionary, often advocated by the populist right. This interpretation of *laïcité* does not focus on egalitarian goals, but centres on banning religious symbols from public places. In their research, Roebroeck and Guimond (2017) demonstrate that these two discourses of *laïcité* have different implications for tolerance of cultural and religious diversity.

Similar to *laïcité*, the discourse of toleration is flexible and can be strategically used to promote higher minority acceptance and inclusion or rather to justify rejection and exclusion. Thus rather than stimulating minority acceptance, an emphasis on toleration can serve to justify negative stereotypes and social exclusion of "intolerant" minority groups.

Reciprocity and a threshold

The slogan "no toleration for the intolerant" is used by populist and mainstream politicians[16] in Europe to argue against minorities and newcomers (e.g. Verkuyten, 2013). For example, in relation to Muslims, the leader of the Dutch populist party stated, "You can only answer intolerance with intolerance, that's just the way it is. . . . We must learn to be intolerant of the intolerant, in the street, in the mosque and in the court",[17] and the then leader of the British populist party UKIP stated, "The Brexit Party is going to be deeply intolerant of intolerance".[18]

These statements indicate that talk about the boundaries of tolerance is not unproblematic. There is always the question of who draws the line against whom, for which reasons, and by what means. Some politicians and opinion makers emphasise the self-defining meaning of national tolerance to criticise Muslim minorities for their intolerance and unwillingness to adapt (Richardson, 2009;

Verkuyten, 2013). They argue that we cannot let the intolerant destroy our tolerant identity and that our tolerance has gone too far leading to segregated and isolated communities (see Blommaert & Verschueren, 1998). Thus, the notion of tolerance can be used to argue not only for acceptance of the beliefs and practices of minority groups but also for drawing a moral boundary between "us, the tolerant" and "them, the intolerant" (Van der Veer, 2006). Notions of tolerance depend on equality and, as populists argue, Islam is unequal to our liberal worldview, and therefore it is not intolerant to treat Islam in a different way (Verkuyten, 2013).

The next quote illustrates these points. It is taken from a focus group discussion among ethnic Dutch residents of an old neighbourhood in Rotterdam who are talking about immigrants living in their area, and Muslims in particular (Verkuyten, 1997).

> I simply believe, we live as Dutch in the Netherlands, and then I think if we would go to Turkey or Saudi Arabia or whatever, we also are not to walk topless on the street, than we have to adapt to the society you go to. Look, and I think that Dutch people, certainly in our neighbourhood, have been tolerant enough, too tolerant even, and then I think I only will be tolerant to a certain degree, but no longer towards everybody because they themselves are not tolerant at all.

There are three aspects in this excerpt that we are worth highlighting. The first one is that the notion of tolerance is employed in which endurance and forbearance of dissenting practices are central. In this discourse, claiming to tolerate others' dissenting beliefs and practices construes these beliefs and practices as transgressing or deviating from what is considered appropriate and right: it "manages the demands of marginal groups in ways that incorporate them without disturbing the hegemony of norms that marginalize them" (Brown, 2006, p. 36). Those requiring tolerance are marked as undesirable, marginal, or inferior. The discourse of toleration can legitimise and reinforce the dominance of those who extend the tolerance (subject of tolerance), and thereby confirms the inequality and relative powerlessness of those that are tolerated (the object of tolerance): "To tolerate someone else is an act of power; to be tolerated is an acceptance of weakness" (Walzer, 1997, p. 52). For example, the discourse of tolerance can be linked to assimilationist demands for immigrants to fully adjust to the dominant national norms and values, similar to what "we" would have to do when emigrating to another country (see the excerpt).

Second, a distinction is made between "us, the tolerant" and "them, the intolerant". Being tolerant is well regarded and typically considered a sign of virtue and moral character. People showing self-restraint and putting up with things that they disapprove of can feel morally superior towards those they tolerate. Those who are tolerated are put in a relative position of moral inferiority whereby they should be thankful for being allowed by a more virtuous other to express their minority identity. So the notion of tolerance can not only be used to argue for acceptance of dissenting beliefs and practices of immigrants and minority groups but also for making a moral intergroup distinction whereby "they" are defined as failing to meet "our" moral standard of tolerance.

Third, at the end of the excerpt, tolerance is linked to reciprocity, which is presented as essential for the practice of tolerance: one cannot tolerate those who are intolerant. Being tolerant towards forces that fail to reciprocate undermines the benefits of civil liberties and equality, and therefore cannot be tolerated. In portraying immigrants and religious minorities as transgressing our traditional and civilised tolerant way of life, minority groups are positioned as subverting our identity and as being incompatible with the essence of who we are. Lay people and populist politicians argue that we have been tolerant enough and that there is a limit beyond which "our" tolerance threatens to self-destroy our liberal society. Having been tolerant enough implies a "threshold" of tolerance whereby the circumstances, unfortunately, would make it no longer possible to continue to live up to one's tolerant identity but rather requires a justified intolerant reaction (Blommaert & Verschueren, 1998). Here, intolerance is used as an understandable and justified boundary to unacceptable dissent. In this discourse, tolerance either would not be reciprocated or would have gone too far and is therefore portrayed as a vice, and intolerance as a virtue.

Tolerance can be construed as a historic national value of "us" that is threatened by the presence of "them", or by "us" having been too accommodating of diversity (Billig et al., 1988). People can be expected to only support and behave in keeping with tolerance up to a certain point. Similar as populist politicians, majority members can emphasise, first, the self-defining meaning of ingroup tolerance in order to criticise Muslim immigrants for their intolerance, and, second, that society has become too indulgent and permissive of dissenting ways of life (Bowskill et al., 2007; Verkuyten, 2004b).

In the former discourse ("reciprocity"), Muslims are portrayed as not being tolerant themselves and therefore as transgressing "our" traditional tolerant way of life and the "social contract" with its norm of reciprocity that guarantees civil liberties for all. Experimental research has found that people are less tolerant if Muslim minorities are portrayed as threatening the self-defining norms of tolerance (Fairlamb & Cinnirella, 2021).

In the second discourse ("a threshold"), society is considered to have been tolerant enough and even too tolerant of dissenting others which fuels segregation and undermines not only social cohesion but in the end also "our" cultural identity (Verkuyten, 2013). Alleged excessive tolerance for deviations from cultural traditions would threaten the national identity and therefore would form a boundary condition to what can be tolerated (Blommaert & Verschueren, 1998; Richardson, 2009). Being too indulgent towards Muslim minorities would mean that tolerance gradually becomes "meaningless" by turning into indifference ("do not care"), resignation ("give up"), or a permissive relativism ("anything goes"). Thus, in order to maintain our self-defining culture and identity, it is argued that we should not led things slide by and become too "soft".

In four studies among Dutch majority members, we examined the relations between the endorsement of these two discourses of national identity of tolerance with the support for Muslim minority practices (Verkuyten et al., 2022a). We expected that stronger endorsement of the notion of "reciprocity" and of "a threshold" are both associated with lower support. Additionally, these two associations were expected to be due to perceived cultural threat. We presented the participants with a short introduction about the Dutch cultural tradition and historical identity of tolerance which was followed by sets of two related items measuring the level of agreement with what is required for maintaining this identity and the possible boundaries.[19] In the introduction and in the items, there was no mentioning of specific minority groups such as Muslims. Subsequently participants were presented with the text "According to some, however, our tolerance is at stake by dissenters who, in turn, are not always so tolerant" which was followed by two items for measuring "reciprocity" (e.g. "In order to maintain our tradition of tolerance we should not accept intolerant people"). Then, it was added that "And according to still others, we have been tolerant enough and rather become *too* tolerant towards dissenters that undermine our society" which was also followed by two items for measuring "a threshold" (e.g. "For maintaining our national culture we should not become indifferent and accept everything").

The findings show, first, that agreement with both discourses are positively correlated but that participants make a distinction between the two. Furthermore, the average level of agreement with the two measures was similar and around the mid-point of the scale. Importantly and as expected, support for Muslim minority practices was lower for participants who more strongly agreed with the importance of reciprocity for maintaining national identity and for those who more strongly agreed with a threshold, over and above individual differences in general tolerance predisposition, national identification and political orientation. Thus, stronger agreement with the notions that maintaining our tolerant tradition implies not tolerating the intolerant (reciprocity notion) and not becoming too indulgent (threshold) were both associated with weaker support for Muslim minority practices.

The likely reason for these associations is that these two discourses emphasise the cultural undermining implications that unconditional tolerance might have. Tolerance without boundaries can be perceived as threatening "our culture". Thus, individuals who more strongly endorse the belief that for maintaining our tolerant identity, we should not tolerate the intolerant or should not become indifferent, might support Muslim minority practices less because they are more concerned about their national culture being transformed into something that is different from what it used to be. In other words, there might be an indirect association between the agreement with these boundary conditions of tolerance and support for minority practices via perceived cultural threat. We found empirical support for this reasoning in two studies: stronger endorsement of each of the two tolerance discourses was associated with higher perceived cultural threat and via threat to lower support of Muslim minority practices.

These findings indicate that an emphasis on the importance of tolerance for supporting minorities can backfire, and for different reasons. The discourse of tolerance can be interpreted in different ways and (mis)used for different purposes and a call for tolerance can not only be beneficial for intergroup relations but can also do more harm than good. However, this does not mean that "tolerance" has only, or mainly, negative effects. In the previous chapter, I have discussed that the notion that one should "practice what one preaches" in order to maintain the historical identity of tolerance is associated with stronger support for minority rights and practices. And also in the current research, we found that the endorsement of living up to "our" Dutch tradition of tolerance was more strongly associated with support for Muslim minority practices, than agreement with the notions of reciprocity and of a threshold were. This suggests that the commitment to uphold the national self-defining norm of tolerance is particularly important for accommodating minorities and supporting their rights. Hence, the implications of the toleration discourses depend on the ways in which these are presented and used for maintaining the national identity. However, the research indicates that the line between tolerance and intolerance can get blurry and that it is easy to slip towards becoming intolerant of things that one is expected to tolerate.

7

A SLIPPERY SLOPE, THREATS, AND CHANGES

It is not easy to put up with things that you disagree with, dislike, or disapprove of. Some people are better able to do this than others, some dissenting practices and beliefs are more easy to tolerate than others, and in some situations, it is more difficult to be tolerant than in other situations. There are many differences between individuals, situations, and circumstances that matter for tolerance. In previous chapters, I have discussed that people can tolerate some practices of a particular group but not other practices of that group, that the perceived reasons for dissenting conduct matters, and that there can be different considerations for either tolerating things or finding them intolerable. What people are asked to tolerate and why matters, and so do when and where people are expected to be tolerant, as well as whom is asked to be tolerant.

The social science literature on cultural diversity and intergroup relations has extensively considered the role of individual differences and situational conditions. Specifically, a great many studies examining prejudice and racism have focused, for example, on authoritarianism, social dominance orientation, and open-mindedness, as well as perceived realistic and symbolic outgroup threat, social status, social norms, and degree of situational (e.g. school and neighbourhood) diversity. These constructs and factors are likely to be also important for tolerance and intolerance. Not everyone will react in the same situation in the same way, and the same person can react differently in different situations. There are individual differences and situational conditions that need to be considered for understanding the tolerance process.

Individual differences

Research, including our own work, reveals that not only individual differences in ingroup identification but also authoritarianism, social dominance, multicultural beliefs, and deprovincialisation are important correlates of tolerance

DOI: 10.4324/9781003335030-7

(e.g. Adelman & Verkuyten, 2020a; Crawford & Pilanski, 2014; Dangubić et al., 2021; Feldman, 2020). Furthermore, research has found that hatred, anger and fear are all associated with lower political tolerance (Gibson et al., 2020b; Halperin et al., 2009; Skitka et al., 2004), and that positive emotions can elevate tolerance (Tenenbaum et al., 2018). Additionally, individual differences in thinking abilities and thinking dispositions can play a role in the tolerance process. For example, across several studies, we have found that open-mindedness and balanced thinking as the tendency to evaluate contrasting reasons (e.g. "I always try to weigh whether there are good reasons to accept or not accept differences") are associated with higher tolerance of a range of minority group practices (e.g. Adelman & Verkuyten, 2020a). Relatedly, research shows that individuals tend to be more tolerant of others and of controversial policies when they habitually engage in dialectic thinking (Ma-Kellams et al., 2011), paradoxical thinking (Hameiri et al., 2019; Swann et al., 1988), situational wise reasoning (Brienza et al., 2021), and exhibit greater wisdom (Staudinger & Glück, 2011), intellectual humility (Hook et al., 2017), and recognise their lack of understanding of controversial policies (Fernbach et al., 2013).

These flexible forms of thinking also imply a greater tendency to be interested in others and a desire to learn about and from them. These interests and desires influence a person's motivation to be involved in reflective thinking in which the relevant considerations for tolerating beliefs and practices that one continues to be negative about are carefully examined and weighted. Individual differences in ability, motivation, and in dispositional modes of thinking imply differences in the habitual tendency to collect and seriously consider information, in seeking various points of views, in thinking extensively about the dissenting conduct, and in weighting the different reasons for objection and acceptance that one has for tolerating or not tolerating the dissenting conduct.

However, being better able to think about controversial issues does not simply have to result in higher tolerance. One of the most replicated and robust findings in the social sciences is that a higher level of education goes together with higher tolerance, and we also consistently have found such a relation in all our studies among national representative samples. This association is not explained by a greater tendency of the higher educated to respond in a socially desirable way (Heerwig & McCabe, 2009; Ostapczuk et al., 2009), but rather by cognitive development and the learning of liberal democratic values. Education is associated with cognitive ability and flexibility (Bobo & Licari, 1989; Ohlander et al., 2005) and cognitive ability has been found to contribute to support for the democratic right of freedom of speech for groups across the ideological spectrum (De Keersmaecker et al., 2021). Education is also a strong correlate of understanding of the values and beliefs that underlie political-ideological differences (Bennett, 1996; Highton, 2009; Osborne & Sibley, 2012). The higher educated are better able to think about the importance of basic norms and values of equality and tolerance underlying the democratic culture, and they are not only more likely to be tolerant in general but also in practice (Gaasholt & Togeby, 1995) and as a matter of principle (Sniderman et al., 1989).

However, the ideological refinement perspective (Jackman & Muha, 1984) views education as endowing majority members with more advanced cognitive skills and ideological commitments to support abstract ideas of equality and justice, while simultaneously using their cognitive skills to protect the status quo and reject ideological opponents. Research on aversive racism (Dovidio & Gaertner, 2004) has shown that aversive racists show relatively strong prejudice on implicit but not on explicit measures (Son Hing et al., 2008), and the higher educated have been found to have lower explicit but not implicit prejudices (Kuppens & Spears, 2014). Higher education is related to a stronger crystallisation of political attitudes and a stronger tendency to rely on ideological beliefs. For example, among a representative sample of Dutch respondents, we found that the endorsement of social conformity and the acceptance of group-based inequality were part of people's political ideological configuration, but more strongly so for the higher compared to the lower educated (Van der Heijden & Verkuyten, 2020). This higher sophistication can imply a stronger tendency to seek out and accept information supporting one's own political position, and to disagree stronger with one's political opponents on specific issues (see Bartels, 2008). Political sophistication helps people identify policies that suit their personality and involves a crystallisation of political attitudes with a tendency towards political polarisation (Henry & Napier, 2017; Jacoby, 1988). Political polarisation tends to be strongest among the most educated, with the higher educated and the more intelligent having stronger negative attitudes towards those at the other side of the left-right political spectrum (Ganzach & Schul, 2021; Henry & Napier, 2017). The higher educated are more able to think in terms of their abstract values and principles and this leads to stronger polarisation when partisanship identity is salient (Luguri & Napier, 2013), especially on questions of social inequality (Chan, 2016).

Thus, there seem to be two routes by which higher education can affect tolerance. A first positive pathway is that cognitive ability and an understanding of the general norms and values underlying the democratic culture lead to higher tolerance. The second negative pathway is that political sophistication leads to a greater awareness of ideological dissimilarities which results in lower tolerance. The relative importance of these two pathways for tolerance is likely to depend on various factors, such as the specific dissenting practice, the psychological distance that one feels to it, political identity importance, and situational circumstances.

Situational conditions

In addition to individual differences, situational and contextual factors are likely to affect the tolerance process. For example, while stressful environments can lead to lower tolerance, safe environments might boost tolerance (Capelos & Van Troost, 2012). Furthermore, intergroup contact, mere exposure, and increased familiarity might over time lead to higher tolerance of things that one disapproves of (e.g. same-sex marriage; Boch, 2020; Janmaat & Keating, 2019). Additionally, threatening situations decrease tolerance and reassuring stimuli increase tolerance.

There is a substantial literature showing that perceived threat (e.g. symbolic, realistic, political) is one of the most consistent and robust correlates and causes of lower tolerance (e.g. Crawford, & Pilanski, 2014; Gibson, 2006a; Gibson et al., 2020a; Sullivan & Transue, 1999). Threat perceptions can be a function of an assessment and analysis of events and situations, and of the attributes and capabilities of opponents or outgroup members. These perceptions do not have to be grounded in emotions but do make, for example, fear, anxiety, and anger more likely. These emotions lead to either withdrawal or a confrontational mindset which reduces reflective thinking about one's objections towards dissenting beliefs and practices. This makes tolerance less likely, irrespective of the values and considerations that one can have for being tolerant (Tenenbaum et al., 2018).

There are, as always, two sets of factors involved in the perception and experience of threats. One is that some people are more than others prone to find things threatening or have predisposing concerns that make them more vigilant and sensitive to any potential threat. The other is that some behaviours, events, or situations actually do have more negative psychological, social, economic, cultural, or political implications and therefore trigger feelings of threat and insecurity. It is of course possible to examine how predisposing factors and situational triggers in combination shape people's reactions to others (Stenner, 2005; Sniderman et al., 2004). For example, the arrival of a great number of refugees can prompt those already concerned about immigration into action, or it can mobilise people who were not already very concerned. Furthermore, uncertainty can lead to lower tolerance when feeling threatened but not when feeling safe (Haas & Cunningham, 2014). And while intolerance among people high in authoritarianism is activated by threats to the social order (nonconformity, cultural diversity), those low in authoritarianism are more intolerant with threats to personal autonomy and freedom (Feldman, 2020; Hetherington & Suhay, 2011).

Additionally, those who do not tend to care much about the country's national identity can become more negative towards newcomers when politicians and the media construe immigration as an economic, cultural, or security threat. In the previous chapter, we have discussed some of our findings on the interplay of national identification and historical national representations with low identifiers, for example, being mobilised in becoming more negative about Muslim minority rights when the nation is defined in Christian terms. In another study, it was found that people who are ordinarily not much concerned about the Dutch way of life, demonstrate much stronger opposition to immigration when they are invited to think in terms of their national rather than their personal identity (Sniderman et al., 2004). And in our research, we found that for people who find the topic of immigration personally important, perceived involuntary (vs. voluntary) migration leads to stronger communitarian concerns which, in turn, is associated with weaker support for the accommodation of immigrants. Additionally, humanitarian considerations are associated with stronger support for immigrants, but especially for people who do not find the topic of immigration very important (Verkuyten et al., 2018).

In addition to all these works and the well-known individual difference constructs that are extensively examined in the literature on prejudice and intergroup relations, I will consider in this chapter the role of the relatively new construct of slippery slope belief. Additionally, I will discuss the role of sociocultural threat and of power threat for supporting Muslim identity enactment and Muslim minority political participation. Subsequently, processes of adaptation and change that make tolerance more likely are considered.

Slippery slope belief

> "The tsunami of Islamization forms a direct threat to the world as we know it and is the beginning of the end of our Western norms and values that are so dear to us".
>
> (Geert Wilders, leader of the Dutch populist Party for Freedom. *GeenStijl*, 23 January 2007)

> "There are so many emerging parallels with early fascist developments that to deny the potential to slide down such a slope would be to have your head firmly in the sand. I don't believe we can yet be said to be sliding but the slope is there".
>
> (thread posting on the topic "Are we on the slippery slope to fascism?", UKC[1])

In the first quote, it is argued that Muslim immigration eventually will lead to the destruction of Western culture, and in the second quote, it is stated that allowing speeches by populist politicians leads us on the path of fascism and ethnic cleansing. These two quotes from respectively the political right and the left, are examples of the so-called "slippery slope" whereby a relatively non-problematic proposal or event is presented as the beginning of an inevitable process of cause and effect that will end in harmful or unacceptable results (Van der Burg, 1998; Volokh, 2003). Similarly, supporters of the Swiss minaret ban (see Chapter 6) argued that allowing the building of new minarets would be a further step on the inevitable road to the Islamisation of the country (Miller, 2014).[2] Furthermore, religious people sometimes argue that the legalisation of same-sex marriage is a further step to the legalisation of pedophilia. And to give one further example, in 2019, the Peace Organisation PAX presented to the United Nations a report on the future of the arms industry titled "*Slippery Slope*".

In the academic literature, the notion of "slippery slope" is predominantly examined as a logical and philosophical investigation of (flawed) argumentations in which a first action is considered to lead to unacceptable consequences, such as by distinguishing the logical, empirical, and apocalyptic types of slippery slope reasoning (e.g. Van der Burg, 1998; Volokh, 2003; Walton, 2015). In psychology, very little research has been conducted on slippery slope reasoning or argumentation (Corner et al., 2011; Haigh et al., 2016). In contrast to this focus on reasoning processes, we considered individual differences in general slippery slope belief and how this relates to intolerance.

Individuals are likely to differ in their general propensity to think that small or unobjectionable actions or events will inevitably lead to negative social consequences. For example, when presented with a proposal for building a new minaret, some individuals might be more likely to believe that if Muslim organisations are permitted to express their religion in this way (unobjectionable action), it will end up by Muslim taking over their neighbourhood and then also the country (harmful consequence). Similarly, when presented with a proposal regarding government spying on suspected terrorists or criminals, some individuals might be more likely to believe that if the government is permitted to spy on known criminals or terror suspects (unobjectionable action), it will end up using that power in an authoritarian manner to spy on ordinary citizens or political opponents (harmful consequence). These individuals will be inclined to perceive this as a likely chain of events, because they in general tend to believe that an unobjectionable or a small action is a first step on an inevitable road to disaster (e.g. Volokh, 2003; Walton, 2015). They are more likely to consider a cascade of dangers as reasonably arising from accepting relatively benign dissenting practices and cultural expressions, making intolerance more likely.

Across six national samples from the Netherlands and Germany, we developed and tested an individual difference measure of slippery slope belief and examined its importance for intolerance of outgroup freedoms and debated minority practices, as well as agreement with real-world slippery slope examples across the political spectrum (Adelman et al., 2021b). We first developed and validated a reliable six item measure of slippery slope belief (e.g. "If you give people one finger, they will eventually take the whole hand", and "If you start to be okay with all sorts of things, you will slowly but surely end up on a slippery slope") that was found to be empirically distinct from generalised trust, sense of control, conspiratorial thinking, present-oriented focus, pessimism, optimism, authoritarianism, open-mindedness, and close-mindedness. Thus, for example, slippery slope belief goes beyond mistrust of other individuals in that it reflects how the world tends to work, beyond malevolent actors.

We further found evidence for the generalisability and stability of our measure of slippery slope belief across the different samples and the two countries, with similar mean scores. Subsequently, slippery slope belief was an independent and relatively strong negative predictor of general tolerance of immigrants, ("Immigrants must be able to preserve traditions and customs that are important to them"), and of Muslim minorities ("Muslims in the Netherlands must be able to show and experience their own faith in public life"), and also predicted debated practices not related to immigrant minority groups (e.g. the installation of gender-neutral toilets in public buildings; replacing words like "manpower" with gender-neutral terms; gay men kissing in public).

The different studies further demonstrated that the general inclination of slippery slope belief was positively related to a more right-wing political orientation and the related predispositions of endorsing status quo conservatism and normative conformity (Jost et al., 2003). However, slippery slope belief does not simply reflect the psychology of the political right because we found that this belief was often the most powerful predictor of minority rights, even when controlling statistically for political orientation. Furthermore, and as indicated by the two aforementioned quotes, slippery slope belief can be used by both the political left and right when it comes to the evaluation of concrete situations that matter ideologically. Both the political left and right have been found to be susceptible to intolerance and biased ways of thinking (e.g. Brandt et al., 2014; Ditto et al., 2019; but see Baron & Jost, 2019). Therefore, for testing whether slippery slope belief is relevant across the political spectrum, we examined its role for the acceptance of situations that are typically of concern among people on the left ("If we allow right-wing extremists to say what they want, fascists will eventually take over") or for people on the right ("If immigrants retain their own language and culture, Dutch culture will eventually change beyond recognition"). To the extent that the propensity towards slippery slope belief reflects a general approach to the world, we would expect to find that slippery slope belief predicts agreement with the concrete examples regardless of the political orientation of the participants and of whether these examples reflect politically left-wing or politically right-wing issues. This is indeed what we found with, for example, slippery slope belief being associated with lower acceptance of immigrants, also among left-wing oriented people. Thus, the findings indicate that people who in general are inclined to think about small or innocuous events and acts as leading inevitably to dangerous consequences can be less tolerant of societal changes, even when these align with their ideological worldview.

Threats and tolerance

Slippery slope belief leads people to see single event as the first step on a dangerous road to a threatening societal outcome, and therefore might reduce people's tolerance of the practices, beliefs, and rights of others. Perceived threat is an important and robust driver of outgroup negativity (Riek et al., 2006), social and political intolerance (e.g. Chanley, 1994; Crawford, 2014; Gibson, 2006a), and support for restricting the human rights and civil liberties of both outgroup and ingroup members, but more strongly for the latter (Carriere et al., 2022).

Tolerance is typically found to be lower when actions of a person or group generate insecurity, fear, and anxiety. People not only tend to be less tolerant in a highly stressful and very threatening context, such as the aftermath of a terrorist attack (Skitka et al., 2004), but also in more ordinary threatening situations (e.g. Capelos & Van Troost, 2012). And the stronger people's sense of threat, the higher their willingness to trade off civil liberties for greater personal security and safety (Davis & Silver, 2004). A person feeling threatened will try to eliminate or control the threat by favouring restrictive measures. A sense of threat directs the attention to contextual information and thus to disliked or disapproved of actions and practices. The perception of threat means that self-restraint and cognitive control are superseded by implicit and contextual emotional responses of fear, anxiety, and anger that justify negative reactions (Pereira et al., 2010). Threat tends to reduce reflective thinking about different considerations and leads to dissonance reduction in which the emotional gut-feelings are less likely to be adapted than the reasons for tolerance. The perception of threat can also lead to morality shifting in the trade-off thinking process, such as from moral principles of harm and fairness to those of ingroup loyalty and authority (Leidner & Castano, 2012). This type of shifting does not only protect the moral image of oneself as an individual and that of one's ingroup, but can also imply that the reasonable grounds for tolerance of particular practices and beliefs change, and intolerant responses are considered justified.

Threats can relate to one's personal situation ("egocentric threat") as well as to the normative community and the larger system ("sociotropic threat"), and can involve competition over scarce resources, opportunities, and safety (realistic threats), and worldviews, culture, and identity (symbolic threats). Furthermore, the perceived power of an outgroup has been identified as a separate form of threat for political tolerance (Gibson, 2006b). In our research, we have examined tolerance in relation to minority identity enactment as a possible source of symbolic threat, and minority political participation as a form of power threat.

Minority identity enactment

In a set of studies, we investigated whether tolerance is lower when minority identity enactment is considered to have more threatening sociocultural implications. For example, in two experimental studies, we presented Dutch adolescents with short stories on various Muslim minority practices (e.g. religious attire at school) that were depicted as having either modest sociocultural implications (e.g. a headscarf that only covers the hair) or more far-reaching consequences (e.g. not only covering the hair but also part of the face; Verkuyten & Slooter, 2007, 2008). The findings showed that the level of tolerance was lower when the practice was described as have larger implications for society. We further tested the importance of sociocultural threats in several other studies in two ways: (1) by examining the difference between tolerance of minority enactment and of persuasion, and (2) by using the distinction between private and public minority identity enactment.

First, we considered people's tolerance of Muslim minority practices (e.g. Islamic attire, wearing a headscarf) as well as their tolerance of minority campaigns trying to persuade other Muslims to enact their religious identity in a similar way (e.g. to also start wearing a headscarf). It is one thing to tolerate religious minority identity enactment, but another to accept campaigns that try to persuade co-believers to express their identity in a similar way. The former can be perceived as a matter of personal choice, while the latter can be considered to imply, for example, mobilising fellow Muslims to engage in the same religious enactment practices, which might be considered as contributing to the "Islamisation" of the country. Research has shown that the perception of minority group size is related to perceived threat (McLaren, 2003; Outten et al., 2012) and that "threat in numbers" predicts negative attitudes towards minorities (Earle & Hodson, 2019). We tested in our research the expectation that tolerance of identity enactment (e.g. "Do you think it is OK that Muslims like Fatma enact their religious identity this way?") will be higher than tolerance of campaigning (e.g. "Do you think it is OK if Muslims like Fatma try to persuade other Muslims to engage with their religion in the same way?").

In different studies, we consistently found that Dutch adolescents were indeed more tolerant of Muslims involved in practices such as the wearing of religious attire (e.g. headscarf) and refusal to shake hands with someone of the opposite gender (i.e. tolerance of enactment), than of Muslims trying to persuade other Muslims to engage in these practices (i.e. tolerance of campaigning). For example, in one study (Gieling et al., 2010), 43% of Dutch adolescents thought that the decision of a female teacher not to shake hands with men should be tolerated, but for the persuasion of fellow Muslims to do the same, this percentage was only 10%. And while 35% thought that the foundation of an Islamic primary school should be accepted, only 18% found it acceptable that people try to convince other Muslims to also found Islamic schools. The difference between tolerance of enactment and tolerance of campaigning was quite consistent across age, gender, and educational level.

We further examined both forms of tolerance among a national sample of Dutch adults and again found higher intolerance for campaigning to persuade fellow Muslims than for Muslim identity enactment. Additionally, higher intolerance for campaigning compared to enactment was not only found in different public contexts (street, work), but also in the private sphere (Velthuis et al., 2022b). This suggests that trying to persuade fellow Muslims to enact their religious identity per se, is perceived as increasing the number of Muslims in society who practice their religion, which is considered by many majority members as being a threatening development (McLaren, 2003; Outten et al., 2012).

Second, we investigated tolerance of Muslim identity enactment in different contexts, reasoning that enactment is likely to be considered more threatening in public contexts (street, work) as compared to private contexts (Velthuis et al., 2022b). Furthermore, we examined whether the expected effect of context on tolerance is especially strong for majority group members who value Dutch culture. Religious expression in public contexts is a visible form of minority identity enactment, while identity enactment in the private sphere has less sociocultural consequences and therefore should be easier to tolerate. Research in the United States has shown that minority groups are construed as less American when expressing their minority identity publicly versus privately and that White American perceivers' national identification elicit more negative explicit and implicit attitudes towards non-White ethnic groups when members embrace their ethnic heritage in public rather than in private (Yogeeswaran et al., 2011). Research has also shown that people are less tolerant when a particular practice is considered to have negative implications for people themselves, their group, or society more generally (Chanley, 1994; Kuklinski et al., 1991).

Thus, the wearing of a headscarf in public may be tolerated less than wearing it in the private sphere. However, there are different sorts of "public" contexts and we therefore additionally examined tolerance of wearing the headscarf in the public context of the street compared to two work contexts (i.e. the general work context, and working as a civil servant). Although the wearing of a headscarf is visible in the street, the consequences for majority members are less obvious and direct, compared to the work context or in social interactions with civil servants. People may perceive the latter two settings as having to be "religious neutral" (i.e. "colour-blind") situations in which religious identity enactment is less appropriate, and research has found that such a perception can lead to lower minority group acceptance (Dovidio et al., 2015). Thus, we expected that tolerance for wearing a headscarf in both work contexts is lower than in the street context.

Using a survey experiment involving a national sample of Dutch majority members, we found that tolerance was indeed significantly lower for religious expression in the street than in the private context, and that religious expression at work and as a civil servant elicited significantly lower tolerance as compared to the street context (Velthuis et al., 2022b). In support of a threat-based interpretation, these context effects were found to be stronger among majority members who highly valued Dutch culture, while people who did not value Dutch culture strongly were generally tolerant and did not seem to clearly consider the different sociocultural implications of the various contexts.

Power threat

Politics deals with questions of influence and the ability to make decisions that affect individuals, groups, and society as a whole. In 2010, the American Immigration Council published a special report titled "*The growing political power of immigrants and their children*". Census projections suggest that the United States will be more ethnically diverse in the near future with more ethnic minority members than White Americans,[3] and there are similar census projections for countries in the European Union.[4] Since the democratic political power of a group is based on its relative size, this development raises important questions for political tolerance as one of the most elusive democratic values.

The mass media, social media, and populist politicians often present Muslims as a cultural, demographic, and safety threat to the West. For example, an analysis of five Australian newspapers in 2017 found almost 3000 articles in which words suggesting threat (violence, terror, radical) were used alongside with Muslims/Islam.[5] And an analysis of the word corpus of British newspaper articles (1998–2009) found that notions related to "conflict" were prominent (Baker et al., 2013). In populist political discourse, an essentialised, homogeneous, and dangerous "Islamic other" is being construed (Verkuyten, 2013; Wood & Finlay, 2008) with an inflated perception of the size of the Muslim minority population. For example, the number of Muslim immigrants in the US (1.2%) and throughout West European nations (<10%) is overestimated with 15% to 20%.[6] There is threat in numbers and this threat might appear greater, as it actually is which increases feelings of vulnerability and reduced support for the equal civil rights and political participation of Muslim minority citizens. Among two representative sample, we found that on average

Dutch majority members were rather negative towards the democratic political organisation of Muslim citizens (Bot & Verkuyten, 2018).

However, minority participation in political systems is widely recognised as crucial for the democratic process, the legitimacy of the political system, and for improving the socio-economic position of disadvantaged groups (Pande, 2003; Petrusevska, 2009). In Europe, immigrant-origin groups are clearly underrepresented in political institutions and this is not a simple reflection of their recent arrival, delayed acquisition of citizenship, educational qualifications, social experiences, or cultural attitudes (Bloemraad & Schönwälder, 2013). Minorities' reception as fully equal citizens by the dominant majority supports or undermines their ability to participate in the democratic process and in party politics. Some sections of the majority population are likely to believe that their ingroup's power is threatened by the political engagement of minorities and therefore will resist minority democratic political participation. Other sections of the population are likely to support immigrant minority's ability to fully participate in society and exercise not only their civic but also their democratic political rights.

In the political domain, majority members can hold a belief in zero-sum competition with minority groups and might fear that the more influence minorities gain, the more power they themselves will lose. Minority members who are seen as being in a position to secure their group interest and enact changes in the status quo are likely to be perceived as potential competitors for influence and power. This would mean, for example, that people will feel most positive about Muslim minorities who disengage from democratic politics. After all, these Muslims do not wish to participate in formal politics and therefore do not pose a challenge to the power position of the majority group. Muslim minorities who do want to participate in the political system and thereby pursue political influence can be expected to be evaluated more negatively. The perceived competition can relate, first, to Muslims wanting to secure their group-specific interests and, second, to Muslims wanting to be represented politically in the democratic political system. We examined majority members' reactions and tolerance towards these two forms of political participation.

Group interests

Political participation in terms of group interests and goals can take different forms and we focused on the distinction between Muslim minorities trying to advance the interests and goals of their religious minority group, of both their own group and the broader society, or only of society as a whole. This distinction is based on the identification of two key issues that immigrant-origin members need to decide on in their acculturation process (Berry, 1997). The first one deals with the extent to which immigrants wish to get involved and have contacts with the dominant majority group, or rather remain primarily among themselves. The second one concerns the extent to which they prefer to maintain their heritage culture compared to adopting the majority culture. Applied to the political domain, immigrants first face the question of whether or not to advance politically their minority group interests and goals. Second, they need to decide on the extent to which they wish to advance interests and goals that benefit society as a whole. When considering these two issues simultaneously, at least three political participation strategies can be identified (e.g. Navas et al., 2007).

Separation is the political strategy in which minority members predominantly wish to advance the interests of their own group. Politically *integrating* minority members advocate for the interests of their own group but also pursue goals that are relevant for society as a whole. The *assimilation* strategy is defined when minority members wish to advance society's interests and not those of their minority group.

Separation directly challenges the political status quo, and with it, the privileged status position of the majority group. Therefore, majority members might evaluate the separation strategy most negatively. By contrast, they can be expected to evaluate political assimilation most positively, as it focuses on the interests of society as a whole. This strategy does not imply advocacy for the interests of the minority group and thereby poses low threat to the existing power relations. Moreover, this strategy signals acceptance of both the existing political system and the dominant culture (Tip et al., 2012). Majority members can be expected to place Muslim minorities adopting the political integration strategy at an intermediate position. With this strategy, minority members advance the interests of their Muslim ingroup, while demonstrating political commitment to the broader society. It follows that majority members can be expected to evaluate this strategy more negatively than the assimilation strategy, yet more positively than the separation strategy.

We tested these expectations in three experimental studies using national samples of Dutch majority members (Hindriks et al., 2015; Verkuyten, 2022b). Participants were presented with a short excerpt from a fictitious interview that "was recently published in a well-known morning newspaper". In this excerpt, a 30-year-old Muslim named Ahmed was interviewed.[7] Ahmed first described himself as being born in Turkey, just like his parents were, but he has been living in the Netherlands for the last 20 years and has Dutch citizenship. When asked by the interviewer if he had a clear idea about Dutch politics, Ahmed answered, "Yes, I do". Next, he was asked if he thinks it is important that Muslims are politically active in the Netherlands. Depending on the experimental condition, Ahmed gave one of three answers that reflected the three political acculturation strategies.[8]

The findings in the three studies were similar with the Dutch public having more positive feelings and also being politically more tolerant of political assimilation, followed by integration, and then segregation of Muslim minorities. For example, in the assimilation condition, more participants (69%) were fully tolerant (on six yes-no questions)[9] compared to the integration condition (51%) and the segregation condition (37%).

The reactions to these three forms of political participation differed quite strongly[10] indicating that it matter much to people. Furthermore, compared to a control condition, participants were more negative about separation and more positive about assimilation. In other words, majority members were more tolerant and even welcoming towards politically active Muslim minority members when they assimilate, but far more intolerant and negative towards those that focus upon and wish to improve the societal situation of their minority group.

Additionally, we also considered whether perceived power threat[11] is a factor that might have an impact on the differential evaluation of the political acculturation strategies. The results showed that the Dutch were more negative about Muslim political participation when they perceived more power threat, especially when they learned about Muslims favouring separation or integration. The effect of perceived threat was consistently weaker in the assimilation condition. This indicates, first, that majority members apparently are not so much threatened by the fact that religious minorities become politically active, but rather fear that they themselves will have to relinquish power and influence to minority groups. Second, perceived threat appears to affect feelings and tolerance as a function of the level of perceived group competition. Among those with strong perceptions of power threat, differences in the evaluation of the three political acculturation strategies were more pronounced.

Concerns about potential limits to political power and influence are not only important for majority group members but for ethnic minorities as well. Minority members might reject political participation of other minority groups because it reduces their own opportunities for political influence. From an intergroup competition perspective, a gain in political power of another minority implies a loss of influence for one's own minority group. In a further study, we examined, therefore, whether the ranking of the political acculturation strategies by ethnic minority members (Moroccan-Dutch and Surinamese-Dutch) is similar to that of the ethnic Dutch. We used the same experimental design with a focus on political acculturation strategies of Turkish-Dutch citizens (Hindriks et al., 2017).

We again found a clear and similar ranking in the evaluation of political acculturation strategies: participants were most rejecting towards Turkish minority members who exclusively advocated for the interests of their ingroup (separation), most accepting about those who only wished to advance societal interests (assimilation), while Turkish minority members advocating for both their ingroup and society as a whole (integration) were evaluated in between. Thus, the more the political acculturation strategy focused on the interests of the minority group, thereby implicitly challenging the existing political status quo, the more negative participants were. This rank ordering was found for the ethnic Dutch and for participants with a Surinamese and Moroccan background. This similar ranking among the three groups is in line with an intergroup competition perspective whereby the gain in political influence and power of another group implies a threat to the influence and power of one's own (majority or minority) group. A further result supporting this interpretation is that Turkish outgroup members were rejected more strongly when the power position of participants' ethnic minority ingroup was perceived to be threatened by other minority groups.

Political representation

There are several ways in which Muslim minorities can participate in the democratic political party system and these are likely to elicit different feelings of intergroup competition. One way has to do with the so-called *descriptive representation* of minority members in existing political parties due to preferential "co-ethnic voting" based on cultural affinity and minority group-based interests (e.g. Bloemraad, 2013; Schildkraut, 2013; Sobolewska, 2013).

Furthermore, in countries with a multi-party political system, there is also the possibility of participating in democratic politics with an ethnic or religious minority party (*group representation*). The Netherlands has a multi-party political system and the Dutch House of Representatives is elected by proportional representation without a threshold. As a consequence, there are 20 political factions currently (2022) represented in Parliament. Voters have a range of parties which fit their beliefs and political orientation, including several small Christian parties and different one-issue parties (e.g. "party for the elderly" and "party for the animals"). Similar to, for example, Spain, Belgium, and Denmark, there are and have been also several political parties in the Netherlands that try to participate in politics by explicitly presenting themselves as Islamic, or that claim, or are perceived, to draw inspiration from Islam. Some of these political parties have secured seats in municipality councils in Dutch local elections (e.g. "NIDA" in Rotterdam, and "Islam Democrats" in The Hague) and in the national election (2021, "DENK"). Thus, Muslim citizens can organise themselves and collectively compete with other parties for influence and power within the democratic political system, similar to what Christian political parties and one-issue parties do.

The perceived political competition is probably highest when Muslims want to participate in the system with their own political party (group representation strategy). In contrast, descriptive representation is likely to elicit lower resistance. This strategy implies that Muslim minorities do not explicitly wish to be represented by their own political party but rather prefer co-believers to participate within existing parties. Therefore, majority group members might view them less as competitors for power and influence than their group representing counterparts. However, the presence of minority representatives within an existing party can activate group-based considerations in the minds of majority members (McConnaughy et al., 2010). For example, in the Netherlands, mainstream political parties can be reluctant to include Muslim minority group candidates because of concerns about clientelism[12] and unwanted influences on the party's agenda-setting and political programme (Michon & Vermeulen, 2013). This means that majority members might be more negative about descriptive representation of Muslim minorities than about political disengagement in which Muslims do not want to be involved in party politics. Thus, the native Dutch are likely to have the most negative feelings and lowest tolerance towards political group representation of Muslim minorities, followed by descriptive representation, and to be least negative about political disengagement.[13]

The findings of four experimental studies, again using national samples and short excerpts from a fictitious interview (Verkuyten et al., 2016; Verkuyten, 2022b), were similar and robust across people's political orientation, level of education, religiosity, age and gender, and across time periods (data collected in 2011, 2012, 2016, and 2020) indicating that the results were not due to specific incidents or tragedies such as the Islamist Paris attacks in November 2015. People responded again quite strongly towards the different forms of political party strategies, with the least negative feelings towards Muslims who opt for the strategy of political party disengagement, followed by those who prefer descriptive (co-religious) representation, whereas the political group representation strategy was evaluated most negatively. Furthermore, participants were more fully tolerant in relation to disengagement (55%) compared to descriptive representation (47%), and group representation (41%), but less fully tolerant than in the control condition (63%). Hence, people were more negative and less tolerant of Muslims in the political disengagement condition in which political party involvement was explicitly rejected compared to the control condition.

In the Netherlands, Muslims are sometimes seen as being politically untrustworthy and as a fifth column trying to secretly Islamise the country (Shadid, 2006; Sniderman & Hagendoorn, 2007). As a result, the mere mentioning of Muslim minorities with party politics might already invoke feelings of power threat and the related lower political intolerance among majority members. That power threat considerations lead majority members to rank the political party strategies differently is also indicated by the finding that higher perceived power threat was related to more negative feelings in the two more competitive political representation situations, but hardly so in the disengagement condition. Thus, when Muslims explicitly stated that they do not want to be involved in Dutch party politics (disengagement), or when there was no mentioning of politics (control condition), higher perceived power threat was not related to more negative outgroup feelings and lower tolerance. Another way of interpreting this finding is that the particular political representation strategy matters much more for individuals who perceive relatively high power threat compared to those who perceive relatively little power threat. In our studies, there is a clear, consistent, and robust ranking of outgroup feelings for the former group of individuals but not for the latter group. These findings indicate that perceived power threat does not has a general negative effect on acceptance of Muslim minorities in general, but rather that the effect is specific to situations in which political influence and power are at stake. This is similar to studies that show, for example, that the role of realistic and symbolic threats for outgroup attitudes depends on the relative importance of these considerations in a particular national context or domain of life (e.g. Sniderman et al., 2004).

In our research, we examined whether individuals react differently to the political party strategies of Muslim citizens depending on their general tendency to perceive power threat. However, thinking about these different strategies might also (temporarily) elicit different feelings of power threat. Specifically, feelings of power threat might explain why the different strategies of political representation lead to different levels of negative feelings and intolerance. Political representation of Muslim immigrants might trigger stronger situational threat feelings about the ingroup's power than descriptive representation and political disengagement.

Using the same design, in a further experimental study among a national sample, I found support for this reasoning (Verkuyten, 2018c). The same rank ordering of acceptance was again found, and in addition, the reaction towards Muslims in the group representation strategy was the most negative because an Islamic party elicited the greatest feelings of threat to the privileged power position of the majority ingroup. This strategy means that Muslim citizens organise themselves and that majority members consequently feel more threatened. Furthermore, the descriptive representation strategy and disengagement strategy elicited similar negative reactions, but the elicited power threat was somewhat stronger in the former compared to the latter condition. This difference suggests that majority members can be made concerned about the likelihood that Muslim representatives influence mainstream party's agenda setting and political programme, or about the possibility of clientelism by minority group politicians (Lemarchand & Legg, 1972).

Dual citizenship

> "To be politically active in the Netherlands, one needs to be Dutch and nothing else. It is unacceptable that people with a double nationality and thus a double loyalty take their place in parliament, government, municipality council, provincial council, and in other representative bodies".
>
> (Geert Wilders leader of the populist Party for Freedom; 15 February 2019)

In the experimental research discussed, we used short vignettes in which it was explicitly stated that the Muslim minority members had Dutch citizenship. And the findings indicate that the liberal democratic ideal of all citizens enjoying equal political rights is not fully endorsed by many majority members in relation to Muslim citizens (Conover et al., 2004). As illustrated by the aforementioned quote, this intolerance might even be stronger for minorities with dual citizenship. An increasing number of countries permit dual citizenship for immigrants, and nowadays tens of millions of persons hold citizenship in more than one country (Harpaz, 2019; Harpaz & Mateos, 2019). Such changes have led to politicised questions about national citizenship[14] and concerns about divided loyalties, especially when dual citizens are perceived as becoming the targets of external political influence, are members of representative bodies, have government employment, and have jobs related to national security.

For native-born individuals, immigrant minorities gaining dual citizenship might lead to political intolerance because of suspicions of contrasting loyalties and the belief that the national unity and security is compromised[15] (Kunst et al., 2019). Loyalty towards a nation implies the moral responsibility and obligation to act in a way that supports its unity, functioning, and continued existence. Behaviour that is partial in enhancing group welfare is considered loyal (Zdaniuk & Levine, 2001) and national loyalty implies the expectations of national commitment, trustworthiness, and sacrifice (Hildreth et al., 2016). Thus, when immigrants are assumed to be only loyal to the country of settlement, it will be easier to politically trust, accept, and tolerate them (e.g. Faist et al., 2004; Kunst et al., 2019).

In an experimental study conducted in Germany, Finland, and the Netherlands (Jasinskaja-Lahti et al., 2020), we investigated whether dual citizenship of immigrants affects how the two national loyalties (country of origin and country of residence) are perceived, and whether perceived loyalties have ramifications for people's trust in immigrants, willingness to accept immigrants in strategic societal positions (e.g. "have important political functions" and "work for the national security service"), and willingness to support immigrants' social influence in society (e.g. "should be heard more often in the [country's] media" and "should be more involved when it comes to important decision-making in society"). Majority members took part in a study related to impression formation in the internet and were randomly allocated to a LinkedIn profile of an immigrant-origin male that included the same photo and personal details but differed in terms of citizenship information: national citizenship (Finnish/Dutch/German), foreign citizenship (Russian/Turkish), dual citizenship (Finnish and Russian/Dutch and Turkish/German and Turkish), or no citizenship information.

Across the three countries, the results first showed that the two perceived loyalties were negatively associated which suggests that people tend to think more in terms of contrasting or divided loyalties rather than dual loyalties. Furthermore, compared to national citizens, dual citizens were perceived as having lower national loyalty and higher foreign loyalty. Compared to foreign citizens, dual citizens were perceived to have higher national loyalty but equally high foreign loyalty.[16] Furthermore, higher foreign loyalty was associated with more distrust, stronger reluctance to accept dual citizens in strategic positions, and lower acceptance of their social influence. Thus, people tended to trust immigrants less, and accept immigrants in strategic positions and accept their social influence less, when they had dual rather than single national citizenship of the country of residence.

In Chapter 6, I have discussed that the perceived reasons behind specific practices and beliefs matter for whether people will be less or more tolerant. Similarly, public concerns about divided loyalties might depend on the perceived reasons that immigrants have for naturalisation and acquiring dual nationality (Ditlmann et al., 2011; Politi et al., 2020). In addition to emotional attachment to the country of settlement and the wish to call it home, there can be instrumental reasons for applying for host society citizenship. Various studies have analysed the practical incentives of obtaining an additional citizenship, such as better opportunities, higher status, more extensive rights, and greater freedom of global movement (Diehl & Blohm, 2003; Harpaz, 2019). It is even argued that there is a worldwide trend to strategic citizenship (Harpaz & Mateos, 2019) in which the acquisition and use of citizenship is driven by the advantages that it brings (Joppke, 2019).

However, majority members can consider this instrumental orientation as lacking true emotional commitment and attachment which citizenship would require or imply. Specifically, immigrants who indicate that they apply for second citizenship mainly out of the emotional desire to belong to the national community might be considered more loyal to the country of settlement and less loyal to the country of origin, compared to those who mainly have instrumental reasons.

Using a survey experiment on a nationally representative sample of the native Dutch, we examined whether perceived national loyalty and political tolerance depend on whether immigrants themselves express emotional or rather instrumental reasons for having applied for and acquired their second, country of residence citizenship (Verkuyten et al., 2022b). We found that the reasons for naturalisation did indeed matter with emotional motivations for dual citizenship leading to higher perceived host country loyalty (and lower country of origin loyalty), compared to instrumental reasons. Furthermore, the perceived loyalties were similar when instrumental reasons or no reasons (control condition) were presented. This suggests that it is commonly assumed that immigrants want to acquire second citizenship mainly for strategic-instrumental reasons (Vink et al., 2019). Additionally, higher perceived host country loyalty was associated with higher political tolerance of immigrants with a dual citizenship.

In short, the reasons that immigrant minorities give for acquiring a second citizenship matter for majority member's perceptions of loyalty and political tolerance. Specifically, instrumental reasons for a second citizenship might be perceived as not demonstrating a readiness to be loyal to the host country which can fuel suspicions making political tolerance more difficult.

Adjustment and change

The clinical literature on so-called distress tolerance indicates that the unwillingness or inability to tolerate emotional distress can be addressed, for example, by adjustments and acceptance-based emotion regulation interventions (Leyro et al., 2010). Change and adjustment also occur in society and everyday life when specific practices and beliefs are no longer considered to be very controversial, threatening or regarded with alarm. Not everything can and will be tolerated, but what is considered intolerable can change. Threats can disappear, fears can fade, and differences that were considered reasons for concern can gradually be seen as common and even interesting; differences that were once unsettling can make little difference any more. Societies are not static and attitudes, beliefs, norms, institutions, and behaviour shift over time, sometimes gradually and sometimes rapidly (Varnum & Grossmann, 2021). Technological innovations, economic changes, and political constellations matter for cultural dynamics and social relationships. For example, in the United States, there has been between 2007 and 2018 a widespread decline in (explicit and implicit) prejudices towards sexual, racial, and age groups (Charlesworth & Banaji, 2021, 2022). This consistent reduction of prejudices across geographic areas and demographic groups indicates the importance of broad sociocultural changes. Furthermore, public opinion research in the US and UK has found a steady increase in tolerance towards a range of groups and practices over the years (Boch, 2020; Chong & Levy, 2018; Janmaat & Keating, 2019), and that the tolerance gap between college-educated and non-college educated has narrowed due to the increasing tolerance among the latter group (Campbell & Johnson, 2018). Additionally, the public acceptance of same-sex marriage and gay rights more generally has changed dramatically in the US which has been described as "moving a mountain" (Rosenfeld, 2017).

Furthermore, forms of positive intergroup contact might not only lead to less group-based prejudice (Al Ramiah & Hewstone, 2013) but also change the basis and strength of the disagreement, dislike, or disapproval of specific outgroup beliefs and practices (Chong, 1994; Ramos et al., 2019). Contact, mere exposure, and increased familiarity might over time lead to higher tolerance of things that one dislikes or disapproves of (e.g. same-sex marriage, gay rights, and building of minarets). The range of groups, beliefs, and practices that people adapt to and come to accept can expand. This change in the direction of greater acceptance implies that things that used to be controversial and intuitively resisted are now allowable variations from a standard: included in people's latitudes of acceptance, for example, by "recasting differences as diversity rather than deviance" (Prislin & Filson, 2009, p. 812). A large-scale study in Europe found that concern about immigration rises in the short to medium run but that there is a longer-term process of habituation and increased support for immigration (Claassen & McLaren, 2022).

People can get used to living around others with different cultural and religious beliefs, customs and practices, and can become more inured to things that once bothered them (e.g. Muslim headscarf). They are able to adapt psychologically to changing social standards and norms. Changes in policies and legal rules can change perceived social norms, which can be internalised and alter how one feels about what one tolerates (Bishin et al., 2016; Ofosu et al., 2019; Tankard & Paluck, 2017). New legal, political, and social norms can lead people to become more tolerant of things they first wanted to censor or repress.

The adjustment process implies that uncertainties, fears, and anxieties are assuaged and that one is able to engage in more reflective thinking; "as fears diminish, tolerance becomes less strained and more easily forthcoming" (Chong, 1994, p. 29). Importantly, this does not have to imply that people give up or compromise on their own convictions and beliefs, or do not continue to prefer their own over the conduct and belief of others. Rather, it means that they will be more likely to tolerate what they once thought was intolerable. They can still have objections, but these might be less strongly felt and thus involve less psychological tension and less need for self-restraint. Psychological adaptation means that people's feelings about the things that they tolerate can gradually change so that things that used to be controversial and intolerable become acceptable, even up to a point where the notion of "tolerance" loses much of its point. There can be a process of ethical fading and demoralisation where individuals increasingly reduce and withdraw their moral concerns about specific conduct (Tenbrunsel & Messick, 2004), as well as processes that works against moral polarisation, such as perspective taking, shared experiences, and cultural learning (see Kovacheff et al., 2018).

Higher tolerance is thus not necessarily based on increased self-restraint, but can be the result of psychological adjustment. The adjustment process diminishes people's objections making them in general more willing to support the right of others to live the life that they want. However, the adjustment process and increased acceptance of diversity may not uniformly change towards all types of difference. For example, in many countries, people have become less tolerant of smoking, soft drugs, and alcohol consumption in public. And while people can display increases in tolerance towards cultural, religious, or sexual differences, they may display higher intolerance towards ideological or viewpoint diversity. Research has found that younger generations tend to be more tolerant of a range of minority groups and minority practices (e.g. Janmaat & Keating, 2019), but at the same time that their tolerance for ideologically opposing points of view has declined (Chong & Levy, 2018). And in political science, there is an ongoing debate about whether political intolerance has decreased over the last decades or rather been redirected towards other least liked groups (e.g. from communists to ideological opponents; Mondak & Sanders, 2004).[17]

Furthermore, the adjustment process can also imply that people get used to radical rhetoric and exclusionary ideologies of the extreme right or the radical left. For example, the things that populist politicians are currently saying about immigrants and minorities and that was considered unacceptable not so long ago, is increasingly adopted by mainstream politicians. There can be a normalisation of radical ideologies which, among other things, negatively affects people's attitudes towards freedom of speech and their political tolerance of ideological opponents (Orazani et al., 2020).

Cultural differences

Social norms change and current beliefs and convictions differ from those in the past making things that were once controversial more common (e.g. same-sex marriage, birth control) and things that were once common no longer socially acceptable (e.g. smoking in public places, driving without a seatbelt, and using certain labels and words for groups of people). Furthermore, there are cultural differences in values, norms, and beliefs that matter for the tolerance process: e.g. smoking in public places is not considered unacceptable in all countries. Diversity of views, beliefs, and practices exist in all societies, and every culture will display some degree of tolerance and intolerance. Yet there are cross-national differences with liberal democracies being on average more open-minded, trustful, and well-disposed towards a range of divergent groups and practices. And there are country and state differences in the degree of tolerance in the social, moral, and political domain (e.g. Peffley & Rohrschneider, 2003; Rapp, 2017; Weldon, 2006; Widmalm, 2016), even between neighbouring countries such as Germany and the Netherlands (Erisen & Kentmen-Cin, 2017). For example, religious identity expression in the workplace is accepted more in European countries that are more religious (Van der Noll et al., 2018), and a history of being a colonial power or being a settler society is associated with being more accommodating where cultural rights for immigrant-origin groups are concerned (Koopmans & Michalowski, 2017). And within the US, followers of Christ in the state of Idaho are allowed to withhold medical care from their children on the basis of their religion, even if this could result in death.

These country and state differences have to do with political, legal, economic, and historical circumstances, the average level of education (i.e. cognitive abilities) and educational content (i.e. citizenship education), and with differences in emphasis and interpretation of specific moral values, as well as with distinct moralities. Tolerance implies a moral standard together with an allowable variation of that standard, and these standards and variations can differ between cultures. For example, individuals who grow up in a more collectivist culture are likely to emphasise tradition and conformity more than personal autonomy and self-determination. This could mean that the trade-off between these competing considerations will have a different outcome for (in)tolerance of divergent conduct, compared to people who are raised in an individualist culture. Furthermore, there can be cultural differences in the meaning and applicability of specific moral values. For example, what is considered "freedom" or "equality" can be interpreted differently,[18] similar to what are considered cases in which tolerance of free speech or intolerance of unequal treatment are at stake.

Additionally, there can be culture-specific moralities. For example, whereas free speech is highly valued in the US and also applies to what some consider "hate speech", this kind of speech is considered beyond tolerance by people in other countries that have hate speech legislation, such as in many European countries (e.g. Douglas-Scott, 1999; Harell, 2010). Furthermore, statements and utterances that in one country are considered unacceptable forms of criticism and disapproval (e.g. microaggressions) are seen very differently in other countries. And there are also more striking country differences. Research in Amman, Jordan, finds that 40% of adolescent boys and 20% of girls believe that killing a daughter, sister, or wife who has dishounored the family can be justified, and this belief is related to having a patriarchal worldview (Eisner & Ghuneim, 2013). Also, among Muslim populations in five Muslim-majority countries and four Western European countries, we found that around 40% (Muslim countries) and 30% (European countries) agreed that suicide bombings and other forms of violence are sometimes justifiable to defend one's religion (Zhirkov et al., 2014). These findings indicate that there can be cultural differences in the forms of violence that are considered virtuous (Fiske & Rai, 2015). And honour and respect for one's self, family, or community are not only more important in some parts of the world, but variability can emerge even within the same country, such as the culture of honour in the American South (Nisbett & Cohen, 1996).

These country and regional differences do not have to imply, however, that the psychological processes underlying tolerance differ. Specifically, the difference between intuitive and deliberative thinking probably is not culture specific, and neither is the cognitive dissonance with the related self-restraint and the need to weigh different reasons involved in tolerance. Cultural differences in reasoning do not presuppose distinct types of thinking, but rather can reflect culturally sensitive modes or styles (Yama, 2018). Cross-cultural research demonstrates that similar types of information can be processed and interpreted quite differently depending on the culture in which an individual grows up in. For example, research suggests that Westerners are more inclined to use rule-based reasoning, while Easterners tend to use dialectical thinking more (Peng & Nisbett, 1999). Dialectic thinking accepts contradiction and that the world is in flux and constantly changing (Spencer-Rogers et al., 2010). This could mean that Easterners tolerate moral disagreements and divergent practices more. For example, one study found that East Asian religiosity, but not Western Christian religiosity, was associated with higher acceptance of contradiction and therefore with higher tolerance of ethnic and moral outgroups (Clobert et al., 2017).

At the same time, it can be argued that Easterners will be less likely to be tolerant than Westerners. Tolerance requires self-restraint that is voluntary and not compelled or socially sanctioned. It involves a reflective thinking process and the internal motivation to refrain from negatively interfering with the disliked or disapproved of conduct of others. This means that tolerance does not depend on external control and social sanctions, making it a critical subjective ingredient for a peaceful diverse society. In collectivist cultures, however, descriptive social norms tend to be more important for behavioural regulation (Bond & Smith, 1996). This could mean that situations of non-interference with others' dissenting way of life are based less on internalised guidelines and more on social norm compliance with its anticipated positive or negative social sanctions. The result might be that tolerance is psychologically less common in Eastern than Western cultures, but it is not clear whether this is indeed the case. There is very little systematic research on cultural differences in tolerance and intolerance and the related psychological processes. However, this is not the only topic on which there is a lack of research. Another example is the important question of what it means to be tolerated, which is the topic of the next chapter.

8

BEING TOLERATED

In Chapter 2, I discussed the case of Felix Ngole who was excluded from a social work course by Sheffield University after posting a series of comments on Facebook on homosexuality and same-sex couples. Ngole appealed to a higher appeal committee in the university and later to the Court on the ground that the decision to exclude him was an interference with his rights to freedom of speech, conscience, and religion. In his online account, he explained that he migrated from Cameroon to Britain because of the opportunities he thought it offered "to be who we want to be" and the "right to exercise freedom of conscience at work" (Verkuyten, 2022a). Furthermore, he argued that it is not he who is intolerant, but rather the university for its "new political orthodoxy" that bars religious people and forces them to forswear their deep beliefs to prevent exclusion.

> They couldn't see the irony of their own intolerance of my views. If this is the way the system operates then it means that people like me and followers of Christ everywhere will be "barred from professions'; deemed "not fit for practise". . . . The new political orthodoxy coerces and compels a "way to think and a way to speak" – if you disagree you're left out in the cold.

He finds his exclusion from the course shocking, because it would mean that the university and country do not live up to their own credo of tolerance and religious freedom. In the online discussion that followed Ngole's account, many people agreed with the university's decision and called Ngole prejudiced, a homophobe, and a bigot (Verkuyten, 2022a). However, in several other posts, those supporting the university decision were accused of the bigotry and intolerance that they accused Ngole of ("Haven't you just practiced or condoned the exact same prejudice, bigotry & intolerance you have deemed Mr Ngole unfit to be a social worker?", "So you think Christians are wrong, bigoted, narrow minded or should just keep quiet about

DOI: 10.4324/9781003335030-8

everything, politics, sex and religion? If so you prove yourself to be bigoted, narrow minded and just as 'phobic' as you say this chap is!"), and that the development of autonomous thinking and freedom of conscience are required in social work. Different contributors to the discussion agreed with Ngole's argument that having and expressing strong beliefs should be tolerated, because it does not necessarily mean that one is negative towards others as human beings and will not treat them with dignity and respect ("He DISAGREES with the lifestyle of lesbian and gays. Did he say he hates LGBT's? No he didn't"; "How can people be so blind not to see that disagreeing with somethings is not the same as hating a person who does it"). For Ngole and his supporters, the university's decision was a clear example of intolerance. What would be needed is tolerance so that people are not afraid to speak their minds about issues that are really important to them and can practice their profession. Otherwise, Muslim social workers, for example, would also not be allowed to provide services to homosexuals, alcoholics, or single parents, and those who are pro-life would not be able to help with the implications of having an abortion.

There are many examples of people having heterodox views arguing for tolerance in light of the "new political orthodoxy" that is considered to censor and bar people and force them to forswear their beliefs to prevent (online) harassment, exclusion, and discrimination. Dissenting opinions and beliefs should be tolerated, it is argued, so that people can be their authentic self and follow their conscience. Experimental research has demonstrated that minority-caused change is more effective when that change increases the community's tolerance for a variety of positions rather than trying to convert community members (Prislin & Filson, 2009; Shafer & Prislin, 2011). Advocating for tolerance is a way of improving one's minority position, because it changes what is considered acceptable so that differences become redefined as diversity rather than deviance. With tolerance, there is a broadening of the standard of acceptability, without community members having to dilute, compromise, or give up on their own beliefs and position. And minorities who successfully increase tolerance within a group (vs. conversion), value the group more, are more likely to consider themselves members of the group and expect less group conflict.

A community, institution, organisation, or society can also be held accountable when not living up to their self-defining virtue of tolerance. The discourse of tolerance can be used by minority groups to argue for acceptance of their dissenting practices and beliefs. Ngole argued that the University, and Britain more generally, does not live up to its own credo of tolerance and religious freedom; Muslim minorities argue against an Euro-Islam by stating that Europe should honour the principles and standards of conduct that European states themselves profess to have developed in response to religious diversity (Yildiz & Verkuyten, 2012); people of colour can morally blame society and majorities for being intolerant rather than tolerant ("For many people of colour, the Netherlands is not so tolerant at all"; Verkuyten & Kollar, 2021); immigrants can resist societal demands for change and assimilation by mobilising the discourse of the self-proclaimed national tradition of tolerance for diversity (Omlo, 2011); and religious individuals and subgroups can argue that their religious community should practice the acceptance that it preaches and tolerate liminal behaviours and beliefs.

Tolerance is a useful discourse for minorities and a critical defence against censorship, oppression, discrimination and persecution of minority voices. It allows people to express their views and beliefs and to enact their identities, provides access to resources and rights, and protects them from violence. Specifically, tolerance gives minorities the freedoms and rights to define and develop their own ways of life, even in the face of irreconcilable differences. The demand and need for tolerance is especially strong in situations, settings, and countries in which people are not fully able to express their views, enact their identities, and live the life that they want. More authoritarian parents will be less likely to condone their children's dissenting behaviour; orthodox religious communities punish dissenters; radical social activists try to silence heterodox views; tribalists relish in the defeat and humiliation of adversaries; municipalities and regions can declare themselves as being LGTB-free zones (Poland); populist movements call for minority and dissident voices to be silenced; authoritarian regimes suppress dissenting political voices and persecute ideological opponents; and religious countries imprison homosexuals and even put them to death.

Sociological theories of protest movements argue that protest and collective action depends on the opportunities and constraints embedded in the societal and political context (Koopmans, 1999; Meyer & Minkoff, 2004; Tarrow, 2011). When the contextual opportunities (e.g. political rights and freedoms) exceed the constraints (e.g. repression and persecution) of participating in collective action, there is a higher chance that minority members will do so. Toleration acts as a barrier against oppression, hostility, and discrimination and therefore provides minority members the opportunity to engage in actions to achieve social change, free of the threat of repression. Furthermore, a tolerant setting might fuel minority group efficacy beliefs about being able to actually address the group-related disadvantages through collective effort (Van Zomeren et al., 2008). Additionally, for majority members, tolerance does not only have to take a "passive" form of not interfering with the disapproved of conduct of others, but can also take a more "active" form in supporting and defending the equal rights of dissenting others to make their case and practice their beliefs. The language of tolerance can provide a moral basis for engaging in struggles for equal treatment and inclusion of all.

Tolerance is necessary for diversity and a liberal society and democracy cannot exist without social and political tolerance in which minorities in particular are able to exercise their civil rights, express their views, and enact who and what they are. Disagreement, criticism, dislike, and disapproval are inevitable, but discrimination, exclusion, oppression, and domination are not: "to be the object of tolerance is a welcoming improvement on being the object of intolerance" (Horton, 1996, p. 35). However, tolerance can also have unintended negative consequences for those who are tolerated,

> Tolerance is like a gift that you don't really want. Many people see tolerance as a positive thing, but is it really? . . . On the one hand, tolerance can prevent oppression, but on the other it means that you see the other as inferior or undesirable.[1]

Considering the possible negative implications is important for a balanced evaluation of the pros and cons of a focus on tolerance as an indispensable ingredient for dealing with diversity.

Beyond mere tolerance

Tolerance is a critical aspect in any human relationship and arguably has become even more important in our increasingly diverse, polarised, and conflict-ridden societies. Nevertheless, for some, tolerance has transformed from a liberal virtue to a vice, making it necessary to go beyond *mere* tolerance. Critics argue that tolerance functions as a subtle social mechanism contributing to domination and inequality (Insel, 2019; Marcuse, 1969; Schirmer et al., 2012; Wemyss, 2006), and to the depoliticisation of diversity by reducing structural disadvantages to cultural group frictions (Brown, 2006). Tolerance would be inescapably patronising and an inadequate substitute for appreciation and full acceptance. Tolerance is considered to be offensive and hurtful for those who are tolerated, because by definition it implies disapproval of what one believes and practices, and can be seen as reproducing inequality and domination (Brown, 2006). Toleration can be considered "a word signifying power, domination and exclusion" (Forst, 2013, p. 3), and a well-known quote from the German thinker and writer, Johann Wolfgang von Goethe, states, "Tolerance should be a temporary attitude only: it must lead to recognition. To tolerate means to insult" (cited in Forst, 2013, p. 3).

Tolerance differs, however, in its normativity, not only between settings, cultures, and countries but also in relation to who is tolerated by whom and in relation to what. Ngole did not criticise the discourse of tolerance but actually asked for tolerance to be able to exercise freedom of conscience at work. Within a liberal democracy, tolerating an opponent that has a different ideological viewpoint or political opinion is expected, making the experience of being tolerated, and thus being able to express one's views and try to persuade others, common, desirable, and positive. In intellectual debates, people with heterodox views want to have the opportunity to express and explain what they think and belief and why. Furthermore, being tolerated can have benefits for people that have undesirable attributes (e.g. pedophilic desires without acting upon them) or have been involved in undesirable behaviour (ex-convicts). The experience of being tolerated can be a positive one when appreciation is not really necessary or feasible and tolerance is socially expected. Tolerance is "intermediate between wholehearted acceptance and unrestrained opposition" (Scanlon, 2003, p. 187) and being tolerated is in many situations and contexts the expected and preferred option.

However, the experience of being tolerated is likely to be different for ethnic, cultural, religious, and sexual minorities in liberal societies.[2] Tolerance might be considered patronising and therefore an inadequate substitute for the appreciation and full acceptance that these minority members need and deserve. For example, a slogan at a gay bar in Utrecht is "Go where you are celebrated, not where you are tolerated", and sexual minorities in Belgium argue,

> That is the problem with toleration: others determine if they tolerate you, which rules and norms you need to meet in order to be allowed to participate. As LGBTs, we do not want to be tolerated; we want to be respected.[3]

And in the next quote, the Turkish–Dutch writer Akyol is talking about his experiences as an ethnic minority member.

> If you say that you tolerate people you are actually saying "you are different, but we accept you." We turn a blind eye and accept that you are different. That's where I think it often goes wrong in the Netherlands. Because you should not say that people are different and we endure you. No, you should accept people because they are different. That is an essential difference. When you fully accept people, you do not tolerate them, if you see people as different human beings than you fully accept them.

Akyol rejects the discourse of tolerance as forbearance, because it involves marking people as different and therefore an "object" for toleration, instead of accepting them as "subjects", because they are different. He contrasts tolerance ("I can live with you") with fully accepting people for who and what they are ("you are okay"). Similarly, the Turkish–Dutch writer Özdil regularly states in debates "I do not want to be tolerated in my own land. I want equality", and "Toleration is no acceptance. Rather, toleration leads to segregation". And as a further example from a Jewish person:

> I do not want to be tolerated, I want to be accepted. Don't patronize me, be genuinely nice. I would prefer it if you even liked me; but if you don't, that's ok, because I don't like everyone, either. I will treat you with the kavod (respect) that you deserve, and I expect you to do the same. You might be different from me, and I might disagree with you, but I will accept that you are who you are.[4]

Ethnic, cultural, religious, and sexual minority members often want to be more than tolerated, whereby they equate tolerance with a lack of respect.[5] They are not so much interested in having their self-defining beliefs and practices being endured, but rather being recognised, welcomed, and appreciated (Bergsieker et al., 2010). Thus, in everyday life, being tolerated may not only have positive implications for some minorities but might also be offensive and hurtful, because it implies disapproval and dislike of what one believes and practices, and can be seen as reproducing inequality and domination. While many people consider it desirable to be tolerant, they typically do not find it desirable to be "put up with" (Honohan, 2013), and describing someone as tolerable has negative connotations.

While there is a substantial literature on the target's perspective that is concerned with the psychological implications of experiencing stigmatisation, rejection, and discrimination, and how social support, personal beliefs, and coping resources shape the meaning of these negative experiences (see Major et al., 2018), there has been little attention on the psychological implications of being the target of toleration. In our theoretical and empirical works, we have focused on the experience of being tolerated among ethnic, cultural, and sexual minorities, and considered the possible (unintended) psychological consequences for those who are tolerated.

To be tolerated

From the target's perspective, the implied devaluation of one's social identity practices and beliefs and the asymmetrical nature of non-interference are the two key aspects of toleration that can be expected to have negative implications (see Figure 8.1). I, therefore, discuss these aspects in more detail.

Devaluation

What is being tolerated transgresses or deviates from what is considered appropriate and right and many "objects" of tolerance are perceived to be deviant, marginal, or undesirable (Brown, 2006). With toleration, the objection towards ethnic, cultural, religious, and sexual minority beliefs and practices is implicitly affirmed and the implied deviance can threaten a valued minority group membership for the target of tolerance. There is clear empirical evidence that identity devaluation and identity threat have negative psychological consequences (e.g. Major et al., 2013; Meyer, 2003), and this might also be the case in relation to being tolerated.

Further and in contrast to discrimination, tolerance creates a moral distinction, which places the target of toleration in a morally disadvantaged position, which might have detrimental psychological consequences. Being tolerant is well

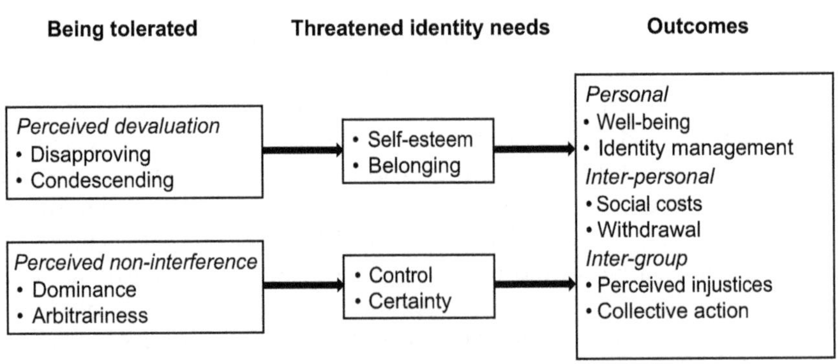

FIGURE 8.1 Process model of being tolerated, social identity needs and outcomes

Source: Taken from Verkuyten et al. (2020b)

regarded by most people, normatively promulgated in many domains of life, and typically considered a sign of virtue and moral character (Horton, 1996). As a result, people can feel morally superior towards those they tolerate, when they endure something they disapprove of:

> When the heterosexual tolerates the homosexual, when Christians tolerate Muslims in the West, not only do the first terms *not* require tolerance but their standing as that which confers tolerance establishes their superiority over that which is said to require tolerance.
>
> *(Brown, 2006, p. 186, emphasis in original)*

It is morally laudable to refrain from interfering with what one could censor or prevent because one has reasons for acceptance (e.g. religious freedom) that outweigh the reasons for objection (e.g. ritual slaughter of animals). Individuals and groups may be strongly motivated to identify and maintain the moral high ground of being those who tolerate, because people do not want to consider themselves or their ingroup less virtuous (see Ellemers, 2017). While this does not have to mean that the tolerated are evil, it introduces a relative interpersonal or intergroup differentiation in favour of those who tolerate (Tajfel & Turner, 1979). As a result, the targets of toleration can feel that they are put in a relative position of moral inferiority. Being tolerated can be experienced as an act of generosity and good will whereby one should be thankful for being allowed to express one's minority identity.

Non-interference

Toleration often has something inescapably patronising about it. This has to do with the inequality involved in toleration and with its conditional nature. First, toleration can legitimise and reinforce the dominance of those who extend the tolerance and thereby confirms the inequality and relative powerlessness of those that are tolerated. With toleration, the practices and policies of toleration can be perceived as confirming and justifying existing power differences and the subordinate position of ethnic, cultural, religious, and sexual minority groups (i.e. second-class citizen). This is expressed in a public speech by Leroy Lucas, a minority activist, saying, "I refuse to be a bit-player who is tolerated in his own house. White Dutch people talk about the tolerant Netherlands. Let me be clear: I refuse to be tolerated in my own country".[6]

The powerful defines the terms and limits of toleration. For example, beliefs and practices related to minority group identities (e.g. not shaking hands with people of the opposite gender, wearing of a headscarf) can be confined to the private domain while the general normative principles and values of the majority group apply to the public sphere. A policy of toleration can thus imply the privatisation of immigrants' cultures (e.g. Yogeeswaran et al., 2011). For instance, Denmark's assimilation policy constitutes toleration with the privatisation of dissenting cultural practices. While minorities are not coerced into adopting the majority culture, they are expected to keep their own culture as much as possible in the private sphere (Tawat, 2014). This would mean that a true minority group believer can only be a Muslim or a Jew at home or in their own religious community.

Second, toleration can operate as an arbitrary exercise of power, because it depends on voluntary self-restraint of those who are able to interfere. The tolerator might at any point decide that there is no need to keep on tolerating the dissenting other. There can always be a sudden or gradual change in the tolerator's inclination not to interfere leaving the tolerated in an insecure position and dependent on the continuing good will of the tolerator.[7] The tolerated may, in turn, experience fear and anxiety that any actions of themselves or their group can risk upsetting the dominant group and losing the permission of following their own way of life: "The barely tolerated must be constantly alert to the moods and policy swings of the barely tolerant, for they know that they avoid serious trouble only at their sufferance" (Oberdiek, 2001, p. 29). Being constantly subject to the threat of intervention is risky and psychologically taxing and can function as a form of oppression (Honohan, 2013; Lovett, 2010).

Awareness and understanding of being tolerated

Ethnic, cultural, religious, and sexual minority members are not passive victims of majority members' negative attitudes and behaviour, but active agents who construe and negotiate their identities and social situations in service of their own goals. For example, research on the target's perspective has considered the ways in which stigmatised and discriminated group members construe negative experiences and cope with the threats they face (Major et al., 2018; Richman & Leary, 2009). Minority members can demonstrate either vulnerability or resilience, and biopsychosocial research has demonstrated that discrimination can also be experienced as a challenge and a possibility for improvement (Scheepers, 2013). The consequences depend on whether the discrimination is recognised and how it is interpreted. For example, not recognising discrimination might protect one's wellbeing (Crocker & Major, 1989), but failing to view events as discrimination also has negative psychological costs (Sechrist et al., 2004). Similarly, the consequences of being tolerated might depend on awareness and interpretation of toleration, the reasons for being tolerated, and the perceived (in)equality of the relevant intergroup relations.

Hence, a first step in our research was to determine whether the experience of being tolerated is familiar to minority group members. We examined this in different ways among ethnic and sexual minorities in Turkey, the Netherlands, and the US, and also among disabled individuals in Turkey (Bağci et al., 2020; Cvetkovska et al., 2020, 2021). For example, following previous research that used straightforward and single questions to measure perceived discrimination, we asked ethnic minority members in the Netherlands, "To what extent do you think that [Turks/Moroccans/Surinamese/Antilleans] are [discriminated against/appreciated/tolerated] in the Netherlands?". Similar to discrimination and acceptance, toleration can mean different things and direct questions allow participants to respond in terms of their own understandings and experiences. Additionally, participants were asked "In your opinion, which of the following best describes how [Turks/Moroccans/Surinamese/Antilleans] are treated in the Netherlands?", and they could choose between the three options of discrimination, tolerance and appreciation.[8] On this latter question, 39.8% indicated that being tolerated is the most common experience of their ethnic minority group (discriminated against, 24.7%; appreciation, 35.5%) and this aligned with the degree to which their group experienced being tolerated. Hence, being tolerated was considered a relatively common experience which we also found in our other studies in which we asked about personal experiences, provided a description of the three experiences and used more extensive measures. Furthermore, the findings show that minority members make a distinction between experiences of being tolerated, appreciated, and discriminated against. Perceived toleration was always seen as in-between being appreciated and being discrimination against, but with tolerance in some contexts being more similar to appreciation and in other contexts as more similar to discrimination.[9]

Experiences of being tolerated

Our findings indicate that the experience of being tolerated is quite common among various minority members. However, given the ambiguity and complexity of tolerance, it is important to further consider whether and how people perceive and interpret being tolerated. Tolerance implies holding objections to others' practices and beliefs but not negatively interfering with their behaviour, and this might be difficult to recognise and evaluate because it manifests in inaction. While situations involving being discriminated against can sometimes be ambiguous, this is even truer in situations where one is being tolerated.

In general, minority individuals can be expected to be aware, for example, of the societal disapproval of their dissenting cultural and religious beliefs and practices. Most Muslim minorities know that many majority members evaluate Islamic beliefs and practices negatively (e.g. Pew, 2017), and most immigrant groups know that some of their cultural beliefs and practices are considered normatively deviant (e.g. Huijnk & Andriessen, 2016). At the same time, it might be more difficult to recognise that these negative evaluations do not lead to exclusion and discrimination, but rather to toleration. The majority can explicitly state that some beliefs and practices will be "put up with", or minority members can experience that they are conditionally allowed to practice their culture or religion (e.g. in private, but not in public). But minority members' awareness that others disapprove, but nevertheless endure, their dissenting cultural practices still force them to determine what interpretations to make about specific situations, events and incidents that they encounter.

Thus, being the target of toleration depends not only on awareness but also on interpretations and construals that provide an understanding of the experience.

While discrimination can be attributed to prejudice, toleration is more ambiguous as it leaves the perceiver with two sets of considerations: the reasons for disapproval of one's minority beliefs and practices and the additional reasons to nevertheless endure these. Or as an interviewee in one of our studies said: "I mean to an extent it's really hard to draw lines between things or even between, for me, between like being tolerated and just not being accepted at all because it's hard to tell what people think".

The resulting ambiguity can be cognitively demanding and taxing and might lead to relatively strong feelings of uncertainty that threatens a sense of predictability and control (Guinote et al., 2006). Furthermore, research has demonstrated that positive behaviours can be attributionally ambiguous, and minorities can sometimes regard such behaviour from majority members with suspicion and uncertainty. To convey a non-prejudiced image, majority members sometimes show support and amplify their positivity towards members of ethnic and other minorities (e.g. Mendes & Koslov, 2013). As a result, it is difficult for minority members to tell whether these positive responses are genuine or should be viewed with scepticism.

Tolerance may be a source of uncertainty and threat when minorities suspect that majority members are motivated by a desire to appear tolerant and are hiding group-based antipathy behind more principled claims of disapproval (see Major & Kunstman, 2013). The uncertainty might make targets on guard during daily interactions. The resulting vigilant state is, for example, typically accompanied by a pattern of maladaptive cardiovascular responses that in time can have negative health outcomes (Derks & Scheepers, 2018). Additionally, the uncertainty can also undermine one's self-confidence and sense of belonging, and reduces one's task motivation and performance (Shelton et al., 2006).

It is unclear what cues targets use to decide whether others are acting out of tolerance, and the experience of being tolerated might have various meanings. In one study, we examined the meaning of being tolerated by conducting in-depth interviews[10] among trans and nonbinary people in the Netherlands[11] (Cvetkovska et al., 2022a). From the perspective of societies structured around binary notions of gender, trans people are usually seen as violating established gender roles and are tolerated at best (Pearce, 2018; Serano, 2007). Non-cisgender people are often considered "anomalies that require explanation and justification" (Serano, 2007, p. 57), rather than part of the normal spectrum of human variation. There often is an expectation for LGBTQ+ people to keep their identities confined to the private sphere and refrain from attempting to destabilise the gendered social order (Buijs et al., 2011; Van Lisdonk et al., 2018).

Using thematic analysis, we identified two main themes in the interviews related to tolerance as perpetuating inequality, and tolerators' misunderstandings of trans identity and experience. First, interviewees were aware of the widely shared positive social representation of tolerance. Comparing tolerance to discrimination, the former was also seen more positively and it was explained, for example, that "Yeah definitely, yeah when someone tolerates me I can just yeah be myself".

However, most interviewees interpreted tolerance as something rather negative and noticed that tolerators usually thought that their tolerant behaviour was virtuous. Several interviewees referred to tolerance as the "bare minimum" while claims of tolerance were also considered "hypocritical" and as "this magical word . . . to say how inclusive you are", without "hav[ing] to do anything". Many interviewees' encounters with being tolerated seemed superficially respectful, but respondents found that "when people tolerate you, they don't necessarily respect you". Tolerance was referred to as a "passive" phenomenon, or "a general let-live-ness, but that's about it". And the conditionality of tolerance would differentiate it from appreciation and full acceptance: whereas "acceptance doesn't come with conditions", with tolerance "there's always like a 'but'". One interviewee explained the difference as follows:

> I think in situations where I'm being tolerated I feel like I feel much more like I'm allowed to be there, but there is some sort of distance. So in the way in the interaction it often feels a bit more distant and very much more formal where I think acceptance being around people that just fully accepting are much more informal and much more I think yeah, and being tolerated yeah it's much more formal way of interacting with others . . . being more like okay I will talk to you about like the weather, I will shake your hand but if I don't have to talk to you or be near you, I won't. I will just leave you and that feels that those moments have felt more like being tolerated in the same space but not really being accepted [which] is more about there's like a person behind it and we can talk about different things and maybe have things in common.

Some interviewees also felt that being tolerated was like "a very insecure place to be" and making them to censor themselves to ensure their safety.

> Being tolerated . . . puts a pressure on me to behave a certain way for [people] to tolerate me. . . . I just feel anxious because I feel like it's kind of something that I could lose in the blink of an eye if I speak up too much or like express myself too much.

Additionally, it was pointed out that others' tolerance was more forthcoming if one did not ask for accommodations: "if you demand any kind of change then you're suddenly an obstruction and then I guess tolerance can be revoked". Tolerance was considered to extend from a position of privilege, which would be threatened by trans people's demands for change. The few interviewees who chose to confront their tolerators recounted facing "huge backlash", which discouraged further attempts at redress. Claims by people of being tolerant would often function as a mechanism preventing a critical discussion about continuing inequalities.

Second, tolerance was considered to be based on a misunderstanding and a lack of recognition of their trans identity. For example, one interviewee recounted being caught between the need to be tolerated and the need to be true to themselves: "I've felt the impulse to present more masculine to make it clearer that I'm not a woman, even though the masculine gender expression did not make me comfortable". Some interviewees also reported feeling disappointed and frustrated when the tolerance of their gender did not resonate with their experiences. The imperative to strive towards a "cis-passing" expression to secure tolerance conveyed that being cisgender was considered the norm while trans people were seen as deviations from that norm. Interviewees reported feeling "lesser than" when they were the objects of tolerance and noted signs of tolerators' disapproval such as stares or negative remarks. They also felt "other" or "exotic" when being tolerated, and as being positioned as "falling outside the norm".

However, it is also possible that trans individuals feel pressured by other trans people, and increasingly also by the wider society, to self-identity as a transgender rather than in terms of the gender they have changed to and prefer. A women who had her transition 30 years ago explains in a newspaper interview: "I am a woman, but not mentioning my transition is not done anymore. Nowadays I am afraid that the reaction is: you are not a women, you are a transgender and you do not accept that". According to her, she is constantly being called a transphobe and a "Terf" (Trans Exclusionary Radical Feminist) which makes any discussion almost impossible.[12] This is another example of the relevance and importance of tolerance of minorities within minorities.

Being tolerated and social identity needs

Misrepresentations of trans experiences can create a number of threats to trans subjects' identities. For example, it can raise the question of how to satisfy different social identity needs, because trying to secure one's safety and belonging might come at the price of invisibility or inauthenticity. There are different possible theoretical frameworks for conceptualising and investigating the psychological consequences of being tolerated, such as the minority stress framework (Meyer, 2003), strain theory (Agnew, 2001), a biopsychological perspective (Clark et al., 1999), and a risk and resilience framework (Masten, 2014). However, a key aspect of being tolerated is that the enactment of one's minority group identity is at stake, which means that social identity processes are involved. Therefore, a social identity perspective can provide a theoretical understanding of the psychological implications of being tolerated. Specifically, notions developed in Identity Process Theory (Breakwell, 2015; Vignoles, 2011) and the concept of social identity threat are useful to discuss the relation between being tolerated and its possible personal, interpersonal, and intergroup consequences (see Figure 8.1).

Social identities can satisfy general psychological needs by providing, for example, a feeling of relatedness, value, efficacy, and security (e.g. Vignoles, 2011; Williams, 2001). One implication is that the negative role of toleration for psychological well-being and functioning depends on the extent to which the fulfilment of social identity needs is undermined or threatened (Greenaway et al., 2016). For example, research has revealed that satisfaction of needs for self-esteem, belonging, efficacy, and meaning predicts higher positive affect, and that identity needs influence possible desired and feared future selves (see Vignoles, 2011). Furthermore, when the fulfilment of those needs are threatened, people engage in various identity management strategies (Breakwell, 2015).

However, the literature on social identity needs is rather fragmented and different needs have been proposed by different theorists. For example, social identity theory emphasises the importance of self-esteem and distinctiveness (Tajfel & Turner, 1979), and others emphasise a sense of belonging, a sense of control and efficacy, and self-certainty that social identities can give. Thus, individuals would be motivated to adopt and construct social identities that allow them, for example, to think positively about themselves in relation to others, give them the feeling that they belong to groups, make them feel competent and in control, and provide them with a sense of certainty about who and what they are.

As discussed, the perceived devaluation and the power imbalance nature of the non-interference are the two key aspects of being tolerated. These two aspects are likely to negatively affect the satisfaction of specific social identity needs for self-esteem and belonging, and for control and certainty (Hogg, 2001; Vignoles, 2011; Williams, 2001). In our research in Turkey among Kurdish minority members, LGTBI members, and disabled people, we found that higher perception of being tolerated is associated with a lower sense of identity-based self-esteem, belonging, and control (Bağci et al., 2020). Importantly, these associations were found over and beyond the negative correlates of the experience of being discriminated against. And in research among racial and ethnic minority members in the United States, we found that independent of perceived discrimination, being tolerated was negatively associated with a sense of control (Cvetkovska et al., 2021).

As shown in Figure 8.1, the two key elements of being tolerated are likely to threaten different identity needs with negative consequences for the tolerated persons. The devaluation aspect of toleration is most likely to be associated with reduced feelings of self-esteem and a reduced sense of belonging. Having one's minority identity questioned or feeling that one is limited in expressing and enacting one's identity or has to conceal it in some (public) situations can be emotionally costly. It lowers self-esteem and self-confidence (Barreto et al., 2006), and can heighten feelings of inauthenticity (Newheiser & Barreto, 2014). Furthermore, the condescending nature of toleration can imply that those who are tolerant are considered morally superior (more virtuous) compared to the dissenting others that are tolerated. For minority members, this unfavourable intergroup comparison can have a negative impact on their self-esteem. Furthermore, the devaluation implied in toleration can have negative consequences for people's need for social belonging and relatedness, which is fundamental for well-being (Baumeister & Leary, 1995). Being tolerated might undermine the fulfilment of this need, as it implies that one is considered deviant and not fully accepted in society. The implied "otherness" means that those who are tolerated are not fully included and do not really belong, which can reduce their sense of belonging and heightens feelings of misfit.

Second, the non-interference aspect of tolerance is likely to be especially problematic for a sense of control and a feeling of certainty. The conditional non-interference can affect people's sense of self-determination, or in attributional terms, their perceived control which is important for psychological well-being and effective functioning (Ryan & Deci, 2017). People's sense of control and efficacy is linked to their social identity and the perceived ability of themselves as group members and of their group as a whole to achieve its goals (Vignoles, 2011). Being tolerated implies that, to some extent, what one can do depends on others' continuing good will and the conditions that they choose to set. This situation can diminish a sense of control and efficacy to freely determine one's own life. It can make minority members feel restricted in their identity choices and less authentic, resulting in negative affect and lower well-being (Sanchez, 2010).

The conditional non-interference might also increase uncertainty. There is the ever-present risk of losing permission that has been granted and fear that prohibitions or restrictions of certain practices may emerge. For example, the last decade has seen a diminishing space for tolerance of Muslim minority practices in various Western countries. There is an increasing sense of conditional acceptance of Muslim practices, which has been described as a new type of liberal intolerance (Mouritsen & Olsen, 2013). Because tolerance depends on the good will or mercy of the dominant group, it can create a sense of uncertainty about whether it will be possible to continue to live the Muslim life that one wants. Feeling uncertainty about the social world, oneself, or one's ingroup is highly aversive and can lead to negative health outcomes (Derks & Scheepers, 2018). It is often linked to feelings of unease, anxiety, and distress and motivates attempts at uncertainty management and resolution (Hogg, 2001).

Outcomes of being tolerated

The nature of being tolerated and the four social identity needs that are most likely to be involved suggest that the experience of being tolerated may have different negative implications at different levels, and the personal, interpersonal, and intergroup level in particular (Figure 8.1).

Personal outcomes

Experiences of overt and subtle discrimination have negative consequences for psychological well-being, including negative physiological stress responses (Harrell et al., 2003), physical and mental health (Pascoe & Smart Richman, 2009), and adolescents biological weathering (Brody et al., 2016). However, discrimination experiences differ considerably in their specific features. For example, having to deal with long-term and pervasive discrimination can be expected to have a more detrimental effect compared to a single incident of discrimination. And facing discrimination in various social contexts, or by many people, is likely to be more problematic than facing discrimination in a single context, or by a single person. Furthermore, individuals differ in their coping strategies and the emotional and practical support that they can draw upon in dealing with discrimination (Major et al., 2018). It is likely that similar factors and conditions are also relevant for understanding the possible negative psychological consequences of being tolerated.

In our research among Kurdish, LGTB, and disabled people in Turkey, we found that independent of perceived discrimination, higher perceived tolerance was associated with lower positive well-being and stronger feelings of depression and anxiety (Bağci et al., 2020). Furthermore, our mini-meta analysis showed small to moderate effect sizes with being tolerated being associated with lower positive well-being through threatened identity needs across the three minority groups.

Similarly, in three studies among racial and ethnic minority members in the United States, we found that perceived toleration was independently associated with higher negative well-being (Cvetkovska et al., 2021). In a first study, and by taking perceived discrimination and trait-like negative emotionality into account, the results showed that being tolerated was independently related to more negative well-being (negative affect and lack of a sense of control). Thus, the negative implications of being tolerated do not simply reflect an underlying trait-like predisposition to see the world in a negative way.

In the second study, we conducted an experiment in order to establish whether the perception of being tolerated negatively affects (situational) well-being. Previous research has found that being reminded of and recalling experiences of discrimination undermine well-being (see Schmitt et al., 2014), and we expected to find this to be the case also for being tolerated. We had minority members recall experiences of being discriminated against, being tolerated, or being appreciated and measured well-being outcomes, while again also assessing the potential confounding role of trait-like negative emotionality. We found that positive affect was lower in the tolerance condition compared to the appreciation condition, but higher compared to the discrimination condition. The pattern for negative affect was reversed with the tolerance condition again being intermediate between appreciation and discrimination.

In the third study, we aimed to experimentally test whether being tolerated (compared to being appreciated and discriminated against) results in lowered well-being because of threatened social identity needs. We used a different experimental manipulation by asking participants to closely read a vignette that clearly illustrated experiences of facing tolerance, discrimination, or appreciation. The results again showed that being tolerated results in more positive affect and less negative affect than being discriminated against, but less positive and more negative affect than being appreciated. However, being tolerated did not differ from being discriminated against in terms of the threat it presented to social identity needs, and both situations were perceived as more threatening than being appreciated. Moreover, we found that higher threat to social identity needs was responsible for the link between increased negative affect and being tolerated as opposed to being appreciated.

In support of our process model (Figure 8.1), the findings of these studies among different minority groups in Turkey and the US indicate that being tolerated can be experienced by ethnic, sexual, and disabled minority members as condescending, conditional, and identity-threatening. For these minority members, being tolerated seems to be an experience that is intermediate between appreciation and discrimination and can have negative psychological consequences compared to being appreciated. In a further study among ethnic minority group members in the Netherlands, we found that being tolerated was associated with more negative affect than being appreciated, because being appreciated was more strongly associated with a sense of national belonging (Cvetkovska et al., 2020). Additionally, when minority members felt that their group was tolerated rather than discriminated against in Dutch society, they showed higher national identification, which was associated with higher well-being.

Interpersonal outcomes

Research shows that claims of having been discriminated against have social costs. Disadvantaged group members who claim discrimination are less valued by majority members (Kaiser & Miller, 2001) and sometimes also by fellow minority group members (Garcia et al., 2005). Those who attribute their disadvantaged situation or unfavourable outcomes to subtle (but also overt) discrimination can be perceived as complainers and troublemakers and as avoiding personal responsibility for their situation and outcomes (Garcia et al., 2005; Kaiser, 2006).

Identifying and confronting "being endured" might have similar interpersonal costs. While people in many places across the world recognise that it is wrong to discriminate (and it is illegal to do so in many countries), they may not as easily recognise the potential harms of being the target of toleration. First, tolerance is typically seen as morally praiseworthy, making it difficult to demonstrate to others how toleration can be harmful. Second, whereas discrimination implies interference, toleration involves non-interference and it might be difficult to convince others, including bystanders (Krolikowski et al., 2016), of the harmful consequences of being tolerated. As a result, complaints about toleration might be seen as unreasonable, unjustified, and demanding, similar to the discrediting of those who face and contest implicit biases or forms of microaggression (Jones et al., 2016). Complaints might result in majority members further limiting the boundaries of toleration and weighing their reasons for objections towards minority practices to be more important than the reasons for acceptance.

Minority members may, therefore, refrain from identifying and discussing the possible negative implications of being tolerated with majority members. But not discussing these implications can cause targets of toleration to feel angry and disappointed, especially among those who think that they should directly confront the treatment (Shelton et al., 2006). People may try to avoid majority group members and start to withdraw from society. Feeling devalued and being conditionally accepted implies a sense of vulnerability which may lead to distancing oneself from people whose acceptance cannot be fully trusted. Research on interracial interactions has found that minority members are wary regarding interactions with majority members in which they might feel devalued, rejected, or conditionally accepted (Shelton & Richeson, 2006). Furthermore, feelings of uncertainty, but also a lack of a sense of belonging and of control, and not being valued, can lead to a more exclusive orientation on one's minority community that is more likely to furnish these feelings and thereby protects one's well-being (Hogg, 2001; Schmitt & Branscombe, 2002). Feeling socially devalued and conditionally accepted may lead people to seek alternative groups that fulfil their various needs, and their minority community is likely to do that.

Being tolerated potentially threatens important motivational goals of cultural, religious, and sexual minority group members leading to identity management strategies (Breakwell, 2015). Specifically, there are various possible forms of protective and avoidance behaviour. For example, the tolerated can try to prevent arbitrary interference in their lives by being relatively invisible and hiding their identity-defining beliefs and practices. It could lead to strategies of identity concealment (e.g. Plante et al., 2014; Quinn & Earnshaw, 2011) and avoidance strategies in fear of provoking the dominant other and to engage in behaviour that reduces or prevents interference in their lives (e.g. taking off one's headscarf in public places). However, it might also lead to confrontation strategies.

In our interview study with trans people, a salient dilemma recounted by several interviewees was whether to confront tolerators or withdraw from them. Both strategies were considered to have benefits and drawbacks. When deciding whether to confront being tolerated, interviewees acknowledged the value of educating cisgender people, for example, by helping them "[get] to know more about [trans] experiences", and providing them with "the right tools and a decent amount of time", and "rather have [people] discuss stuff with [me] than like making their minds up on their own". It was said that they would try to "plant a seed" of understanding, but that it was the other person's responsibility to nurture that seed. Participants were more likely to advocate for themselves if they perceived the tolerating person as receptive to "having their assumptions challenged". Receptivity was a sign of "respecting someone enough to make an effort for them", while a lack of receptivity threatened peoples' self-efficacy making avoidance strategies more likely (Minson & Chen, 2022).

Outside of these sorts of teaching moments, most interviewees preferred to remain within a "bubble" of fellow trans people. Some favoured a strategy of psychological withdrawal and avoiding the topic: "With family, I just kind of like bury [my feelings]. . . . I'm just kind of like well, we're seeing the family today so we're gonna struggle". Others went a step further and withdrew physically: "[There are] people in my family that I completely cut contact with. . . . I feel that it's such a drain on my mental health to even try [to make them understand]". When supportive environments were not available, interviewees chose to isolate themselves from threats to identity and safety. It was explained that one tried to "disappear" in order to avoid censure or would "try to change the subject" because "these are issues where once you start talking, it can easily become a huge argument". Rather, being alone would make it possible to be oneself and nurture resilience: "I want to find my own space where I can feel and be myself and where I don't feel those kinds of negative energies".

Intergroup outcomes

According to one trans interviewee, tolerance "take[s] the side of the oppressor" by not standing against inequality: "tolerance is the status quo. Tolerance is like, okay you fought for this . . . but you still gotta fight for all the other things that you haven't achieved yet". Some of our interviewees publicly opposed tolerance and were involved in protest in the form of collective action and advocacy. They would "show up to protests", contribute by "filling up the crowd", call upon so-called "deviants" to "aggressively fight against tolerance" and proclaiming "I refuse to be tolerated". For them, "the principal thing behind the fight against tolerance is about equity and justice", and protesting tolerance "Is effort and hassle and it might not endear me to people but yeah, I feel that this is work that I need to do". Furthermore, policies advocating tolerance rather than acceptance were criticised by some: "I've been cursing the tolerance discourse of COC [mainstream Dutch LGBT organization] for a long time and finally, hopefully also thanks to my always cursing them for that, they gave in and they changed their discourse". The tolerance discourse was considered inadequate for active resistance and for empowering as a source of efficacy and esteem. Toleration would be a discourse and practice of depoliticisation preventing a real critical discussion and actual change, also because

> the Dutch tend to fall back on like "but we're so tolerant so we don't have to discuss this, we're tolerant" so it's kind of like a defense mechanism also almost where a lot of the times Dutch people will hide behind their shield of tolerance where they say "but we don't, we aren't racist", or "we aren't homophobic or transphobic or xenophobic" or all of those things because we're tolerant, we're tolerant people, we're a tolerant country, we accept everyone.

These statements resemble the critical analysis of the discourse of tolerance as repressive (Marcuse, 1969), being a "velvet glove" (Jackman, 1994), and a strategy for regulating aversion (Brown, 2006), that I discussed in Chapter 2. In social psychology, the process of politicisation is typically examined in terms of the endorsement of, and participation in, actions that aim to improve the rights, power and influence of disadvantaged minority groups (Tajfel & Turner, 1979). Successful social change typically requires raising one's voice and collective action by minority members, and this is most likely when the intergroup structure is considered unjust and unstable. The social identity model of collective action (Van Zomeren et al., 2008) proposes that perceived injustice, a sense of collective efficacy, and a strong (politicised) minority identity, independently, and in combination, drive collective action.

As discussed earlier in relation to the importance of opportunity structures, tolerance makes collective action more feasible and likely and can fuel a sense of collective efficacy. After all, tolerance is a barrier against discrimination, oppression, and persecution which makes it possible to act together for social change. And when recognition and appreciation rather than tolerance is normatively expected, it is more likely that those who are tolerated react to the negative evaluation involved in being tolerated. Sexual minority members have much more opportunities for protests and collective action in a liberal democracy than within an authoritarian or a so-called illiberal democratic regime: in this respect, there is a large difference between liberal democracies and countries such as Poland, Hungary, Turkey, and Russia, let alone most Islamic countries.

However, and despite the opportunity structure, the three aspects of the social identity model of collective action might imply that in comparison to, for example, experiences with overt forms of discrimination, toleration could lead minority members in liberal democracies to attend less to group-based disparities and thereby decrease forms of collective action that challenge disparities.

First, tolerance is typically presented as a strategy of protection against oppression and for promoting equality in a culturally diverse society (Vogt, 1997). The value of tolerance is often understood as a value of justice, and tolerance would serve justice by reducing group-based inequalities. This means that toleration makes it more difficult to perceive and understand intergroup devaluation and injustices that result from toleration than from discrimination. Furthermore, tolerance implies the "good grace" and virtuous nature of the majority which provides little justification for direct action against them (Wright & Baray, 2012), even if structural disadvantages persist. It is psychologically more difficult to question and stand up against those who are considered virtuous and with good intent than towards those who are considered to discriminate, dominate and oppress. According to our interviewees the notion of tolerance as virtuous presents difficulties for making demands; "I feel like a lot of people who tolerate me expect me to be kind of grateful", and "You're allowed to take the train, so can't complain there, right?".

Second, tolerance places minorities in a dependent position and thereby reduces their perceived sense of group-based control and related feelings of collective efficacy. A perceived lack of control undermines a sense of group efficacy and can reduce the willingness of the tolerated group to act collectively against social injustice and inequality. Furthermore, the toleration discourse emphasises that people are permitted as much as possible to live the life that they want. This might stimulate the belief in an individual mobility structure in which societal failure stems from individual shortcomings rather than group disadvantages that should be addressed as a collective (Tajfel & Turner, 1979). It can lead minority members to attend less to group-based disparities and to engage less in collective action that challenge these disparities.

Third, tolerance runs the risk of reducing minority identification needed for collective action. Social identity theory proposes that identification with the disadvantaged group predicts engagement in collective action (Tajfel & Turner, 1979).

Stronger group identification is associated with a greater commitment to one's group and stronger involvement in trying to achieve group-related goals. Identification serves to mobilise people for social change, especially when there is a politicised collective identity that focuses on the struggle for power in the public domain (Simon & Klandermans, 2001). Being discriminated against tends to increase minority group identification and thereby engagement in collective action (e.g. Stronge et al., 2016). In contrast, in our research among ethnic minority groups in the United States and the Netherlands, we have found that being tolerated is not associated with minority group identification (Cvetkovska et al., 2020, 2021). Rather, being tolerated was found to be associated with a stronger feeling of being part of the larger society which makes collective action less likely.

Further experimental tests

The experience of being tolerated as a minority member occurs in many different situations and can be based on other characteristics than ethnicity, culture, or sexual orientation. It is likely that in a situation of more equal relations, the experience of being tolerated is less negative than in an unequal situation. And whereas being tolerated for one's political and ideological views is expected and common, appreciation might be more normative for religious beliefs or sexual orientations. Furthermore, there are various situations in which tolerance can be important, such as in organisational and institutional contexts. Considering these sorts of contexts makes it possible to further examine and conceptually replicate our findings on what it means to be tolerated in liberal societies such as the US and the Netherlands.

We set out to do so in six studies (Adelman et al., 2022b; Cvetkovska et al., 2022b) that used the same experimental design, namely an adaptation of the well-known cyberball paradigm[13] that was developed for examining the psychological impact that the experience of being ostracised can have (Williams & Jarvis, 2006). We manipulated minority experiences of being tolerated in a working team context, in comparison to the experience of being appreciated and of being rejected, in order to examine the effects of toleration on minority well-being (personal outcome), on their future interactions with the majority members (interpersonal outcome), and on raising their voice for articulating discontent at the treatment as a form of collective action (intergroup outcome).

Appreciation, toleration, and rejection each comprises of two components: an initial attitude and the corresponding behaviour (Table 8.1). Appreciation is when you are welcoming in attitude and accepting and inclusive in behaviour. Rejection is when you are rejecting in attitude and exclusive in behaviour. Tolerance sits in between, with the tolerating attitude involving the negativity of rejection that is combined with the acceptance and inclusion in behaviour. We focused on the context of work and simulated the experience of being a minority group member in terms of typical working style ("people-oriented") interacting with majority group member teammates ("task-oriented" working style) who express appreciation ("we welcome diversity"), toleration ("we will put up with people like you"),

TABLE 8.1 Experimentally manipulating the experience of being appreciated, tolerated, and rejected using a novel ostracism paradigm through attitudinal and behavioural components

	Appreciation	*Tolerance*	*Rejection*
Attitude to other	Positive and inclusive	Disapproving but begrudgingly inclusive	Negative and exclusive
Behaviour towards Other	Full inclusion	Full inclusion	Full exclusion

or rejection ("we do not want to work with people like you"). In doing so, we were able to manipulate minority experiences of being tolerated versus appreciated versus rejected and test its effects on the three key dependent outcomes for minority group members: subjective well-being, motivation for future participation and engagement, and voice through assessing the willingness to reveal one's experiences to others.

In general, we expected the experience of being tolerated to have a more negative effect on situational well-being compared to being appreciated, but a less negative effect compared to being rejected. Furthermore, we were interested in people's expectations of future treatment by their majority teammates and expected that being tolerated (compared to being appreciated) inhibits expectations of being a valued and included member of the group (but less so compared to being rejected). Additionally, we examined whether the experience of being tolerated (compared to being rejected) undermines minority voice and collective action against one's teammates, and against the research context itself.

The findings of the different studies were very similar and robust across different measures and among people in the Netherlands and the US. The results demonstrated that compared to those who were rejected, the tolerated people strongly displayed less threat to their well-being, had moderately higher expectations of being treated well by their teammates, and were less willing to engage in raising their voice about their treatment. However, compared to those who were appreciated, the tolerated displayed weak-to-moderate greater threats to their well-being, had moderately lower expectations of being treated well by their teammates, and were not more willing to engage in raising their voice over their treatment. Hence, being tolerated had more negative implications than that of being appreciated, with more negative expectations of future treatment and more negative well-being. However, being tolerated was better for minority group members' well-being and expectations of future treatment than being rejected. Furthermore, there was some evidence for the depoliticising effects of tolerance, as people who were tolerated were not more willing to raise their voice in protest of being begrudgingly included on the basis of their identity than those who were appreciated. Importantly, this pattern was found using a strict test of tolerance, where the target was aware of disapproval against their working style in the tolerance relative to the appreciation condition, but the actual behavioural treatment in the cyberball game was identical inclusive in both conditions.

One limitation of this experimental work is that we examined the experience of being tolerated in relation to an alleged dissenting working style that is likely not a very important identity for the participants. It might be that the consequences of being tolerated are different, for example, when one's gender of sexual orientation is involved. We therefore conducted a fifth study in which only women were involved with a focus on a stereotypical female working-style ("people-oriented") in a team of task-oriented men (Cvetkovska et al., 2022b). The findings of this study were similar to the previous ones: for example, being tolerated resulting again in more positive interactional implications (indexed by enactment of the tolerated female identity, expectations for future treatment, and trust for outgroup teammates) than being rejected, but had more negative implications than being appreciated. Being tolerated also resulted in a reduced inclination to raise one's voice against one's teammates compared to being rejected, but a stronger inclination to raise one's voice compared to being appreciated. Thus, the experience of being tolerated again had negative implications for how minorities feel compared to being appreciated, and positive implications compared to being rejected.

Another limitation of these experimental studies is that they offered people a single experience (being tolerated, rejected, or appreciated), whereas in real life, people have many experiences that follow each other and that can influence each other's meanings. For example, it is likely that the experience of being tolerated is much more positive after first being rejected compared to first being appreciated and included. People tend to evaluate and make sense of particular experiences by comparing these with what they experienced in the past. A previous experience is likely to affect the meaning and impact of the next one. Therefore, we conducted a further study in which we again used the same cyberball paradigm, but this time having participants experiencing being tolerated after first being appreciated or rather being rejected (Adelman et al., 2022b). The results showed that being tolerated was indeed a more positive experience after first having experienced rejection, and that being tolerated after being appreciation did not matter for the social psychological impact that tolerance had. In fact, being tolerated after first being rejected appeared to be equally positive to being appreciated only, while tolerance following appreciation did not have a comparable negative impact.

Tolerance from the target's perspective

While there is a relatively large social psychological literature on the targets' perspective examining what it means to be stigmatised, rejected, excluded, ostracised, and discriminated against, such work has not examined the impact of the distinct yet common experience of being tolerated. This is unfortunate for theoretical and applied reasons. Toleration implies a specific form of disapproval and non-interference ("putting up with") which makes it different from other behaviours, including microaggressions for which the actual intention or attitude behind the microaggression is considered not to matter (Freeman & Stewart, 2021; Mekawi & Todd, 2021). However, the difference in attitude is exactly what matters for the distinction between being tolerated and being appreciated. Specific for the experience of being tolerated is that the behaviour is accepting and inclusive but the attitude is not, making being tolerated different from forms of microaggression.

Tolerance protects minority and marginalised group members from oppression, discrimination, and violence, provides access to rights and resources, and gives opportunities to live the life that they want. It is therefore understandable that tolerance is widely promoted and embraced across a wide range of countries and settings for trying to establish equality and peaceful coexistence. This makes it important to systematically consider the different complexities and paradoxes involved in toleration, including the question what it means to be tolerated and the possible negative implications for minority and disadvantaged group members.

Acknowledging the continued and increased importance of toleration does not mean that we should ignore the possible drawbacks. On the contrary, a focus on negative consequences allows us to make progress in finding more viable approaches to forms of diversity and in our theoretical thinking and in the development of novel research questions. The interest in toleration is not driven by normative pathos, but because toleration is an indispensable strategy for living with meaningful and irreconcilable cultural, religious, and ideological differences. Examining the various aspects and implications of toleration is important for productive dialogue on differences in majority and marginalised realities and helps to minimise misunderstandings, tensions, and conflicts.

The experience of being tolerated will not be the same for different individuals and different minority groups and will differ between intergroup settings (e.g. power and status differences), and social contexts (e.g. schools, neighbourhoods, and countries). Thus, there are various avenues for future work on the complexities involved in the processes of what it means to be tolerated. Such work could systematically examine why, when, and how exactly people experience that they are being tolerated, and why, how, and when this affects their thinking, feeling and doing in positive or rather negative ways. For example, the potential negative implications of being "put up with" can occur not only in a societal majority–minority context but also within minority groups and communities. The "in-group domination objection" towards policies of toleration implies that majority group members' non-interference in minority beliefs and practices can create, maintain, and justify relations of dependency and conditional non-interference within minority communities (Lovett, 2010). Through intragroup communication and so-called norm talk (Keblusek et al., 2017), minority members can control and negotiate normativity, enabling them to define appropriate conduct, deviance, and the conditions for the experience of being tolerated.

Furthermore, it is likely that there are contextual differences in the social psychological impact that the experience of being tolerated has. Being tolerated in the context of one's work, at school or in one's neighbourhood might be different, because the expectations and norms in these contexts differ. For example, the negative experience of "being put up with" might be more difficult to avoid but more easy to challenge in the context of one's school compared to one's neighbourhood. Furthermore, being tolerated in culturally diverse or rather more homogeneous social contexts might also matter for the meaning of being tolerated. Additionally, there will be cross-national differences that matter for the degree and meaning of being a target of toleration. For example, toleration can go together with a relatively secure status for members of minorities as citizens with equal rights and opportunities. Respect for their legal status together with the necessary institutional safeguards ensures (to some degree) that minority members do not live with the constant threat of arbitrary interference. And this is even more likely when there are strong societal norms of solidarity and civility (Honohan, 2013; Petit, 1997). Similarly, the effects of being tolerated on minority outcomes may vary depending on the extent to which society is characterised by authoritarian versus egalitarian norms and ideals. In liberal nations characterised by relatively low power distance and egalitarian ideals, minority groups may experience more negative psychological outcomes due to the mismatch between societally driven expectations and actual experiences. However, in autocratic nations characterised by high power distance and hierarchical relations, being tolerated may be experienced more strongly as a much-needed and welcoming concession from the dominant group.

9

THE INDISPENSABILITY OF TOLERANCE

Tolerance is generally considered a beacon of justice and equality in Western plural societies and foundational for peaceful functioning. Arguably, the increase in types and forms of diversity and the growing polarisation make tolerance more critical than ever. Tolerance is a barrier against discrimination, repression, oppression, and violence and an indispensable aspect of a liberal democracy, of positive intergroup relations, and of everyday life. The relevance and importance of tolerance for living with diversity can be easily understood if one thinks about the blaming and shaming, harassment and outright threats on social media, and the situations and societies in which diversity is rejected and ideological adversaries and ethnic, religious, cultural, and sexual minorities face serious forms of exclusion, persecution, and criminalisation. Without tolerance, there is cancelling, silencing, unrestrained opposition, and threats and violence, as can be witnessed among the radical right and radical left, among populist and authoritarian political movements and regimes (e.g. Russia, Hungary, and China), and in countries that officially or implicitly define their state in religious terms (e.g. Poland, India, Iran, and Turkey).[1]

There is every reason to promote tolerance as part of a peaceful solution to the challenges of living with diversity grounded in substantial and sometimes irreconcilable differences. However, the nature of these differences matter. Tolerating ideological and political opponents is something else than accepting heterodox viewpoints in academic debates, which differs from tolerating cultural and religious minority beliefs and practices, from accepting sexual minorities, and tolerating those who have fundamental different views about moral issues such as abortion, euthanasia, and the death penalty. Furthermore, the research discussed indicates that it matters not only what people are asked to tolerate but also why they should do so, in which sort of settings, and what the (perceived) reasons are behind the dissenting conduct. There are many things that vary and matter with people being tolerant or not towards some practices, in some contexts, and depending on the

DOI: 10.4324/9781003335030-9

motives of the people engaging in these practices. Individuals also differ in their general predisposition to tend to accept things they object to and in their belief that dissenting others should be able to live the life that they want. The research clearly shows that tolerance judgements and tolerant behaviour depend on who, what, when, and why people are asked to be tolerant. Individual differences matter as do types of dissenting conduct, situational circumstances, and societal conditions.

Three considerations

I started this book with citing Walzer – "Toleration makes difference possible; difference makes toleration necessary" – because this quote clearly summarises what I have tried to argue theoretically and demonstrate empirically. At least three things are important for evaluating the argument and empirical evidence that has been presented and discussed: the conceptualisation of tolerance, the social psychological perspective on tolerance, and possible negative consequences of tolerance.

Conceptualisation

Tolerance and intolerance are familiar labels that are easily pasted over various attitudes, beliefs, and behaviours highlighting the importance of unpacking its variations for productive societal and theoretical debates, systematic research, and successful interventions. How one conceptualises attitudes and actions as representing tolerance and intolerance has an impact on theoretical questions and debates, on the empirical research that is conducted, on a meta-analytical assessments of the field, and on the applied implications. Scientific research and progress depend on clear conceptualisations which prevents obscure thinking, lack of precision, misunderstandings, and unproductive discussions.

The concept of tolerance used to have the specific meaning of forbearance, endurance, and self-restraint but gradually the meaning of being non-judgemental, broad minded, and appreciative has also been introduced. Whereas the former meaning is still dominant in political science and philosophy, the latter predominates in social psychology and intergroup research. Using the same term for different phenomena and processes is of course not exceptional, as is illustrated in the different ways in which terms such as "identity", "diversity", "acceptance", "recognition", "respect", and "inclusion' are used. Often authors use these concepts without pointing out what they mean by them, assuming that the concepts speak for themselves or are plainly understood. This is not very useful, however. The issue here is not whether one conceptualisation is right and the other is not, because one grasps the nature of a phenomenon. Rather, the issue is being clear about what the focus is and the argument is about, and to prevent conceptual overreach and conceptual inflation which reduces the analytical value of concepts. Tolerance as forbearance and tolerance as appreciation are often and easily mixed up in public, political, and academic debates. Yet the related phenomena and processes clearly differ and this should be recognised for providing accurate descriptions and explanations of psychological and social reality, and for thinking about applied implications.

The interpretation of the concept of tolerance as appreciation often detracts from its unique, original meaning. By equating tolerance with positively valuing diversity, the concept becomes quite similar to being non-prejudiced and open-minded, thereby losing its distinctive analytical value. However, tolerance is not an issue in matters that people appreciate and value. Moreover, this equalisation largely eliminates the great social importance of tolerance. Difficult as it may be, promoting acceptance despite a negative evaluation or critical judgement is usually more realistic than changing that evaluation or judgement. The way of tolerance seems more realistic than that of conversion, especially in pluriform societies where people can fundamentally differ from each other in opinions, preferences, beliefs, convictions, and practices. Furthermore, it is a moral and political question whether it is desirable to try to make people more positive about things that go against their own conscience and deep beliefs, rather than ask them to tolerate those things nonetheless. It is precisely from the perspective of tolerance as forbearance that it is crucial to accept that things can be perceived and evaluated in opposite ways. The focus in this book is on tolerance as forbearance, which unfortunately has been largely ignored in social psychology and psychology more generally.

Social psychological perspective

There is a tendency in the social psychological literature to consider all sorts of disagreement, dislike, and disapproval as forms of (subtle, implicit) prejudice. Furthermore, forms of justice-based opposition tend to be considered as rationalisations that merely mask prejudice, and inaction as being the result of suppressed antipathy that is released with the right justification. This tendency implies a pessimistic and one-sided perspective on human functioning and assigns, for example, only a justificatory or secondary role to values. It misses out on understanding some of the principled and nuanced conditions involved in how people perceive, understand, and respond to various differences.

The meaning of prejudice is broad and has been expanded over the years to include modern, aversive, symbolic, subtle, benevolent, and non-conscious forms. There are good and valid reasons for doing so, but this conceptual broadening has ambivalent implications (Haslam, 2016). Theoretically, for example, it becomes difficult to develop an understanding of those situations in which negative evaluations of groups (e.g. pedophiles, terrorists, and extremists) are considered warranted and appropriate. And it also becomes difficult to consider those situations in which people object to specific outgroup beliefs and practices (abortion, religious education, building of minarets, and ritual slaughter of animals), but not of the outgroup as a category of people (e.g. Christians, Muslims, and Jews). Objection can arise from pragmatic considerations, principle commitments, and basic values that have little to do with negative feelings towards specific social categories or groups of people as people. Furthermore, people can also be tolerant or intolerant of specific beliefs, behaviours, and practices of ingroup members and members of their family, their partner, and their children.

The psychology of prejudice-reduction and group-based antipathy should be complemented with the psychology of practice-based objections and tolerance. I have tried to argue that the negativity of objection differs from the antipathy of prejudice, the reasoning to tolerate differs from processes of prejudice, and the considerations behind what is considered intolerable differ from the justifications to express prejudice. Jones (2010) proposes to think about the adequacy of tolerance in terms of three zones. The middle zone is the proper zone of toleration (e.g. dissenting conduct, religious worship, and civil rights), the lower zone is defined by the intolerable (assault, oppression, and violence), and the upper zone is defined not by reasonable objections but rather by group-based antipathy for which the need for toleration does not arise (racism, sexism, and Islamophobia).

A focus on tolerance advances the social psychology of diversity, inclusion, and intergroup relations and generates new directions for theory development and research (Jackman, 1977; Verkuyten & Yogeeswaran, 2017). It draws attention to the ways in which people try to evaluate and weigh the different reasons for and against accepting dissenting beliefs and practices. Specifically, research on tolerance requires a close examination of the reasons (e.g. civil liberties, personal, and group autonomy) to nevertheless accept beliefs and practices that one continues to disagree with or disapprove of. The psychological processes involved in these competing reasons and motivations and how these differ from self-regulation processes in prejudice should be considered and taken seriously. And it requires a focus on the reasons that people have for drawing boundaries to what can be tolerated (e.g. harms and rights principle, reciprocity, and identity continuity), and when particular beliefs and practices become intolerable for them.

It also requires a closer examination of the specific considerations people give to object to others' beliefs and practices, how these are similar or different from feelings of group-based antipathy, and when and why individuals object towards outgroup beliefs and practices that are incompatible with their own, without necessarily rejecting the category of outgroup people. Prejudice might make it more difficult to accept the equal rights of others, and perceived social consequences of particular outgroup practices might fuel outgroup antipathy. Furthermore, perceptions of outgroup threat might make tolerance more difficult and processes of prejudice justification more likely. Perceived threat is one of the strongest and robust predictors of reduced tolerance, and much social psychological research has demonstrated that threat increases prejudice. In contrast, forms of positive intergroup contact might make that people distinguish more between group-based antipathy and disapproval-based tolerance. Contact does not have to mean that people no longer have objections, but these might be less strongly felt and thus involve less psychological tension and less need for balanced thinking and self-restraint. Psychological adaptation implies that people's feelings about the things that they tolerate can gradually change and the boundaries of what they tolerate can alter.

Negative consequences of tolerance

Acknowledging the continuing and even increased importance of toleration does not mean that we should ignore possible negative consequences, intended or unintended. On the contrary, a focus on these consequences is important for making theoretical progress and for finding viable ways for living together.

Toleration implies a perceived asymmetrical relationship, because we can only tolerate what we think we can prohibit. Some individuals or groups (e.g. majority members; dominant members in minority communities; the far right and the far left; ideological activists) are more able to negatively interfere with the way of life of others (e.g. minority members, vulnerable minorities within minority communities, mainstream politicians, and heterodox viewpoints). Tolerance inevitably raises questions of status and power, whereby some people and groups conditionally permit others to live the life that they want. This qualified permission affirms the dominant position of the tolerator and the dependent position of the one who is tolerated. Therefore, some critics argue that tolerance functions as a subtle social mechanism contributing to domination and inequality (Marcuse, 1969), and to the depoliticisation of structural disadvantages (Brown, 2006). Other critics argue that those who themselves claim to be tolerant represent the "new orthodoxy" and are involved in "cancel culture" practices and thus the ones that are intolerant towards questioning diversity policies, heterodox opinions, religious beliefs, and conservative views (Carson, 2012; McWhorter, 2021).

One implication is that tolerance should be studied not only in terms of the psychological processes of weighing moral values and self-restraint but also in terms of social discourses and processes of influence and power. For example, claims of being the victim of intolerance can provide moral capital to minorities that can be used to argue for societal change and induce a sense of guilt among majorities. Furthermore, the notion of tolerance is useful not only to argue for the acceptance of minority group practices and beliefs but also for construing an ingroup favouring moral distinction between "us" and "them". As frequently argued in debates about immigration and diversity, western societies would coalesce around core values of equality, freedom, and tolerance. This argument is typically made in comparison to the alleged intolerance of some immigrant groups, and Muslims in particular (Verkuyten, 2004b, 2013). Moreover, it is also argued that "we" have been tolerant enough, even too indulgent or "soft". That "we" have let things slide and that it is time to again reaffirm what "we" believe in and define the boundaries of what can be accepted. The discourse of tolerance can be deployed in the service of justifying double standards and exclusionary measures (Augoustinos, 2022).

However, the power of the toleration discourse depends on the meanings that are put forward, the way in which these are used, and who is using them and for which purposes. Similar to diversity discourses (e.g. colour-blindness and multiculturalism), tolerance and intolerance are a language with different meanings which can be used for progressive or oppressive ends and therefore is not by definition desirable or undesirable. Sometimes, the struggle for equality and inclusion will benefit from deploying the tolerance discourse, and sometimes this discourse is used for repressive and depoliticising ends: tolerance discourse "has always had a dominating and disciplining effect *as well as* the effect of resisting domination and disciplining" (Forst, in Di Blasi & Holzhey, 2014, p. 65; original italics).

Other implications of "tolerance" have to do with the possible negative impact on those who are being tolerated. Toleration has many positive implications for minority group members. After all, it provides the freedoms to define and develop their own ways of life, allows them to express and enact their identities, provides access to resources and rights, and protects them from violence. Yet, for some minority groups, there are also negative social psychological consequences because of the patronising and condescending nature of tolerance. Being tolerated in the political domain and in public debates is something else than being tolerated as a cultural or sexual minority group member. Being able to participate, speak up, and present one's case are what matters in the former context, while in the latter one, more is at stake which can make the experience of being tolerated offensive and hurtful.

Is tolerance enough?

The notion of tolerance is not only criticised for maintaining and justifying inequalities and power relations and for having (unintended) negative consequences for those who are tolerated, but also because it would not be enough and not appropriate anymore. It is argued that it might have been a good idea in the past, but the judgemental nature of "mere" tolerance is considered inadequate for inclusive communities that would require the full acceptance, appreciation, and respect for differences: tolerance as forbearance should be replaced by tolerance as appreciation. However, this claim is too general, rather unrealistic, and based upon misunderstandings.

First, the claim is much too general, because the relevance and importance of tolerance depend on what, when, where, why, and how people are asked to accept what they disagree with, dislike, or disapprove off. The importance of tolerance in the political domain and for managing ideological polarisation is something else than tolerating the lifestyle of cultural, religious, or sexual minorities. Furthermore, political tolerance is foundational in a liberal democracy, and tolerance is also higher in more stable democracies and when people have more experience with democracy (Marquartz-Pyatt & Paxton, 2007; Peffley & Rohrschneider, 2003). In contrast, the lack of tolerance of political and ideological opponents and of ethnic, religious, and sexual minorities in illiberal democracies and authoritarian settings implies oppression, suppression, and criminalisation of differences. Similar to most of the social psychological theorising and research (Henrich et al., 2010), the scholarly and public debates about diversity, inclusion, and tolerance predominantly relate to liberal western societies and its organisational and educational settings. However, these societies represent only a fraction of the world, and the most recent Freedom House report (2021) is titled "*Democracy under Siege*" to indicate that since

2005, there are more countries that have become autocratic than democratic. Of the 196 UN member states, only 23 are considered full-fledged democracies, representing 8.5% of the world population.

Second, it is unrealistic to ask people not to judge things and expect them to value and appreciate all sorts of diversity. This is psychologically and logically impossible, and also problematic. No one can really value and appreciate everything and at the same time be committed to their own convictions and beliefs: valuing everything means valuing nothing. Socialisation and enculturation imply that the new generation learns cultural commitments, convictions, beliefs, and practices for being able to live a meaningful and valuable life. This will inevitably mean that they will encounter people with quite different cultural, religious, and ideological worldviews. Not all beliefs and moral codes will be considered and treated as equal, because this precludes the commitment to particular beliefs and codes in the first place. Also people who argue for full acceptance, appreciation, and inclusion are critical, dismissive, and intolerant towards those who question the benefits of diversity and the related policies. Asking people to value, appreciate, and fully accept all differences can mean asking them to be inauthentic by compromising or giving up on what they sincerely believe in and what gives meaning to their life. Yet what can be expected and asked for is civility and being well disposed towards dissenting others, and to not negatively interfere with the things that one disagrees with, dislikes, or disapproves of. Thus, what can and should be asked for is the hard and often psychological painful work of toleration in which negative attitudes and objections are not translated in interference, obstruction, and rejection.

Third, the argument that full acceptance and respect, rather than "mere" tolerance, are required is often based on a misunderstanding of what tolerance entails. Specifically, it is argued that tolerance would imply a lack of respect and an unwillingness to engage with the lives of others (e.g. Ramadan, 2010; Schirmer et al., 2012). There is no doubt that in practice tolerance does indeed come to be presented, understood, and used in this way: tolerance as a cover for a lack of respect and an excuse for not having to take others seriously. However, tolerance implies that one does not consider all viewpoints and beliefs as equally valuable while treating and respecting all people as equally valuable. Tolerance requires the recognition of other's basic human dignity and the unconditional respect for their personal autonomy and inalienable human rights, which is something else than respecting their specific achievements, views, beliefs, commitments, and practices.

Furthermore, tolerance should not lead to turning a blind eye or living segregated lives. Tolerance does not mean indifference or a lack of interest, and neither giving in nor giving up, but rather forms the necessary basis for engaging with and discussing contrasting viewpoints, beliefs, and convictions. Tolerance is not about "mind your – or mine – own business", because behaviour inevitably has consequences for many people. If some people vaccinate against an infectious disease and some don't, it affects us all. Similarly, even if only some of us pollute, the result is pollution for everyone, and if only some of us smoke, it can affect the health of many others. Thus, tolerance is more than being indifferent and acting as though what people please to do does not affect anyone. Rather, tolerance makes it possible that one does not use coercion and pressure for regulating others and interfering in their lives, but rather argument and debate for convincing them and finding mutual accommodating solutions. Tolerance is compatible with active engagement, because it provides a basis from which to mitigate meaningful, deep differences and engage in debates about substantive issues rather than about avoiding discomfort and trying to please others (Laegaard, 2010a, 2010b). A tendency to silence unsettling opinions and to close down dissent and debate about contentious moral issues stands in the way of critical thinking and productive change. Tolerance allows debate and to deliberate with equanimity or "calm passion" which helps us to change our opinions and develop more adequate views and better solutions.

However, tolerance will have a very limited scope if conflict and radical change, rather than finding peaceful solutions, are considered necessary for societal development and social justice. In situations of long-term oppression, severe (existential) threats, unsuccessful nonviolent resistance and governmental corruption, more extreme or even violent methods can be called for and will be supported for achieving justice and social change (e.g. Thomas & Louis, 2014; Vollhardt et al., 2020; Wohl et al., 2014). And more generally, beyond these extreme situations, relentless conflict between self-interested groups of unequal power can be the starting assumption about the nature of every society, even liberal democratic ones.[2] It is then argued that all groups in all societies are involved in a continuous struggle to impose social arrangements that benefit themselves which makes tolerance a sham or even a trick of the powerful to prevent structural change:

> tolerance represents the well-meaning but ultimately illusory liberal hope of resisting "by intercommunication" the reactionary violence embedded in capitalist democracy (also known as the dictatorship of capital). Tolerance implies that we can achieve lasting progressive social change, all without serious social conflict, and especially without social or socialist revolution. Of that kind of "tolerance," I remain firmly intolerant.[3]

Tolerance is inadequate if the aim is to radically change society, in whatever direction, rather than trying to find peaceful ways of coexistence within diversity. Radical activists do not ask for, or practice, tolerance but rather want to have it their way and try to threaten, silence, and punish those who question their new dogma.

Tolerance as an intermediate step

The fact that tolerance is critically important in all sorts of settings, relationships, and for all sorts of differences does not mean, of course, that tolerance is *the* solution to all complex and multifaceted questions related to diversity and polarisation. In social relations and human societies, there are no silver bullets or panacea that solve all problems: human beings are no machines and social developments are unpredictable. A focus on tolerance cannot replace the struggle against systematic oppression, inequality and social injustices, or anti-racism and prejudice reduction interventions and strategies. However, these struggles and strategies also do not make tolerance superfluous. Criticising a measure for not curing a "disease" it was not meant for does not make sense. Tolerance as forbearance is not appropriate for addressing systemic racism and generalised antipathy and negativity towards, for example, racial, ethnic, national, or gender categories. Group-based negativity and beliefs about outgroup inferiority should be addressed for what they are. A racist bigot should not become more tolerant but change their racist feelings and beliefs, and a misogynist should change his negative views about women. Tolerance is concerned with the acceptance of opinions, beliefs, convictions, behaviours, and practices that one disagrees with, dislikes, or disapproves off. And although questions of tolerance and intolerance are most visible and urgent in relation to negatively evaluated minority outgroups, they also occur in relation to positively evaluated outgroups, minorities within minorities, ingroup members, neighbours, colleagues, family members, and in many other relationships.

In situations where there are clear moral differences, tolerance is not only necessary but also the right response and most likely endpoint. When ways of life collide, "each believes that what the other believes is right, is wrong; indeed, an affront to how decent people should live" (Sniderman & Hagendoorn, 2007, p. 134). These sorts of situations need a commitment to tolerance as a peaceful way for dealing with conflicting and irreconcilable convictions, beliefs, and practices: a respectful "agree to disagree".

However, tolerance does not have to be the endpoint for differences that are not strongly moralised. Tolerance can be considered a second-best solution, because the underlying feelings of dislike and disapproval are not changed but only hold in check: biting one's lip but not changing one's mind. It could be argued that it would be better to eliminate the negative feelings and learn to appreciate differences. But tolerance might actually be an important step on the way to encouraging people to change their dislike and disapproval (Sandel, 1989). This step implies that people personally recognise that there are good reasons to learn to "bite one's lip" and allow others to live the life that they want, rather than being socially pressured to do so which easily backfires (Legault et al., 2011). The practicing of tolerance might make people more sensitive and aware of the freedoms and equal rights of others and gradually diminish their objections. When people themselves experience the value of tolerance, they might become more accepting of cultural, religious, and ideological others but without becoming uncritical: what we have called "critical inclusiveness" (Chapter 4). And with regular reflection and re-evaluation of different reasons for what should be tolerated and why, people might end up with re-considering and re-evaluating their objections.

However, reasons are often used for rationalisations that, for example, make morally divisive problems worse and constitute a real enemy of tolerance. Our moral emotional gut reactions are often provided with rational-sounding, plausible justifications (Haidt, 2012). Furthermore, asking people to justify their views with explicit reasons or presenting them with alternative arguments might do little to change their strong views and intolerance, and can even do the opposite. For example, calls for tolerance can help build support for public policies among the already tolerant, but simultaneously weaken the support among the intolerant (Djupe et al., 2015). Similarly, asking people to consider reasons to allow practices they disapprove of can backfire and increase intolerance towards the very group that one is trying to benefit (Kuklinski et al., 1991).

This does not mean that tolerance is impossible and that we must give up on deliberation, but rather that we need to find ways to use our thinking and reasoning ability adequately. For this, learning to recognise rationalisations among oneself and others, establishing ground rules for thinking and debate, understanding the perspective of others, reducing fears and (self-)uncertainties, and trying as much as possible to bracket personal prestige and group identity are useful and important (e.g. Feinberg & Willer, 2015; Rauch, 2021). Furthermore, research shows that outgroup acceptance can be increased by encouraging people to think about the amplified, exaggerated, and even absurd implications of their beliefs (paradoxical thinking; Hameiri et al., 2019), to think in terms of contradictions (dialectical thinking; Ma-Kellams et al., 2011), to think about pros and cons of things (Xu & Petty, 2022), to engage in analytic thinking (Pennycook et al., 2015), and by stimulating high-quality listening (Itzchakov et al., 2017), receptiveness to opposing views (Minson & Chen, 2022), intellectual humility (Hook et al., 2017), and wise reasoning (Staudinger & Glück, 2011). Furthermore, tolerance of controversial beliefs, practices, and policies might be increased by confronting people with their illusion of explanatory depth with the preferred single-cause interpretations (Fernbach et al., 2013). These findings provide various directions for trying to stimulate and increase tolerance, but more can be done.

What can be done?

An emphasis on tolerance and toleration is extremely important and useful in many contexts and for many types of differences. It forms a barrier against discrimination, hostility, conflict, and a critical condition for citizenship and democracy. Tolerance requires a standard, based on our beliefs and values, of what we think is best, together with establishing an allowable variation from that standard, including when something is no longer tolerable. It is difficult to know what to tolerate without establishing standards and allowable variations of it. In the absence of such specifications, one might find it easier to simply reject things that you disapprove of or rather try to take the seemingly moral high ground by just accepting almost everything. Successful policies and interventions for improving tolerance need to set norms and stimulate the willingness and ability to discuss disagreements and put up with group differences (Verkuyten et al., 2019). Based on the theoretical and empirical literature discussed, I will briefly indicate some issues that might be important to consider in policy development and implementation, and especially in the context of education.

Policies

The European *Statute for the Promotion of Tolerance* was developed by experts of the European Council on Tolerance and Reconciliation for adoption by all European member states. Although the member states were committed to the principle of tolerance, this principle was nowhere defined in clear terms. Yet, for establishing the distinction between what should and should not be tolerated, it was considered important to have a common point of reference for the member states. Therefore, the main aim of the Model Statute was to fill a vacuum by spelling out the meaning of "tolerance" with the related (legal) obligations for addressing the problems of extremism and intolerance in European societies. There are similar policy documents and initiatives for the promotion of tolerance and the suppression of intolerance from other international organisations (UNESCO), various countries, local authorities (e.g. municipalities), and organisations and institutions.

Some of these documents focus on tolerance and others discuss tolerance as part of, for example, inclusion, diversity, citizenship, and democracy. Furthermore, whereas some documents focus on tolerance as forbearance (e.g. Modal Statute), others emphasise tolerance as appreciation (UNESCO), and most often, the two meanings of tolerance are not clearly distinguished. The latter is unfortunate, because it can easily lead to misunderstandings about the aims, implementations, and evaluations of policy initiatives. Policies on tolerance and diversity should explain very clearly and convincingly *what* they try to achieve, *why* they are necessary, and *how* exactly they affect people's life. This also means that the focus should be on concrete cases, events, or situations rather than only abstract principles. It is one thing to promote, for example, the ideal of freedom, equality, and tolerance, and something quite different to argue for the actual enactment of those ideals with regard to specific dissenting beliefs, behaviours, and practices (Luguri et al., 2012; Yogeeswaran & Dasgupta, 2014).

Tolerance can be promoted as a general ideal and even civic virtue, but the practicing of tolerance depends on whom, what, why, and when people are asked to tolerate dissenting beliefs and practices. Additionally, policies that moralise issues are likely to be less successful, because people might feel externally pressured and controlled to have to accept things that they do not agree with, rather than having self-determined and autonomous reasons for being tolerant (Cobb et al., 2020; Legault et al., 2011). There are several other issues that policies and interventions should consider. One is that it should be recognised that tolerance is much more vulnerable than intolerance: it is often easier to convince tolerant people to give up their tolerant attitudes than to persuade intolerant people to become more tolerant. Another issue relates to the possible dark sides of toleration discourses and policies: the different strategic usages of these discourses and the negative implications that these can have for social relations in society and the well-being of those who are tolerated.

Successfully implementing tolerance in policies and interventions is not easy, can backfire, and can have various unintended negative consequences. For example, a permissive policy approach to minorities can lead to a backlash and increase citizens' intolerance. Citizens can consider policies towards specific minority practices as too liberal or "soft", leading to resentment towards minorities and polarisation among the public (Traunmüller & Helbling, 2017). Alternatively, regulations and policy approaches that are viewed as being illiberal and overly restrictive towards minority groups may evoke feelings of increased commitment and solidarity with minority citizens (Bishin et al., 2016).

Policies and interventions have to take many factors into account (e.g. legal, political, historical, economic, and cultural) and must have (control) mechanisms in place ensuring that the policy or intervention does not remain confined to abstract principles but is actually carried out as intended. Tolerance should not be a substitute for justice and substantive equality, and policy makers should emphasise that not everything can and should be tolerated. Tolerance is not the same as indulgence and should not be an excuse for letting things slide by. There are basic values and principles that are the foundations of a society. One's own freedom should not be at the expense of someone else's, and the right to religious freedom goes together with a duty to recognise and respect the beliefs of others. Furthermore, liberal values such as gender equality, freedom of expression, free choice of a partner, and the right to apostasy cannot be violated without consequences. For public and political debates, this implies that people should be able to critically and freely question each other and set standards together.

People's tolerance or intolerance of contested minority practices and beliefs can depend on the proposed policy approach, which is the responsibility of political actors. This means, for example, that disagreements and conflicts about controversial issues are a struggle not only between groups of citizens but also between citizens and the political elites. Authorities, politicians, and policy makers play an important role in setting toleration norms and building inclusive institutions and egalitarian citizenship regimes. Experimental research has found that people are more likely to express and act upon their negative attitudes in the presence of prejudiced and inflammatory elite speech that is tacitly condoned by other elite political actors (Newman et al., 2021), and that trust in the government matters for people's commitment to democratic values (Davis & Silver, 2004).

Authorities and elites can in various ways have an impact on the beliefs and behaviour of lay people, and it matters whether they communicate explicitly that discussions about (un)acceptable practices should take place within legal boundaries defining human rights and individual freedoms embedded in constitutional laws. However, it should also be recognised that the degree to which the dominant culture or religion is institutionalised in the laws, rules, and state policies can negatively affect people's tolerance towards, for example, immigrant minorities (Helbling & Traunmüller, 2016; Weldon, 2006).

Educational context

Formal (primary and secondary) education represents an institutional context in which the relevance of toleration for diverse societies is most often put forward and discussed.[4] For example, the UNESCO *Declaration of Principles of Tolerance* states:

> Education is the most effective means of preventing intolerance. The first step in tolerance education is to teach people what their shared rights and freedoms are so that they may be respected and to promote the will to protect those of others.
>
> *(1995, Article 4.1)*

This emphasis on education is understandable given the importance of the formative years for political socialisation, for developing an understanding of the critical role of tolerance in society, and for learning to practice tolerance in the familiar context of the school.

The promotion of tolerance in education is, for example, part of civics courses, education for democratic citizenship, and human rights education (Barrett, 2020; Drerup, 2018; Dutch Educational Council, 2021; Hess & McAvoy, 2015). Schools aim the promotion of tolerance and the suppression of intolerance by creating a positive school atmosphere, providing opportunities for intergroup contacts, developing intercultural competencies, and using forms of multicultural education, project-based learning, cooperative learning, student-to-student dialogue, peer education, and relevant curricula (Van Driel et al., 2016; Verkuyten & Thijs, 2013). In relation to tolerance and diversity, students need to learn "that dilemmas and clashes of values can be insoluble, that people can fundamentally disagree with each other and can nevertheless respect each other", and that one has to accept "that people (may) do or find things that you yourself disapprove of" (Dutch Educational Council, 2021, p. 32). Furthermore, it is important that students realise that situations and context matter, that not all types of differences are similar, and that the reason for tolerating one type of difference (e.g. religious beliefs) can differ from the reason to tolerate another type of difference (political views).

To create and evaluate age appropriate tools and educational practices for stimulating tolerance, we also need to understand children's thinking about the diversity of belief and how children's acceptance of discrepancies in beliefs and dissenting practices develops over time (see Verkuyten & Killen, 2021). Children are committed to their own convictions and beliefs and engage in practices based on these beliefs. However, this does not have to mean that they want to exclude or reject those who have a conflicting worldview. Already young children can and do tolerate dissenting beliefs and conduct which means that there are possibilities for trying to further stimulate the development of tolerance.

There is some experimental evidence that school-based interventions can increase tolerance (e.g. Al Said & Basit, 2013; Osler, 2010). However, learning to be tolerant is far from easy, and educational initiatives can also have unintended consequences. For example, in a study among early adolescents, it was found that egalitarian and equality messages stimulated self-endorsed reasons for accepting outgroups, whereas explicit prosocial prescriptions (e.g. "You should be nice and honest to people from other groups") only led to concerns about social sanctions and compliance (Jargon & Thijs, 2021). And teaching middle-school students about the norms and principles of democracy was found to enhance their political tolerance of groups they disliked, but also made their dislike of the groups in question stronger (Avery et al., 1992).

Furthermore, in school practices, the focus is often on appreciating differences and celebrating diversity rather than tolerance as forbearance (Weissberg, 2008). Discouraging evaluation and judgement and having to consider all views as equally valuable increasingly replaces learning to critically consider evidence, arguments, and contrasting moral values. As a result, some of the more difficult and challenging moral, social, and political questions of living with meaningful differences and what it means to be a responsible citizen are avoided (Balint, 2010). It matters whether children are encouraged to tolerate things they disagree with and disapprove of or rather whether they are discouraged from having any objections to things.

Additionally, teachers face many challenges when trying to promote discussions and deliberations about controversial issues, while maintaining a supportive classroom environment (Hess & McAvoy, 2015). Some topics are seen by teachers as too controversial, because these divide society with different groups offering conflicting explanations and solutions based on alternative understandings (Stradling, 2003). Uncertainty about the content of the controversy, strong emotions of students or fear of the reactions of parents can make teachers reluctant to discuss these issues in class. For example, in some US school districts, teachers are hesitant to discuss topics related to sexuality, abortion, and religion, or are required to offer "opposing" viewpoints on evolution and even on the holocaust. And in western Europe, there are many examples of teachers who avoid discussing the holocaust, terrorist attacks, freedom of speech, and sexuality in classes with Muslim students:

> We have to teach a course about conflicting fundamental rights. Half of the colleagues said during the team meeting: we are not going to talk about cartoons in relation to freedom of expression. That's really a no-go. Half of the students are Islamic. There is a lot of fear.[5]

Discussing controversial themes is sometimes avoided, because these "hot" topics can make students (and also teachers) feel threatened in their ethnic, religious, or sexual identity (e.g. Orlenius, 2008). Emotions can run high if there is not only a difference of opinion, but also those differences (implicitly or explicitly) are linked to who and what you are. Students who feel attacked and threatened in their identity during a discussion are less open to perspectives and arguments of others. A sense of threat leads students to be more focused on defending who and what they are in their own eyes and makes them less willing to really listen to others and critically reflect on their views and beliefs and what these are based on. However, avoiding the discussion about controversial topics and themes deprives students of the opportunity to learn to determine why and when things should be tolerated, and why and when things are considered intolerable. Children should learn to care about the right things, and this means that they should also learn not to tolerate the wrong things (Schinkel, 2021).

When discussing conflicting perspectives, it is probably best to start as much as possible with "cold" debated topics with which students do not identify too strongly which makes it easier to seriously consider different viewpoints (Wansink et al., 2018). What is considered as a "cold" or rather "hot" topic can of course differ greatly between settings and students, but there are also subjects that do not evoke too strong feelings in most students, such as the struggle for women's rights, the abolition of slavery, and clear forms of exclusion, oppression, and discrimination. Thinking about civil liberties and the importance of letting other students say what is on their mind might form paradigmatic examples of tolerance. Thus, discussing relatively straightforward "cold" cases of tolerable conduct (e.g. tastes and hobbies) and intolerable conduct (e.g. bullying and theft) is probably a good starting point.

There are relatively uncontroversial cases of intolerable conduct and there are many examples in which intolerance is inappropriate, because the objection is hard to defend. These can form the impetus for evaluating more complex real-world issues, although there is always the possibility that thinking about these issues and their consequences leads students to consider a range of other principles and values (e.g. social order and cultural tradition) which reduce their tolerance (Kuklinski et al., 1991). And even with relatively "cold" topics, there can be irreconcilable opinions and views. This means that it is important that teachers discuss with the students how you can disagree with each other: that students are not expected to give up or adjust their own views, only that they accept that others do not have to do the same. The importance of tolerance can be made clear and tangible by discussing it as a core aspect of a decision-making process in which everyone is equal and has the same right to put forward and defend his or her views and interests (Jones, 2010). The experience of not being allowed to express one's own views in class or having one's opinions simply dismissed, makes the relevance of tolerance and free speech vividly clear.

What is important is that students feel safe to express their opinions and views and that there are clear norms for how to discuss controversial topics. For example, in discussions, it is useful to first make an inventory of the different perspectives and considerations of the students. Students and teachers must be able to make their judgements and opinions known, but without condemning others or attacking them directly or indirectly. There must be a willingness to listen openly to each other and to engage in genuine debate over substantive differences, while recognising areas of agreement and commonality and the facts of the matter (Hess & McAvoy, 2015; Kugler & Coleman, 2020). Subsequently, students should not only express their emotional feelings but also learn to reflect on exactly what the arguments are for their own perspective on the controversy, and to critically question each other about it (Weinstock et al., 2017). Additionally, it is possible to discuss together about why a common framework of the rule of law and human and civil rights with freedom of thought and speech is important for peaceful coexistence.

In general, students should be given the opportunity to thoroughly immerse themselves in the content of the discussed controversies, and to learn to speak less and listen more, to accuse less and think more, to feel hurt less and be interested more, and to look beyond their own horizon and understand the perspective of others (Eyal et al., 2018; Hess & McAvoy, 2015; Weston, 2018). This is of course not only important for students in the contexts of education, but for all citizens in relation to real-world controversies in which the stakes can be high and emotions can run high, and polarisation, threats, and even violence are likely outcomes.

A final word

The key diversity question of "How should we live together with our many differences?" does inevitably raise the topic of tolerance and its boundaries. There are many types of differences and these can be more superficial or rather deep, interesting or unsettling, stimulating or threatening, and easy to accommodate or difficult to bridge. Tolerance makes it possible to live with a range of differences without resolving them: to allow others to be themselves while being yourself. It is grounded in the acknowledgement of each other as equal and free in the face of sometimes fundamental disagreements about the value of commitments, beliefs, and practices.

Tolerance is a minimal but much more attractive condition for living with diversity than many alternatives. It is not only necessary in challenging social circumstances but also in many everyday situations, in various domains of life, and in relation to various persons and groups. Tolerance is not the silver bullet or an unqualified good for a diverse society, but one of those things that we "cannot not want", even as we recognise its limitations and boundaries, the difficulties in practicing tolerance, and the disturbing political reversals and appropriations of the tolerance discourse for contradictory political ends: "I believe in tolerance despite its risks, because it seems to me that any alternative would put me in an antagonistic and alienated relation to my fellow citizens, friends as well as foes" (Scanlon, 2003, p. 201). Tolerance is a necessary condition for any plural society, an indispensable link of a chain, the lube oil that makes things function in an equal and peaceful way. But tolerance is of course not a sufficient condition, because much more is required, including addressing prejudices, racisms and forms of discrimination at individual, institutional, cultural, and structural levels.

In contrast to political scientists and the vast theoretical and empirical literature on prejudice and discrimination, social psychologists have not focused much on understanding the tolerance process. Yet, the disagreements, tensions, and conflicts arising from meaningful cultural, religious, and other differences heed a focus on toleration in many settings. The theoretical, empirical, and practical questions raised by the toleration approach differ from those raised by prejudice-reduction, anti-racism, intergroup contact, and cultural diversity approaches that are much studied in social psychology. Systematic attention to questions of tolerance can enhance social psychology's contribution to the development of positive relations in our increasingly diverse and polarised societies. Understanding the relevant social psychological processes and people's subjective realities in actually living with diversity is not only important for theory development but also forms the impetus for wise interventions.

REFERENCES

Aarøe, L. (2012). Does tolerance of religion in the public space depend on the salience of the manifestation of religious group membership? *Political Behavior, 22*, 585–606.

Accetti, C.I., & Zuckerman, I. (2017). What's wrong with militant democracy? *Political Studies, 65*, 182–199.

Adelman, L., & Verkuyten, M. (2020a). Prejudice and the acceptance of Muslim minority practices: A person-centered approach. *Social Psychology, 51*, 185–198.

Adelman, L., & Verkuyten, M. (2020b). Rules of engagement: Reactions to internal and external criticism in public debate. *British Journal of Social Psychology, 59*, 405–424.

Adelman, L., Verkuyten, M., Cardenas, D., & Yogeeswaran, K. (2021b). On a slippery slope to intolerance: Individual difference in slippery slope beliefs predict outgroup negativity. *Journal of Research in Personality, 94*, 104–141.

Adelman, L., Verkuyten, M., & Yogeeswaran, K. (2021a). Moralization and moral trade-offs explain (in)tolerance of Muslim minority behaviours. *European Journal of Social Psychology, 51*, 924–935.

Adelman, L., Verkuyten, M., & Yogeeswaran, K. (2022a). Distinguishing active and passive outgroup tolerance: Understanding its prevalence and the role of moral concern. *Political Psychology, 43*, 731–750.

Adelman, L., Yogeeswaran, K., & Verkuyten, M. (2022b). The unintended consequences of tolerance: The experience and repercussions of being tolerated (manuscript under review).

Agerström, J., & Björklund, F. (2009). Moral concerns are greater for temporary distant events and are moderated by value strength. *Social Cognition, 27*, 261–282.

Agnew, R. (2001). Building on the foundation of general strain theory: Specifying the types of strain most likely to lead to crime and delinquency. *Journal of Research in Crime and Delinquency, 38*, 319–361.

Akrami, N., Ekehammar, B., & Bergh, R. (2011). Generalized prejudice: Common and specific components. *Psychological Science, 22*, 57–59.

Alba, R. (2005). Bright vs blurred boundaries: Second-generation assimilation and exclusion in France, Germany and the United States. *Ethnic and Racial Studies, 28*, 20–49.

Alba, R. (2020). The great demographic illusion: Majority, minority, and the expanding American mainstream. Princeton, NJ: Princeton University Press.

Alba, R., & Foner, N. (2015). Strangers no more: Immigration and the challenges of integration in North America and Western Europe. Princeton, NJ: Princeton University Press.

Al Ramiah, A., & Hewstone, M. (2013). Intergroup contact as a tool for reducing, resolving, and preventing intergroup contact. Evidence, limitations, and potential. *American Psychologist, 68*, 527–542

Al Said, F.H., & Basit, T.N. (2013). Religious tolerance in Oman: Addressing religious prejudice through educational intervention. *British Educational Research Journal, 39*, 447–472.

Allport, G.W. (1954). The nature of prejudice. Reading: Addison-Wesley.

Alvarez M.J., & Kemmelmeier, M. (2018). Free speech as a cultural value in the United States. *Journal of Social and Political Psychology, 5*, 707–735.

Amnesty International (2012). Choice and prejudice: Discrimination against Muslims in Europe. London: Amnesty International.

Anderson, B. (1983). Imagined communities. London: Verso.

Andreassen, R. (2012). Gender as a tool in Danish debates about Muslims. In J.S. Nielsen (Ed.), Islam in Denmark: The challenge of diversity (pp. 143–160). Lanham, MD: Lexington Books.

Andreouli, E. (2019). Social psychology and citizenship: A critical perspective. Social and Personality Compass, 13, e12432.

Arnett, J.J. (2008). The neglected 95%: Why American psychology needs to become less American. *American Psychologist, 63*, 602–614.

Augoustinos, M. (2022). Concluding remarks: The future of multiculturalism. In K. Pettersson & E. Nortio (Eds.), The far-right discourse of multiculturalism in intergroup interactions: A critical discursive perspective (pp. 241–256). New York, NY: Palgrave Macmillan.

Augoustinos, M., & Tileagă, C. (2012). Twenty five years of discursive psychology. *British Journal of Social Psychology, 51*, 405–412.

Avery, P.G., Bird, K., Johnstone, S., Sullivan, J.L., & Thalhammer, K. (1992). Exploring political tolerance with adolescents. *Theory and Research in Social Education, 20*, 386–420.

Avramenko, R., & Promisel, M. (2018). When toleration becomes a vice: Naming Aristotle's third unnamed virtue. *American Journal of Political Science, 62*, 849–860.

Bader, V. (2013). Moral minimalism and more demanding moralities: Some reflections on tolerance/toleration. In J. Dobbernack & T. Modood (Eds.), Tolerance, intolerance and respect (pp. 23–51). New York, NY: Palgrave Macmillan.

Bağci S.C., Verkuyten, M., Koc, Y., Turnuklu, A., Piyale, Z.E., & Bekmezci, E. (2020). Being tolerated and being discriminated against: Links to psychological well-being through threatened social identity needs. *European Journal of Social Psychology, 50*, 1463–1477.

Bai, H. (2021). When racism and sexism benefit black and female politicians: Politicians' ideology moderates prejudice's effect more than politicians' demographic background. *Journal of Personality and Social Psychology, 120*, 1480–1520.

Baker, P., Gabrielatos, C., & McEnery, T. (2013). Sketching Muslims: A corpus-driven analysis of representations around the word "Muslim" in the British press 1998–2009. *Applied Linguistics, 34*, 255–278.

Balint, P.A. (2010). Avoiding an intolerant society: Why respect of difference may not be the best approach. *Educational Philosophy and Theory, 42*, 129–141.

Bamberg, K., & Verkuyten, M. (2022). Internal and external motivation to respond without prejudice: A person-centered approach. *The Journal of Social Psychology, 162*, 435–454.

Barbacan, M. (2022). Young Turks in Britain and Islamophobia: Perceptions, experiences and identity strategies. PhD Dissertation, University of Bristol, UK.

Barkey, K. (2008). Empire of differences: The Ottomans in comparative perspective. Cambridge, UK: Cambridge University Press.

Baron, J., & Jost, J.T. (2019). False equivalence: Are liberals and conservatives in the United States equally biased? *Perspectives on Psychological Science, 14*, 292–302.

Baron, J., & Ritov, I. (2004). Omission bias, individual differences, and normality. *Organizational Behavior and Human Decision Processes, 94*, 74–85.

Baron, J., Scott, S., Fincher, K., & Metz, S.E. (2015). Why does the cognitive reflection test (sometimes) predict utilitarian moral judgment (and other things)? *Journal of Applied Research in Memory and Cognition, 4*, 265–284.

Baron, J., & Spranca, M. (1997). Protected values. *Organizational Behavior and Human Decision Processes, 70*, 1–16.

Barreto, M., Ellemers, N., & Banal, S. (2006). Working undercover: Performance-related self-confidence among members of contextually devalued groups who try to pass. *European Journal of Social Psychology, 36*, 337–352.

Barrett, M. (2020). The Council of Europe's reference framework for competences in democratic culture: Policy context, content and impact. *London Review of Education, 18*, 1–17.

Barrow, R. (2005). On the duty of not taking offence. *Journal of Moral Education, 34*, 265–275.

Bartels, L.M. (2008). Unequal democracy: The political economy of the new gilded age. New York, NY: Russell Sage.

Baumeister, R.F. (2001). Evil: Inside human violence and cruelty. New York, NY: Henry Holt.

Baumeister, R.F., & Leary, M.R. (1995). The need to belong: Desire for interpersonal attachments as a fundamental motivation. *Psychological Bulletin, 117*, 497–529.

Baumgartner, J.N., & Morgan, G.S. (2019). Mindfulness and cognitive depletion shape the relationship between moral conviction and intolerance of dissimilar others. *Studia Psychologica, 61*, 31–41.

Baumgartner, M., & Epple, R. (2014). A coincidence analysis of a causal change: The Swiss minaret vote. *Sociological Methods and Research, 43*, 280–312.

Beattie, P. (2017). Anti-Semitism and opposition to Israel government policies: The roles of prejudice and information. *Ethnic and Racial Studies, 40*, 2749–2767.

Bell, J.M., & Hartmann, D. (2007). Diversity in everyday discourse: The cultural ambiguities and consequences of 'happy talk'. *American Sociological Review, 72*, 895–914.

Bendersky, C. (2014). Resolving ideological conflicts by affirming opponents' status: The Tea party, Obamacare and the 2013 Governmental shutdown. *Organizational Behavior and Human Decision Processes, 53*, 163–168.

Bennett, S.E. (1996). Know-nothings revisited again. *Political Behavior, 18*, 219–233

Bergh, R., & Akrami, N. (2016). Generalized prejudice: Old wisdom and new perspectives. In C.G. Sibley & F.K. Barlow (Eds.), Cambridge handbook of the psychology of prejudice (pp. 1–33). Cambridge, UK: Cambridge University Press.

Bergsieker, H.B., Shelton, J.N., & Richeson, J.A. (2010). To be liked versus respected: Divergent goals in interracial interactions. *Journal of Personality and Social Psychology, 99*, 248–264.

Berry, J.M., & Sobieraj, S. (2014). The outrage industry: Political opinion media and the new incivility. Oxford, UK: Oxford University Press.

Berry, J.W. (1997). Immigration, acculturation, and adaptation. *Applied Psychology: An International Review, 46*, 5–68.

Bertin, P., Marinthe, G., Biddlestone, M., & Delouvée, S. (2022). Investigating the identification-prejudice link through the lens of national narcissism: The role of defensive group beliefs. *Journal of Experimental Social Psychology, 98*, 104–252.

Bilgrami, A. (1992). What is a Muslim? Fundamental commitment and cultural identity. *Critical Inquiry, 18*, 821–842.

Biliński, A. (2021). Cultural origins and immigrant integration in the west: Towards emergence of ethnically divided societies? Pittsburg: Independently Published.

Billig, M. (1988). The notion of 'Prejudice': Some rhetorical and ideological aspects. *Text, 8*, 91–110.

Billig, M. (1995). Banal nationalism. London, UK: Sage.

Billig, M., Condor, S., Edwards, D., Gane, M., Middleton, D., & Radley, A. (1988). Ideological dilemmas: A social psychology of everyday thinking. London, UK: Sage.

Bilodeau, A., Turgeon, L., White, S., & Henderson, A. (2018). Strange bedfellows? Attitudes toward minority and majority religious symbols in the public sphere. *Politics and Religion, 11*, 309–333.

Bishin, B.G., Hayes, T.J., Incantalupo, M.B., & Smith, C.A. (2016). Opinion backlash and public attitudes: Are political advances in gay rights counterproductive? *American Journal of Political Science, 60*, 625–648.

Bizumic, B., Kenny, A., Iyer, R., Tanuwira, J., & Huxley, E. (2017). Are the ethnically tolerant free of discrimination, prejudice and political intolerance? *European Journal of Social Psychology, 47*, 457–471.

Blackford, R. (2019). The tyranny opinion: Conformity and the future of liberalism. London, UK: Bloomsbury Academic.

Blair, G., & Imai, K. (2012). Statistical analysis of list experiments. *Political Analysis, 20*, 47–77

Bliuc, A.-M., McGarty, C., Reynolds, K., & Muntele, D. (2007). Opinion based group membership as a predictor of commitment to political action. *European Journal of Social Psychology, 37*, 19–32.

Bloemraad, I. (2013). Accessing the corridors of power: Puzzles and pathways to understanding minority representation. *West European Politics, 36*, 652–670

Bloemraad, I. (2015). Theorizing and analyzing citizenship in multicultural societies. *The Sociological Quarterly, 56*, 591–606.

Bloemraad, I., & Schönwälder, K. (2013). Immigrant and ethnic minority representation in Europe: Conceptual challenges and theoretical approaches. *West European Politics, 36*, 564–579.

Blommaert, J., & Verschueren, J. (1998). Debating diversity: Analysing the discourse of tolerance. London: Routledge.

Bobo, L., & Licari, F.C. (1989). Education and political tolerance: Testing the effects of cognitive sophistication and target group affect. *Public Opinion Quarterly, 53*, 285–308

Bobocel, D.R., Son Hing, L.S., Davey, L.M., Stanley, D.J., Zanna, M.P. (1998). Justice-based opposition to social policies: Is it genuine? *Journal of Personality and Social Psychology, 75*, 653–669.

Boch, A. (2020). Increasing American political tolerance: A framework excluding hate speech. *Socius, 6*, 1–12.

Bond, R., & Smith, P.B. (1996). Culture and conformity: A meta-analysis of studies using Asch's (1952b, 1956) line judgment task. *Psychological Bulletin, 119*, 111–137.

Bot, W., & Verkuyten, M. (2018). Evaluating the political organization of Muslim citizens in the Netherlands: The role of political orientation, education and multiculturalism. *Journal of Social and Political Psychology, 6*, 364–382

Bouchard, G. (2011). What is interculturalism? *McGill Law Journal, 56*, 435–468.

Bowskill, M., Lyons, E., Coyle, A. (2007). The rhetoric of acculturation: When integration means assimilation. *British Journal of Social Psychology, 46*, 793–813

Brandt, M.J., Reyna, C., Chambers, J.R., Crawford, J.T., & Wetherell, G. (2014). The ideological-conflict hypothesis: Intolerance among both liberals and conservatives. *Current Directions in Psychological Science, 23*, 27–34.

Brandt, M.J., & Van Tongeren, D.R. (2017). People both high and low on religious fundamentalism are prejudiced toward dissimilar groups. *Journal of Personality and Social Psychology, 112*, 76–97.

Breakwell, G.M. (2015). Coping with threatened identities (2nd ed.). London, UK: Methuen.

Breton, C., & Eady, G. (2015). Is support for banning religious symbols in the public sphere prejudiced? Nashville, TN: Vanderbilt University: Department of Political Science.

Brienza, J.P., Kung, F.Y.H., & Chao, M.M. (2021). Wise reasoning, intergroup positivity, and attitude polarization across contexts. Nature Communications, 12, 3313.

Brody, G.H., Miller, G.E., Yu, T., & Beach, S.R., & Chen, E. (2016). Supportive family environments ameliorate the link between racial discrimination and epigenetic aging. *Psychological Science, 27*, 530–541.

Brown, R. (2010). Prejudice: Its social psychology (2nd ed.). Oxford, UK: Wiley-Blackwell.

Brown, W. (2006). Regulating aversion: Tolerance in the age of identity and empire. Princeton, NJ: Princeton University Press.

Brown, W. (2015). Tolerance as such does not exist. Contemporary Political Theory, 14, 159–196.

Bruce, S. (2011). Secularization: In defence of an unfashionable theory. Oxford, UK: Oxford University Press.

Buijs, L., Hekma, G., & Duyvendak, J.W. (2011). 'As long as they keep away from me': The paradox of antigay violence in a gay-friendly country. *Sexualities, 14*, 632–652.

Butz, D.A., Plant, E.A., & Doerr, C.E. (2007). Liberty and justice for all? Implications of exposure to the U.S. flag for intergroup relations. *Personality and Social Psychology Bulletin, 33*, 396–408.

Bybee, J. (2010). Language, usage and cognition. Cambridge, UK: Cambridge University Press.

Byrd, N., & Conway, P. (2019). Not all who ponder count costs: Arithmetic reflection predicts utilitarian tendencies, but logical reflection predicts both deontological and utilitarian tendencies. *Cognition, 192,* 103995.

Campbell, B., & Manning, J. (2018). The rise of victimhood culture: Microaggressions, safe spaces, and the new culture wars. Cham; Palgrave, Macmillan.

Campbell, C., & Johnson, J. (2018). Trends in the association between college education and political tolerance, 1976–2016. *Socius: Sociological Research for a Dynamic World, 4*, 1–3.

Capdevila, R., & Callaghan, J.E.M. (2008). "It's not racist. It's common sense'. A critical analysis of political discourse around asylum and immigration in the UK. *Journal of Community and Applied Social Psychology, 18*, 1–16.

Capelos, T., & Van Troost, D.M. (2012). Reason, passion, and Islam: The impact of emotionality and values on political tolerance. In C. Flood, S. Hutchings, G. Miazhevich, & H. Nickles (Eds.), Political and cultural representations of Muslims (pp. 75–79). Amsterdam: Brill.

Capoccia, G. (2013). Militant democracy: The institutional bases of democratic self-preservation. *Annual Review of Law and Social Sciences, 9*, 207–226.

Capraro, V., Everett, J., & Earp, B. (2019). Priming intuition disfavors instrumental harm but not impartial beneficence. *Journal of Experimental Social Psychology, 83*, 142–149

Carriere, K.R., Hallahan, A., & Moghaddam, F.M. (2022). The effect of perceived threat on human rights: A meta-analysis. *Group Processes and Intergroup Relations, 25*, 247–279.

Carson, D.A. (2012). The intolerance of tolerance. Cambridge, UK: Eerdmans.

Castanho Silva, B. (2018). The (non) impact of the 2015 Paris terrorist attacks on political attitudes. *Personality and Social Psychology Bulletin, 44*, 838–850.

Ceci, S.J., & Williams, W.M. (2018). Who decides what is acceptable speech on campus? Why restricting free speech is not an answer. *Perspectives on Psychological Science, 13*, 299–323.

Ceobanu, A.M., & Escandell, X. (2010). Comparative analyses of public attitudes toward immigrants and immigration using multinational survey data: A review of theories and research. *Annual Review of Sociology, 36*, 309–328.

Cesario, J. (2022). What can experimental studies of bias tell us about real-world group disparities? *Behavioral and Brain Sciences, 45,* 1–20.

Chakraborti, N., & Zempi, I. (2012). The veil under attack: Gendered dimensions of Islamophobic victimization. *International Review of Victimology, 18*, 269–284.

Chambers, J.R., & Schlenker, B.R. (2015). Political homogeneity can nurture threats to research validity. *Behavioral and Brain Sciences, 38*, 21–22.

Chan, E.Y. (2016). Re-constructing politics: The dual impacts of abstraction on political ideology. *European Journal of Social Psychology, 46*, 649–656.

Chanley, V. (1994). Commitment to political tolerance: Situational and activity-based differences. *Political Behavior, 16*, 343–363.

Charlesworth, T.E.S., & Banaji, M.R. (2021). Patterns of implicit and explicit attitudes II. Long-term change and stability, regardless of group membership. *American Psychologist, 76*, 851–869.

Charlesworth, T.E.S., & Banaji, M.R. (2022). Patterns of implicit and explicit stereotypes III: Long-term change in gender stereotypes. *Social Psychological and Personality Science, 13*, 14–26.

Choi, D.D., Poertner, M., & Sambanis, N. (2021). The Hijab penalty: Feminist backlash to Muslim immigrants. *American Journal of Political Science*. Retrieved from https://doi.org/10.1111/ajps.12627

Chong, D. (1994). Tolerance and social adjustment to new norms and practices. *Political Behavior, 16*, 21–53.

Chong, D., & Levy, M. (2018). Competing norms of free expression and political tolerance. *Social Research, 85*, 197–227.

Christmann, A., Danaci, D., & O. Krömler, O. (2011). Ein Sonderfall? Das Stimmverhalten bei der Minarettverbots-Initiative im Vergleich zu andern Abstimmungen und Sachfragen. In A. Vatter (Ed.), Vom Schacht – zum Minarettverbot: Religiöse Minderheiten in der direkten Demokratie (pp. 171–190). Zurich: Verlag Neue Zurcher Zeitung.

Cichocka, A. (2016). Understanding defensive and secure ingroup positivity: The role of collective narcissism. *European Review of Social Psychology, 27*, 283–317.

Citrin, J., Johnston, R., & Wright, M. (2012). Do 'patriotism' and 'multiculturalism' collide? Competing perspectives from the U.A. and Canada. *Canadian Journal of Political Science, 45*, 531–552.

Claassen, C., & McLaren, L. (2022). Does immigration produce a public backlash or public acceptance? Time-series, cross-sectional evidence from thirty European democracies. *British Journal of Political Science, 52,* 1013–1031.

Clark, R., Anderson, N., Clark, V., & Williams, D. (1999). Racism as a stressor for African Americans: A biopsychosocial model. *American Psychologist, 54*(10), 805–816.

Clobert, M., Saroglou, V., & Hwang, K-K. (2017). East Asian religious tolerance versus western monotheistic prejudice: The role of (in)tolerance of contradiction. *Group Processes and Intergroup Relations, 20*, 216–232.

Cobb, C.L., Frisby, C., Lilienfeld, S.O., Sanders, G.L., & Schwartz, S.J. (2020). Rethinking multiculturalism: Toward a balanced approach. *American Journal of Psychology, 133*, 275–293.

Cohen, A.J. (2004). What toleration is. *Ethics, 115*, 68–95.

Cohen, J. (1988). Statistical power analysis for the behavioral sciences. Hillsdale, NJ: Erlbaum.

Colombo, C. (2021). Principled or pragmatic? Morality politics in direct democracy. *British Journal of Political Science, 51*, 584–603.

Condor, S. (1996). Social identity and time. In W.P. Robinson (Ed.), Social groups and identities: Developing the legacy of Henri Tajfel (pp. 285–315). Oxford, UK: Butterworth Heinemann.

Conover, P.J. (2009). The politics of recognition: A social psychological perspective. In E. Borgida, C.M. Federico, & J.L. Sullivan (Eds.), The political psychology of democratic citizenship (pp. 176–204). New York, NY: Oxford University Press.

Conover, P.J., Searing, D.D., & Crewe, I. (2004). The elusive ideal of equal citizenship: Political theory and political psychology in the United States and Great Britain. *The Journal of Politics, 66*, 1036–1068.

Cooper, M.L. (2015). Editorial. *Journal of Personality and Social Psychology, 110*, 431–434.

Corner, A., Hahn, U., & Oaksford, M. (2011). The psychological mechanism of the slippery slope argument. *Journal of Memory and Language, 64*, 133–152.

Costello, M., & Dillard, C. (2019). Assessing – An interrupting – Intolerance at school. *American Educator, 43*, 4–7.

Crandall, C.S., & Eshleman, A. (2003). A justification-suppression model of the expression and experience of prejudice. *Psychological Bulletin, 129*, 414–446.

Crandall, C.S., Eshleman, A., & O'Brien, L. (2002). Social norms and the expression and suppression of prejudice: The struggle for internalization. *Journal of Personality and Social Psychology, 82*, 359–378.

Crandall, C.S., & Sherman, J.W. (2016). On the scientific superiority of conceptual replications for scientific progress. *Journal of Experimental Social Psychology, 66*, 93–99.

Crane, T. (2017). The meaning of belief: Religion from an atheist's point of view. Cambridge, MA: Harvard University Press.

Crawford, J.T. (2014). Ideological symmetries and asymmetries in political intolerance and prejudice toward political activists groups. *Journal of Experimental Social Psychology, 55*, 284–298.

Crawford, J.T., & Pilanski, J.M. (2014). The differential effects of right-wing authoritarianism and social dominance orientation on political intolerance. *Political Psychology, 35*, 557–576.

Creighton, M.J., Fahey, E., & McGinnity, F. (2022). Immigrantion, identity, and anonymity: Intentionally masked intolerance in Ireland. *International Migration Review, 56*, 881–910.

Crocker, J., & Major, B. (1989). Social stigma and self-esteem: The self-protective properties of stigma. *Psychological Review, 96*, 608–630.

Cushman, F., Young, L., & Hauser, M. (2006). The role of conscious reasoning and institution in moral judgment. *Psychological Science, 17*, 1082–1089.

Cvetkovska, S., Adelman, L., Verkuyten, M., & Yogeeswaran, K. (2022b). Can't complain: The interpersonal and collective consequences of being tolerated. Utrecht, The Netherlands: Ercomer, Utrecht University.

Cvetkovska, S., Jaspal, R., Verkuyten, M., & Adelman, L. (2022a). Coping with being tolerated: Trans experiences. *Psychology of Sexual Orientation and Gender Diversity*. Retrieved from https://doi.org/10.1037/sgd0000580

Cvetkovska, S., Verkuyten, M., & Adelman, L. (2020). Being tolerated and minority well-being: The role of group identifications. *International Journal of Intercultural Relations, 74*, 161–173.

Cvetkovska, S., Verkuyten, M., Adelman, L., & Yogeeswaran, K. (2021). Being tolerated: Implications for well-being among ethnic minorities. *British Journal of Psychology, 112*, 781–803.

Dahab, R., & Omori, M. (2019). Homegrown foreigners: How Christian nationalism and nativist attitudes impact Muslim civil liberties. *Ethnic and Racial Studies, 42*, 1727–1746.

Dangubić, M., Verkuyten, M., & Stark, T. (2020). Rejecting Muslim or Christian religious practices in five West European countries: A case of discriminatory rejection? *Ethnic and Racial Studies, 43*, 306–326.

Dangubić, M., Verkuyten, M., & Stark, T. (2021). Understanding (in)tolerance of Muslim minority practices: A latent profile analysis. *Journal of Ethnic and Migration Studies, 47*, 1517–1538.

Dangubić, M., Verkuyten, M., & Stark, T. (2022a). Critical inclusiveness: Gender values and the social inclusion of Muslim minorities (manuscript under review).

Dangubić, M., Yogeeswaran, K., Verkuyten, M., & Sibley, C. (2022b). The rejection and acceptance of Muslim minority practices: A person-centered approach. *Group Processes and Intergroup Relations*. Retrieved from https://doi.org/10.1177/13684302211067967

Danniels, E., & Perlman, M. (2021). Because everybody believes in different things: Examining tolerance of divergent preferences, beliefs, and morals in kindergarten students. *Social Development, 30*, 973–993.

Davis, D.W., & Silver, B.D. (2004). Civil liberties vs. Security: Public opinion in the context of the terrorist attacks on America. *American Journal of Political Science, 48*, 28–46.

De Hardt, J., Van Houwelingen, P., & Versantvoort, M. (2019). Denkend aan Nederland [Thinking about the Netherlands]. The Hague, Netherlands: Social and Cultural Planning Office.

De Keersmaecker, J., Bostyn, D.H., Van Hiel, A., & Roets, A. (2021). Disliked but free to speak: Cognitive ability is related to supporting freedom of speech for groups across the ideological spectrum. *Social Psychological and Personality Science, 12*, 34–41.

Dellantonio, S., & Job, R. (2012). Moral intuitions vs. moral reasoning. A philosophical analysis of the explanatory models intuitionism relies on. In L. Magnani & P. Li (Eds.), Philosophy and cognitive science. Studies in applied philosophy, epistemology and rational ethics, vol 2 (pp. 239–262). Berlin: Springer.

Derks, B., & Scheepers, D. (2018). Neural and cardiovascular pathways from stigma to health. In B. Major, J.F. Dovidio, & B.G. Link (Eds.), The handbook of stigma, discrimination and health. Oxford, UK: Oxford University Press.

DeVos, G.A. (1995). Ethnic pluralism: Conflict and accomodation. In L. Romanucci-Ross & G. DeVos (Eds.), Ethnic identity: Creation, conflict and accommodation (pp. 15–47). Walnut Creek, CA: Altamira.

Di Blasi, L., & Holzhey, C.F.E. (2014). Wendy Brown/Rainer Forst: The power of tolerance. Berlin: Turia and Kant.

Diehl, C., & Blohm, M. (2003). Rights or identity? Naturalization processes among "labor migrants" in Germany. *International Migration Review, 37*, 133–162.

Diehl, C., Koenig, M., & Ruckdeschel, K. (2009). Religiosity and gender equality: Comparing natives and Muslim migrants in Germany. *Ethnic and Racial Studies, 32*, 278–301

Diehl, M. (1990). The minimal group paradigm: Theoretical explanations and empirical findings. *European Review of Social Psychology, 1*, 263–292.

Diener, E., Northcott, R., Zyphur, M.J., & West, S.G. (2022). Beyond experiments. *Perspectives on Psychological Science, 17*, 1101–1119.

Ditlmann, R., Purdie-Vaughns, V., and Eibach, R. 2011. Heritage- and ideology-based national identities and their implications for immigrant citizen relations in the United States and in Germany. *International Journal of Intercultural Relations, 35*, 395–405.

Ditto, P.H., Liu, B.S., Clark, C.J., Wojcik, S.P., Chen, E.E., Grady, R.H., Celniker, J.B., & Zinger, J.F. (2019). At least bias is bipartisan: A meta-analytical comparison of partisan bias in liberals and conservatives. *Perspectives on Psychological Science, 14*, 273–291

Dixon, J. (2017). 'Thinking ill of others without sufficient warrant?' Transcending the accuracy-inaccuracy dualism in prejudice and stereotyping research. *British Journal of Social Psychology, 56*, 4–27

Dixon, J., Durrheim, K., & Thomae, M. (2017). The principle-implementation gap in attitudes towards racial equality (and how to close it). Advances in Political Psychology, 38, 91–126.

Dixon, J., & Levine, M. (Eds.) (2012). Beyond prejudice: Extending the social psychology of conflict, inequality and social change. Cambridge, UK: Cambridge University Press.

Dixon, J., Levine, M., Reicher, S., & Durrheim, K. (2012). Beyond prejudice: Are negative evaluations the problem and is getting us to like one another the solution? *Behavioral and Brain Science, 35*, 411–425.

Djupe, P.A., Lewis, A.R., & Jelen, T.G. (2016). Rights, reflection, and reciprocity: Implications of the same-sex marriage debate for tolerance and the political process. *Politics and Religion, 9*, 630–648.

Djupe, P.A., & Neiheisel, J.R. (2022). The dimensions and effects of reciprocity in political tolerance judgments. *Political Behavior, 44*, 895–914.

Djupe, P.A., Neiheisel, J.R., & Olson, L.R. (2015). Carriers of the creed? The effects of urging tolerance on persuasion. In P.A. Djupe (Ed.), Religion and political tolerance in America: Advances and state of the art (pp. 183–199). Philadelphia, PA: Temple University Press.

Doré, N., Satherley, N., Yogeeswaran, K., Vonasch, A., Verkuyten, M., & Sibley, C. (2022). Free speech or offensive speech: Profiling support for speech restrictions. *International Journal of Public Opinion Research*. (in press).

Dovidio, J.F., & Gaertner, S.L. (2004). Aversive racism. In M.P. Zanna (Ed.), Advances in experimental social psychology (Vol. 36, pp. 1–52). San Diego, CA: Academic Press.

Dovidio, J.F., Gaertner, S.L., & Saguy, T. (2015). Color-blindness and commonality: Included but invisible? *American Behavioral Scientist, 59*, 1518–1538

Doving, C.A. (2015). The wat they treat their daughters and wives: Radicalisation of Muslims in Norway. *Islamophobia Studies Journal, 3*, 62–77.

Douglas-Scott, S. (1999). The hatefulness of protected speech: A comparison of American and European approaches. *William and Mary Bill of Rights Journal*, 7, 305–346.

Dreger, A. (2015). Galileo's middle finger: Heretics, activists, and the search for justice in science. New York, NY: Penguin.

Drerup, J. (2018). Education for democratic tolerance, respect and the limits of political liberalism. *Journal of Philosophy of Education, 52*, 515–532.

Driel, E., & Verkuyten, M. (2020). Local identity and the welcoming reception of refugees: The example of Riace. Identities: Global Studies in Culture and Power, 27, 614–632

Driel, E., & Verkuyten, M. (2022). Contact theory and the multi-ethnic community of Riace, Italy: An ethnographic examination. *Journal of Community Psychology, 50*, 2326–2343.

Duckitt, J. (1992). The social psychology of prejudice. London, UK: Praeger.

Duerte, J.L., Crawford, J.T., Stern, C., Haidt, J., Jussim, L., & Tetlock, P. (2015). Political diversity will improve social and personality psychological science. *Behavioral and Brain Sciences, 38*, 1–13.

Dunn, K.M., Diallo, T.M., Sharples, R. (2021). Segmenting anti-Muslim sentiment in Australia: Insights for the diverse project of countering Islamophobia. *Ethnicities, 21*(3), 538–562.

Dunn, K.P., & Singh, S.P. (2011). The surprising non-impact of radical right-wing populist party representation on public tolerance of minorities. *Journal of Elections, Public Opinion, and Parties, 21*, 313–331.

Dutch Educational Council (2021). Sets limits, allow freedom. The Hague, The Netherlands: Educational Council.

Dworkin, R. (1993). Life's dominion. London, UK: Harper Collins.

Eagly, A.H., & Karau, S.J. (2002). Role congruity theory of prejudice toward female leaders. *Psychological Review, 109*, 573–598.

Earle, M., & Hodson, G. (2019). Right-wing adherence and objective numeracy as predictors of minority group size perceptions and size threat reactions. *European Journal of Social Psychology, 49*, 760–777.

Edgell, P., Gerteis, J., & Hartmann, D. (2006). Atheists as „other": Moral boundaries and cultural membership in American society. *American Sociological Review, 71*, 211–234.

Eisner, M., & Ghuneim, L. (2013). Honor killing attitudes amongst adolescents in Amman, Jordan. *Aggressive Behavior, 39*, 405–417.

Eitan, O., Viganola, D., Inbar, Y., Dreber, A., Johannesson, M., Pfeiffer, T., Thau, S., & Uhlmann, E.L. (2018). Is research in social psychology politically biased? Systematic empirical tests and a forecasting survey to address the controversy. *Journal of Experimental Social Psychology, 79*, 188–199.

Elchardus, M., & Spruyt, B. (2014). Universalism and anti-Muslim sentiment. *International Journal of Intercultural Relations, 38*, 75–85.

Ellemers, N. (2017). Morality and the regulation of social behaviour: Groups as moral anchors. London, UK: Routledge.

Erisen, C., & Kentmen-Cin, C. (2017). Tolerance and perceived threat toward Muslim immigrants in Germany and the Netherlands. *European Union Politics, 18*, 73–97.

Eronen, M.I. (2020). Causal discovery and the problem of psychological interventions. New Ideas in Psychology, 59, 100785

Eronen, M.I., & Bringmann, L.F. (2021). The theory crisis in psychology: How to move forward. *Perspectives in Psychological Science, 16*, 779–788.

Eskelinen, V., Renvik, T.A., Pauha, T., Jetten, J., Kunst, J., Van der Noll, J., Rohmann, A., & Jasinskaja-Lahti, I. (2022). Disentangling national and religious identification as predictors of support for religious minority rights among Christian majority groups. *British Journal of Social Psychology, 61*, 550–568.

Eskelinen, V., & Verkuyten, M. (2020). Support for democracy and liberal sexual mores among Muslims in Western Europe. *Journal of Ethnic and Migration Studies, 46*, 2346–2366.

Eugster, B. (2021). Variations in public opinion towards face veiling: Arguments in the Swiss debate. *Swiss Political Science Review, 27*, 712–730.

Evans, J.B.T. (2008). Dual-processing accounts of reasoning, judgment and social cognition. *Annual Review of Psychology, 59*, 255–278.

Evans, J.B.T., & Stanovich, K.E. (2013). Dual-process theories of higher cognition: Advancing the debate. *Perspectives on Psychological Science, 8*, 223–241.

Everett, J.A.C., Schellhaas, F.M.H., Earp, B., Ando, V., Memarzia, J., Parise, C.V., Fell, B., & Hewstone, M. (2015). Covered in stigma? The impact of differing levels of Islamic head-covering on explicit and implicit biases toward Muslim women. *Journal of Applied Social Psychology, 45*, 90–104.

Eyal, T., Liberman, N., & Trope, Y. (2008). Judging near and distant virtue and vice. *Journal of Experimental Social Psychology, 44*, 1204–1209.

Eyal, T., Steffel, M., & Epley, N. (2018). Perspective mistaking: Accurately understanding the mind of another requires getting perspective, not taking perspective. *Journal of Personality and Social Psychology, 114*, 547–571.

Fairlamb, S., & Cinnirella, M. (2021). To be or not to be tolerant? A terror management perspective exploring the ideological dilemma of tolerance and prejudice. *British Journal of Social Psychology, 60*, 360–382.

Faist, T., Gerdes, J., & Rieple, B. (2004). Dual citizenship as a path-dependent process. *International Migration Review, 38*, 913–944.

Fasel, N., Green, E.G.T., & Sarrasin, O. (2013). Unveiling naturalization: A multilevel study on minority proportion, conservative ideologies, and attitudes toward the Muslim veil. *Zeitschrift für Psychologie, 221*, 242–251.

Feinberg, M., & Willer, R. (2015). From gulfe to bridge: When do moral arguments facilitate political influence. *Personality and Social Psychology Bulletin, 41*, 1665–1681.

Feinberg, M., Willer, R., & Kovacheff, C. (2020). The activist's dilemma: Extreme protest actions reduce popular support for social movements. *Journal of Personality and Social Psychology, 19*, 1086–1111.

Feldman, G., & Albarracín, D. (2017). Norm theory and the action-effect: The role of social norms in regret following action and inaction. *Journal of Experimental Social Psychology, 69*, 111–120

Feldman, S. (2020). Authoritarianism, threat, and intolerance. In E. Borgida, C.M., Federico, & J.M. Miller (Eds.), At the forefront of political psychology. New York, NY: Routledge.

Felson, R.B. (1991). Blame analysis: Accounting for the behavior of protected groups. *American Sociologist, 22*, 5–23.

Ferguson, M.A., Branscombe, N.R., & Reynolds, K.J. (2019). Social psychological research on prejudice as collective action supporting emergent ingroup members. *British Journal of Social Psychology, 58*, 1–32.

Fernandez, S. (2009). The crusade over the bodies of women. *Patterns of Prejudice, 43*, 269–286

Fernbach, P.M., Rogers, T., Fox, C.R., & Sloman, S.A. (2013). Political extremism is supported by an illusion of understanding. *Psychological Science, 24*, 939–946

Ferrar, J.W. (1976). The dimensions of tolerance. *Pacific Sociological Review, 19*, 63–78.

Festinger, L. (1962). A theory of cognitive dissonance. Stanford, CA: Stanford University Press.

Fetzer, J.S., & Soper, J.C. (2003). The roots of public attitudes toward state accommodation of European Muslims' religious practices before and after September 11. *Journal for the Scientific Study of Religion, 42*, 247–258.

Figgou, L., & Condor, S. (2006). Irrational categorization, natural intolerance and reasonable discrimination: Lay representations of prejudice and racism. *British Journal of Social Psychology, 45*, 219–243.

Finkel, E.J., Bail, A., Cikara, M., Ditto, P.H., Iyengar, S., Klar, S., Mason, L., McGrath, M.C., Nyhan, B., Rand, D.G., Skitka, L.J., Tucker, J.A., Van Bavel, J., Wang, C.S., & Druckman, J.N. (2020). Political sectarism in America: A poisonous cocktail of othering, aversion, and moralization poses a threat to democracy. *Science, 370*, 533–536.

Fiske, A.P., & Rai, T.S. (2015). Virtuous violence. Cambridge, UK: Cambridge University Press.

Fleischmann, F., & Phalet, K. (2016). Identity conflict or compatibility: A comparison of Muslim minorities in five European cities. *Political Psychologist, 37*, 447–463

Forst, R. (2001). Tolerance as a virtue of justice. *Philosophical Explorations, 3*, 193–206.

Forst, R. (2013). Toleration in conflict: Past and present. Cambridge, UK: Cambridge University Press

Fraser, N. (2003). Recognition without ethics? In C. McKinnon & D. Castiglione (Eds.), The culture of toleration in diverse societies (pp. 86–109). Manchester, UK: Manchester University Press.

Freeman, L., & Stewart, H. (2021). Toward a harm-based account of microaggressions. *Perspectives on Psychological Science, 16*, 1008–1023.

Frimer, J.A., & Skitka, L.J. (2018). The Montagu principle: Incivility decreases politicians' public approval, even with their political base. *Journal of Personality and Social Psychology, 115*, 845–866.

Funder, D.C. (2009). Naïve and obvious questions. *Perspectives on Psychological Science, 4*, 340–344.

Furedi, F. (2011). On tolerance: A defence of moral independence. London, UK: Bloomsbury.

Gaasholt, O., & Togeby, L. (1995). Interethnic tolerance, education, and political orientation. *Political Behavior, 17*, 265–285.

Galeotti, A. (2002). Toleration as recognition. Cambridge, MA: Cambridge University Press.

Gampa, A., Wojcik, S.P., Motyl, M., Nosek, B.A., & Ditto, P.H. (2019). (Ideo)logical reasoning: Ideology impairs sound reasoning. *Social Psychological and Personality Science, 10*, 1075–1083.

Ganzach, Y., & Schul, Y. (2021). Partisan ideological attitudes: Liberals are tolerant; the intelligent are intolerant. *Journal of Personality and Social Psychology, 120*, 1551–1566.

Garcia, D.M., Reser, A.H., Amo, R.B., Redersdorff, S., & Branscombe, N.R. (2005). Perceivers' responses to in-group and out-group members who blame a negative outcome on discrimination. *Personality and Social Psychology Bulletin, 31*, 769–780.

Gardikiotis, A, (2011). Minority influence. *Social and Personality Psychology Compass, 5*, 679–693.

Gest, J. (2016). The new minority: White working-class politics in an age of immigration and inequality. Oxford, UK: Oxford University Press.

Gibson, J.L. (2005a). On the nature of tolerance: Dichotomous or continuous. *Political Behavior, 27*, 313–323.

Gibson, J.L. (2005b). Parsimony in the study of tolerance and intolerance. *Political Behavior, 27*, 339–345.

Gibson, J.L. (2006a). Enigmas of intolerance: Fifty years after Stouffer's communism, conformity, and civil liberties. *Perspectives on Politics, 4*, 21–34.

Gibson, J.L. (2006b). Do strong group identities fuel intolerance? Evidence from the South African case. *Political Psychology, 27*, 665–705.

Gibson, J., Claassen, C., & Barceló, J. (2020a). Putting groups back into the study of political intolerance. In E. Borgida, C.M., Federico, & J.M. Miller (Eds.), At the forefront of political psychology. New York, NY: Routledge.

Gibson, J., Claassen, C., & Barceló, J. (2020b). Deplorables: Emotions, Political sophistication, and political intolerance. *American Politics Research, 48*, 252–262.

Gibson, J.L., & Gouws, A. (2001). Making tolerance judgments: The effects of context, local and national. *The Journal of Politics, 63*, 1067–1090.

Gieling, M., Thijs, J., & Verkuyten, M. (2010). Tolerance of practices by Muslim actors: An integrative social-developmental perspective. *Child Development, 81*, 1384–1399.

Gieling, M., Thijs, J., & Verkuyten, M. (2011). Voluntary and involuntary immigrants and adolescents' endorsement of cultural maintenance. *International Journal of Intercultural Relations, 35*, 259–267.

Gieling, M., Thijs, J., & Verkuyten, M. (2012). Dutch adolescents' tolerance of practices by Muslim actors: The effect of issue framing. *Youth and Society, 44*, 348–365.

Gijsberts, M., & Lubbers, M. (2009). Wederzijdse beeldvorming (mutual images). The Hague, The Netherlands: Netherlands Institute for Social Research.

Glick, P., & Fiske, S.T. (2001). An ambivalent alliance: Hostile and benevolent sexism as complementary justifications for gender inequality. *American Psychologist, 56*, 109–118.

Golec de Zavala, A., Dyduch-Hazar, & Lantos, D. (2019). Collective narcissism: Political consequences of investing self-worth in the ingroup's image. Advances in Political Psychology, 40(Suppl. 1), 37–74

Goodwin, G.P., & Darley, J.M. (2008). The psychology of meta-ethics: Exploring objectivism. *Cognition, 106*, 1339–1366.

Goodwin, G.P., & Darley, J.M. (2012). Why are some moral beliefs perceived to be more objective than others? *Journal of Experimental Social Psychology, 48*, 250–256.

Górska, P., Stefaniak, A., Marchlewska, M., Matera, J., Kocyba, P., Lukianow, M., Malinowska, K., & Lipowska, K. (2022). Refugees welcome: Narcissistic and secure national commitment differently predict collective action against immigrants and refugees. *International Journal od Intercultural relations, 86*, 258–271.

Götz, F.M., Gosling, S.D., & Rentfrow, P.J. (2022). Small effects: The indispensable foundation for a cumulative psychological science. *Perspectives on Psychological Science, 17*, 205–215.

Gouldner, A.W. (1960). The norm of reciprocity: A preliminary statement. *American Sociological Review, 25*, 161–178.

Graham, J., Haidt, J., Koleva, S., Motyl, M., Iyer, R., Wojcik, S., & Ditto, P. (2013). Moral foundations theory: The pragmatic validity of moral pluralism. *Advances in Experimental Social Psychology, 47*, 55–130.

Greenaway, K.H., Cruwys, T., Haslam, S.A., & Jetten, J. (2016). Social identities promote well-being because they satisfy global psychological needs. *European Journal of Social Psychology, 46*, 294–307.

Greenberg, J., Simon, L., Pyszczynski, T., Solomon, S., & Chatel, D. (1992). Terror management and tolerance: Does mortality salience always intensify negative reactions to others who threaten one's worldview? *Journal of Personality and Social Psychology, 63*, 212–220.

Greene, J. (2013). Moral tribes: Emotion, reason and the gap between us and them. London: Penguin.

Grey, M., Devlin, M., & Goldsmith, A. (2009). Postville U.S.A.: Surviving diversity in small-town America. Boston, MA: Gemma.

Guimond, S., de la Sablonnière, R., & Nugier, A. (2014). Living in a multicultural world: Intergroup ideologies and the societal context of intergroup relations. *European Review of Social Psychology, 25*, 142–188.

Guinote, A., Brown, M., & Fiske, S. (2006). Minority status decreases sense of control and increases interpretive processing. *Social Cognition, 24*, 169–186.

Gustavsson, G., Van der Noll, J., & Sundberg, R. (2016). Opposing the veil in the name of liberalism: Popular attitudes to liberalism and Muslim veiling in the Netherlands. *Ethnic and Racial Studies, 39*, 1719–1737.

Haas, I.J., & Cunningham, W.A. (2014). The uncertainty paradox: Perceived threat moderates the effect of uncertainty on political tolerance. *Political Psychology, 35*, 291–302.

Hagendoorn, L., & Poppe, E. (2011). Consistency of tolerance, public opinion on immigrants in the Netherlands and the turn of the millennium. *Politics, Culture and Socialization, 2*, 367–387.

Haidt, J. (2001). The emotional dog and its rational tail: A social intuitionist approach to moral judgment. *Psychological Review, 108*, 814–834.

Haidt, J. (2012). The righteous mind: Why good people are divided by politics and religion. New York, NY: Pantheon Book

Haidt, J., Koller, S.H., & Dias, M. (1993). Affect, culture, and morality, or is wrong to eat your dog? *Journal of Personality and Social Psychology, 65*, 613–628.

Haidt, J., Rosenberg, E., & Hom, H. (2003). Differentiating diversities: Moral diversity is not like other kinds. *Journal of Applied Social Psychology, 33*, 1–36.

Haig, B.D. (2013). Detecting psychological phenomena: Taking bottom-up research seriously *The American Journal of Psychology, 126*, 135–153.

Haigh, M., Wood, J., & Stewart, A. (2016). Slippery slope arguments imply opposition to change. *Memory & Cognition, 44*, 819–836

Halperin, E., Canetti-Nisim, D., & Hirsch-Hoefler, S. (2009). The central role of group-based hatred as an emotional antecedent of political tolerance: Evidence from Israel. *Political Psychology, 30*, 93–123.

Hameiri, B., Bar-Tal, D., & Halperin, E. (2019). Paradoxical thinking interventions: A paradigm for societal change. *Social Issues and Policy Review, 113*, 36–62

Haré, R.M. (1981). Moral thinking. Oxford, UK: Oxford University Press.

Harell, A. (2010). The limits of tolerance in diverse societies: Hate speech and political tolerance norms among youth. *Canadian Journal of Political Science, 43*, 407–432.

Harmon-Jones, E., & Mills, J. (Eds.) (1999). Cognitive dissonance: Progress on a pivotal theory in social psychology. Washington, DC: American Psychological Association.

Harrell, J.P., Hall, S., & Taliaferro, J. (2003). Physiological responses to racism and discrimination: An assessment of the evidence. *American Journal of Public Health, 93*, 243–248.

Harpaz, Y. (2019). Compensatory citizenship: Dual nationality as a strategy of global upward mobility. *Journal of Ethnic and Migration Studies, 45*, 897–916.

Harpaz, Y., & Mateos, P. (2019). Strategic citizenship: Negotiating membership in the age of dual nationality. *Journal of Ethnic and Migration Studies, 45*, 843–857.

Harris, A. (2012). Young people and everyday multiculturalism. New York, NY: Routledge.

Harris, L.H. (2012). Recognizing conscience in abortion provision. *New England Journal of Medicine, 367*, 981–983.

Haslam, N. (2016). Concept creep: Psychology's expanding conceptions of harm and pathology. *Psychological Inquiry, 27*, 1–17.

Haslam, N., Rothschild, L., & Ernst, D. (2002). Are essentialist beliefs associated with prejudice? *British Journal of Social Psychology, 41*, 87–100

Haslam, N., Vylomova, E., Zyphur, M., & Kashima, Y. (2021). The cultural dynamics of concept creep. *American Psychologist, 76*, 1013–1026.

Havermans, W., & Verkuyten, M. (2021). Positive and negative behavioral intentions towards immigrants: A question of ethnic categorization or worldview conflict. *International Journal of Psychology, 56*, 633–641.

Hayden, R.M. (2002). Antagonistic tolerance: Competitive sharing of religious sites in South Asia and the Balkans. *Current Anthropology, 43*, 205–219.

Heerwig, J.A., & McCabe, B.J. (2009). Education and social desirability bias: The case of black presidential candidate. *Social Science Quarterly, 90*, 674–686.

Helbling, M. ((2014). Opposing Muslims and the Muslim headscarf in Western Europe. *European Sociological Review, 30*, 242–257.

Helbling, M., & Traunmüller, R. (2016). How state support of religion shapes attitudes toward Muslim immigrants: New evidence from a sub-national comparison. *Comparative Political Studies, 49*, 391–424.

Helbling, M., & Traunmüller, R. (2020). What is islamophobia? Disentangling citizens' feelings toward ethnicity, religion and religiosity using a survey experiment. *British Journal of Political Science, 50*, 811–828.

Helwig, C.C. (2008). The development of personal autonomy throughout cultures. *Cognitive Development, 21*, 458–473.

Helwig, C.C., & Prencipe, A. (1999). Children's judgments of flags and flag-burning. *Child Development, 70*, 132–143.

Henry, P.J. (2008). College sophomores in the laboratory redux: Influences of a narrow data base on social psychology's view of the nature of prejudice. *Psychological Inquiry, 19*, 49–71.

Henry, P.J., & Napier, J.L. (2017). Education is related to greater ideological prejudice. *Public Opinion Quarterly, 81*, 930–942.

Henrich, J., Heine, S.J., & Norenzayan, A. (2010). The weirdest people in the world? Behavioral and Brain Sciences, 33, 61–83.

Hess, D.E., & McAvoy, P. (2015). The political classroom: Evidence and ethics in democratic education. New York, NY: Routledge.

Hetherington, M., & Suhay, E. (2011). Authoritarianism, threat, and Americans' support for the war on terror. *American Journal of Political Science, 55*, 546–560.

Heyder, A., & Eisentraut, M. (2016). Islamophobia and criticism of Islam: An empirical study of explanations using representative surveys from Germany. *Islamophobia Studies Journal, 3*(2), 178–198.

Highton, B. (2009). Revisiting the relationship between educational attainment and political sophistication. *The Journal of Politics, 71*, 1564–1576

Hildreth, J.A.D., Gino, F., & Bazerman, M. (2016). Blind loyalty? When group loyalty makes us see evil or engage in it. *Organizational Behavior and Human Decision Processes, 132*, 16–36.

Hindriks, P., Verkuyten, M., & Coenders, M. (2015). The evaluation of immigrants' political acculturation strategies. *International Journal of Intercultural Relations, 47*, 131–142.

Hindriks, P., Verkuyten, M., & Coenders, M. (2017). Evaluating political acculturation strategies: The perspective of the majority and other minority groups. *Political Psychology, 38*, 741–756.

Hirsch, M., Verkuyten, M., & Yogeeswaran, K. (2019). To accept or not to accept: Level of moral concern impacts on tolerance of Muslim minority practices. *British Journal of Social Psychology, 58*, 196–210.

Hjerm, M., Eger, M.A., Bohman, A., & Connolly, F.F. (2020). A new approach to the study of tolerance: Conceptualizing and measuring acceptance, respect, and appreciation of difference. *Social Indicators Research, 147*, 897–919.

Hochschild, A.R. (2016). Strangers in their own land. New York, NY: The New Press.

Hodgson, D. (2002). Comparative perspectives on the indigenous rights movement in Africa and the Americas. *American Anthropologist, 104*, 1037–1049.

Hodson, G., & Dhont, K. (2015). The person-based nature of prejudice: Individual difference predictors of intergroup negativity. *European Review of Social Psychology, 26*, 1–42.

Hogg, M.A. (2001). Uncertainty-identity theory. *Advances in Experimental Social Psychology, 39*, 69–126.

Honneth, A. (1995). The struggle for recognition: The moral grammar of social conflicts. Cambridge, UK: Polity Press.

Honohan, I. (2013). Toleration and non-domination. In J. Dobbernack & T. Modood (Eds.), Tolerance, intolerance and respect (pp. 77–100). New York, NY: Palgrave Macmillan.

Hook, J.N., Farrell, J.E., Johnson, K.A., Van Tongeren, D.R., Davis, D.E., & Aten, J.D. (2017). Intellectual humility and religious tolerance. *The Journal of Positive Psychology, 12*, 29–35

Horowitz, M., Haynor, A., & Kickham, K. (2018). Sociology's sacred victims and the politics of knowledge: Moral foundations theory and disciplinary controversies. *American Sociologist, 49*, 459–495.

Horton, J. (1996). Toleration as a virtue. In D. Heyd (Ed.), Toleration: An elusive virtue (pp. 28–43). Princeton, NJ: Princeton University Press.

Howard, E. (2012). Banning Islamic veils: Is gender equality a valid argument? *International Journal of Discrimination and the Law, 12*, 147–165.

Howard, K.A., Cervone, D., & Motyl, M. (2022). On the varieties of diversity: Ideological variations in attitudes toward, and understandings of diversity. Personality and Social Psychology Bulletin, 48, 1039–1053.

Hughes, J.M., Alo, J., Krieger, K., & O'Leary, L. (2016). Emergence of internal and external motivations to respond without prejudice in White children. *Group Processes and Intergroup Relations, 19*, 202–216.

Hunsberger, B., & Jackson, L.M. (2005). Religion, meaning and prejudice. *Journal of Social Issues, 61*, 807–826.

Huntington, S.P. (1993). The clash of civilizations? *Foreign Affairs, 72*, 22–49.

Huijnk, W., & Andriessen, I. (2016). Integratie in zicht? De integratie van migranten in Nederland op acht terreinen bekeken (Integration in sight?). The Hague, Netherlands: Social and Cultural Planning Office.

Hurwitz, J., & Mondak, J.J. (2002). Democratic principles, discrimination and political intolerance. *British Journal of Political Science, 32*, 93–118.

Imhoff, R., & Recker, J. (2012). Differentiating islamophobia: Introducing a new scale to measure islamoprejudice and secular Islam critique. *Political Psychology, 33*, 811–824.

Insel, A. (2019). Tolerated but not equal. *Philosophy & Social Criticism, 45*, 511–515.

Itzchakov, G., Kluger, A.N., & Castro, D.R. (2017). I am aware of my inconsistencies but can tolerate them: The effect of high quality listening on speakers' attitude ambivalence. *Personality and Social Psychology Bulletin, 43*, 105–120.

Ivarsflaten, E., & Sniderman, P.M. (2017). The challenge of Muslim inclusion: A study in thresholds (Digsscore Working Paper Series 7). www.uib.no/sites/w3.uib.no/files/attachments/working_paper_2017-7.pdf.

Jackman, M.R. (1977). Prejudice, tolerance, and attitudes toward ethnic groups. *Social Science Research, 6*, 145–169.

Jackman, M.R. (1994). The velvet glove: Paternalism and conflict in gender, class, and race relations. Berkeley, CA: University of California Press.

Jackman, M.R., & Muha, M.J. (1984). Education and intergroup attitudes: Moral enlightenment, superficial democratic commitment, or ideological refinement. *American Sociological Review, 49*, 751–769

Jacoby, W.G. (1988). The sources of liberal-conservative thinking: Education and conceptualization. *Political Behavior, 10*, 316–332

Janmaat, J.G., & Keating, A. (2019). Are today's youth more tolerant? Trends in tolerance among young people in Britain. *Ethnicities, 19*, 44–65.

Janoff-Bulman, R., Sheikh, S., Hepp, S. (2009). Proscriptive versus prescriptive morality: Two faces of moral regulation. *Journal of Personality and Social Psychology, 93*, 521–537

Jargon, M., & Thijs, J. (2021). Antiprejudice norm and ethnic attitudes in preadolescents: A matter of stimulating the "right reasons". *Group Processes and Intergroup Relations, 24*, 468–487.

Jasinskaja-Lahti, I., Renvik, T.A., Van der Noll, J., Eskelinen, V., Rohmann, A., & Verkuyten, M. (2020). Dual citizenship and perceived loyalty of immigrants. *Group Processes and Intergroup Relations, 23*, 996–1013.

Jetten, J., & Wohl, M.J.A. (2012). The past as a determinant of the present: Historical continuity, collective angst, and opposition to immigration. *European Journal of Social Psychology, 42*, 442–450.

Jetten, J., Spears, R., & Manstead, A.S.R. (1997). Strength of identification and intergroup differentiation: The influence of group norms. *European Journal of Social Psychology, 27*, 603–609.

Jones, C.W., & Bejan, T.M. (2021). Reconsidering tolerance: Insights from Political theory and three experiments. *British Journal of Political Science, 51*, 604–623.

Jones, K.P., Peddie, C.I., Gilrane, V.L., King, E.B., & Gray, A.L. (2016). Not so subtle: A meta-analytic investigation of the correlates of subtle and overt discrimination. *Journal of Management, 42*, 1588–1613

Jones, P.N. (2010). Toleration and recognition: What should we teach? *Educational Philosophy and Theory, 42*, 38–56.

Joppke, C. (2004). The retreat of multiculturalism in the liberal state: Theory and policy. *The British Journal of Sociology, 55*, 237–257

Joppke, C. (2019). The instrumental turn of citizenship. *Journal of Ethnic and Migration Studies, 45*, 858–878.

Jordan, C., Spencer, S., & Zanna, M. (2005). Types of high self-esteem and prejudice: How implicit self-esteem relates to ethnic discrimination among high explicit self-esteem individuals. *Personality and Social Psychology Bulletin, 31*(5), 693–702.

Jost, J.T. (2017). Ideological asymmetries and the essence of political psychology. *Political Psychology, 38*, 167–208.

Jost, J.T., & Banaji, M.R. (1994). The role of stereotyping in system-justification and the production of false consciousness. *British Journal of Social Psychology, 33*, 1–27.

Jost, J.T., Glaser, J., Kruglanski, A.W., & Sulloway, F.J. (2003). Political conservatism as motivated social cognition. *Psychological Bulletin, 129*, 339–375

Jowett, A. (2017). 'One can hardly call them homophobic': Denials of antigay prejudice in within the same-sex marriage debate. *Discourse & Society, 28*, 281–295.

Jussim, L., Cain, T., Crawford, J., Harber, K., & Cohen, F. (2009). The unbearable accuracy of stereotypes. In T. Nelson (Ed.), Handbook of prejudice, stereotyping, and discrimination (pp. 199–227). Hillsdale, NJ: Erlbaum.

Jussim, L., Crawford, J.T., & Rubenstein, R.S. (2015). Stereotype (in)accuracy in perceptions of groups and individuals. *Current Directions in Psychological Science, 24*, 490–497.

Kachanoff, F.J., Gray, K., Koestner, R., Kteily, N., & Wohl, M.J.A. (2021). Collective autonomy: Why groups fight for power and status. Social and Personality Psychology Compass, w12652.

Kahan, D.M. (2012). Ideology, motivated reasoning, and cognitive reflection: An experimental study. *Judgment and Decision making, 8*, 407–424.

Kahneman, D., & Miller, D.T. (1986). Norm theory: Comparing reality to its alternatives. Psychological Review, 93, 136.

Kahneman, D., & Tversky, A. (1982). The psychology of preferences. *Scientific American, 246*, 160–173

Kaiser, C.R. (2006). Dominant ideology threat and the interpersonal consequences of attributions to discrimination. In S. Levin & C. van Laar (Eds.), Stigma and group inequality: Social psychological perspectives (pp. 45–64). Mahwah, NJ: Erlbaum.

Kaiser, C.R., & Miller, C.T. (2001). Stop complaining! The social costs of making attributions to discrimination. *Personality and Social Psychology Bulletin, 27*, 254–263.

Kalla, J.L., & Broockman, D.E. (2020). Reducing exclusionary attitudes through interpersonal conversation: *Evidence from Three Field Experiments, 114*, 410–425.

Kata, A. (2012). Anti-vaccine activists, Web 2.0, and the postmodern paradigm: An overview of tactics and tropes used online by the anti-vaccination movement. *Vaccine, 30*, 3778–3789.

Kauff, M., Asbrock, F., & Schmid, K. (2020). Pro-diversity beliefs and intergroup relations. European Review of Social Psychology, 32, 269–304.

Keblusek, L., Giles, H., & Maass, A. (2017). Communication and group life: How language and symbols shape intergroup relations. *Group Processes & Intergroup Relations, 20*, 632–643.

Keinan, R., & Bereby-Meyer, Y. (2017). Perceptions of active versus passive risks, and the effect of personal responsibility. *Personality and Social Psychology Bulletin, 43*, 999–1007

Kelman, H.C. (2001). The role of national identity in conflict resolution: Experiences from Israeli-Palestinian problem-solving workshops. In R.J. Ashmore, L. Jussim, & D. Wilder (Eds.), Social identity, intergroup conflict and conflict reduction (pp. 187–212). Oxford, UK: Oxford University Press.

Kessler, T., Neumann, J., Mummendey, A., Berthold, A., Schubert, T., & Waldzus, S. (2010). How do we assign punishment? The impact of minimal and maximal standards on the evaluation of deviants. *Personality and Social Psychology Bulletin, 36*, 1213–1224.

Kim, H-K., & Wreen, M. (2003). Relativism, absolutism, and tolerance. *Metaphilosophy, 34*, 447–459.

King, P. (2012). Toleration. London: Routledge.

Kirchner, A., Freitag, M., & Rapp, C. (2011). Crafting tolerance: The role of political institutions in a comparative perspective. *European Political Science Review, 3*, 201–227

Klein, A., & Zick, A. (2013). Toleranz versus Vorurteil? Eine empirische Analyse zum Verhälnis von Toleranz und Vorurteil. *Kölner Zeitschrift für Soziologie und Sozialpsychology, 65*, 277–300

Kleiner, B. (1998). The modern racist ideology and its reproduction in "pseudo-argument". *Discourse and Society, 9*, 187–215

Knowles, E.D., Lowery, B.S., Hogan, C.M., & Chow, R.M. (2009). On the malleability of ideology: Motivated construals of color blindness. *Journal of Personality and Social Psychology, 96*, 857–869.

Koopmans, R. (1999). Political opportunity structure: Some splitting to balance the lumping. *Sociological Forum, 14*, 93–105.

Koopmans, R., & Michalowski, I. (2017). Why do states extend rights to immigrants? Institutional settings and historical legacies across 44 countries worldwide. *Comparative Political Studies, 50*, 41–74.

Kordes-de Vaal, J.H. (1996). Intention and the omission bias: Omissions perceived as non-decisions. *Acta Psychologica, 93*, 161–172

Kosnick, K. (2004). 'Speaking in One's Own Voice': Representational strategies of Alevi Turkish migrants on Open-Access Television in Berlin. *Journal of Ethnic and Migration Studies, 30*, 979–994.

Kovacheff, C., Schwartz, S., Inbar, Y., & Feinberg, M. (2018). The problem of morality: Impeding progress and increasing divides. *Social Issues and Policy Review, 12*, 218–257.

Kraft, P.W., Klemmensen, R., & Larsen, E.G. (2019). Everyone cares about fairness: Why morality doesn't fit in a bag of words. Milwaukee, WI: University of Wisconsin.

Krolikowski, A.M., Rinella, M., & Ratcliff, J.J. (2016). The influence of expression of subtle and blatant sexual prejudice on personal prejudice and identification with the expresser. *Journal of Homosexuality, 63*, 228–249.

Krosnick, J.A. (1999). Survey research. *Annual Review of Psychology, 50*, 537–567

Krylov, A.I. (2021). The peril of politicizing science. *The Journal of Physical Chemistry Letters, 12*, 5371–5376.

Kugler, K.G., & Coleman, P.T. (2020). Get complicated: The effects of complexity on conversations over potentially intractable moral conflicts. *Negotiation and Conflict Management Research, 13*, 211–230.

Kuklinski, J.H., Riggle, E., Ottati, V., Schwarz, N., & Wyer, R.S. (1991). The cognitive and affective basis of political tolerance judgments. *American Journal of Political Science, 35*, 1–27.

Kumar, R., Seay, N., & Karabenick, S.A. (2015). Immigrant Arab adolescents in ethnic enclaves: Physical and phenomenological contexts of identity negotiation. *Cultural Diversity and Ethnic Minority Psychology, 21*, 201–212.

Kunst, J.R., Thomsen, L., & Dovidio, J.F. (2019). Divided loyalties: Perceptions of disloyalty underpin bias toward dually-identified minority-group members. *Journal of Personality and Social Psychology, 117*, 807–838

Kuppens, T., & Spears, R. (2014). You don't have to be well-educated to be an aversive racist, but it helps. *Social Science Research, 45*, 211–223.

Kuyper, L. (2012). Transgenders in Nederland: Prevalentie en attitudes (Transgenders in the Netherlands: Prevalence and attitudes). *Tijdschrift voor Seksuologie, 36*, 129–135.

Laegaard, S. (2010a). Recognition and toleration: Conflicting approaches to diversity in education? *Educational Philosophy and Theory, 42*, 22–37.

Laegaard, S. (2010b). 'Grand mosque' projects in Copenhagen: Intersections of respect, tolerance and intolerance in the distribution of public space. *Politics in Central Europe, 6*, 60–80.

Lalljee, M., Laham, S., & Tam, T. (2007). Unconditional respect for persons: A social psychological analysis. *Gruppendynamik und Organisationsberatung, 38*, 451–464.

Lalljee, M., Tam, T., Hewstone, M., Laham, S., & Lee, J. (2009). Unconditional respect for persons and the prediction of intergroup action tendencies. *European Journal of Social Psychology, 39*, 666–683

Lautenschlager, G.J., & Flaherty, V.L. (1990). Computer administration of questions: More desirable or more social desirability? *Journal of Applied Psychology, 75*, 310–314.

Lay, C., & Nguyen, T. (1998). Acculturated-related and acculturation non-specific hassles: Vietnamese-Canadian students and psychological distress. *Canadian Journal of Behavioral Science, 30*, 172–181.

Lee, F.L.F. (2014). "Tolerated one way but not the other": Levels and determinants of social and political tolerance in Hong Kong. *Social Indicators Research, 118*, 711–727.

Legate, N., Weinstein, N., Sendi, K., & Al-Khouja, M. (2020). Motives behind the veil: Women's affective experiences wearing a veil depend on their reasons for wearing one. *Journal of Research in Personality, 87*, 103969, 1–5.

Legault, L., Gutsell, J.N., Inzlicht, M., (2011). Ironic effects of antiprejudice messages: How motivational interventions can reduce (but also increase) prejudice. *Psychological Science, 22*, 1472–1477.

Leidner, B., & Castano, E. (2012). Morality shifting in the context of intergroup violence. *European Journal of Social Psychology, 42*, 82–91

Lemarchand, R., & Legg, K. (1972). Political clientelism and development: A preliminary analysis. *Comparative Politics, 4*, 149–178.

Lenard, P.T., & Balint, P. (2020). What is (the wrong of) cultural appropriation? *Ethnicities, 20*, 331–352.

Levari, D.E., Gilbert, D.T., Wilson, T.D., Sievers, B., Amodio, D.M., & Wheatly, T. (2018). Prevalence-induced concept change in human judgment. *Science, 360*, 1465–1567.

Levie, K. (2021, June 29). Transgenderzorg onder vuur: "Anderen beslissen over onze lichamen". OneWorld. Retrieved from www.oneworld.nl/lezen/seks-gender/lhbti/transgenderzorg-onder-vuur-psychologen-beslissen-over-onze-lichamen/

Levine, E.E., Barasch, A., Rand, D., Berman, J.Z., & Small, D.A. (2018). Signaling emotion and reason in cooperation. *Journal of Experimental Psychology: General, 147*, 702–719

Levine, M., & Manning, R. (2014). Social identity, group processes, and helping in emergencies. *European Review of Social Psychology, 24*, 225–251.

Leyro, T.M., Zvolensky, M.J., & Bernstein, A. (2010). Distress tolerance and psychopathological symptoms and disorders: A review of the empirical literature among young adults. *Psychological Bulletin, 136*, 576–600.

Lichtenberg, J. (2010). Negative duties, positive duties, and the "new harms". *Ethics, 120*, 557–578

Lin, H., Werner, K.M., & Inzlicht, M. (2021). Promises and perils of experimentation: The mutual-internal-validity problem. *Perspectives on Psychological Science, 16*, 854–863.

Lindner, N.M., & Nosek, B. (2009). Alienable speech: Ideological variations in the application of free-speech principles. *Political Psychology, 30*, 67–92.

Littlejohn, S. (2009). Speech act theory. In S. Littlejohn, & K. Foss (Eds.), Encyclopedia of communication theory (pp. 919–921). Thousand Oaks, CA: Sage.

Liu, J.H., & Hilton, D.J. (2005). How the past weighs on the present: Social representations of history and their role in identity politics. *British Journal of Social Psychology, 44*, 537–556.

Louis, W.R., Duck, J.M., Terry, D.J., Schuller, R.A., & Lalonde, R.N. (2007). Why do citizens want to keep refugees out? Threats, fairness and hostile norms in the treatment of asylum seekers. *European Journal of Social Psychology, 37*, 53–73.

Loury, G.C. (1994). Self-censorship in public discourse: A theory of "political correctness" and related phenomena. *Rationality and Society, 6*, 428–461.

Lovett, F. (2010). Cultural accommodation and domination. *Political Theory, 38*, 243–267.

Luguri, J.B., & Napier, J.L. (2013). Of two minds: The interactive effect of construal level and identity on political polarization. *Journal of Experimental Social Psychology, 49*, 972–977.

Luguri, J.B., Napier, J.L., & Dovidio, J.F. (2012). Reconstruing intolerance: Abstract thinking reduces conservatives' prejudice against nonnormative groups. *Psychological Science, 23*, 756–763.

Lui, P.P., & Quezada, L. (2019). Associations between microaggression and adjustment outcomes: A meta-analytic and narrative review. *Psychological Bulletin, 145*, 45–78.

Lukes, S. (2008). Moral relativism. London: Profile Books.

Machado, A., & Silva, F.J. (2007). Toward a richer view of the scientific method: The role of conceptual analysis. *American Psychologist, 62*, 671–681.

Ma-Kellams, C., Spencer-Rodgers, J., & Peng, K. (2011). I am against us? Unpacking cultural differences in ingroup favoritism via dialecticism. *Personality and Social Psychology Bulletin, 37*, 15–27

Marcuse, H. (1969). Repressive tolerance. In R.P. Wolfe, B. Moore jr., & H. Marcuse (Eds.), A critique of pure tolerance (pp. 81–123). Boston: Beacon.

Marcus, G.E., Theiss-Morse, E., Sullivan, J.L., & Wood, S.L. (1995). With malice toward some: How people make civil liberties judgments. Cambridge University Press.

Major, B., Dovidio, J.F., & Link, B.G. (Eds.) (2018). The Oxford Handbook of Stigma, Discrimination, and Health. Oxford, UK: Oxford University Press.

Major, B., Kaiser, C.R., O'Brien, L.T., & McCoy, S.K. (2007). Perceived discrimination as worldview threat or worldview confirmation: Implications for self-esteem. *Journal of Personality and Social Psychology, 92*, 1068–1086.

Major, B., & Kunstman, J.W. (2013). Suspicion in interracial interactions: Using measures of cardiovascular reactivity to index threat. In B. Derks, D. Scheepers, & N. Ellemers (Eds.), Neuroscience of prejudice and intergroup relations (pp. 316–333). New York, NY: Psychology Press.

Major, B., Mendes, W.B., & Dovidio, J.F. (2013). Intergroup relations and health disparities: A social psychological perspective. *Health Psychology, 32*, 514–524.

Malle, B.F. (2021). Moral judgments. *Annual Review of Psychology, 72*, 293–318.

Marshall, T.H. (1964). *Class, citizenship and social development*. New York, NY: Anchor books.

Marchlewska, M., Cichocka, A., Furnham, A., & Cislak, A. (2022). Who respects the will of the people? Support for democracy is linked to high secure national identity but low national narcissism. *British Journal of Social Psychology, 62,* 599–621.

Marcia, J. (1966). Development and validation of ego identity status. *Journal of Personality and Social Psychology, 3*, 551–558.

Marfouk, A. (2019). I'm neither racist nor xenophobic, but: Dissecting European attitudes towards a ban on Muslims' immigration. *Ethnic and Racial Studies, 42*, 1747–1765

Margalit, A., & Halbertal, M. (1994). Liberalism and the right to culture. *Social Research, 61*, 491–513.

Marquartz-Pyatt, S., & Paxton, P. (2007). In principle and in practice: Learning political tolerance in Eastern and Western Europe. *Political Behavior, 29*, 89–113.

Marques, J.M., & Paez, D. (1994). The 'black sheep effect': Social categorization, rejection of ingroup deviates, and perception of ingroup variability. *European Review of Social Psychology, 5*, 37–68.

Martinovic, B., & Verkuyten, M. (2012). Host national and religious identification among Turkish Muslims in Western Europe: The role of ingroup norms, perceived discrimination and value incompatibility. *European Journal of Social Psychology, 42*, 893–903.

Masten, A.S. (2014). Global perspectives on resilience in children and youth. Child Development, 85, 6–20.

Mather, D.M., & Tranby, E. (2014). New dimensions of tolerance: A case for a broader, categorical approach. *Sociological Science, 1*, 512–531.

Matthews, J. (2015). Framing alleged Islamist plots: A case study of British press coverage since 9/11. *Critical studies on Terrorism, 8*, 266–283.

McConnaughy, C., White, I.K., Leal, D.L., & Casellas, J.P. (2010). A Latino on the ballot: Explaining co-ethnic voting among Latinos and the response of White Americans. *The Journal of Politics, 72*, 1–13.

McCutcheon, A.L. (1985). A latent class analysis of tolerance for nonconformity in the American public. *Public Opinion Quarterly, 49*, 474–488.

McLaren, L.M. (2003). Anti-immigrant prejudice in Europe: Contact, threat perception, and preferences for the exclusion of migrants. *Social Forces, 81*, 909–936

McPheters, J., Conway, P., Hughes, J., & Zuckerman, M. (2018). Reflecting on God's will: Reflective processing contributes to religious people's deontological dilemma responses. *Journal of Experimental Social Psychology, 79*, 301–314

McWhorter, J. (2021). Woke racism: How a new religion has betrayed black America. New York, NY: Penguin

Meeusen, C., Meuleman, B., Abts, K., & Bergh, R. (2017). Comparing a variable-centered and a person-centered approach to the structure of prejudice. *Social Psychological and Personality Science, 9*, 645–655

Mekawi, Y., & Todd, N.R. (2021). Focusing the lens to see more clearly: Overcoming definitional challenges and identifying new directions in racial microaggressions research. *Perspective on Psychological Science, 16*, 972–990.

Mendes, W.B., & Koslov, K. (2013). Brittle smiles: Positive biases toward stigmatized and outgroup targets. *Journal of Experimental Psychology*, 923–933.

Meyer, D.S., & Minkoff, D.C. (2004). Conceptualizing political opportunity. *Social Forces, 82*, 1457–1492

Meyer, I.H. (2003). Prejudice, social stress, and mental health in lesbian, gay, and bisexual populations: Conceptual issues and research evidence. *Psychological Bulletin, 129*, 674–697.

Michel, J-B., Shen, Y.K., Aiden, A.P., Veres, A., Gray, M.K., The Google Books Team, Pickett, J.P., Hoiberg, D., Clancy, D., Norvig, P., Orwant, J., Pinker, S., Nowak, M.A., & Lieberman Aiden, E. (2011). Quantitative analysis of culture using millions of digitized books. *Science, 331*(6014), 176–182.

Michon, L., & Vermeulen, F. (2013). Explaining different trajectories in immigrant political integration: Moroccans and Turks in Amsterdam. *West European Politics, 36*, 597–614.

Mill, J.S. (1859/1978). On liberty. London: Penguin.

Miller, D. (2014). Majorities and minarets: Religious freedom and public space. *British Journal of Political Science, 46*, 437–456.

Minson, J.A., & Chen, F.S. (2022). Receptiveness to opposing views: Conceptualization and integrative review. *Personality and Social Psychology Review, 26*, 93–111.

Modood, T. (2014). Multiculturalism, interculturalism and the majority. *Journal of Moral Education, 43*, 302–315.

Modood, T., Beishon, S., & Virdee, S. (1994). Changing ethnic identities. London, UK: Policy Studies Institute.

Molden, D.C., & Higgins, E.T. (2012). Motivated thinking. In K.J. Holyoak & R.G. Morrison (Eds.), The Oxford handbook of thinking and reasoning (pp. 390–409). Oxford, UK: Oxford University Press.

Mondak, J.J., & Hurwitz. J. (1998). Values, acts, and actors distinguishing generic and discriminatory intolerance. *Political Behavior 20*, 313–339.

Mondak, J.J., & Sanders, M.S. (2004). Tolerance and intolerance, 1976–1998. *American Journal of Political Science, 47*, 492–502.

Mondak, J.J., & Sanders, M.S. (2005). The complexity of tolerance and intolerance in judgments: A response to Gibson. *Political Behavior, 27*, 325–337.

Morin, F., & Saladin d'Anglure, B. (1997). Ethnicity as a political tool for indigenous peoples. In C. Govers & H. Vermeulen (Eds.), The politics of ethnic consciousness (pp. 157–193). London, UK: Palgrave Macmillan.

Morris, M.W., Chiu, C-y., & Liu, Z. (2015). Polycultural psychology. Annual Review of Psychology, 66, 24.1–24.29.

Morton, T.A., Hornsey, M.J., & Postmes, T. (2009). Shifting grounds: The variable use of essentialism in contexts of inclusion and exclusion. *British Journal of Social Psychology, 48*, 35–59.

Morton, T.A., & Postmes, T. (2009). When differences become essential: Minority essentialism in response to majority treatment. *Personality and Social Psychology Bulletin, 35*, 656–668.

Moscovici, S., & Pérez, J.A. (2007). A study of minorities as victims. *European Journal of Social Psychology, 37*, 725–746.

Mosley, A.J., & Biernat, M. (2020). The new identity theft: Perceptions of cultural appropriation in intergroup contexts. *Journal of Personality and Social Psychology, 121,* 308–33.

Moss, A.J., Blodorn, A., Van Camp, A.R., & O'Brien, L.T. (2019). Gender equality, value violations, and prejudice toward Muslims. *Group Processes and Intergroup Relations, 22,* 288–301.

Mouritsen, P., & Olsen, T.V. (2013). Liberalism and the diminishing space of tolerance. In J. Dobbernack & T. Modood (Eds.), Tolerance, intolerance and respect (pp. 127–156). New York, NY: Palgrave MacMillan.

Muldoon, R., Borgida, M., & Cuffaro, M. (2011). The conditions of tolerance. *Politics, Philosophy and Economics, 11,* 322–344.

Mullinix, K.J., Leeper, T.J., Druckman, J.N., & Freese, J. (2015). The generalizability of survey experiments. *Journal of Experimental Political Science, 2,* 109–138.

Munzer, S.R. (2015). Secularization, anti-minority sentiment, and cultural norms in the German circumcision controversy. *University of Pennsylvania Journal of International Law, 37,* 503–582.

Murphy, S., & Genius, S.J. (2013). Freedom of conscience in health care: Distinctions and limits. *Bioethical Inquiry, 10,* 347–354.

Napier, J.L., & Luguri, J.B. (2012). Moral mind-sets: Abstract thinking increases a preference for 'individualizing' over 'binding' moral foundations. *Social Psychological and Personality Science, 4,* 754–759.

Nash, K., Yogeeswaran, K., Adelman, L., & Verkuyten, M. (2022). Tolerance is associated with increased activity in ACC, right DLPFC, and right insula. Manuscript in preparation.

Navas, M.S., Rojas, A.J., García, M.C., & Pumares, P. (2007). Acculturation strategies and attitudes according to the relative acculturation extended model (RAEM): The perspectives of natives versus immigrants. *International Journal of Intercultural Relations, 31,* 67–86.

Nehushtan, Y. (2007). The limits of tolerance: A substantive-liberal perspective. *Ratio Juris, 20,* 230–257.

Nelson, T.E., Clawson, R.A., & Oxley, Z.M. (1997). Media framing of a civil liberties conflict and its effect on tolerance. American Political Science Review, 567–583.

Newheiser, A.K., & Barreto, M. (2014). Hidden costs of hiding stigma: Ironic interpersonal consequences of concealing a stigmatized identity in social interactions. *Journal of Experimental Social Psychology, 52,* 58–70.

Newman, B., Merolla, J.L., Shah, S., Lemi, D.S., Collingwood, L., & Ramakrishnan, S.K. (2021). The Trump effect: An experimental investigation of the emboldening effect of racial inflammatory elite communication. *British Journal of Political Science, 51,* 1138–1159.

Ng Tseung Wong, C., & Verkuyten, M. (2018). Diversity ideologies and intergroup attitudes: When multiculturalism is beneficial for majority group members. *Group Processes and Intergroup Relations, 21,* 336–350

Ngole, P. (2018). Felix Ngole behand the scenes: The story of one social worker's battle with his university. London, UK: Christian Legal Centre.

Nicolle, A., Fleming, S.M., Bach, D.R., Driver, J., & Dolan, R.J. (2011). A regret-induced status quo bias. *Journal of Neuroscience, 31,* 3320–3327.

Nisbett, R.E., & Cohen, D. (1996). Culture of honor: The psychology of violence in the South. Boulder, CO: Westview Press.

Norris, P., & Inglehardt, R. (2004). Sacred and secular: Religion and politics worldwide. Cambridge, UK: Cambridge University press.

Obeid, N., Argo, N., & Ginges, J. (2017). How moral perceptions influence intergroup tolerance: Evidence from Lebanon, Morocco, and the United States. *Personality and Social Psychology Bulletin*, *43*, 381–391.

Oberdiek, H. (2001). Tolerance between forbearance and acceptance. Lanham, MD: Rowman and Littlefield.

OECD. (2020, June). Over the rainbow? The road to LGBTI inclusion. Retrieved from www.oecd.org/netherlands/OECD-LGBTI-2020-Over-The-Rainbow-Netherlands.pdf

Ofosu, E.K., Chambers, M.K., Chen, J.M., & Hehman, E. (2019). Same-sex marriage legalization associated with reduced implicit and explicit antigay bias. *PNAS*, *116*(18), 8845–8851.

Ogan, C., Willnat, L., Pennington, R., & Bashir, M. (2014). The rise of anti-Muslim prejudice: Media and Islamophobia in Europe and the United States. *The International Communication Gazette*, *76*, 27–46.

Ohlander, J., Batalova, J., & Treas, J. (2005). Explaining educational influences on attitudes toward homosexual relations. *Social Science Research*, *34*, 781–799.

Okin, S.M. (1999). Is multiculturalism bad for women? Princeton, NJ: Princeton University Press.

Omlo, J. (2011). Integratie en uit de gratie? Perspectieven van Marokkaans-Nederlandse jongvolwassenen (Integratie and no acceptance?). Delft, The Netherlands: Eburon

O'Neill, D.I. (1999). Multicultural liberals and the Rushdie affair: A critique of Kymlicka, Taylor, and Walzer. *Review of Politics*, *61*, 219–250.

Orazani, N., Tabri, M., Wohl, M.J.A., & Leidner, B. (2021). Social movement strategy (nonviolent vs. violent) and the garnering of third-party support: A meta-analysis. *European Journal of Social Psychology*, *51*, 645–658.

Orazani, S.N., Wohl, M.J.A., & Leidner, B. (2020). Perceived normalization of radical ideologies and its effect on political tolerance and support for freedom of speech. *Group Processes and Intergroup Relations*, *23*, 1150–1170.

Orgad, L. (2015). The cultural defense of nations: A liberal theory of majority rights. Oxford, UK: Oxford university press.

Orlenius, K. (2008). Tolerance of intolerance: Values and virtues at stake in education. *Journal of Moral Education*, *37*, 467–484.

Osborne, D., & Sibley, C.G. (2012). Does personality matter? Openness correlates with vote choice but particularly for politically sophisticated voters. *Journal of Research in Personality*, *46*, 743–751

Osborne, D., & Sibley, C.G. (2017). Identifying "types" of ideologies and intergroup biases: Advancing a person-centred approach to social psychology. *European Review of Social Psychology*, *28*, 288–332.

Osler, A. (2010). Students' perspectives on schooling. Maidenhead, UK: Open University Press.

Ostapczuk, M., Musch, J., & Moshagen, M. (2009). A randomized-response investigation of the education effect in attitudes towards foreigners. *European Journal of Social Psychology*, *39*, 920–931

Outten, H.R., Schmitt, M.T., Miller, D.A., & Garcia, A.L. (2012). Feeling threatened about the future: White's emotional reactions to anticipated ethnic demographic changes. *Personality and Social Psychology Bulletin*, *38*, 14–25

Pande, R. (2003). Can mandated political representation increase policy influence for disadvantaged minorities? Theory and evidence from India. *The American Economic Review*, *93*, 1132–1151

Park, B., & Judd, C.M. (2005). Rethinking the link between categorization and prejudice within the social cognition perspective. *Personality and Social Psychology Review, 9*, 108–130.

Pascoe, E.A., & Smart Richman, L. (2009). Perceived discrimination and health: A meta-analytic review. *Psychological Bulletin, 135*, 531–554.

Patten, A. (2020). Populist multiculturalism: Are there majority cultural rights? *Philosophy and Social Criticism, 46*, 1–14.

Pearce, R. (2018). Understanding trans health: Discourse, power and possibility. Bristol, UK: Policy Press.

Peffley, M., Knigge, P., & Hurwitz, J. (2001). A multiple values model of political tolerance. *Political Research Quarterly, 54*, 379–406

Peffley, M., & Rohrschneider, R. (2003). Democratization and political tolerance in seventeen countries: A multi-level model of democratic learning. *Political Research Quarterly, 56*(3), 243–257

Peng, K., & Nisbett, R.E. (1999). Culture, dialects, and reasoning about contradiction. *American Psychologist, 54*, 741–754.

Pennycook, G. (2020). Belief bias and its significance for modern social science. *Psychological Inquiry, 31*, 57–60.

Pennycook, G., Cheyne, J.A., Barr, N., Koehler, D.J., & Fugelsang, J.A. (2014). The role of analytic thinking in moral judgements and values. *Thinking & Reasoning, 20*, 188–214

Pennycook, G., Fugelsang, J.A., & Koehler, D.J. (2015). Everyday consequences of analytic thinking. *Current Directions in Psychological Science, 24*, 425–432.

Pennycook, G., & Rand, D.G. (2019). Lazy, not biased: Susceptibility to partisan fake news is better explained by lack of reasoning than by motivated reasoning. *Cognition, 188*, 39–50.

Pereira, C., Vala, J., & Costa-Lopes, R. (2010). From prejudice to discrimination: The legitimizing role of perceived threat in discrimination against immigrants. *European Journal of Social Psychology, 40*, 1231–1250.

Petersen, M., Slothuus, R., Stubager, R., & Togebey, L. (2011). Freedom for all? The strength and limits of political tolerance. *British Journal of Political Science, 41*, 581–597.

Petit, P. (1997). Republicanism. Oxford, UK: Oxford University Press.

Petrusevska, T. (Ed.) (2009). A guide to minorities and political participation in South-East Europe. Brussels, Belgium: King Baudouin Foundation

Pew Research Center (2017). U.S. Muslims concerned about their place in society, but continue to believe in the American dream. Washington, DC: Pew Research Center.

Phinney, J.S., Jacoby, B., & Silva, C. (2007). Positive intergroup attitudes: The role of ethnic identity. *International Journal of Behavioral Development, 31*, 478–490.

Pizarro, D.A., & Bloom, P. (2003). The intelligence of the moral intuitions: Comment on Haidt (2001). *Psychological Review, 110*, 193–196.

Plant, E.A., & Devine, P.G. (1998). Internal and external motivation to respond without prejudice. *Journal of Personality and Social Psychology, 75*, 811–832.

Plante, C.N., Roberts, S., Reysen, S., & Gerbasi, K. (2014). Interaction of socio-structural characteristics predicts identity concealment and self-esteem in stigmatized group members. *Current Psychology, 33*, 3–19

Pluckrose, H., & Lindsay, J. (2020). Cynical theories: How activist scholarship made everything about race, gender and identity. Durham, NC: Pitchstone.

Politi, E., Roblain, A., Gale, J., Licata, L., and Staerklé, C. 2020. If you want to be one of us, then become like us: The evaluation of naturalization applicants by host nationals. *European Journal of Social Psychology, 50*, 839–856

Popan, J.R., Coursey, L., Acosta, J., & Kenworthy, J. (2019). Testing the effects of incivility during internet political discussion on perceptions of rational argument and evaluations of a political outgroup. *Computers in Human Behavior, 96*, 123–132.

Popper, K.R. (1945). The open society and its enemies. London, UK: George Routledge & Sons.

Prislin, R., & Filson, J. (2009). Seeking conversion versus advocating tolerance in the pursuit of social change. *Journal of Personality and Social Psychology, 97*, 811–822.

Quinn, D.M., & Earnshaw, V.A. (2011). Understanding concealable stigmatized identities: The role of identity in psychological, physical, and behavioral outcomes. *Social Issues and Policy Review, 5*, 160–190.

Ram, A., & Ross, H.S. (2001). Problem solving, contention, and struggle: How siblings resolve a conflict of interest. *Child Development, 72*, 1710–1722.

Ramadan. T. (2010). The quest for meaning. Harmondsworth, UK: Penguin.

Ramos, M.R., Bennett, M.R., Massey, D.S., & Hewstone, M. (2019). Humans adapt to social diversity over time. *PNAS, 116*, 12244–12249.

Rapp, C. (2017). Shaping tolerant attitudes towards immigrants: The role of welfare state expenditure. *Journal of European Social Policy, 27*, 40–56.

Rauch, J. (2021). The constitution of knowledge: A defense of truth. Washington, DC: Brookings Institute Press.

Raz, J. (1994). Ethics in the public domain. Oxford, UK: Oxford University Press.

Reicher, S., Cassidy, C., Wolpert, I., Hopkins, N., & Levine, M. (2006). Saving Bulgaria's Jews: An analysis of social identity and the mobilisation of social solidarity. *European Journal of Social Psychology, 36*, 49–72.

Reicher, S., & Hopkins, N. (2001). Self and nation. London, UK: Sage.

Reicher, S., Spears, R., & Haslam, S.A. (2010). The social identity approach in social psychology. In M. Wetherell & C.T. Mohanty (Eds.), The Sage handbook of identities (pp. 45–62). London, UK: Sage.

Rhee, J.J., Schein, C., & Bastian, B. (2019). The what, how, and why of moralization: A review of current definitions, methods, and evidence in moralization research. Social Personality and Psychology Compass, e12511.

Ribberink, E., Achterberg, P., & Houtman, D. (2017). Secular tolerance? Anti-Muslim sentiment in Western Europe. *Journal for the Scientific Study of Religion, 56*, 259–276.

Richardson, J.E. (2009). 'Get shot of the lot of them': Election reporting of Muslims in British newspapers. *Patterns of Prejudice, 43*, 367–377.

Richman, L.S., & Leary, M.R. (2009). Reactions to discrimination, stigmatization, ostracism, and other forms of interpersonal rejection: A multimotive model. *Psychological Review, 116*, 365–383

Ricoeur, P. (1996). The erosion of tolerance and the resistance of the intolerable. *Diogenes, 44*, 189–201.

Riek, B.M., Mania, E.W., & Gaertner, S.L. (2006). Intergroup threat and outgroup attitudes: A meta-analytic review. *Personality and Social Psychology Review, 10*, 336–353.

Rinaldis, A. 2016. Riace il paese di accoglienza, Un modello alternativo di integrazione (Riace place of hospitality: An alternative model of integration). Reggio Emilia: Imprimatur.

Robertson, A.D., & Hairston, W.T. (2022). Observing whiteness in introductory physics: A case study. Physics Review Physics Educational Research, 18, 010119.

Roccas, S., & Amit, A. (2011). Group heterogeneity and tolerance: The moderating role of conservative values. *Journal of Experimental Social Psychology, 47*, 898–907.

Röder, A., & Spierings, N. (2022). What shapes attitudes toward homosexuality among European Muslims? The role of religiosity and destination hostility. *International Migration Review, 56*, 533–561.

Rodriguez, C.G., & Ditto, P.H. (2019). Another kind of diversity: A case study on abortion attitudes. Retrieved from www.spssi.org/index.cfm?pageID=2406&nodelD=1&fuseaction=page.viewPage.

Roebroeck, E., & Guimond, S. (2017). Intergroup threat, social dominance, and the malleability of ideology: The importance of conceptual replication. *European Journal of Social Psychology, 48*, 134–149.

Roets, A., & Van Hiel, A. (2011). Allport's prejudiced personality today: Need for closure as the motivated cognitive basis of prejudice. *Current Directions in Psychological Science, 20*(6), 349–354.

Roggeband, C., & Verloo, M. (2007) Dutch Women are liberated, migrant women are a problem: The evolution of policy frames on gender and migration in the Netherlands (1995–2005). *Social Policy & Administration, 41*, 271–288

Rosenfeld, M.J. (2017). Moving a mountain: The extraordinary trajectory of same-sex marriage approval in the United States. *Socius, 3*, 1–22.

Rothberg, H. (2013). Tolerism: The ideology revealed (2nd ed.). London, UK: Mantua Books

Rozin, P. (1999). The process of moralization. *Psychological Science, 10*, 218–221.

Rozin, P. (2009). What kind of empirical research should we publish, fund, and reward? A different perspective. *Perspectives on Psychological Science, 4*, 435–439.

Ryan, R.M., & Deci, E.L. (2017). Self-determination: Basic psychological needs in motivation, developments and wellness. New York, NY: Guildford.

Sanchez, D.T. (2010). How do forced-choice dilemma affect multiracial people? The role of identity autonomy and public regard in depressive symptoms. *Journal of Applied Social Psychology, 40*, 1657–1677.

Sandel, M.J. (1989). Moral argument and liberal toleration: Abortion and homosexuality. *California Law Review*, 77, 521–538

Sandel, M.J. (1996). Judgmental toleration. In R.P. George (Ed.), Natural law, liberalism, and morality: Contemporary essays. Oxford, UK: Clarendon Press.

Sani, F. (Ed.) (2008). Self continuity: Individual and collective perspectives. New York, NY: Psychology Press.

Sani, F., Bowe, M., & Herrera, M. (2008). Perceived collective continuity: Seeing groups as temporally enduring entities. In F. Sani (Ed.), Self continuity: Individual and collective perspectives (pp. 159–172). Hove, UK: Psychology Press.

Sani, F., & Reicher, S. (1999). Identity, argument and schisms: Two longitudinal studies of the split of the church of England over the ordination of women to the priesthood. *Group Processes and Intergroup Relations, 2*, 279–300.

Saroglou, V., Lamkaddem, B., Van Pachterbeke, M., & Buxant, C. (2009). Host society's dislike of the Islamic veil: The role of subtle prejudice, values and religion. *International Journal of Intercultural Relations, 33*, 419–428.

Sasso, C. (2012). Riace, terra di accoglienza (Riace, land of hospitality). Turin, Italy: Edizioni Gruppo Abele.

Savelkoul, M., te Grotenhuis, M., & Scheepers, P. (2022). Has the terrorist attack on Charlie Hebdo fuelled resistance towards Muslim immigrants in Europe? Results from a natural experiment in six European countries. Acta Sociologica. Retreived from https://doi.org/10.1177/00016993221088447.

Scanlon, T.M. (2003). The difficulty of tolerance: Essays in political philosophy. Cambridge, UK: Cambridge University Press.

Scanlon, T.M. (2004). Reasons: A puzzling duality. In R.J. Wallace, S. Scheffler, & M. Smith (Eds.), Reason and value: Themes from moral philosophy of Joseph Raz (pp. 231–246). Oxford, UK: Oxford University Press.

Scheepers, D. (2013). Studying social identity-based threats and challenges using cardiovascular measures. In B. Derks, D. Scheepers, & N. Ellemers (Eds.), Neuroscience of prejudice and intergroup relations (pp. 243–259). New York, NY: Psychology Press.

Schildkraut, D.J. (2013). Which birds of a feather flock together? Assessing attitudes about descriptive representation among Latinos and Asian Americans. *American Politics Research, 41*, 699–729.

Schinkel, A. (2021). Leer je kinderen minder tolereren! (Lear your children to tolerate less!). *Pedagogiek, 41*, 243–250.

Schirmer, W., Weidenstedt, L., & Reich, W. (2012). From tolerance to respect in inter-ethnic contexts. *Journal of Ethnic and Migration Studies, 38*, 1049–1065.

Schlueter, E., & Schmidt, P. (2010). Special issue: Survey experiments [Editorial]. *Methodology: European Journal of Research Methods for the Behavioral and Social Sciences, 6*, 93–95.

Schmitt, M.T., & Branscombe, N.R. (2002). The meaning and consequences of perceived discrimination in disadvantaged and privileged social groups. *European Review of Social Psychology, 12*, 167–199.

Schmitt, M.T., Branscombe, N.R., Postmes, T., & Garcia, A. (2014). The consequences of perceived discrimination for psychological well-being: A meta-analytic review. *Psychological Bulletin, 140*, 921–948.

Schneider, J., Fokkema, T., Matias, R., Stojcic, S., Ugrina, D., & Vera-Larrucea, C. (2012). Identities: Urban belonging and intercultural relations. In M. Crul, J. Schneider, & F. Lelie (Eds.), The European second generation compared: Does the integration context matter? (pp. 285–340). Amsterdam, The Netherlands: Amsterdam University Press.

Schuyt, K. (1997). Continuïteit en verandering in de idee van tolerantie (Continuity and change in the idea of toleration). In N. Wilterdink, J. Heilbron, & A. de Swaan (Eds.), Alles verandert (Everything changes)(pp. 167–178). Amsterdam, The Netherlands: Meulenhoff.

SCP, WODC & CBS. (2005). Jaarrapport integratie 2005 [Year report on integration 2005]. The Hague, The Netherlands: Social Cultural Planning office.

Sears, D.O., & Henry, P.J. (2003). The origins of symbolic racism. *Journal of Personality and Social Psychology, 85*, 259–275.

Sechrist, G.B., Swim, J.K., & Stangor, C. (2004). When do the stigmatized make attributions to discrimination occurring to the self and others? The roles of self-presentation and need for control. *Journal of Personality and Social Psychology, 87*, 111–122.

Serano, J. (2007) Whipping girl: A transsexual woman on sexism and the scapegoating of femininity. Emeryville, CA: Seal Press.

Shadid, W.A. (2006). Public debates over Islam and the awareness of Muslim identity in the Netherlands. *European Education, 38*, 10–22.

Shafer, E.S., & Prislin, R. (2011). Conversion vs. Tolerance: Minority-focused influence strategies can affect group loyalty. *Group Processes and Intergroup Relations, 14*, 755–766.

Shaver, J.H., Sibley, C.G., Osborne, D., & Bulbulia, J. (2017). News exposure predicts anti-Muslim prejudice. *PLoS One, 12*(3), e0174606

Shaver, J.H., Troughton, G., Sibley, C.G., & Bulbulia, J. (2016). Religion and unmaking of prejudice toward Muslims: Evidence from a large national sample. PLoS One, 11, e0150209.

Shelton, J.N., & Richeson, J.A. (2006). Interracial interactions: A relational approach. In M.P. Zanna (Ed.), Advances in experimental social psychology, vol. 38 (pp. 121–181). San Diego, CA: Elsevier.

Shelton, J.N., Richeson, J.A., Salvatore, J., & Hill, D.M. (2006). Silence is golden: The intrapersonal consequences of not confronting prejudice. In S. Levin & C. van Laar (Eds.), Stigma and group inequality: Social psychological perspectives (pp. 65–81). Mahwah, NJ: Erlbaum.

Shynkaruk, J.M., & Thompson, V.A. (2006). Confidence and accuracy in deductive reasoning. *Memory & Cognition, 34*, 619–632

Sidanius, J., & Pratto, F. (1999). Social dominance: An intergroup theory of social hierarchy and oppression. New York, NY: Cambridge University Press.

Siebers, H. (2017). 'Race' versus 'ethnicity'? Critical race essentialism and the exclusion and oppression of migrants in the Netherlands. *Ethnic and Racial Studies, 40*, 369–387.

Silver, L. (2018, 22 October). Immigration concerns fall in Western Europe, but most see need for newcomers to integrate into society. Pew Research Center. Retrieved from www.pewresearch.org/fact-tank/2018/10/22/immigration-concerns-fall-in-western-europe-but-most-see-need-for-newcomers-to-integrate-into-society/

Simon, B. (2020). A new perspective on intergroup conflict: The social psychology of politicized struggles for recognition. *Theory & Psychology, 30*, 147–163.

Simon, B., Eschert, S., Schaefer, C.D., Reininger, K.M., Zitzmann, S., & Smith, H.J. (2019). Disapproved, but tolerated: The role of respect in outgroup tolerance. *Personality and Social Psychology Bulletin, 45*, 406–415.

Simon, B., & Klandermans, B. (2001). Politicized collective identity: A social-psychological analysis. *American Psychologist, 56*, 319–331.

Simpson, B., Willer, R., & Feinberg, M. (2018). Does violent protest backfire? Testing a theory of public reactions to activist violence. *Socius, 4*, 1–14.

Sindic, D., Reicher, S.D. (2009). 'Our way of life is worth defending': Testing a model of attitudes towards superordinate group membership through a study of Scots' attitudes towards Britain. *European Journal of Social Psychology, 39*, 114–129.

Skitka, L.J. (2002). Do the means always justify the ends, or do the ends sometimes justify the means? A value protection model of justice reasoning. *Personality and Social Psychology Bulletin, 28*, 588–597.

Skitka, L.J., Bauman, C.W., & Mullen, E. (2004). Political tolerance and coming to psychological closure following the September 11, 2002, terrorist attacks: An integrative approach. *Personality and Social Psychology Bulletin, 30*, 743–756.

Skitka, L.J., Hanson, B.E., Morgan, G.S., & Wisneski, D.C. (2021). The psychology of moral conviction. *Annual Review of Psychology, 72*, 347–366

Skitka, L.J., Liu, J.H., Yang, Y., Chen, H., Liu, L., & Xu, L. (2013). Exploring the cross-cultural generalizability and scope of morally motivated intolerance. *Social Psychological and Personality Science, 4*, 324–331.

Skitka, L.J., Mullen, E. (2002). Understanding judgments of fairness in a real-world political context: A test of the value protection model of justice reasoning. *Personality and Social Psychology Bulletin, 28*, 1419–1429.

Sleijpen, S., Verkuyten, M., & Adelman, L. (2020). Accepting Muslim minority practices: A case of discriminatory or normative intolerance? *Journal of Community and Applied Social Psychology, 30*, 405–418.

Sloman, S.A. (1996). The empirical case for two systems of reasoning. *Psychological Bulletin, 119*, 3–22.

Smeekes, A., & Verkuyten, M. (2014a). Collective self-continuity, group identification and in-group defense. *Journal of Experimental Social Psychology, 49*, 984–994.

Smeekes, A., & Verkuyten, M. (2014b). When national culture is disrupted: Cultural continuity and resistance to Muslim immigrants. *Group Processes and Intergroup Relations, 17*, 45–66.

Smeekes, A., Verkuyten, M., & Poppe, E. (2011). Mobilising opposition towards Muslim immigrants: National identification and the representation of national history. *British Journal of Social Psychology*, *50*, 265–280.

Smeekes, A., Verkuyten, M., & Poppe, E. (2012). How a tolerant past affects the present: Historical tolerance and the acceptance of Muslim expressive rights. *Personality and Social Psychology Bulletin*, *38*, 1410–1422.

Sniderman, P. (2018). Some advances in the design of survey experiments. *Annual Review of Political Science*, *21*, 259–275.

Sniderman, P.M., & Hagendoorn, L. (2007). When ways of life collide. Princeton, NJ: Princeton University Press.

Sniderman, P., Hagendoorn, L., & Prior, M. (2004). Predisposing factors and situational triggers: Exclusionary reactions to immigrant minorities. *American Political Science Review*, *98*, 35–49.

Sniderman, P.M., Petersen, M.B., Slothuus, R., & Stubager, R. (2014). Paradoxes of liberal democracy: Islam, Western Europe, and the Danish cartoon crisis. Princeton, NJ: Princeton University Press.

Sniderman, P.M., & Tetlock, P.E. (1986). Symbolic racism: Problems of motive attribution in political analysis. *Journal of Social Issues*, *42*, 129–150.

Sniderman, P.M., Tetlock, P.E., Glaser, J.M., Green, D.P., & Hout, M. (1989). Principled tolerance and the American mass public. *British Journal of Political Science*, *19*, 25–45.

Sobolewska, M. (2013). Party strategies and the descriptive representation of ethnic minorities: The 2010 British general election. *West European Politics*, *36*, 615–633.

Sökefeld, M. 2008. Struggling for recognition: Alevi movement in Germany and in transnational space. New York, NY: Berghan Books.

Solomon, S.S. (2016). Shifting discourses of tolerance: The framing of Muslim minorities in the US and the UK before and after national traumas. Carlisle, PA: Dickinson College Honors Theses. Paper 226.

Son Hing, L.S., Chung-Yan, G.A., Hamilton, L.K., & Zanna, M.P. (2008). A two-dimensional model that employs explicit and implicit attitudes to characterize prejudice. *Journal of Personality and Social Psychology*, *94*, 971–987

Spencer-Rogers, J., Williams, M., & Peng, K. (2010). Cultural differences in expectations of change and tolerance for contradiction: A decade of empirical research. *Personality and Social Psychology Review*, *14*, 296–312.

Spiegler, O., Christ, O., & Verkuyten, M. (2022). National identity exploration attenuates the identification-prejudice link. *Group Processes and Intergroup Relations, 25,* 902–923.

Spiegler, O., Verkuyten, M., Thijs, J., & Leyendecker, B. (2016). Low ethnic identity exploration undermines positive interethnic relations: A study among Turkish immigrant-origin youth. *Cultural Diversity and Ethnic Minority Psychology*, *22*, 495–503

Spruyt, B., & Elchardus, M. (2012). Are anti-Muslim feelings more widespread than anti-foreigner feelings? Evidence from two split-sample experiments. *Ethnicities*, *12*, 800–820.

Staetsky, L.D. (2012). Antisemitism in contemporary Great Britain: A study of attitudes towards Jews and Israel. London, UK: Institute for Jewish Policy Research.

Stanovich, K.E., & West, R.F. (1997). Reasoning independently of prior belief and individual differences in actively open-minded thinking. *Journal of Educational Psychology*, *89*, 342–357

Stark, T.H., van Maaren, F.M., Krosnick, J., & Sood, G. (2022). The impact of social desirability pressures on whites' endorsement of racial stereotypes: A comparison between oral and ACASI reports in a national Survey. *Sociological Methods & Research, 51,* 605–631.

Staudinger, U.M., & Glück, J. (2011). Psychological wisdom research: Commonalities and differences in a growing field. *Annual Review of Psychology*, *62*, 215–241.

Stein, J-P., & Appel, M. (2021). How to deal with researcher harassment in the social sciences. *Human Nature Behaviour, 5*, 178–180.

Stenner, K. (2005). The authoritarian dynamic. New York, NY: Cambridge University Press.

Stephan, W., Stephan, C. (2000). An integrated threat theory of prejudice. In S. Oskamp (Ed.), Reducing prejudice and discrimination (pp. 23–46). Hillsdale, NJ: Lawrence Erlbaum.

Stephan, W.G., Ybarra, O., & Bachman, G. (1999). Prejudice towards immigrants. *Journal of Applied Social Psychology, 29*, 2221–2237.

Stouffer, S.A. (1955). Communism, conformity, and civil liberties. New York, NY: Doubleday.

Strabac, Z., & Listhaug, O. (2008). Anti-Muslim prejudice in Europe: A multilevel analysis of survey data from 30 countries. *Social Science Research, 37*, 268–286

Stradling, R. (2003). Multiperspectivity in history teaching: A guide for teachers. Strasbourg, France: Council of Europe.

Stronge, S., Sengupta, N.K., Barlow, F.K., Osborne, D., Houkamau, C.A., & Sibley, C.G. (2016). Perceived discrimination predicts increased support for political rights and life satisfaction mediated by ethnic identity: A longitudinal analysis. *Cultural Diversity and Ethnic Minority Psychology, 22*, 359–368

Sturgis, P., Roberts, C., & Smith, P. (2014). Middle alternatives revised: How the neither/nor response acts as a way of saying "I don't know"? *Sociological Methods & Research, 43*, 15–38.

Suarez-Orozco, M. (1991). Migration, minority status, and education: European dilemmas and responses in the 1990s. *Anthropology & Education Quarterly, 22*, 99–120.

Suhay, E., & Jayaratne, T.E. (2013). Does biology justify ideology? The politics of genetic attribution. *Public Opinion Quarterly, 77*, 497–521

Sullivan, J.L., Piereson, J., & Marcus, G.E. (1979). An alternative conceptualization of political tolerance: Illusory increases 1950s-1970s. *American Political Science Review, 73*, 781–794.

Sullivan, J.L., & Transue, J.E. (1999). The psychological underpinnings of democracy: A selective review of research on political tolerance, interpersonal trust, and social capital. *Annual Review of Psychology, 50*, 625–650.

Swann, W.B., Pelham, B.W., & & Chidester, T.R. (1988). Change through paradox: Using self-verification to alter beliefs. *Journal of Personality and Social Psychology, 54*, 268–273.

Syed, M. (2021). The logic of microaggressions assumes a racist society. *Perspectives on Psychological Science, 16*, 926–931.

Syed, M., Walker, L.H., Lee, R.M., Umaña-Taylor, A.J., Zamboanga, B.L., Schwartz, S.J., Armenta, B.E., & Huynh, Q.-L. (2013). A two-factor model of ethnic identity exploration: Implications for identity coherence and well-being. *Cultural Diversity & Ethnic Minority Psychology, 19*, 143–154

Tajfel, H. (1978). The social psychology of minorities. London, UK: Minority Rights Group.

Tajfel, H., & Turner, J. (1979). An integrative theory of intergroup conflict. In W.G. Austin & S. Worchel (Eds.), The social psychology of intergroup relations (pp. 33–47). Monterey, CA: Brooks/Cole.

Takahashi, K., & Jefferson, H. (2021). When the powerful feel voiceless: White identity and feelings of racial voicelessness (Pre-print February 4th). Retrieved from https://pdf.manuscriptpro.com/search/Author-Hakeem-Jefferson/1/90bbfcc2

Tankard, M.E., & Paluck, E.L. (2017). The effect of a Supreme Court decision regarding gay marriage on social norms and personal attitudes. *Psychological Science, 28*, 1334–1344.

Tarrant, M., Dazeley, S., & Cottom, T. (2009). Social categorization and empathy for outgroup members. *British Journal of Social Psychology, 48*, 427–446.

Tarrow, S. (Ed.) (2011). Power in movement. Cambridge, UK: Cambridge University Press.

Tawat, M. (2014). Danish and Swedish immigrants' cultural policies between 1960 and 2006: Toleration and the celebration of difference. *International Journal of Cultural Policy, 20*, 202–220.

Taylor, C. (1992). Multiculturalism and the politics of recognition. Princeton, NJ: Princeton University Press.

Taylor, C. (2012). Interculturalism or multiculturalism? *Philosophy and Social Criticism, 38*, 25–73.

Taylor, D.M., & de la Sablonnière, R. (2014). Towards constructive change in Aboriginal communities: A social psychology perspective. Montreal, Canada: McGill-Queen's University Press.

Tenbrunsel, A.E., & Messick, D.M. (2004). Ethical fading: The role of self-deception in unethical behavior. *Social Justice Research, 17*, 223–236

Tenenbaum, H., Capelos, T., Lorimer, J., & Stocks, T. (2018). Positive thinking elevates tolerance: Experimental effects of happiness on adolescents' attitudes towards asylum seekers. *Clinical Child Psychology and Psychiatry, 23*, 346–357.

Terpstra, M., & de Wit, T. (2019). Waarom tolerantie niet de hoogste waarde kan zijn (Why tolerance cannot be the highest value). Eindhoven, The Netherlands: Damon.

Tetlock, P.E. (2003). Thinking the unthinkable: Sacred values and taboo cognitions. *Trends in Cognitive Sciences*, 7, 320–324.

Thalmayer, A.G., Toscanelli, C., & Arnett, J.J. (2021). The neglected 95% revisited: Is American psychology becoming less American? *American Psychologist, 76*, 116–129.

Thijs, J., Wansink, B., & Verkuyten, M. (2021). Verdraagzaamheid in het secundair onderwijs. *Pedagogiek, 41*, 317–340.

Thomas, E.F., & Louis, W.R. (2014). When will collective action be effective? Violent and nonviolent protests differentially influence perceptions of legitimacy and efficacy among sympathizers. *Personality and Social Psychology Bulletin, 40*, 263–227

Thompson, V.A. (2013). Why it matters: The implications of autonomy processes for dual process theories: Commentary on Evans & Stanovich, 2013). *Perspectives on Psychological Science, 8*, 253–256.

Thompson, V.A., Prowse Turner, J.A., & Pennycook, G. (2011). Intuition, reason, and metacognition. *Cognitive Psychology, 63*, 107–140.

Tibi, B. (2002). Muslim migrants in Europe: Between Euro-Islam and ghettoization. In B. Tibi (Ed.), Muslim Europe or Euro Islam: Politics, culture, and citizenship in the age of globalization (pp. 31–52). Lanham, MD: Lexington.

Tiemeijer, W. (2021). Project Nederland: van feitelijke naar gewenste identiteit (Project Netherlands: From actual to desired national identity). The Hague, Netherlands: WRR.

Tileagă, C., Augoustinos, M., & Durrheim, K. (Eds.) (2021). The Routledge international handbook of discrimination, prejudice, and stereotyping. London, UK: Routledge

Tip, L.K., Zagefka, H., González, R., Brown, R., Cinnirella, M., & Na, X. (2012). Is support for multiculturalism threatened by . . . threat itself? *International Journal of Intercultural Relations, 36*, 22–30.

Togeby, L. (1998). Prejudice and tolerance in a period of increasing ethnic diversity and growing unemployment: Demark since 1970. *Ethnic and Racial Studies, 21*(6), 1137–1154.

Tønder, L. (2013). Tolerance: A sensorial orientation to politics. Oxford, UK: Oxford University Press.

Traunmüller, R., & Helbling, M. (2017). Public opinion backlash to liberal policy: The case of Muslim political rights in the UK. *SSRN*. Retrieved from https://dx.doi.org/10.2139/ssrn.2906365

Treanor, B., & Sweetman, B. (2021). Gabriel (-Honoré) Marcel. Stanford Encyclopedia of Philosophy. Retrieved from https://plato.stanford.edu/entries/marcel/

Trémolière, B., De Neys, W., & Bonnefon, J.F. (2018). Reasoning and moral judgment: A common experimental toolbox. In J. Ball & V.A. Thompson (Eds.), The Routledge international handbook of thinking and reasoning (pp. 575–589). London, UK: Routledge.

Trope, Y., & Liberman, N. (2010). Construal level theory of psychological science. *Psychological Review, 117*, 440–463.

Turiel, E. (2002). The culture of morality. Cambridge, UK: Cambridge University Press.

Turiel, E., Killen, M., & Helwig, C.C. (1987). Morality: Its structure, function, and vagaries. In J. Kagan & S. Lamb (Eds.), The emergence of morality in young children (pp. 155–243). Chicago, IL: University of Chicago Press.

Turner, J.C., Hogg, M.A., Oakes, P.J., Reicher, S.D., & Wetherell, M.S. (1987). Rediscovering the social group: A self-categorization theory. Oxford, UK: Blackwell.

Uenal, F., Bergh, R., Sidanius, J., Zick, A., Kimel, S., & Kunst, J.R. (2021). The nature of Islamophobia: A test of a tripartite view in five countries. *Personality and Social Psychology Bulletin, 47*, 275–292.

Uhlmann, E.L., Pizarro, D.A., Tannenbaum, D., & Ditto, P.H. (2009). The motivated use of moral principles. *Judgment and Decision Making, 4*, 476–491.

UNESCO (1995, 16 November). Declaration of principles on tolerance. Retrieved from https://portal.unesco.org/en/ev.php-URL_ID=13175&URL_DO=DO_TOPIC&URL_SECTION=201.html.

United Nations (2001). Gender mainstreaming: Strategy for promoting gender equality. In office of the special advisor on gender issues and advancement of women. Rome, Italy: United Nations. Retrieved from www.un.org/womenwatch/osagi/pdf/factsheet1.pdf

Unkelbach, C., Schneider, H., Gode, K., & Senft, M. (2010). The turban effect, too: Selection biases against women wearing Muslim headscarves. *Social Psychology and Personality Science, 1*, 378–383

Uzarevic, F., Saroglou, V., & Pichon, I. (2020). Rejecting opposite ideologies without discriminating against ideological opponents? Understanding nonbelievers' outgroup attitudes. *Basic and Applied Social Psychology, 42*, 62–77.

Van Bavel, J.J., Mende-Siedlecki, P., Brady, W.J., & Reinero, D.A. (2016). Contextual sensitivity in scientific reproducibility. *PNAS, 113*, 6454–6459.

Van der Burg, W. (1998). Slippery slope arguments. In R. Chadwick (Ed.), International encyclopedia of applied ethics (pp. 129–142). San Diego, CA: Academic Press.

Van der Heijden, E., & Verkuyten, M. (2020). Educational attainment, political sophistication and anti-immigrant attitudes. *Journal of Social and Political Psychology, 8*, 600–616.

Van der Noll, J. (2010). Public support for a ban on headscarves: A cross-national perspective. *International Journal of Conflict and Violence, 4*, 191–204.

Van der Noll, J. (2014). Religious toleration of Muslims in the German public sphere. *International Journal of Intercultural Relations, 38*(1), 60–74.

Van der Noll, J., Rohmann, A., & Saroglou, V. (2018). Societal level of religiosity and religious identity expression in Europe. *Journal of Cross-Cultural Psychology, 49*, 959–975.

Van der Noll, J., & Saroglou, V. (2015). Anti-Islam or anti-religion? Understanding objection against Islamic education. *Journal of Ethnic and Migration Studies, 41*, 219–238.

Van der Noll, J., Verkuyten, M., & Poppe, E. (2010). Political tolerance and prejudice: Differential reactions toward Muslims in the Netherlands. *Basic and Applied Social Psychology, 32*, 46–56.

Van der Veer, P. (2006). Pim Fortuyn, Theo van Gogh, and the politics of tolerance in the Netherlands. *Public Culture, 18*, 111–124

Van Doorn, M. (2016). Accepting the disliked. The practice and promotion of tolerance. PhD Dissertation, Free University, Amsterdam, Amsterdam, The Netherlands.

Van Driel, B., Darmody, M., & Kerzil, J. (2016). Education policies and practices to foster tolerance, respect for diversity and civic responsibility in children and young people in the EU (NESET II report). Luxembourg: Publications Office of the European Union.

Van Lisdonk, J., Nencel, L., & Keuzenkamp, S. (2018). Labeling same-sex sexuality in a tolerant society that values normality: The Dutch case. *Journal of Homosexuality, 65*, 1892–1915.

Van Meeteren, M.J., & Van Oosterdorp, L.N. (2019). Are Muslims in the Netherlands constructed as a 'suspect community'? An analysis of Dutch political discourse on terrorism in 2004–2015. *Crime, Law and Social Change, 71*, 525–540.

Van Zalk, M., Walte, H., & Kerr, M. (2014). Developmental trajectories of prejudice and tolerance toward immigrants from early to late adolescence. *Journal of Youth and Adolescence, 43*, 1658–1671

Van Zomeren, M., Postmes, T., & Spears, R. (2008). Toward and integrative social identity model of collective action: A quantitative research synthesis of three socio-psychological perspectives. *Psychological Bulletin, 134*, 504–535.

Varnum, M.E.W., & Grossmann, I. (2021). The psychology of cultural change: Introduction to the special issue. *American Psychologist, 76*, 833–837.

Vatter, A., Milic, T., & Hirter, H. (2011). Das Stimmverhalten bei der Minarettverbots Initiative unter der Lupe. In Vatter, A. (Ed.), Vom Schacht zum Minarettverbot: Religiöse Minderheiten in der direkten Demokratie (pp. 144–170). Zürich, Switzerland: Verlag Neuer Zürcher Zeitung.

Veenvliet, S.G. (2008). Intrinsic religious orientation and religious teaching: Differential judgments toward same-gender sexual behavior and gay men and lesbians. *International Journal for the Psychology of Religion, 18*, 53–65.

Velthuis, E., Van der Nol, J., & Verkuyten, M. (2022b). Tolerance of Muslim minority identity enactment: The roles of social context, type of action, and cultural continuity concern. *Journal of Community and Applied Social Psychology*. Retrieved from https://doi.org/10.1002/casp.2605

Velthuis, E., Verkuyten, M., & Smeekes, A. (2020). Supporting immigrant cultural rights: The roles of deprovincialization and identity continuity. *Journal of Applied Social Psychology, 50*, 733–743.

Velthuis, E., Verkuyten, M., & Smeekes, A. (2021). The different faces of social tolerance: Conceptualizing and measuring respect and coexistence tolerance. *Social Indicators Research, 158*, 1105–1125.

Velthuis, E., Verkuyten, M., Van der Noll, J., & Smeekes, A. (2022a). Tolerance of the Muslim headscarf: Reasons for wearing a headscarf matter. *International Journal of Intercultural Relations* (in print).

Verkuyten, M. (1995). Symbols and social representations. *Journal for the Theory of Social Behaviour, 25*, 263–284.

Verkuyten, M. (1997). "Redelijk racisme": Gesprekken over allochtonen in oude stadswijken ("Reasonable racism": Talking about ethnic minorities in the inner city). Amsterdam, The Netherlands: Amsterdam University Press.

Verkuyten, M. (1998). Personhood and accounting racism in conversation. *Journal for the Theory of Social Behavior, 28*, 147–167.

Verkuyten, M. (2003). Discourses about ethnic group (de-)essentialism: Oppressive and progressive aspects. *British Journal of Social Psychology, 42*, 371–391.

Verkuyten, M. (2004a). Emotional reactions to and support for immigrant policies: Attributed responsibilities to categories of asylum seekers, *Social Justice Research, 17*, 293–314.

Verkuyten, M. (2004b). Everyday ways of thinking about multiculturalism. *Ethnicities, 4*, 53–74.

Verkuyten, M. (2013). Justifying discrimination of Muslim immigrants: Outgroup ideology and the five-step social identity model. *British Journal of Social Psychology, 52*, 345–360.

Verkuyten, M. (2018a). The social psychology of ethnic identity (2nd ed.). London, UK: Routledge.

Verkuyten, M. (2018b). The benefits of studying immigration for social psychology. *European Journal of Social Psychology, 48*, 225–239

Verkuyten, M. (2018c). The struggle over political power: Evaluating immigrants' political party representation. *Social Psychological and Personality Science, 9*, 419–425

Verkuyten, M. (2021). Anti-Muslim sentiments in Western societies. In C. Tileagă, M. Augoustinos, & K. Durrheim (Eds.), The Routledge international handbook of discrimination, prejudice, and stereotyping (pp. 118–135). London, UK: Routledge

Verkuyten, M. (2022a). The meanings of tolerance: Discursive usage in a case of 'identity politics'. *Journal for the Theory of Social Behaviour, 52*, 224–236.

Verkuyten, M. (2022b). Are different forms of Muslim political participation differently accepted? Public attitudes in the Netherlands. Utrecht, The Netherlands: Ercomer.

Verkuyten, M., Adelman, L., & Yogeeswaran, K. (2022a). Intolerance of transgressive protest actions: The differential roles of deontological and utilitarian morality. *Personality and Social Psychology Bulletin*. Retrieved from https://doi.org/10.1177/01461672221099709

Verkuyten, M., Altabatabaei, H.G., & Nooitgedagt, W. (2018). Supporting the accommodation of voluntary and involuntary migrants: Humanitarian and host society considerations. *Social Psychological and Personality Science, 9*, 267–274

Verkuyten, M., Gale, J., Yogeeswaran, K., & Adelman, L. (2022a). Maintaining a tolerant national identity: Positive and negative attitudes towards minority group practices (manuscript under review).

Verkuyten, M., Gale, J., Yogeeswaran, K., & Adelman, L. (2022b). The impact of emotional versus instrumental reasons for dual citizenship on the perceived loyalty and political tolerance of immigrant-origin minorities. *Journal of Experimental Political Science*. Retreived from https://doi.org/10.1017/XPS.2022.17

Verkuyten, M., Hindriks, P., & Coenders, M. (2016). Majority members' feelings about political representation of Muslim immigrants. *Social Psychology, 47*, 257–269

Verkuyten, M., & Killen, M. (2021). Tolerance, dissenting beliefs, and cultural diversity. *Child Development Perspectives, 15*, 51–56.

Verkuyten, M., & Kollar, R. (2021). Tolerance and intolerance: Cultural meanings and discursive usage. *Culture & Psychology, 27*, 172–186.

Verkuyten, M., Kollar, R., Gale, J., & Yogeeswaran, K. (2022). Right-wing political orientation, national identification and the acceptance of immigrants and minorities. *Personality and Individual Differences, 184, 111217*, 1–9.

Verkuyten, M., Maliepaard, M., Martinovic, B., & Khoudja, Y. (2014). Political tolerance among Muslim minorities in Western Europe: The role of denomination and religious and host national identification. *Politics and Religion, 7*, 265–286.

Verkuyten, M., & Martinovic, B. (2012). Immigrants' national identification: Meanings, determinants and consequences. *Social Issues and Policy Review, 6*, 82–112.

Verkuyten, K., Mepham, K., & Kros, M. (2018b). Public attitudes towards support for migrants: The importance of perceived voluntary and involuntary migration. *Ethnic and Racial Studies, 41*, 901–918.

Verkuyten, M., Schlette, A., Adelman, L., & Yogeeswaran, K. (2022a). Deliberative thinking increases tolerance of minority group practices: Testing a dual-process model of tolerance. *Journal of Experimental Psychology: Applied*. Retrieved from http://dx.doi.org/10.1037/xap0000429

Verkuyten, M., Schlette, A., Adelman, L., & Yogeeswaran, K. (2022b). With rhyme and reason: Recognizing reasons for disliked practices increases tolerance. *British Journal of Social Psychology, 61,* 471–490.

Verkuyten, M., & Slooter, L. (2007). Tolerance of Muslim beliefs and practices: Age related differences and context effects. *International Journal of Behavioral Development, 31*, 467–477.

Verkuyten, M., & Slooter, L. (2008). Muslim and non-Muslim adolescents' reasoning about freedom of speech and minority rights. *Child Development, 79*, 514–528.

Verkuyten, M., & Thijs, J. (2010). Religious group relations among Christian, Muslim and non-religious early adolescents in the Netherlands. *Journal of Early Adolescence, 30*, 27–49.

Verkuyten, M., & Thijs, J. (2013). Multicultural education and inter-ethnic attitudes: An intergroup perspective. *European Psychologist, 18*, 179–190

Verkuyten, M., Thijs, J., & Gieling, M. (2018a). Early adolescents' evaluation of parental regulation. Utrecht, The Netherlands: Ercomer, Utrecht University

Verkuyten, M., Voci, A., & Pettigrew, T.F. (2022c). Deprovincialization: It's importance for plural societies. *Social Issues and Policy Review, 16*, 289–309.

Verkuyten, M., & Yogeeswaran, K. (2020). Cultural diversity and its implications for intergroup relations. *Current Opinion in Psychology, 32*, 1–5

Verkuyten, M., & Yogeeswaran, K. (2017). The social psychology of intergroup toleration: A roadmap for theory and research. *Personality and Social Psychology Review, 21*, 72–96

Verkuyten, M., Yogeeswaran, K., & Adelman, L. (2019). Intergroup toleration and its implications for culturally diverse societies. *Social Issues and Policy Review, 13*, 5–35

Verkuyten, M., Yogeeswaran, K., & Adelman, L. (2020a). Toleration and prejudice-reduction: Two ways of improving intergroup relations. *European Journal of Social Psychology, 50*, 239–255.

Verkuyten, M., Yogeeswaran, K., & Adelman, L. (2020b). The negative implications of being tolerated: Tolerance from the target's perspective. *Perspectives on Psychological Science, 15*, 544–561

Verkuyten, M., Yogeeswaran, K., & Adelman, L. (2022a). Tolerance as forbearance: Overcoming intuitive versus deliberative objection to cultural, religious and ideological differences. *Psychological Review, 129*, 368–387.

Verkuyten, M., Yogeeswaran, K., & Adelman, L. (2022b). Does deliberative thinking increase tolerance? Political tolerance toward individuals with dual citizenship. *Social Cognition, 40,* 396–409.

Vertovec, S. (2007). Super-diversity and its implications. *Ethnic and Racial Studies, 30,* 1024–1054.

Vignoles, V.L. (2011). Identity motives. In K. Luycke, S.J. Schwartz, & V.L. Vignoles (Eds.), Handbook of identity theory and research (pp. 403–432). New York, NY: Springer.

Vink, M., Schmeets, H., & Mennes, H. (2019). Double standards? Attitudes towards immigrant and emigrant dual citizenship in the Netherlands. *Ethnic and Racial Studies, 42*, 83–11.

Vogt, W.P. (1997). Tolerance and education: Learning to live with diversity and difference. London, UK: Sage.

Vollhardt, J.R., Okuyan, M., & Ünal, H. (2020). Resistance to collective victimization and oppression. *Current Opinion in Psychology, 35*, 92–97.

Von Bergen, C.W., Van Bergen, B.A., Stubblefield, C., & Bandow, D. (2012). Authentic tolerance: Between forbearance and acceptance. *Journal of Cultural Diversity, 19,* 111–117.

Volokh, E. (2003). The mechanisms of the slippery slope. Harvard Law Review, 116, 1026.

Wagner, W. (2021). Groups in contact: Meta-representations, interobjectivity, and cultural incompatibilities. *Journal for the Theory of Social Behaviour, 51*, 2–24.

Wainryb, C. (1993). The application of moral judgments to other cultures: Relativism and universality. *Child Development, 64*, 924–933.

Wainryb, C. (2006). Moral development in culture: Diversity, tolerance, and justice. In M. Killen, J.G. Smetana, M. Killen, & J.G. Smetana (Eds.), Handbook of moral development (pp. 211–240). Mahwah, NJ: Lawrence Erlbaum Associates Publishers.

Wainryb, C., Shaw, L.A., Langley, M., Cottam, K., & Lewis, R. (2004). Children's thinking about diversity of belief in the early school years: Judgments of relativism, tolerance, and disagreeing persons. *Child Development, 75*, 687–703.

Wainryb, C., Shaw, L.A., Laupa, M., & Smith, K.R. (2001). Children's, adolescents, and young adults' thinking about different types of disagreement. *Developmental Psychology, 37*, 373–386.

Wainryb, C., Shaw, L.A., & Maianu, C. (1998). Tolerance and intolerance: Children's and adolescents' judgments of dissenting beliefs, speech, persons, and conduct. *Child Development, 69*, 1541–1555.

Wallrich, L., West, K., & Rutland, A. (2020). Painting all foreigners with one brush? How the salience of Muslims and refugees shapes judgements. *Journal of Social and Political Psychology, 8*, 246–265.

Walton, D. (2015). The basic slippery slope argument. *Informal Logic, 35*, 273–311

Walton, G.M. (2014). The new science of wise psychological interventions. *Current Directions in Psychological Science, 23*, 73–82.

Walzer, M. (1997). On toleration. New Haven, CT: Yale University Press.

Wansink, B., Akkerman, S., Zuiker, I., & Wubbels, T. (2018). Where does teaching multiperspectivity in history education begin and end? An analysis of the uses of temporality. *Theory & Research in Social Education, 46*, 495–527.

Wasow, O. (2020). Agenda seeding: How 1960s Black protest moved elites, public opinion and voting. *American Political Science Review, 114*, 638–659.

Weinstock, M., Kienhues, D., Feucht, F., & Ryan, M. (2017). Informed reflexivity: Enacting epistemic virtue. *Educational Psychologist, 52*, 284–298.

Weissberg, R. (2008). Pernicious tolerance: How teaching to "accept differences" undermines civil society. London, UK: Routledge.

Weldon, S.A. (2006). The institutional context of tolerance for ethnic minorities: A comparative, multilevel analysis of Western Europe. *American Journal of Political Science, 50*, 331–349.

Wemyss, G. (2006). The power to tolerate: Contests over Britishness and belonging in East London. *Patterns of Prejudice, 40*, 215–236.

Wenger, J.L., & Daniels, A.L. (2006) Who distinguishes between sinners and sins at the implicit level of awareness? *The Journal of Social Psychology, 146*, 657–669

Weston, A. (2018). A 21st century ethical toolbox (4th ed.). Oxford, UK: Oxford University Press.

White, M.H., & Crandall, C.S. (2017). Freedom of racist speech: Ego and expressive threats. *Journal of Personality and Social Psychology, 113*, 413–429.

Whitehead, K.A., Ainsworth, A.T., Wittig, M.A., & Gadino, B. (2009). Implications of ethnic identity exploration and ethnic identity affirmation and belonging for intergroup attitudes among adolescents. *Journal of Research on Adolescence, 19*, 123–135.

Widmalm, S. (2016). Political tolerance in the global south: Images of India, Pakistan and Uganda. London, UK: Routledge.

Wike, R., & Simmons, K. (2015, November 18). Global support for principle of free expression, but opposition to some forms of speech. Pew Research Center. Retrieved from www.pewresearch.org/global/2015/11/18/global-support-for-principle-of-free-expression-but-opposition-to-some-forms-of-speech/

Williams, B. (1996). Tolerations: An impossible virtue? In D. Heyd (Ed.), Toleration: An elusive virtue (pp. 19–27). Princeton, NJ: Princeton University Press.

Williams, K.D. (2001). Ostracism: The power of silence. New York, NY: Guilford.

Williams, K.D., & Jarvis, B. (2006). Cyberball: A program for use in research on interpersonal ostracism and acceptance. *Behavior Research Methods, Instruments, and Computers, 38*, 174–180.

Wimmer, A. (2009). Herder's heritage and the boundary-making approach: Studying ethnicity in immigrant societies. *Sociological Theory, 27*, 244–270.

Wise, A., & Velayutham, S. (Eds.) (2009). Everyday multiculturalism. New York, NY: Palgrave Macmillan.

Wohl, M.J.A., Branscombe, N.R., & Reysen, S. (2010). Perceiving your group's future to be in jeopardy: Extinction threat induces collective angst and the desire to strengthen the ingroup. *Personality and Social Psychology Bulletin, 36*, 898–910

Wohl, M.J.A., King, M., & Taylor, D.M. (2014). Expressions of political practice: Collective angst moderated politicized collective identity to predict support for political protest (peaceful or violent) among diaspora group members. *International Journal of Intercultural Relations, 43*, 114–125

Wood, C., & Finlay, W.M.L. (2008). British national party representations of Muslims in the month after the London bombings: Homogeneity, threat, and the conspiracy tradition. *British Journal of Social Psychology, 47*, 707–726.

Wright, J.C. (2012). Children's and adolescents' tolerance for divergent beliefs: Exploring the cognitive and affective dimensions of moral conviction in our youth. *British Journal of Developmental Psychology, 30*, 493–510.

Wright, J.C., Cullum, J., & Schwab, H. (2008). The cognitive and affective dimensions of moral conviction: Implications for attitudinal and behavioral measures of interpersonal tolerance. *Personality and Social Psychology Bulletin, 34*, 1461–1476.

Wright, J.C., McWhite, C.B., & Grandjean, P.T. (2014). The cognitive mechanisms of intolerance: Do our meta-ethical commitments matter? In T. Lombrozo, J. Knobe, & S. Nichols (Eds.), Oxford experimental studies in philosophy, vol. 1. Oxford, UK: Oxford University Press.

Wright, S.C., & Baray, G. (2012). Models of social change in social psychology: Collective action or prejudice reduction? In J. Dixon & M. Levine (Eds.), Beyond prejudice: Extending the social psychology of conflict, inequality, and social change. Cambridge, UK: Cambridge University Press.

Xiao, Y.J., Coppin, G., & Van Bavel, J.J. (2016). Perceiving the world through-colored glasses: A perceptual model of intergroup relations. *Psychological Inquiry, 27*, 255–274.

Xu, M., & Petty, R.E. (2022). Two-sided messages promote openness for morally based attitudes. *Personality and Social Psychology Bulletin, 48*, 1151–1166.

Yama, H. (2018). Thinking and reasoning across cultures. In J. Ball & V.A. Thompson (Eds.), The Routledge International handbook of thinking and reasoning (pp. 624–838). London, UK: Routledge.

Yildiz, A.A., & Verkuyten, M. (2011). Inclusive victimhood: Social identity and the politicization of collective trauma among Turkey's Alevis in Western Europe. *Peace and Conflict: Journal of Peace Psychology, 17*, 243–269.

Yildiz, A.A., & Verkuyten, M. (2012). Conceptualizing Euro-Islam: Managing the societal demand for religious reform. *Identities: Global Studies in Culture and Power, 19*, 360–376.

Yogeeswaran, K., & Dasgupta, N. (2014). The devil is in the details: Abstract versus concrete construals of multiculturalism differentially impact intergroup relations. *Journal of Personality and Social Psychology, 106*, 772–789.

Yogeeswaran, K., Dasgupta, N., Adelman, L., Eccleston, A., & Parker, M.T. (2011). To be or not to be (ethnic): Public vs. private expressions of ethnic identification differentially impact national inclusion of white and non-white groups. *Journal of Experimental Social Psychology, 47*, 908–914.

Yogeeswaran, K., Nash, K., Jia, H., Adelman, L., & Verkuyten, M. (2021). Intolerant of being tolerant? Examining the impact of intergroup toleration on relative left frontal activity and outgroup attitudes. *Current Psychology*. Retreived from https://doi.org/10.1007/s12144-020-01290-2

Zaller, J.R. (1992). The nature and origins of mass opinion. Cambridge, UK: Cambridge University Press.

Zdaniuk, B., & Levine, J.M. (2001). Group loyalty: Impact of members' identification and contributions. *Journal of Experimental Social Psychology, 37*, 502–509.

Zembylas, M. (2011). Toleration and coexistence in conflicting societies: Some tensions and implications for education. *Pedagogy, Culture & Society, 19*, 385–402.

Zhirkov, K., Verkuyten, M., & Weesie, J. (2014). Perceptions of World Politics and Support for Terrorism among Muslims: Evidence from Muslim Countries and Western Europe. *Conflict Management and Peace Science, 31*, 481–501.

Zhou, H., & Fishbach, A. (2016). The pitfall of experimenting on the web: How unattended selective attrition leads to surprising (yet false) research conclusions. *Journal of Personality and Social Psychology, 111*, 493–504

Zilli Ramirez, C., & Verkuyten, M. (2011). Values, media framing and political tolerance for extremist groups. *Journal of Applied Social Psychology, 41*, 1583–1602.

Zitzmann, S., & Loreth, L. (2021). Regarding an "almost anything" goes attitude toward methods in psychology. *Frontiers in Psychology*. Retrieved from https://doi.org/10.3389/fpsyg.2021.612570.

Zitzmann, S., Loreth, L., Reininger, K.M., & Simon, B. (2022). Does respect foster tolerance? (Re)analyzing and synthesizing data from a large research project using meta-analytic techniques. *Personality and Social Psychology Bulletin, 84*, 823–843.

Zlatev, J.J. (2019). "I may not agree with you, but I trust you": Caring about social issues signals integrity. *Psychological Science, 30*, 880–892.

Zmigrod, L. (2022). A psychology of ideology: Unpacking the psychological structure of ideological thinking. *Perspectives on Psychological Science, 17*, 1072–1092.

Zolberg, A.R., & Woon, L.L. (1999). Why Islam is like Spanish: Cultural incorporation in Europe and the United States. *Politics and Society, 27*, 5–28.

Zuquete, J.P. (2008). The European extreme-right and Islam: New directions. *Journal of Political Ideologies, 13*, 321–344.

1. Introduction

1 www.youtube.com/watch?v=ihaB8AFOhZo
2 https://books.google.com/ngrams/info#
3 https://assets.publishing.service.gov.uk/government/uploads/system/uploads/attachment_data/file/380595/SMSC_Guidance_Maintained_Schools.pdf
4 https://au.int/sites/default/files/documents/36541-doc-au_tj_policy_eng_web.pdf
5 https://bpd.de/publikationen/40QIUX,2,0,Leitkultur_als_Wertekonsens.html#art2
6 https://epthinktank.eu/2015/11/16/promoting-tolerance-in-the-eu/
7 An earlier version was called "A European Model Law for the Promotion of Tolerance and the Suppression of Intolerance".
8 www.learningforjustice.org/magazine/our-new-name-learning-for-justice. Retrieved 9-12-2021.

9 www.theguardian.com/politics/ng-interactive/2015/oct/07/david-cameron-speech-at-tory-conference-what-he-said-and-what-he-meant
10 For example, in 2019, a representative public opinion poll among the Dutch showed that "asocial behaviour and a lack of tolerance" was considered the most important issue on a list of ten issues before, for example, climate change. www.issuemakers.nl/nieuws/asociaal-gedrag-belangrijkste-issue-van-2019/. And as another example, teachers in the US have noted a disturbing surge of intolerance in the form of derogatory language, bigotry, harassment, swastikas, and Nazi salutes (Costello & Dillard, 2019); www.splcenter.org/sites/default/files/tt_2019_hate_at_school_report_final_0.pdf.
11 I use the term "Muslim practices and beliefs" to refer to the way the public tends to perceive these practices and beliefs, without suggesting that these are necessarily part of Islam or that all Muslim think and act alike.
12 www.pewresearch.org/fact-tank/2017/07/26/american-muslims-are-concerned-but-also-satisfied-with-their-lives/
13 www.abc.net.au/news/2015-11-30/muslims-discrimination-three-times-more-than-other-australians/6985138
14 www.unisa.edu.au/siteassets/episerver-6-files/global/eass/mnm/publications/islamophobia_report.pdf
15 Pew Research centre: www.pewforum.org/2018/05/29/being-christian-in-western-europe/
16 This is illustrated in the finding that compared to a long list of ethnic or racial (e.g. Hispanics and African Americans), religious (Muslims and Jews), and other minority groups (e.g. homosexuals and recent immigrants), atheist are less likely to be accepted, both publicly and privately (Edgell et al., 2006).
17 An analysis of articles in six major psychology journals indicates that the authors and samples represent some 11% of the world's population and that 89% of the world's population continues to be neglected (Thalmayer et al., 2021).
18 This is not always appreciated or recognized by US scholars, reviewers, and Journal editors who not seldom have a quite strong US-centric perspective. For example, it is often taken for granted that multiculturalism is a hierarchy-attenuating ideology, whereas in some local and national contexts, it functions in a hierarchy justifying way (e.g. Ng Tseung Wong & Verkuyten, 2018). Similarly, the research and debates on colour-blindness, whiteness, and forms of microaggression are strongly US-based and not simply translatable to other countries, including European ones.
19 See also the description and analysis of white working-class people as "the new minority" (e.g. Gest, 2016).

2. Why tolerance matters

1 Unfortunately the Riace model has come under serious attack after around 2018, due to general political, financial, institutional, and legal changes, including the prosecution of the Riace mayor. A somewhat similar small town case of living together in unparalleled diversity that sparked international attention is Postville, Iowa, in the US (Grey et al., 2009).
2 In the past, there have also been objections from orthodox protestants who considered the feast as a form of Roman-Catholic idolatry since St Nicolaus is a Catholic bishop. However, this led not to proposals to alter the tradition.
3 www.communitycare.co.uk/2016/03/10/views-gay-marriage-shouldnt-stop-social-worker/.
4 See for various other examples in the context of the US: https://academicfreedom.org/public-statements/
5 Nigel Farage, the then leader of the British populist UKIP party: May 18, 2016, www.theneweuropean.co.uk/top-stories/nigel-farage-says-his-new-party-will-be-intolerant-of-intolerance-1–5992933

6 In 2020, a long list of high-profile scholars and intellectuals published "*A letter on Justice and Open Debate*" in Harper's magazine's October issue. The letter argues against the new dogma that "weakens our norms of open debate and toleration of differences in favor of ideological conformity", and that "The democratic inclusion we want can be achieved only if we speak out against the intolerant climate that has set in on sides".
7 There are also conservative demands for bans on classroom instruction on "sexual orientation and gender identity", and in April 2022, the state of Florida adopted the "Stop WOKE (Wrongs to Our Kinds and Employees) against act".
8 In some cases, this can entirely erase the difference between a person and an opinion which closes down conversation and debate: criticizing a view put forward by a women is then simply denounced as "toxic masculinity" or "male attitude", and those questioning the benefits of immigration are dismissed as being xenophobes and propagators of hate.

3. The meaning of tolerance

1 Honneth and Taylor also discuss the importance of recognition of cultural particularity in relation to social esteem. However, there is a difference between respect based on shared personhood and esteem based on specific traits, accomplishments and contributions. To respect everyone as a person equally is appropriate and sensible, but to socially esteem everyone equally (e.g. racists and murderers) is self-defeating.
2 We have described this distinction also in terms of "weak" and "strong" tolerance (Verkuyten & Yogeeswaran, 2017).
3 www.google.com/search?q=tolerance+word+cloud&source=lnms&tbm=isch&sa=X&ved=2ahUKEwj8_d3Eu-DrAhUONOwKHcQLA48Q_AUoAXoECAsQAw&biw=128.
4 www.google.com/search?q=tolerance+word+cloud&source=lnms&tbm=isch&sa=X&ved=2ahUKEwj8_d3Eu-DrAhUONOwKHcQLA48Q_AUoAXoECAsQAw&biw=1280.
5 www.google.com/search?q=intolerance+word+cloud&tbm=isch&ved=2ahUKEwjW78bFu-DrAhVSyKQKHVS0CD4Q2-cCegQIABAA&oq=intolerance+word+cloud&gs. For intolerance, there are also many word clouds that contain medical terms and that refer to lactose intolerance and so on.
6 This is also labelled as "authentic tolerance" (Von Bergen et al., 2012).
7 These interviews were conducted by Sara Cvetkovska.
8 See for a list of various examples: www.canceledpeople.com/cancelations.
9 For example, no longer teach "Newton's laws" but rather the "three fundamental laws of physics" (Krylov, 2021). And three coloured students working on a mundane physical problem in an introductory course has been analysed from the perspective of white supremacy whereby, for example, instructions for focusing students' attention on a well-defined task or tool are being interpreted as a manifestation of whiteness (Robertson & Hairston, 2022).
10 A striking example is the removal of the word "normal" from beauty products, because according to Unilever (the company), the word would make "*most* people feel excluded" (my italics).
11 www.dailymail.co.uk/news/article-2019547/Anjem-Choudary-Islamic-extremists-set-Sharia-law-zones-UK-cities.html
12 For example, children are asked to indicate on a multiple choice question which punishment is the right one (a) whipping, (b) stoning,(c) kill with a sword.
13 There are more than 50 of these Mosque schools in which thousands of young children follow each weekend Islamic lessons (NRC-Handelsblad, Wednesday, 11 September 2019).
14 *NRC-Handelsblad*, Saturday, 21 September 2021.
15 Forst talks about "respect tolerance" and also distinguishes a coexistence and an esteem conception of tolerance.

4. Tolerance and prejudice

1 People might not express negative outgroup feelings due to social desirability concerns, but this would imply that the research is partly about describing and explaining individual differences in the tendency to respond in a social desirable way rather than about prejudice per se.
2 Here, I follow United Nations definition of gender equality, which entails "equal rights, responsibilities and opportunities of women and men and girls and boys" and implies that "the interests, needs and priorities of both women and men are taken into consideration" (United Nations, 2001).
3 The list technique (also known as the item-count technique; Blair & Imai, 2012) entails randomly dividing participants into two experimental conditions. In the control condition, respondents are presented a list of items (groups or social issues) people can feel negative about. In the treatment condition, respondents are presented with the same list of items plus one "sensitive" item added. In both conditions, participants are asked to only indicate *the number* of items they are negative about and not which items these are. The difference in means between the treatment and the control condition corresponds to the percentage of people who are negative about the sensitive item. This technique has been found to yield higher levels of prejudice compared to direct measures which has been interpreted in terms of the list technique circumventing socially desirable reponding that can affect direct self-report measures.
4 www.pewglobal.org/2006/11/20/europeans-debate-the-scarf-and-the-veil/.
5 It might be argued that an emphasis on secular principles is a form of, or justification of, prejudice towards religion in general. However, such an argument would label all secular people as being prejudiced and assigns only a secondary or justificatory role to values.
6 Hoksbergen and Tillie. (2012). *EURISLAM Survey-Data & Codebook*. https://doi.org/10.17026/dans-xx7–5×27.
7 Additionally, the Hebdo attacks did lead to higher resistance towards Muslim immigrants in Ireland and Czech Republic, but did not have any effect in Austria, Germany, and Finland (Savelkoul et al., 2022).
8 https://europarl.europa.eu/election-results-2019/en/national-results/netherlands/2019-2024/https://europarl.europa.eu/election-results-2019/en/national-results/germany/2019-2024/

5. Practicing tolerance

1 Similarly, among a large representative sample in New Zealand, we found that the great majority of the public (73.2%) expresses very strong support for tolerating free speech of opinions that one disagrees with, together with moderate to low support for banning offensive speech for minority groups (Doré et al., 2022).
2 It might be argued that these findings partly reflect social desirable responding. However, the provision of complete anonymity in online surveys has been found to minimize social desirability pressures (e.g. Lautenschlager & Flaherty, 1990; Stark et al., 2022), which we also found in a survey-embedded experiment in Germany and the Netherlands (Bamberg & Verkuyten, 2022) and which was found in a research on attitudes towards Muslim immigrants in Ireland, but not towards Black and Polish immigrants (Creighton et al., 2022).
3 Furthermore, experimental research has found that a prime using these sorts of general tolerant statements leads to less negative reactions towards a target criticizing the ingroup (Greenberg et al., 1992; see also Fairlamb & Cinnirella, 2021).
4 The shared variance between tolerance in general and measures of tolerance of specific dissenting practices and beliefs tends to be around 20%.
5 Forst (2013) also distinguished *esteem* and *permission tolerance* which we did not examine. *Esteem tolerance* with its emphasis on valuing diversity is very similar to appreciation and

full recognition (Klein & Zick, 2013), and *permission tolerance* refers to the hierarchical intergroup context of tolerance rather than to an underlying reason for being tolerant. In addition to principled and pragmatic reasons, Nehushtan (2007) also identifies tolerance out of mercy whereby one tolerates other people's physical or mental limitations just out of feeling sorry for them.

6 For the peaceful coexistence in conflict settings, the term "antagonistic tolerance" has also been used (Hayden, 2002; Zembylas, 2011), and in addition to this pragmatic consideration, it has also been argued that rational and economic self-interests can prevent acting upon one's objections and therefore can underlie tolerance (Muldoon et al., 2011).

7 In this paper, we report on the findings of three studies and four samples, but we collected more recent data in an additional study and the findings were similar.

8 Participants received the following introduction: "Below are several reasons for tolerating dissenting ways of life of cultural minorities. To what extent do you agree or disagree with each of these reasons?". A sample item for *respect tolerance* is "because they have the equal right to live their own life", and a sample item for *coexistence tolerance* is "in order to avoid social conflict".

9 In a second scenario, participants were asked to consider a positive figure in their life before considering something that person does they disapprove of, followed by considering reasons why despite their disapproval, they tolerate this practice. In a further scenario, participants were asked to reflect on any group in society they like or feel neutrally toward but engage in something they personally disapprove of, and then consider reasons why despite their disapproval, we should nevertheless tolerate it.

10 The trolley problem implies a stylized dilemma of whether to sacrifice one person to save a larger number. The typical scenario involves a runaway tram or trolley that is on course to collide with and kill a number of people down the track (five or six), but a driver or bystander can intervene and divert the vehicle to kill just one person on a different track.

11 The focus on a male person was for reasons of relevance, because men are more likely than women to be involved in these sorts of protest actions.

12 Veiling has historically been associated with Islam but can be traced to various cultural traditions and can be a form of cultural identity enactment.

13 The narrative of Riace as having a history of migration does not only involve immigration and the reception of newcomers but also emigration to which locals also refer for explaining their hospitality towards refugees. The town's history of emigration would define a commonality with the refugees. Many locals have experienced what it feels like to migrate, either directly or by the stories from parents, family, and close friends who sometimes returned to Riace after retirement. Hence, being a migrant provides a shared experience with refugees which works against the rejection and exclusion of these newcomers, and makes providing help and support "a normal thing to do".

14 Also internationally, there is a recognition of the famous "Dutch tolerance": a term that was used one of the first times in 1890 by the *New York Times* which since then published more than 700 related articles.

15 Historically, the Netherlands had a large Catholic population that mainly lived in the south of the country and a large protestant population that mainly lived in the north.

16 www.pewforum.org/2018/10/29/eastern-and-western-europeans-differ-on-importance-of-religion-views-of-minorities-and-key-social-issues/

17 The introduction was:

> The Netherlands is known in the world as a tolerant country. That was already so in the past (17e century) when dissidents and dissenters fled to the Netherlands. And this is demonstrated, for example, by the fact that the Netherlands was the first to allow euthanasia, legalized same-sex marriage, and allowed coffeeshops [that sell soft drugs].

18 Measured with items such as "I am concerned about the continuation of the Dutch culture", and "The future of the Dutch way of life is under threat".
19 Items, e.g. "Muslims and the Dutch are like a jigsaw puzzle. They may differ, but they fit together well", "The fact that the Dutch and Muslim way of life differ does not mean that they are necessarily in opposition" (reversed scored).

6. Boundaries of tolerance

1 The then vice president Mike Pence: Tweet, referencing the Minnesota case and the February shooting death of a black jogger in Georgia, May 2020. https://eu.usatoday.com/story/news/politics/2020/05/28/george-floyd-donald-trump-twitter-jacob-frey-thugs/5281374002/
2 Canadian Prime minister Trudeau. https://pm.gc.ca/en/news/statements/2017/03/10/statement-prime-minister-canada-purim.
3 Statement of the rector of Utrecht University, 26 January 2022.
4 Taylor and de la Sablonnière (2014) provide a short discussion of the origins and criticisms of the notion of "zero tolerance" and related policies in North America. They also argue for the importance of zero tolerance in disadvantaged school settings plagued with problems of drugs, weapons, violence and bullying, and as a first step towards constructive social change of dysfunctional behaviours within Aboriginal communities.
5 For example, in everyday thinking, people tend to apply Bayesian logic in which there is an a priori belief that forms a starting point and that can be gradually changed based on the evidence that is observed. Chapter 3).
7 Although the pattern of findings was similar in both countries, Germans did not differentiate as clearly between the two levels of low and medium dissenting behaviours compared to the Dutch. The reason for this country difference is that the Germans were less inclined to prioritize freedom over social cohesion, compared to the Dutch.
8 www.pewforum.org/2018/05/29/being-christian-in-western-europe/
9 www.pewresearch.org/fact-tank/2018/07/24/in-western-europe-familiarity-with-muslims-is-linked-to-positive-views-of-muslims-and-islam/
10 www.gatestoneinstitute.org/7861/british-muslims-survey
11 Deprovincialization means diminished provincialism in which people have developed a more nuanced and fresh perspective on their ingroup culture by recognizing that their group's norms, customs, and lifestyles are not the only ways to manage the social world successfully. For an overview of the existing research on deprovincialization, see Verkuyten et al. (2022c).
12 www.cbsnews.com/news/many-british-muslims-put-islam-first
13 The well-known least liked group technique examines political tolerance by first asking people to indicate which group they like the least and subsequently whether they are willing to grant people of that group the full rights of citizenship (Sullivan et al., 1979). This content-controlled approach allows the examination of political tolerance of groups that people themselves dislike and disidentify with. However, there are also limitations to this approach such as ignoring the type of disliked group (e.g. democratic or undemocratic) that people choose and that can matter for their tolerance (Gibson et al., 2020a).
14 Sunni Muslims ideally adhere to the pillars of Islam: the declaration of faith, prayer (five times a day), fasting during the month of Ramadan, the Hajj (visiting Mecca), and Zakat (giving alms). Orthopraxis is central in the Sunni faith, which is not to say that all Sunni Muslims adhere to it. Bruce (2011) has argued that this emphasis on orthopraxy restricts a personal interpretation of Islam, creating higher levels of social conformity to religious dogmas than in other religions. In contrast, almost none of the Alevis who self-identify as Muslims practice the ritual prayer five times a day, go to a mosque, fast during the Ramadan, or go on the Hajj. These are not Alevi religious customs. For most of them, the love of God and how a person treats other humans and whether he or she acts as a

responsible and caring human being is central. Some argue therefore that "Alevis share with Germans and Europeans a democratic, laicist and egalitarian outlook" (Kosnick, 2004, p. 985).

15 In this research, among a large national sample of Creole, Muslim, and Hindu Mauritians, we found that people of all three groups make a distinction between social and political tolerance and that both forms of tolerance are positively associated (around r = .20) with the endorsement of cultural essentialist beliefs (e.g. "The way people think and behave is strongly determined by the culture they grow up in", "Due to cultural differences, individuals who are brought up in one culture develop different mentalities than individuals who are brought up in another culture").

16 For example, two members of the Dutch liberal party wrote in 2003 (12 April) a common manifesto in the quality daily newspaper (*NRC Handelsblad*) titled "The time has come for a liberal jihad" in which they argued for a war against what they saw as the "intolerance of the radical Islam".

17 Geert Wilders, leader of the populist Dutch Party for Freedom.

18 Nigel Farage: www.theneweuropean.co.uk/top-stories/nigel-farage-says-his-new-party-will-be-intolerant-of-intolerance-1–5992933

7. A slippery slope, threats, and changes

1 www.ukclimbing.com/forums/off_belay/are_we_on_the_slippery_slope_to_fascism-707323?v=1

2 The same argument was made, for example, in the Danish "grand mosque" debate in which it was argued that the alleged Islamization is financed by the Iranian regime, and also Iranian exiles in Denmark demonstrated and warned against this link (Laegaard, 2010b).

3 But see Alba (2020) for a critical discussion of what he calls the "great demographic illusion" in the US.

4 See Eurostat: https://ec.europa.eu/eurostat/data/database.

5 www.onepathnetwork.com/islam-in-the-media

6 www.economist.com/blogs/graphicdetail/2015/01/daily-chart2?fsrc=scn%2Fwl1%2Fislamineurope

7 The focus on a male person was for reasons of relevance, because Muslim males are more likely to be involved in politics than females.

8 In the *separation* condition, Ahmed answered: "Yes, absolutely. They have to advocate especially and as much as possible for the interests of Muslims in the Netherlands". In the *integration* condition, Ahmed answered: "Yes, absolutely. They have to advocate for the interests of Muslims, but not exclusively. They should also advocate for general societal issues". In the *assimilation* condition, Ahmed answered: "Yes, absolutely. But they should advocate for general societal issues and not for the interests of Muslims". In the fourth control condition, participants only received the beginning of the interview in which the interviewee introduced and described himself. The excerpt ended before the question was asked about the importance of Muslims becoming politically active in the Netherlands.

9 Measure: "Apart from your negative or positive feelings: do you think that in the Netherlands people like Ahmed should have the possibility to": "organize political meetings", "to give public speeches", "hold public demonstrations", "work as a civil servant at a ministry", "Have a high-ranking military position", and "work for homeland security". Response categories yes vs. no.

10 There were relatively large effect sizes, with up to *partial eta2* = .31.

11 Items used, e.g.: "Because many immigrants live here, native Dutch people have less and less influence", "Due to an increasing number of immigrants, native Dutch can determine what happens in the Netherlands to a lesser extent".

12 Turkse politici intimideren bestuurders Rotterdamse deelgemeente (Turkish politicians intimidate administrators in Rotterdam district). NRC-handelsblad, February 16, 2013. Retrieved from www.nrc.nl/nieuws/2013/02/16/turkse-politici-intimideren-bestuurders-rotterdamse-deelgemeente/
13 In the *group representation* condition, Ahmed answered: "Yes, they should try to exercise as much influence as possible through an Islamic political party". In the *descriptive representation* condition, Ahmed answered: "Yes, they should try to exercise as much influence as possible through an existing political party". In the *political disengagement* condition, Ahmed answered: "No, they should not get involved in party politics". In the fourth control condition, participants only received the beginning of the interview in which the interviewee introduced and described himself.
14 To give one example, in 2018, the Australian Supreme Court ruled that the Australian vice president Barnaby Joyce had to resign because he also had a New Zealand passport. The Australian constitution does not allow dual citizens to be members of parliament.
15 Such feelings are also fuelled, for example, by Turkish Dutch people demonstrating against the Dutch state and the Netherlands more generally when there is a conflict between Turkey and the Netherlands, and by being allowed to vote also in Turkey and having to serve in the Turkish military.
16 What is likely to also matter for these loyalty perceptions is the relationship between two countries. Having both a Dutch and Belgian passport is probably considered much less problematic than having a Dutch and Turkish passport.
17 This debate involves, among other things, measurement issues, the question whether political tolerance ought to be considered a dichotomous or continuous variable, and whether an absolute absence of any intolerance is possible in real life (e.g. Gibson, 2005a, 2005b; Mondak & Sanders, 2005).
18 Different interpretations and usages can also exist within a culture and even in legal debates. For example, in 1984 as a protest against nuclear armament G.L. Johnson was convicted for burning the national flag of the US at a Republic convention in Dallas. The judge sentenced Johnson to a fine and a year imprisonment. However, in 1989, five of the nine judges of the Supreme Court decided that demonstrators cannot be punished for burning since there is freedom of speech. The majority decision was expressed by judge Brennan who wrote that one does not honour the flag by punishing its violation, because such punishment would mean a repression of the freedom that the flag symbolizes. The four minority judges argued that it is the flag in particular that gives expression to the ideal of freedom and equality and should therefore be protected against unnecessary violation.

8. Being tolerated

1 Lavèn, 7 March 2017. https://i-d.vice.com/nl/article/mbgwgb/waarom-we-van-het-woord-tolerantie-af-moeten
2 And this is even more obvious in intimate personal relationships: when your partner or friend is putting up with you rather than genuinely appreciating and loving you.
3 De Sutter and De Lille in Magazine *Knack*, 16 May 2015: www.knack.be/nieuws/belgie/wij-willen-niet-getolereerd-worden-wij-willen-respect/article-normal-570685.html?cookie_check=1547197763
4 http://jewishspecialneeds.blogspot.com/2013/10/do-you-want-to-be-tolerated-or-accepted.html
5 Chapter 3 on the importance of equal dignity and respect for tolerance and the critical distinction between respect for others as equal human beings and respect for their worldviews.
6 At a protest against what he calls the colonial and nationalistic film "Michiel de Ruyter". www.doorbraak.eu/ik-weiger-een-figurant-te-zijn-die-zijn-eigen-huis-wordt-getolereerd/

7 A historical example is the Ottoman empire. Barkey (2008, p 110), a famous Ottoman historian, argued that toleration in the Ottoman context as well as in other imperial contexts refers to the "absence of persecution of people but not their acceptance into society as full and welcomed members of community". This would still characterize present day Turkey (Insel, 2019). The Turkish nation then, and now, would tolerate non-Muslims, non-Sunni-Muslims and non-Turks as long as they did, and do, not disturb or go against the Sunni Islam-Turkish order. If ethno-cultural and religious minorities did, or do, transgress, their recognition would easily turn into suppression and persecution.
8 The three options were: "[Turks/Moroccans/Surinamese/Antilleans] are discriminated against: they are often treated negatively and do not have the same opportunities as others"; "[Turks/Moroccans/Surinamese/Antilleans] are tolerated: they are not appreciated, but they do get the same opportunities as others"; and "[Turks/Moroccans/Surinamese/Antilleans] are appreciated: they are respected and get the same opportunities as others".
9 This can also be due, however, to differences in operationalizations and measures used.
10 The interviews were conducted and transcribed by Sara Cvetkovska.
11 The Netherlands generally fares better in providing legal protections to trans people than other European countries (OECD, 2020). However, trans people are still marginalized in Dutch society. A fifth of Dutch people report disapproval of non-cisgender individuals (Kuyper, 2012) and trans people are less likely to be employed and earning as much as their cisgender counterparts despite being equally educated. Nearly half of those seeking transition-related care report negative experiences with service users contend with gatekeeping and a lack of autonomy in care (Levie, 2021).
12 In *NRC Handelsblad*, 8 January 2022.
13 The paradigm involves having a participant play a toss-ball game with two virtual others and in which the participant playing the game is ignored and left out in the exclusion condition (not receiving the ball), but they are included in the inclusion condition (receiving the ball equally).

9. The indispensability of tolerance

1 One strong example is that people who criticize the still-existing forms of slavery in the Islamic republic of Mauritania are sometimes considered to criticize Islam, which is an extremely risky thing to do.
2 See also Syed (2021) for a discussion of how different starting assumptions about the nature of society underlie the debate on microaggressions.
3 Blog post at https://s-usih.org/2015/04/against-tolerance-history-politics-and-the-specter-of-charles-a-ellwood/
4 See, for example, the special issue of the journal "*Educational Philosophy and Theory*" (2010, 42, 1) and Weissberg (2008).
5 In *NRC Handelsblad*, 7 November 2020.

INDEX

Note: Page numbers in *italics* refer to figures. Numbers in **bold** refer to tables.

Lightning Source UK Ltd.
Milton Keynes UK
UKHW010624011222
413028UK00019B/133

9 781032 370439